HOLINESS AND PENTECOSTAL MOVEMENTS

STUDIES IN THE HOLINESS AND PENTECOSTAL MOVEMENTS

Editors
DAVID BUNDY, *Manchester Wesley Research Centre*
GEORDAN HAMMOND, *Manchester Wesley Research Centre* AND *Nazarene Theological College*
DAVID SANG-EHIL HAN, *Pentecostal Theological Seminary*

The Holiness and Pentecostal movements have influenced most Christian churches since the 1830s and have been a central force in the global spread of Christianity. The histories and theologies of the Holiness, Pentecostal, Charismatic, and related movements are intertwined. Yet, they are often studied as distinct movements in relative isolation from each other.

Studies in the Holiness and Pentecostal Movements seeks to enhance our understanding of both traditions by examining the two movements, and their complex relationship, through multidisciplinary approaches. Bringing these traditions into critical comparison and dialogue opens up extensive possibilities for scholarly research. The series publishes original work from a variety of scholarly disciplines and geographical perspectives.

Advisory Board
DANIEL ÁLVAREZ, *Pentecostal Theological Seminary, US*
KWABENA ASAMOAH-GYADU, *Trinity Theological Seminary, Ghana*
CANDY GUNTHER BROWN, *Indiana University, US*
DALE M. COULTER, *Pentecostal Theological Seminary, US*
NAOMI HAYNES, *University of Edinburgh, UK*
MARK HUTCHINSON, *Alphacrucis College, Australia*
MELISSA WEI-TSING INOUYE, *University of Auckland, New Zealand*
GIANCARLO RINALDI, *University of Naples, Italy*
CHERYL J. SANDERS, *Howard University School of Divinity, US*
ELIZABETH SALAZAR SANZANA, *Comunidad Teológica Evangélica de Chile*

For more information about the series, please visit https://www.psupress.org/books/series/book_SeriesStudiesInHolinessAndPentecostalMovements.html.

HOLINESS AND PENTECOSTAL MOVEMENTS

Intertwined Pasts, Presents, and Futures

DAVID BUNDY, GEORDAN HAMMOND,
AND DAVID SANG-EHIL HAN

The Pennsylvania State University Press | *University Park, Pennsylvania*

The editors thank Fernando Carvalho and Mark K. Olson for their help with editing the index.

Library of Congress Cataloging-in-Publication Data

Names: Bundy, David D., editor. | Hammond, Geordan, editor. | Han, David Sang-Ehil, editor.
Title: Holiness and Pentecostal movements : intertwined pasts, presents, and futures / [edited by] David Bundy, Geordan Hammond, and David Sang-Ehil Han.
Other titles: Studies in the Holiness and Pentecostal movements.
Description: University Park, Pennsylvania : The Pennsylvania State University Press, [2022] | Series: Studies in the Holiness and Pentecostal movements | Includes bibliographical references and index.
Summary: "A collection of essays examining the Holiness, Radical Holiness, and Pentecostal movements, focusing on the circulation of ideas among these movements in the United States, the United Kingdom, India, and Southeast and East Asia"—Provided by publisher.
Identifiers: LCCN 2021047971 | ISBN 9780271092157 (hardback) | ISBN 9780271092164 (paper)
Subjects: LCSH: Holiness movement. | Holiness movement—History. | Pentecostalism. | Pentecostalism—History.
Classification: LCC BX7990.H6 H57 2022 | DDC 280/.4—dc23/eng/20211014
LC record available at https://lccn.loc.gov/2021047971

Copyright © 2022 The Pennsylvania State University Press
All rights reserved
Printed in the United States of America
Published by The Pennsylvania State University Press,
University Park, PA 16802–1003

The Pennsylvania State University Press is a member of the Association of University Presses.

It is the policy of The Pennsylvania State University Press to use acid-free paper. Publications on uncoated stock satisfy the minimum requirements of American National Standard for Information Sciences—Permanence of Paper for Printed Library Material, ANSI Z39.48–1992.

CONTENTS

List of Illustrations   *vii*

Introduction: Intertwined History, Theology, and Scholarship   *1*
David Bundy, Geordan Hammond, and David Sang-Ehil Han

AT THE BEGINNING

1. The Preachers and Their Students: God's Bible School as a Seedbed of Radical Holiness and Pentecostal Leaders, 1892–1910   *27*
David Bundy

2. Pandita Ramabai, the Holiness Movement, and the Mukti Revival of 1905   *52*
Robert A. Danielson

3. Alexander A. Boddy, the Pentecostal League of Prayer, and the Wesleyan Roots of British Pentecostalism   *72*
Kimberly Ervin Alexander

4. A World Tour of Evangelism: Henry Clay Morrison's Radical Holiness Meets "Global Holiness," 1909–10   *96*
Luther Oconer

UNITY AND DIVERSITY

5. "Spiritual Railroading": Trains as Metaphor and Reality in the Holiness and Pentecostal Movements, ca. 1880–ca. 1920   *119*
Daniel Woods

6. Black Radical Holy Women at the Intersection of Christian Unity and Social Justice   *138*
Cheryl J. Sanders

7. Pneumatology as a Basis for Ecumenical Dialogue Between the Korean Methodist, Holiness, and Pentecostal Traditions   *159*
Insik Choi

THEOLOGICAL ENGAGEMENT

8. Baptized in the Spirit and Fire: The Relevance of Spirit Baptism for a Holiness and Pentecostal View of the Atonement   *187*

   Frank D. Macchia

9. The Presence of the Kingdom: Optimism of Grace in the Holiness and Pentecostal Movements   *208*

   Henry H. Knight III

10. Fulfilling the Full Gospel: The Promise of the Theology of the Cleveland School   *229*

    Chris E. W. Green

List of Contributors   *253*

Index   *255*
Christopher D. Rodkey

ILLUSTRATIONS

1.1. God's Tabernacle and Men's Dormitory, early twentieth century *29*

1.2. Martin Wells Knapp, frontispiece of A. M. Hills, *A Hero of Faith and Prayer; Or, Life of Rev. Martin Wells Knapp* (Cincinnati: Mrs. M. W. Knapp, 1902) *32*

2.1. Inset image of Pandita Ramabai, in The Woman's International Council, *Frank Leslie's Illustrated Newspaper* (New York) 66 (April 7, 1888), 120–21 *54*

2.2. Ward family, frontispiece of Ernest F. Ward, *Echoes from Bharatkhand* (Chicago: Free Methodist Publishing House, 1913) *60*

3.1. A. A. Boddy family portrait outside their home, ca. 1913 *73*

3.2. Reader Harris, frontispiece of his book, *Daniel the Prophet* (London: S. W. Partridge, 1909) *74*

4.1. Holiness evangelist Henry Clay Morrison with members of the Philippine Islands Annual Conference of the Methodist Episcopal Church (MEC), Knox Memorial MEC, Manila, March 2–8, 1910. From *The Official Journal of the Third Session of the Philippine Islands Annual Conference of the Methodist Episcopal Church* (Manila: Methodist Publishing House, 1910), 10 *99*

5.1. "Lost, Saved, Sanctified." From Martin Wells Knapp, *Lightning Bolts from Pentecostal Skies* (Cincinnati: Revivalist, 1898), 32 *120*

5.2. Frontispiece of Olin Marvin Owen, *The Great Celestial Railroad . . .* (Syracuse, NY: A. W. Hall, 1893) *122*

6.1. Amanda Berry Smith, frontispiece of her *An Autobiography: The Story of the Lord's Dealings with Mrs. Amanda Smith; The Colored Evangelist* (Chicago: Meter and Brother, 1893) *142*

6.2. Mother Lizzie Robinson, ca. 1930s *144*

6.3. Mother Lillian Brooks Coffey standing in front of her home, ca. 1960s *144*

7.1. The Rev. Seong-bong Lee [이성봉] *167*

7.2. Yong-gi Cho [조용기] speaking at the World Assemblies of God Congress in Seoul, South Korea, October 1994 *170*

10.1. Steven J. Land speaking at the 2018 Society for Pentecostal Studies meeting *230*

10.2. Cheryl Bridges Johns *230*

10.3. Rickie D. Moore at the 2018 Society for Pentecostal Studies meeting *230*

10.4. John Christopher Thomas *230*

Introduction

Intertwined History, Theology, and Scholarship

David Bundy, Geordan Hammond, and David Sang-Ehil Han

Historically and theologically, the Holiness and Pentecostal movements are closely related and intertwined. They have been cordial and hostile "cousins" and competitors—and, at times, exclusivist regarding one another. This combination of shared heritage and tension has made scholarly discussion of the commonalities and differences between them challenging. Yet there are common values, histories, theologies, and practices, even as these shared elements have often been defined over against one another. Conversation at local and church leadership levels as well as in scholarly gatherings has been difficult. While there have been examples of respectful and fruitful church and scholarly dialogue between the two traditions, cooperative research, thinking, and publishing have languished. We hope this book contributes to filling this gap in the scholarship.

The volume presents chapters demonstrating that one way to understand the Holiness, Radical Holiness, and Pentecostal movements is to analyze them in relation to one another. The chapters support the thesis that the movements are indeed intertwined. The chapters are arranged under three rubrics: (1) "At the Beginning," focusing on geographically diverse historical case studies; (2) "Unity and Diversity," examining cultural images and metaphors, struggles with manifesting unity and social justice, and pneumatology; and (3) "Theological Engagement," analyzing theologies of Spirit baptism and atonement, grace, and "full gospel."

This book does not present an argument for, or critique of, the three most popular scholarly theories of the origins of Pentecostalism. That is beyond the purview of this work. The primary theses remain: the Parham thesis, the Seymour/Azusa thesis, and the multiple origins thesis.[1] What can perhaps be deduced from the studies presented in this volume is that these theses require further research and reflection. Investigations that incorporate a larger base of more precise definitions, questions, and data may shed new light on the origins of Pentecostalism and its relationship to the Holiness Movement.

The introduction to this volume has three goals: (1) to describe the intertwining sources and trajectories of the Holiness and Pentecostal movements; (2) to discuss the rise and fall of scholarly interaction between the two traditions in the United States since about 1970; and (3) to provide an orientation to the chapters in this volume.

INTERTWINED SOURCES AND TRAJECTORIES OF THE HOLINESS AND PENTECOSTAL MOVEMENTS

Throughout the history of the Christian churches, there have been networks of earnest Christians formed to correct what they perceive to be the churches' shortcomings. Some Protestant reform networks developed to revive and challenge the older churches of the sixteenth to twenty-first century. These reform movements often had their origins in the Pietist and Moravian experience (Ward) or that of French Protestantism following the Revocation of the Edict of Nantes (Vuilleumier).[2] These movements were influential in Methodism and the Great Awakening. However, the Quakers, Baptists, and Congregationalists—as well as the Catholic Brethren of the Common Life in the Low Countries and Catholic orders—had similar goals. Inspiration from the Catholic tradition was drawn upon (e.g., Thomas à Kempis, Madame Guyon, François Fénelon, Catherine of Siena, St. John of the Cross) by many of these reformers, as were the theology and practice of the Protestant Reformation. French scholar Bernard Cottret has argued that there were three reformations: those of Luther, Calvin, and Wesley, with that led by the latter being more definitive.[3] Significantly for later developments, the reforming or renewing movements generally had prominent pneumatic elements. As Finnish Pentecostal scholar Juhani Kuosmanen has demonstrated, pneumatic reformist and renewal movements have had a long history.[4] Many nineteenth-century networks seeking to reform the churches and enhance the quality of Christian faith drew upon the diverse reformist sources, both Protestant and Catholic, of earlier centuries. Throughout their history, the Holiness Movement, the Radical Holiness Networks, and Methodists have had ambiguous relationships with John Wesley, Wesleyan spirituality, and Wesleyan theological foci. Individuals and networks might claim varying aspects of this legacy, but rarely was that identity paramount. Historical, theological, and cultural analysis of the diverse holiness networks is a complicated project.

Holiness Movements: Reforming the Churches in North America

In North America, the Methodists, heirs of reformist networks, quickly attracted a following that eclipsed most colonial churches, including Anglicans, Congregationalists, and Presbyterians. Within Bishop Francis Asbury's (1745–1816) lifetime, a network of not very prosperous lay and ordained preachers (women, men, white, black) developed to correct the Methodist Episcopal Church's ill treatment of German "Methodist" Brethren and African American Methodists, as well as to provide alternatives to the silencing of women, most of whom understood the doctrine of sanctification (baptism with the Holy Spirit) as giving them freedom to address religious and wider moral issues.[5] They found an unlikely leader/model in Lorenzo Dow (1777–1834), who was perhaps seen in person by a larger number of people than anyone before the development of television. He preached a combination of Methodist doctrine and "Americanism" (he did not always distinguish!) and reported converts in all denominations within the developing infrastructure of the new United States of America.[6] Many of the next generation of religious leaders, including Brigham Young and Charles G. Finney, were influenced by him, probably indirectly.[7] Dow requires extensive research to establish more clearly his role in developments in the United States during the early nineteenth century. His work in encouraging the formation of Primitive Methodism in the United Kingdom out of Wesleyan Methodism is well documented.[8]

A decade after Dow, from 1830 to the Civil War, the Methodist Episcopal Church erupted with a new network of reformers, including Orange Scott, La Roy Sunderland, Timothy Merritt, Sarah Worrall Lankford, Phoebe Worrall Palmer, and B. T. Roberts, some of whom left the Methodist Episcopal Church or were forced out. From outside of Methodism came figures such as William Boardman (Presbyterian), Asa Mahan (Presbyterian, Congregationalist), Thomas Upham (Congregationalist), and Charles G. Finney (Presbyterian, Congregationalist). Methodists and non-Methodists in these networks (with the possible exception of the Worrall sisters) understood sanctification (baptism with the Holy Spirit) to require the abolition of slavery, economic justice, and freedom for women to minister.⁹

From these leaders and their followers, the Holiness Movement emerged. It was a diverse network with multiple nodes. Often, they worked together to achieve goals, and sometimes they did not. A central driving force for them was the question, Can we not be better Christians tomorrow than we are today? All believed that sanctification required living lives of love for God and for their neighbor. They trumpeted their concerns in periodicals, including *The True Wesleyan* (Scott), *Guide to Christian Perfection* (Merritt), and *Earnest Christian* (Roberts). The movement was also promoted through a series of books: Merritt's *Christian's Manual: A Treatise on Christian Perfection* (1824), Mahan's *The Scriptural Doctrine of Christian Perfection* (1839), Upham's *Principles of the Interior or Hidden Life* (1843), Palmer's *The Way of Holiness* (1843), and William E. Boardman's *The Higher Christian Life* (1858), to name just a few. Timothy Smith, Victor Howard, and Douglas Strong have argued that this diverse Holiness Movement played a significant role in achieving its goal of emancipation of enslaved African Americans.¹⁰

From the Holiness Movement to the Radical Holiness Networks

After the Civil War, around the edges of the Methodist Episcopal Church, the National Camp Meeting Association for the Promotion of Holiness (1867), which became the National Holiness Association (NHA), developed a more Methodist-focused version of the Holiness Movement. While it attracted participants from other churches (Baptists, Quakers, Congregationalists, Presbyterians, among others), the focus was Methodist theology and practice. The understanding of sanctification came to focus on personal purification and power for ministry, rather than engagement with social change. Many Methodists (and Free Methodists) in cooperation with disaffected Holiness advocates in the older churches developed Radical Holiness Networks. These people and groups were usually alienated from their own churches, due to social location, education, and conceptions of Christian ministry and mission. They adopted ideas that were not prominent in Methodist churches, including faith healing and premillennialism. By the 1890s, loose networks of Radical Holiness churches and ministries were forming into regional denominations, with diverse theologies and publications. These new networks and denominations constituted the Radical Holiness Networks.¹¹ Holiness churches founded before the Civil War (Wesleyan Methodist Church [1843], Free Methodist Church [1860]) firmed up their Holiness boundaries. Many members of the older Methodist churches, both white and black, remained faithful Holiness Movement–style Methodists.

Those outside the Methodist folds who were enthusiastic about sanctification/baptism with the Holy Spirit had diverse understandings of the experience. They were minimally interested in classic Methodist theology, and became proponents of the ministry of women, faith healing, "self-supporting" or "faith" mission, and premillennialism. Most relativized their earlier religious involvements, even while retaining connections and/or credentials in older denominations. The Radical Holiness Networks became their primary identity. Defections from the Methodist Episcopal Church were many; those from the Free Methodist Church included the Vanguard Mission (1881) and Pentecost Bands (1882). The Salvation Army (1880 in the United States), Church of God (Anderson [Indiana]) (1881), and the Christian and Missionary Alliance (1887) grew quickly. The Radical Holiness Networks and denominations gathered significant numbers of committed Christians from diverse denominations. Quaker Yearly Meetings became Radical Holiness as did Baptist Associations (e.g., Georgia and Arkansas). Both the Holiness and Radical Holiness movements established large numbers of educational institutions, rescue missions, and foreign mission agencies throughout the United States, as well as camp meetings.[12] Crucial to maintaining the networks were the periodical publications. Every group and emerging denomination had one or several. Among those with significant national circulation were the *Christian Witness and Advocate of Bible Holiness* (Boston, Chicago, University Park [Iowa]), *God's Revivalist* (Cincinnati), *Pentecostal Herald* (Louisville), and *Burning Bush* (Chicago, Waukesha).

The conflict between the NHA Methodist-oriented Holiness Movement and the Radical Holiness Movements came to a head in Chicago in 1901. William Kostlevy described the trauma of the two networks sharing meeting and ministry venues as they competed for the heart and minds of the religious seekers of Chicago, church people, and donors. The Radical Holiness Networks "won" these contests and the NHA became more Radical Holiness.[13]

Holiness, Radical Holiness, and Pentecostal

Pentecostalism as we now know it was arguably initially defined for the United States during the period 1906–19. There were certainly earlier revivals in which glossolalia and other elements claimed as Pentecostal "distinctives" played important roles. However, the Azusa Street Revival in Los Angeles provided crucial, if brief and illusory, cohesiveness. Azusa Street served as a quasi-historical (mythic) icon within which converts to Pentecostalism sometimes sought to understand their spirituality.[14] Most of the leadership of this and other similar revivals around the world involved Radical Holiness believers and leaders. The unity through the experience of baptism with the Holy Spirit envisaged by William Seymour (1870–1922) and his team splintered quickly into Hispanic, European American, African American, and other ethnic and language traditions. It also fragmented theologically (between Trinitarian and Oneness Pentecostals, and between Holiness and "Finished Work" views of sanctification) and regionally in the United States. Within a short time, there were Pentecostal denominations and ministries on six continents.[15] Those who identified with the Azusa Street icon were, at the same time, independent of it. There was no magisterium to enforce uniformity, even within the United States, much less beyond.

The Radical Holiness churches lost much of a generation of charismatic leaders to the new movement. Many of the newer and smaller Holiness denominations consolidated in the Pentecostal Church of the Nazarene or in the Pilgrim Holiness Church. New networks formed out of the Pentecostal revival in Los Angeles. In 1919, the Pentecostal Church of the Nazarene left the term *Pentecostal* behind, and took firmer stances against religious enthusiasm in its midst.[16] In the context of the larger American culture, which understood them as "Holy Rollers," a term reborn following the 1904–6 trials of Franz Creffield and George Mitchell in Portland and Seattle,[17] both the Radical Holiness and Pentecostal movements were considered deviant by the older churches, not only for their religious enthusiasm and theologies but also for their multiracial ministry efforts, women preachers, and lower-class adherents.[18] Both movements were caught between the mainline churches and the Fundamentalists, which, despite their differences, generally agreed on their negative views of the Holiness, Radical Holiness, and Pentecostal churches. The shared general (but not absolute) alienation from North American religious culture only increased their competition and tendency toward differentiation.

Some of the predominantly white Holiness and Pentecostal churches sought refuge from American religious conflict and hoped for a more unified future within the National Association of Evangelicals (NAE) following its establishment in 1942. It was founded by the ecumenically committed leader of the New England Fellowship, J. Elwin Wright, whose father left the Free Methodist Church and became Pentecostal with the assistance of, among others,

Bishop Leslie R. Marston (Free Methodist) and Harold John Ockenga, who grew up in the Methodist Episcopal Church and graduated from the Holiness, Methodist-related Taylor University (1927).[19] The NAE worked to make space for the Holiness and Pentecostal churches. It is important to note that most denominations of both traditions did not join, including the Church of the Nazarene, Salvation Army, Church of God in Christ, and Pentecostal Assemblies of the World.

Outside North America, relationships between Radical Holiness and Pentecostal movements and other churches varied from country to country and are too diverse to summarize here. Despite occasional irenic moments, Holiness, Radical Holiness, and Pentecostal churches remained largely divided along racial and class lines. Actualizing the dream of all these movements at the beginning of the century to transcend the divisions of humanity through baptism with the Holy Spirit remained, and remains, elusive.

Another opportunity appeared with the development of the Charismatic Movements and Jesus People networks. Some local relationships developed between Holiness and Pentecostal churches and Jesus People. Occasionally, positive connections were made between Pentecostals and Charismatics, but usually not between Charismatics and Holiness churches.[20]

BRINGING SCHOLARSHIP ON THE HOLINESS AND PENTECOSTAL
MOVEMENTS TOGETHER

Despite the shared history, theology, and praxis, as well as limited engagement within the NAE and other agencies, the development of Holiness and Pentecostal historiography has been fragmented.[21] As the churches evolved separately along class, racial, regional, and denominational lines, demarcations were made clear by differentiated theologies. Scholars, whose financial survival often depended on the denominations, wrote extensively for publication within the denominations. They tended perforce to ignore connections to other parts of the traditions and focused on the part of the movement to which they were confessionally tied.[22] Radical Holiness and Pentecostal students had difficulty being accepted into doctoral programs of the universities. While a few succeeded in gaining access, it was not until the late 1950s and 1960s that a critical mass had the education that could support creative intellectual work.[23] On the model of other scholarly societies, the Wesleyan Theological Society (WTS) was organized in 1965.[24] The Society for Pentecostal Studies (SPS) was founded in 1970.[25] SPS had a larger vision, including dialogue with the Charismatic Movement and

Wesleyan-Holiness scholars. The early dialogues were published in *Aspects of Pentecostal-Charismatic Origins* and in *Pneuma*, the scholarly journal of SPS.[26]

There were three primary centers for this initial Wesleyan-Holiness and Pentecostal encounter: Cleveland, Tennessee; Franklin Springs, Georgia; and Wilmore, Kentucky. At Franklin Springs College, Vinson Synan (1934–2020), with his PhD degree from the University of Georgia, was beginning to reach out to other scholars, primarily through the publication of his thesis, about which more is said below. At Lee College (now University) in Cleveland, R. Hollis Gause (1925–2015) was celebrating more than two decades of teaching, as he and others worked to found what is now known as Pentecostal Theological Seminary. He was also in his own educational transition as a PhD student at Emory University. There he encountered the Wesleyan tradition of the Methodists. He was crucial to the founding of SPS. At the 1972 SPS, his presidential address, "Issues in Pentecostalism," noted that there were some connections between Pentecostalism and "Wesleyanism."[27] Through his life, thanks primarily to his discussions with Henry H. Knight III and Steven J. Land, he moved from being a Holiness-Pentecostal to being a Wesleyan-Holiness-Pentecostal, as is evidenced in a 1970 lecture on "Worldliness" and the two editions of his book, *Living in the Spirit*.[28] In the words of historian and archivist David Roebuck, Gause moved toward "situating his identity in a historical movement."[29]

At the same time, developments were taking place at Asbury Theological Seminary, a Wesleyan-Holiness institution, that led to early exploration of histories, theologies, and concerns of the Holiness, Keswick, and Pentecostal movements. Dr. Susan A. Schultz Rose (1911–2011), a Librarian and Professor at Asbury Theological Seminary, employed Donald W. Dayton (1942–2020) (a Collection Development Librarian), D. William Faupel (Reference Librarian), and David Bundy (as a work study student bibliographer).[30] She understood the connections among the three religious movements and commissioned her three disciples to write about them: Dayton on the Holiness Movement, Faupel on the Pentecostal Movement, and Bundy on the Keswick-Higher Life Movements. To avoid criticism from the senior faculty, all were written and published as bibliographical essays.[31]

Then, on the same day, Dayton and Bundy purchased the first two copies of a version of the University of Georgia doctoral dissertation of Vinson Synan, *The Holiness-Pentecostal Movement in the United States* (1971), to arrive at the seminary bookstore.[32] Now, half a century later, it is difficult to imagine the excitement produced by this book that hyphenated the two movements in its title. Among other things, it provoked the work of Herbert McGonigle, followed by Timothy L. Smith (1924–1997), and Donald Dayton in the WTS to insist on varying degrees of commonality and distance among the Methodist, Wesleyan-Holiness, and Pentecostal churches, an analysis based, in part, on perceived differences in language between John Wesley and John Fletcher.[33] Out of this grew Dayton's *Theological Roots of Pentecostalism* (1987).[34]

Another formative moment was Donald Dayton and David Bundy's visit to Franklin Springs, Georgia, in January 1972, to meet Vinson Synan. He received us graciously and we discussed his book. During the discussion, Bundy asked whether Synan would come to lecture at Asbury Theological Seminary in March 1972 if a way could be found to invite him. At the time, Asbury required all Pentecostals and Charismatics to undergo psychological testing and therapy if they were admitted at all. Bundy, editor of *The Short Circuit*, the Asbury Seminary student newspaper, widely circulated in Wilmore, Kentucky, organized the "*Short Circuit* Forum," which paid Synan's transportation and guestroom. Susan Schultz agreed that the library lecture room could be used if "Don as a member of the library staff would take responsibility." The audience overflowed into the hallways and library. The next morning Bundy was summoned to the president's office to explain the "irrational and unwise decision."[35]

This event marked a beginning of friendships, dialogues, and intensified historical research. It was not easy. Later that year, at the Wesleyan Theological Society, Donald Dayton moved that the WTS send greetings to its "sister" society, SPS. Only two people (Dayton and Bundy) voted for the motion; a motion to expunge the motion, the discussion, and vote from the record passed. The next year (1973) a group of Asbury Theological Seminary faculty (David Bundy, D. William Faupel, Delbert R. Rose, and future faculty member Melvin E. Dieter) as well as Donald W. Dayton, by then a librarian at North Park Theological Seminary and doctoral student at the University of Chicago, attended the SPS meeting in Cleveland, Tennessee.[36] The WTS, which had very restrictive membership policies, refused to allow Vinson Synan to join and rescinded an invitation for him to give a paper. The next decade saw some thawing of relationships from the Wesleyan-Holiness side. In 1988, the Wesleyan-Holiness Studies Project, created by Bundy and Faupel at Asbury Theological Seminary, hosted both WTS and SPS, albeit at different times. At that SPS meeting, a "Post-Meeting Session," cochaired by Howard A. Snyder and Vinson Synan, featured presentations and discussion of "The Holiness and Pentecostal Traditions in Dialogue."[37]

In Cleveland, R. Hollis Gause was developing (from 1975) the Church of God School of Theology (later Pentecostal Theological Seminary), often team teaching with Steven J. Land, who for some of this time was a PhD student at Emory University. Crucial to the shift to "Wesleyan" were the discussions begun in 1983 between Henry H. Knight III and Land in the context of Emory University. Gause and Knight were both on Land's doctoral examination committee in 1991.[38] Knight, a United Methodist, taught courses on John Wesley's theology and subsequent Wesleyan movements at Church of God Theological Seminary as an adjunct professor in 1990, 1995–96, and 2000. Land's theological perspective was refined in extensive discussions with Knight.

Most of the faculty and Church of God leadership were shaped by Gause and Land, especially through Land's book, *Pentecostal Spirituality*.[39] Among these was Cheryl Bridges Johns, a prolific scholar and ecumenist. She was already involved in discussion with Dayton, Bundy, Faupel, and Knight. In the summer of 1992, she and Jo Anne Lyon, future General Superintendent of the Wesleyan Church, participated in the summer workshop "Ecumenism Within Us," sponsored by the Institute for Ecumenical and Cultural Research held at Saint John's Abbey and University in Collegeville, Minnesota. They developed an enduring friendship as they discussed the estrangement of the Wesleyan-Holiness and Pentecostal traditions.

A year later at the Fifth World Conference on Faith and Order, which took place at Santiago de Compostela, Spain, August 3–14, 1993, with the theme "Towards Koinonia in Faith, Life and Witness," Cheryl Bridges Johns met Susie C. Stanley, a prolific author, founder of Wesleyan-Holiness Women Clergy, and then Professor at Western Evangelical Seminary, near Portland, Oregon. They discussed the possibility of SPS and WTS having a joint meeting as a form of ecumenical affirmation of their common heritages and missions. In 1992–93, they were presidents of the two societies: Susie C. Stanley headed WTS, and Cheryl Bridges Johns, SPS. Their energy and vision for enlarging the discussion made possible the first joint meeting of SPS and WTS at the Church of God Theological Seminary in Cleveland, Tennessee, in 1998.

The cooperation between the two societies was facilitated by a close working relationship between William Kostlevy (WTS) and D. William Faupel (SPS). Kostlevy, an Archivist, Special Collections Librarian, affiliate Professor of Church History, and Associate Director of the Wesleyan / Holiness Studies Center at Asbury Theological Seminary, was elected Secretary-Treasurer of WTS (1991), and Faupel, Librarian and Professor at Asbury Seminary, was elected Executive Secretary of SPS (1997). The offices of the two organizations were in the B. L. Fisher Library of Asbury Theological Seminary.

After the success of the initial event, a second joint WTS-SPS meeting (2003) was hosted by the Wesleyan / Holiness Studies Center of Asbury Theological Seminary. As in the initial joint gathering, there were common themes, sessions featured both WTS and SPS scholars, and plenary addresses were scheduled so that all participants could attend all plenary events. The third joint meeting held in 2008 at Duke Divinity School continued that tradition.

Some scholars worked to further build these bridges. From 2004 to 2009, Henry H. Knight III hosted "The Wesleyan/Pentecostal Consultation," an annual two-day event that met at the conference center of Nazarene Theological Seminary in Kansas City, Missouri. Funded by a grant from the Louisville Institute given to Saint Paul School of Theology, where Knight is on the faculty, thirty scholars and pastors, representing twelve denominational traditions, discussed the intersections of the Wesleyan and Pentecostal traditions. Most presentations appeared in *From Aldersgate to Azusa Street* (2010). Long-lasting scholarly friendships and collaborations resulted. Knight's *Anticipating Heaven Below* (2014) is best understood as arising from the context of that Consultation.[40]

After changes of leadership in the two societies, the fourth joint meeting of SPS and WTS in 2013 at Seattle Pacific University featured two societies meeting on the same campus, about a half-mile apart. There was little collaboration in programming or visioning. The same occurred at the 2018 joint meeting at Pentecostal Theological Seminary, Cleveland, Tennessee. During the 2020 WTS meeting, the Executive Committee put forward a motion to discontinue joint meetings with SPS. No discussion was allowed. The motion passed.

Wanting to promote fruitful engagement between the Wesleyan-Holiness and Pentecostal traditions and perceiving a decline of discussions and shared research between SPS and WTS scholars, David Sang-Ehil Han, the Dean of the Faculty, Vice-President for Academics, and Professor of Theology and Pentecostal Spirituality at Pentecostal Theological Seminary; Geordan Hammond, a Senior Lecturer in Church History and Wesley Studies at Nazarene Theological College and Director of the Manchester Wesley Research Centre; and David Bundy, Associate Director of the Manchester Wesley Research Centre, met during the March 2018 joint WTS-SPS meeting to discuss the possibilities of a program of research. Since the Manchester Wesley Research Centre was already a "Related Scholarly Organization" of the American Academy of Religion, it was agreed to create an AAR Annual Meeting session sponsored by the Manchester Wesley Research Centre and Pentecostal Theological Seminary on the intertwined Holiness and Pentecostal movements.

THE PRESENT VOLUME

The diachronic and synchronic histories sketched above provide context for the chapters in this volume. The contributions are arranged into three sections: (1) "At the Beginning," (2) "Unity and Diversity," and (3) "Theological Engagement." The chapters in the first section, "At the Beginning," focus on the shared experiences of Holiness and Pentecostal leaders at the turn of the twentieth century. They reveal that while the intertwined elements of the Radical Holiness and Pentecostal movements evolved differently in the United States, India, South and Southeast Asia, and the United Kingdom, the two movements had deep and complex connections.

The second group of chapters, "Unity and Diversity," reveals that the Radical Holiness and Pentecostal movements shared cultural images, struggles with manifesting unity and social justice, and pneumatology. The final contributions, gathered as "Theological Engagement," examine the concepts of Spirit baptism and atonement, grace, and "full gospel," demonstrating that commonalities of theological language, values, and methods shape the theological reflection of the Holiness and Pentecostal movements.

At the Beginning

David Bundy, "The Preachers and Their Students: God's Bible School as a Seedbed of Radical Holiness and Pentecostal Leaders, 1892–1910," focuses on the Cincinnati ministry and institution founded by Martin Wells Knapp that trained several formative leaders for both the Radical Holiness and Pentecostal movements. Examining the theology and social commitments of Knapp and the God's Bible School faculty members, Bundy places the Radical Holiness Movement in Populist and Progressive America, indicating parallels to the Industrial Workers of the World (Wobblies).

Robert A. Danielson, "Pandita Ramabai, the Holiness Movement, and the Mukti Revival of 1905," examines the library of Ramabai as well as some of her relationships with people connected to the Holiness and Radical Holiness movements. Particular attention is paid to Albert Norton, who worked closely with and visited her at the Mukti Mission, E. F. and Phebe Ward, the Pentecost Bands, and William Godbey, a peripatetic Radical Holiness theologian and professor at God's Bible School. Danielson argues that the Mukti Revival of 1905 is better understood in the context of those relationships.

Kimberly Ervin Alexander, "Alexander A. Boddy, the Pentecostal League of Prayer, and the Wesleyan Roots of British Pentecostalism," examines the understudied relationship between Richard Reader Harris, Harris's Pentecostal League of Prayer, and Alexander A. Boddy, one of the founders of Pentecostalism in the United Kingdom. The study provides an example of the separation between the Holiness and Pentecostal movements in the United Kingdom.

Finally, Luther Oconer, "A World Tour of Evangelism: Henry Clay Morrison's Radical Holiness Meets 'Global Holiness,' 1909–10," discusses the significance of the eleven-month "world tour of evangelism" by Morrison, soon to be elected president of Asbury College, conducting "Pentecostal meetings" in Asia, most particularly in India, Korea, and Japan. The chapter argues that Morrison's tour provides an opportunity to examine not only a brand of Radical Holiness that developed after the birth of the Pentecostal Movement (1906), but also the contours of a different form of holiness spirituality that persisted in the mission field, or what has been called "global holiness." It also demonstrates that the reception of Morrison's work in countries where he found great success serves as a barometer for understanding how Pentecostalism would take root in these locations. It establishes that the rise and growth of Pentecostalism in these countries depended initially on the preexistent "global holiness" networks. The work of Danielson, Alexander, and Oconer demonstrate the complex Holiness and Pentecostal interaction outside the United States.

Unity and Diversity

Daniel Woods, "'Spiritual Railroading': Trains as Metaphor and Reality in the Holiness and Pentecostal Movements, ca. 1880–ca. 1920," continues the focus on the early twentieth century. He examines in detail the relationships between Holiness and Pentecostal language developed around railroads and the engagement of the two movements with modernity during the Progressive Era. Woods demonstrates that this language served as a vehicle for developing and communicating theological ideas, social analysis, and religious practices, all in dialogue with the biblical texts. The chapter provides an example of the complex relationship between the two religious movements and modernity.

Cheryl J. Sanders, "Black Radical Holy Women at the Intersection of Christian Unity and Social Justice," explores the contributions of black women leaders whose social witness influenced the emergence of the Radical Holiness Movement in the nineteenth century and of Pentecostalism in the twentieth century.

Three models of Christian social witness explore their exilic ecclesiology of being "in the world, but not of it": (1) the cosmopolitan evangelism of Amanda Berry Smith; (2) the egalitarian revivalism of the Azusa Street washwomen; and (3) the sanctified civic engagement of the Church of God in Christ church mothers, Lizzie Robinson and Lillian Brooks Coffey. H. Richard Niebuhr's *Christ and Culture* provides a framework for analyzing the exilic ecclesiologies of these women. Because of their race, gender, and social class, these black radical holy women were uniquely positioned to confront and dismantle barriers to Christian unity and social transformation.

Insik Choi, "Pneumatology as a Basis for Ecumenical Dialogue Between the Korean Methodist, Holiness, and Pentecostal Traditions," argues that the shared pneumatical heritages, differentiated because of cultural contexts, the work of non-Korean theologians, and the internal logic of the Korean expressions of the three traditions, provide a place to begin ecumenical discussions. The chapter briefly discusses the development of the three traditions in Korea in relation to each other.

Theological Engagement

Frank D. Macchia, "Baptized in the Spirit and Fire: The Relevance of Spirit Baptism for a Holiness and Pentecostal View of the Atonement," argues that historically, Christology in the West was secured as the redemptive event through the linkage between the incarnation and the atonement. This connection protected Christology from adoptionism or the subordination of Christology to pneumatology. Left unanswered by this linkage was the role of Jesus as the Baptizer in the Spirit and fire as announced by John the Baptist. Macchia addresses this question drawing from Holiness and Pentecostal sources, developing the idea that Jesus is sanctified in his own baptism in the Spirit and fire through his passage from death to life in order to baptize others in the Spirit.

Henry H. Knight III, "The Presence of the Kingdom: Optimism of Grace in the Holiness and Pentecostal Movements," insists the two movements are shaped and motivated by the promise that through the power of the Holy Spirit, the life of the coming kingdom of heaven is already being realized in this age. This optimism of grace, centered in the presence and power of God, grounds a spirituality of openness to God and expectant faith and hope. The reception of new life in turn provides motivation for mission, enabled by the reception of power from the Spirit, in which the good news of Jesus Christ is proclaimed through word and deed, the church is renewed, and there is ministry to bodies as well as souls. These movements are a distinct alternative to both liberal theologies shaped by the Enlightenment and Reformed scholasticism.

Chris E. W. Green, "Fulfilling the Full Gospel: The Promise of the Theology of the Cleveland School," describes and analyzes the development of theologians, all shaped by and shapers of Pentecostal Theological Seminary, which is self-defined as Wesleyan-Pentecostal. He explores and evaluates the key theological claims of the Cleveland School—especially its Christ-centeredness, synergism, liberationism, apocalypticism, and affectivity—and asks what those claims mean for the future of Pentecostal theology in particular, and the Christian tradition more broadly. Attention is given to the limits of the fivefold gospel paradigm, which some in the Cleveland School consider essential, and an alternative paradigm is suggested, one that privileges the apocalyptic.

CONCLUSION

These studies demonstrate elements of the shared historical and theological experience of the Holiness and Pentecostal movements. They provide evidence that the movements are closely related and intertwined, sharing values, histories, theologies, sources, and practices. The chapters also point to important differences of this common heritage. Both movements are diverse within themselves. This diversity relates to theology, geography, race, gender, class, and many other factors, including charismatic leadership, a subject implicit in these chapters, but requiring additional analysis. Because of the intertwined trajectories of the two movements for more than a century, these divided and subdivided traditions have often defined the larger movements from which they came in relationship to the key issues that led to separation. These chapters suggest that nuanced approaches to historical and theological analysis of the two movements and their relationships remain desiderata for research.

The Penn State University Press series, "Studies in the Holiness and Pentecostal Movements," seeks to honor complexities of the movements and the multidimensionality of their internal and external relationships. The purpose of this series is to examine particularities of each movement and tradition, as well as the relationships between them in a multidisciplinary fashion. The goal is a better understanding of the Holiness and Pentecostal movements as global religious traditions, together and separately.

NOTES

1. James R. Goff Jr., *Fields White unto Harvest: Charles F. Parham and the Missionary Origins of Pentecostalism* (Fayetteville: University of Arkansas Press, 1988); Cecil M. Robeck Jr., *The Azusa Street Mission and Revival: The Birth of the Global Pentecostal Movement* (Nashville: Thomas Nelson, 2006); Allan Anderson, *Spreading Fires: The Missionary Nature of Early Pentecostalism* (Maryknoll, NY: Orbis, 2007). The Parham thesis is generally not presently supported by scholars.

2. W. R. Ward, *The Protestant Evangelical Awakening* (Cambridge: Cambridge University Press, 1992); Henri Vuilleumier, *L'Histoire de l'Église Réformée du Pays de Vaud sous le Régime Bernois* (Lausanne: Éditions La Concorde, 1930), 3:183–234. See also Hillel Schwartz, *The French Prophets: The History of a Millenarian Group in Eighteenth-Century England* (Berkeley: University of California Press, 1980); Lionel Laborie, *Enlightening Enthusiasm: Prophecy and Religious Experience in Early Eighteenth-Century England* (Manchester: Manchester University Press, 2015). The "French Prophets," perhaps because of their controversial legacy, have not figured prominently in twentieth- and twenty-first-century discussions of the roots of Methodist, Holiness, or Pentecostal movements.

3. Bernard Cottret, *Histoire de la Réforme protestante: Luther, Calvin, Wesley, XVIe–XVIIIe siècle* (2001; repr., Paris: Perrin, 2010), 339–99, 537–67; Jérôme Grosclaude, *Le Méthodisme: Un tison tire du feu*, pref. Bernard Cottret (N.p.: Éditions Ampelos, 2017).

4. Juhani Kuosmanen, *Herätyksen Historia* (Tikkurila, Finland: Ristin Voitto, 1979).

5. The definitions of "entire sanctification" and "baptism with the Holy Spirit" became foci of differentiation in the Wesleyan, Radical Holiness, and Pentecostal traditions, largely depending on interpretations of the biblical Pentecost narratives. Methodists and Methodist Holiness believers understood them as equivalent terms referring to a postconversion experience. Generally, Wesleyan Pentecostals, Sanctified Churches, and Oneness Pentecostals also understood them to be subsequent to conversion, with sanctification being the prerequisite for baptism with the Holy Spirit accompanied by glossolalia. On the other hand, the Assemblies of God and similar groups merged conversion and sanctification, to be followed by another experience, baptism with the Holy Spirit, evidenced by glossolalia.

6. Dow has not received the scholarly attention he deserves. No one has yet definitively established the bibliography and biography of Dow. The best treatment is Nathan O. Hatch, *The Democratization of American Christianity* (New Haven: Yale University Press, 1989).

7. Marilla Marks, ed., *Memoirs of the Life of David Marks, Minister of the Gospel* (Dover, NH: Free-Will Baptist Publishing, 1846), 110–12. The younger brother of Brigham Young was named Lorenzo Dow Young. See James Amasa Little, "Biography of Lorenzo Dow Young," *Utah Historical Quarterly* 14 (1946): 118–21.

8. The best treatments of his transatlantic engagements are Richard Carwardine, *Transatlantic Revivalism: Popular Evangelicalism in Britain and America, 1790–1865* (Westport, CT: Greenwood, 1978), 104–7, 134–35, 198–200, and Tim Woolley, "'Have Our People Been Sufficiently Cautious?' Wesleyan Responses to Lorenzo Dow in England and Ireland, 1799–1819," *Wesley and Methodist Studies* 9, no. 2 (2017): 141–62.

9. For information on each of these individuals, except Dow, see William Kostlevy, ed., *The A to Z of the Holiness*

Movement, A–Z Guide Series 164 (Lanham, MD: Scarecrow Press, 2010).

10. Timothy L. Smith, *Revivalism and Social Reform in Mid-Nineteenth-Century America* (Nashville: Abingdon Press, 1957); Victor B. Howard, *Religion and the Radical Republican Movement, 1860–1870* (Lexington: University Press of Kentucky, 1990); Douglas M. Strong, *Perfectionist Politics: Abolitionism and the Religious Tensions of American Democracy* (Syracuse: Syracuse University Press, 1999).

11. William Kostlevy, *Holy Jumpers: Evangelicals and Radicals in Progressive Era America* (Oxford: Oxford University Press, 2010), 17–36; David Bundy and Masaya Fujii, "Barclay Fowell Buxton, Japanese Christians, and the Japan Evangelistic Band," *Journal of World Christianity* 8, no. 1 (2018): 47–74; David Bundy, "Sophia Chambers, Founder of the Holiness Church: A Case Study of Victorian Entrepreneurial Religious Leadership," *Wesley and Methodist Studies* 11, no. 1 (2019): 24–49.

12. Melvin E. Dieter, *The Holiness Revival of the Nineteenth Century*, Studies in Evangelicalism 1 (Metuchen, NJ: Scarecrow Press, 1980), 2nd ed., 1996; Norman H. Murdock, *Origins of the Salvation Army* (Knoxville: University of Tennessee Press, 1994); Lillian Taiz, *Hallelujah Lads and Lassies: Remaking the Salvation Army in America, 1880–1930* (Chapel Hill: University of North Carolina Press, 2001); David Bundy, "Pauline Missions: The Wesleyan Holiness Vision," in *The Global Impact of the Wesleyan Traditions and Their Related Movements*, ed. Charles Yrigoyen Jr., Pietist and Wesleyan Studies 14 (Lanham, MD: Scarecrow Press, 2002), 13–26; David Bundy, *Visions of Apostolic Mission: Scandinavian Pentecostal Mission to 1935*, Studia Historico-Ecclesiastica Upsaliensia 45 (Uppsala: Uppsala Universitet, 2009), 31–132; Kostlevy, *Holy Jumpers*, 17–36.

13. Kostlevy, *Holy Jumpers*, 60–73.

14. David Bundy, "California Pentecostalism as Icon: Toward an Understanding of the Function of the Azusa Street Revival in Pentecostal Mythology," unpublished lecture presented at the Society for Pentecostal Studies, 1986.

15. Anderson, *Spreading Fires*.

16. Floyd T. Cunningham, Stan Ingersol, Harold E. Raser, and David P. Whitelaw, *Our Watchword and Song: The Centennial History of the Church of the Nazarene* (Kansas City, MO: Beacon Hill Press of Kansas City, 2009).

17. Jim Phillips and Rosemary Gartner, *Murdering Holiness: The Trials of Franz Creffield and George Mitchell* (Vancouver: UBC Press, 2003); T. McCracken and Robert B. Blodgett, *Holy Rollers: Murder and Madness in Oregon's Love Cult* (Caldwell, ID: Caxton Press, 2002). The term "Holy Roller" was first used in the 1840s but gained new currency in the twentieth century because of sensationalized worldwide press coverage of a murder trial that included reference to several Radical Holiness and future Pentecostal leaders of the Pacific Northwest.

18. Douglas Frank, *Less Than Conquerors: How Evangelicals Entered the Twentieth Century* (Grand Rapids, MI: Eerdmans, 1986); Grant Wacker, "Travail of a Broken Family: Evangelical Responses to Pentecostalism in America, 1906–1916," *Journal of Ecclesiastical History* 47, no. 3 (1996): 505–28.

19. J. Elwin Wright succeeded his father as leader of the New England Fellowship. See Elizabeth Evans, *The Wright Vision: The Story of the New England Fellowship* (Lanham: University Press of America, 1991); George L. Ford, *Like a Tree Planted: The Life Story of Leslie Ray Marston* (Winona Lake, IN: Light and Life Press, 1985); John Marion Adams, "The Making of a Neo-Evangelical Statesman: The Case of Harold John Ockenga" (PhD diss., Baylor University, 1994); Garth M. Rosell, *Surprising Work of God: Harold*

John Ockenga, Billy Graham, and the Rebirth of Evangelicalism (Grand Rapids, MI: Baker Academic, 2008).

20. Walter Hollenweger, *New Wine in Old Wineskins: Protestant and Catholic Neo-Pentecostalism* (Gloucester: Fellowship Press, 1973); P. D. Hocken, "Charismatic Movement," in *The New International Dictionary of Pentecostal and Charismatic Movements*, ed. Stanley M. Burgess and Eduard M. van der Maas (Grand Rapids, MI: Zondervan, 2002), 477–519; Allan Anderson, *An Introduction to Pentecostalism: Global Charismatic Christianity* (Cambridge: Cambridge University Press, 2004), 144–65, 187–286; David Di Sabatino, *The Jesus People Movement: An Annotated Bibliography and General Resource* (Westport, CT: Greenwood Press, 1999); Larry Eskridge, *God's Forever Family: The Jesus People Movement in America* (Oxford: Oxford University Press, 2013).

21. Among those who have contributed to this section through discussions, interviews, and emails are Kimberly Ervin Alexander, Dale M. Coulter, Donald W. Dayton, D. William Faupel, David Sang-Ehil Han, Cheryl Bridges Johns, Henry (Hal) Knight III, William Kostlevy, Jo Anne Lyon, David Roebuck, and Vinson Synan. David Bundy has personal notes for many of the events discussed. These are cited only when direct quotations are used. Most people interviewed were also present at several of the events discussed. We are grateful for their contributions.

22. The two most important exceptions were Walter J. Hollenweger, "Handbuch der Pfingstbewegung" (PhD diss., Universitat Zurich, 1965), https://archive.org/details/pts_handbuchderpfings_1422_1, and the bibliographies of Charles Edwin Jones, *A Guide to the Study of the Pentecostal Movement*, ATLA Bibliography Series 6 (Metuchen, NJ: Scarecrow Press, 1983); Charles Edwin Jones, *Black Holiness: A Guide to the Study of Black Participation in Wesleyan Perfectionist and Glossolalic Pentecostal Movements*, ATLA Bibliography Series 18 (Metuchen, NJ: Scarecrow Press, 1987); Charles Edwin Jones, *The Charismatic Movement: A Guide to the Study of Neo-Pentecostalism with Emphasis on Anglo-American Sources*, ATLA Bibliography Series 30 (Metuchen, NJ: Scarecrow Press, 1995); Charles Edwin Jones, *The Wesleyan Holiness Movement: A Comprehensive Guide*, ATLA Bibliography Series 50 (Lanham, MD: Scarecrow Press, 2005); Charles Edwin Jones, *The Keswick Movement: A Comprehensive Guide*, ATLA Bibliography Series 52 (Lanham, MD: Scarecrow Press, 2007); Charles Edwin Jones, *The Holiness-Pentecostal Movement: A Comprehensive Guide*, ATLA Bibliography Series 54 (Lanham, MD: Scarecrow Press, 2008).

23. See, for example, *Rudolph Nelson*, "Fundamentalists at Harvard: The Case of Edward J. Carnell," *Quarterly Review* 2, no. 2 (1982): 79–98; David Bundy, "Blaming the Victim: The Wesleyan/Holiness Movement in American Culture," *Wesleyan Theological Journal* 32, no. 1 (1997): 161–78. Neither mention Pentecostal developments.

24. Barry L. Callen and William C. Kostlevy, *Heart of the Heritage: Core Themes of the Wesleyan/Holiness Tradition as Highlighted by the Wesleyan Theological Society, 1965–2000* (Salem, OH: Schmul, 2001); Barry L. Callen and Steve Hoskins, *Wesleyan Theological Society: The Fiftieth Anniversary Celebration Volume* (Lexington, KY: Emeth Press, 2015).

25. D. William Faupel and Kate McGinn, "The Society for Pentecostal Studies: A Brief History," in *The Society for Pentecostal Studies: Commemorating Thirty Years of Annual Meetings, 1971–2001*, ed. Mark E. Roberts (N.p.: Society for Pentecostal Studies, 2001), 4–6; Russell P. Spittler, "Society for Pentecostal Studies," in *The New International Dictionary of Pentecostal and Charismatic Movements*,

ed. Stanley M. Burgess and Eduard M. van der Maas (Grand Rapids, MI: Zondervan, 2002), 1979–80; Vinson Synan, "The Beginnings of the Society for Pentecostal Studies," presented at the 34th Annual Meeting of the Society for Pentecostal Studies (2005), June 25, 2020, http://storage.cloversites.com/societyforpentecostalstudies/documents/synan_sps_beginnings.pdf.

26. Vinson Synan, ed., *Aspects of Pentecostal-Charismatic Origins* (Plainfield, NJ: Logos International, 1975).

27. R. Hollis Gause, "Issues in Pentecostalism," in *Perspectives on the New Pentecostalism*, ed. Russel P. Spittler (Grand Rapids, MI: Baker, 1976), 106–16.

28. R. Hollis Gause, "Worldliness," paper and panel discussion presented at "Seminar on Holiness," Mount Paran Church of God, Atlanta, Georgia, November 16, 1970, Dixon Pentecostal Research Center, Cleveland, Tennessee; R. Hollis Gause, *Living in the Spirit: The Way of Salvation*, rev. ed. (Cleveland, TN: 1980; repr. CPT Press, 2009). See the important discussion in Kimberly Ervin Alexander, "Under the Authority of the Word and in Response to the Spirit: The Written Work and Worship of R. Hollis Gause," in *Passover, Pentecost and Parousia: Studies in Celebration of the Life and Ministry of R. Hollis Gause*, ed. Steven J. Land, Rickie D. Moore, and John Christopher Thomas, Journal of Pentecostal Theology Supplement Series 36 (Blandford Forum, UK: Deo, 2010), 1–31.

29. Oral history interview with David Roebuck, July 7, 2020.

30. On Schultz, see Frank Bateman Stranger, "A Tribute to Dr. Susan A. Schultz," *Asbury Seminarian* 33, no. 3 (1978): 3–5.

31. Donald W. Dayton, *The American Holiness Movement: A Bibliographical Introduction*, Occasional Bibliographic Papers of the B. L. Fisher Library 1 (Wilmore, KY: B. L. Fisher Library, 1971); David W. Faupel, *The American Pentecostal Movement: A Bibliographical Essay*, Occasional Bibliographic Papers of the B. L. Fisher Library 2 (Wilmore, KY: B. L. Fisher Library, 1972); David D. Bundy, *Keswick: A Bibliographic Introduction to the Higher Life Movements*, Occasional Bibliographic Papers of the B. L. Fisher Library 3 (Wilmore, KY: B. L. Fisher Library, 1975).

32. Vinson Synan, *The Holiness-Pentecostal Movement in the United States* (Grand Rapids, MI: Eerdmans, 1971).

33. Herbert McGonigle, "Pneumatological Nomenclature in Early Methodism," *Wesleyan Theological Journal* 8 (1973): 61, 72; Donald W. Dayton, "Asa Mahan and the Development of American Holiness Theology," *Wesleyan Theological Journal* 9, no. 1 (1974): 60–69; Donald W. Dayton, "From 'Christian Perfection' to the 'Baptism of the Holy Ghost': A Study in the Origins of Pentecostalism," in Synan, *Aspects of Pentecostal-Charismatic Origins*, 54–63; Donald W. Dayton, "The Doctrine of the Baptism of the Holy Spirit: Its Emergence and Significance," *Wesleyan Theological Journal* 13 (1978): 114–26; Timothy L. Smith, "The Doctrine of the Sanctifying Spirit: Charles G. Finney's Synthesis of Wesleyan and Covenant Theology," *Wesleyan Theological Journal* 13 (1978): 92–113; Timothy L. Smith, "How John Fletcher Became the Theologian of Wesleyan Perfectionism, 1770–1776," *Wesleyan Theological Journal* 15, no. 1 (1980): 77–87. Smith gave several papers at the Wesleyan Theological Society, 1973–80, which were not published. See also David Bundy, "Wesleyan Perspectives on the Holy Spirit," *Asbury Seminarian* 30, no. 2 (1975): 31–41.

34. Donald W. Dayton, *Theological Roots of Pentecostalism* (Metuchen, NJ: Scarecrow Press, 1987).

35. Synan, "Beginnings of the Society for Pentecostal Studies," 18.

36. Dieter's lecture was published as Melvin E. Dieter, "Wesleyan-Holiness Aspects of Pentecostal Origins: As Mediated Through the Nineteenth-Century Holiness Revival," in Synan, *Aspects of Pentecostal-Charismatic Origins*, 55–80. Dayton's mentor at the University of Chicago, Martin Marty, gave an address: "Pentecostalism in the Context of American Piety."

37. Roberts, *Society for Pentecostal Studies*, 25.

38. Steven J. Land, "A Passion for the Kingdom: An Analysis and Revision of Pentecostal Spirituality" (PhD diss., Emory University, 1991), published as *Pentecostal Spirituality: A Passion for the Kingdom* (Sheffield: Sheffield Academic Press, 1993).

39. Land, *Pentecostal Spirituality*.

40. Henry H. Knight III, ed., *From Aldersgate to Azusa Street: Wesleyan, Holiness, and Pentecostal Visions of the New Creation* (Eugene, OR: Pickwick Publications, 2010); Henry H. Knight III, *Anticipating Heaven Below: Optimism of Grace from Wesley to the Pentecostals* (Eugene, OR: Cascade, 2014). Henry Knight has provided the details of this paragraph.

BIBLIOGRAPHY

Adams, John Marion. "The Making of a Neo-Evangelical Statesman: The Case of Harold John Ockenga." PhD diss., Baylor University, 1994.

Alexander, Kimberly Ervin. "Under the Authority of the Word and in Response to the Spirit: The Written Work and Worship of R. Hollis Gause." In *Passover, Pentecost, and Parousia: Studies in Celebration of the Life and Ministry of R. Hollis Gause*, edited by Steven J. Land, Rickie D. Moore, and John Christopher Thomas, 1–31. Journal of Pentecostal Theology Supplement Series 36. Blandford Forum, UK: Deo, 2010.

Anderson, Allan. *An Introduction to Pentecostalism: Global Charismatic Christianity*. Cambridge: Cambridge University Press, 2004.

———. *Spreading Fires: The Missionary Nature of Early Pentecostalism*. Maryknoll, NY: Orbis, 2007.

Bundy, David. "Blaming the Victim: The Wesleyan/Holiness Movement in American Culture." *Wesleyan Theological Journal* 32, no. 1 (1997): 161–78.

———. "California Pentecostalism as Icon: Toward an Understanding of the Function of the Azusa Street Revival in Pentecostal Mythology." Unpublished lecture presented at the Society for Pentecostal Studies, 1986.

———. *Keswick: A Bibliographic Introduction to the Higher Life Movements*. Occasional Bibliographic Papers of the B. L. Fisher Library 3. Wilmore, KY: B. L. Fisher Library, 1975.

———. "Pauline Missions: The Wesleyan Holiness Vision." In *The Global Impact of the Wesleyan Traditions and Their Related Movements*, edited by Charles Yrigoyen Jr., 13–26. Pietist and Wesleyan Studies 14. Lanham, MD: Scarecrow Press, 2002.

———. "Sophia Chambers, Founder of the Holiness Church: A Case Study of Victorian Entrepreneurial Religious Leadership." *Wesley and Methodist Studies* 11, no. 1 (2019): 24–49.

———. *Visions of Apostolic Mission: Scandinavian Pentecostal Mission to 1935*. Studia Historico-Ecclesiastica Upsaliensia 45. Uppsala: Uppsala Universitet, 2009.

———. "Wesleyan Perspectives on the Holy Spirit." *Asbury Seminarian* 30, no. 2 (1975): 31–41.

Bundy, David, and Masaya Fujii. "Barclay Fowell Buxton, Japanese Christians, and the Japan Evangelistic Band." *Journal of World Christianity* 8, no. 1 (2018): 47–74.

Callen, Barry L., and Steve Hoskins. *Wesleyan Theological Society: The Fiftieth Anniversary Celebration Volume.* Lexington, KY: Emeth Press, 2015.

Callen, Barry L., and William C. Kostlevy. *Heart of the Heritage: Core Themes of the Wesleyan/Holiness Tradition as Highlighted by the Wesleyan Theological Society, 1965–2000.* Salem, OH: Schmul, 2001.

Carwardine, Richard. *Transatlantic Revivalism: Popular Evangelicalism in Britain and America, 1790–1865.* Westport, CT: Greenwood, 1978.

Cottret, Bernard. *Histoire de la Réforme protestante: Luther, Calvin, Wesley XVIe–XVIIIe siècle.* Paris: Perrin, 2010. First published 2001.

Cunningham, Floyd T., Stan Ingersol, Harold E. Raser, and David P. Whitelaw. *Our Watchword and Song: The Centennial History of the Church of the Nazarene.* Kansas City, MO: Beacon Hill Press of Kansas City, 2009.

Dayton, Donald W. *The American Holiness Movement: A Bibliographical Introduction.* Occasional Bibliographic Papers of the B. L. Fisher Library 1. Wilmore, KY: B. L. Fisher Library, 1971.

———. "Asa Mahan and the Development of American Holiness Theology." *Wesleyan Theological Journal* 9, no. 1 (1974): 60–69.

———. "The Doctrine of the Baptism of the Holy Spirit: Its Emergence and Significance." *Wesleyan Theological Journal* 13 (1978): 114–26.

———. "From 'Christian Perfection' to the 'Baptism of the Holy Ghost': A Study in the Origins of Pentecostalism." In *Aspects of Pentecostal-Charismatic Origins*, edited by Vinson Synan, 54–63. Plainfield, NJ: Logos International, 1975.

———. *Theological Roots of Pentecostalism.* Metuchen, NJ: Scarecrow Press, 1987.

Dieter, Melvin E. *The Holiness Revivals of the Nineteenth Century.* Studies in Evangelicalism 1. Metuchen, NJ: Scarecrow Press, 1980; 2nd ed., 1996.

———. "Wesleyan-Holiness Aspects of Pentecostal Origins: As Mediated Through the Nineteenth-Century Holiness Revival." In *Aspects of Pentecostal-Charismatic Origins*, edited by Vinson Synan, 55–80. Plainfield, NJ: Logos International, 1975.

Di Sabatino, David. *The Jesus People Movement: An Annotated Bibliography and General Resource.* Westport, CT: Greenwood Press, 1999.

Eskridge, Larry. *God's Forever Family: The Jesus People Movement in America.* Oxford: Oxford University Press, 2013.

Evans, Elizabeth. *The Wright Vision: The Story of the New England Fellowship.* Lanham: University Press of America, 1991.

Faupel, David W. *The American Pentecostal Movement: A Bibliographical Essay.* Occasional Bibliographic Papers of the B. L. Fisher Library 2. Wilmore, KY: B. L. Fisher Library, 1972.

Faupel, D. William, and Kate McGinn. "The Society for Pentecostal Studies: A Brief History." In *The Society for Pentecostal Studies: Commemorating Thirty Years of Annual Meetings, 1971–2001*, edited by Mark E. Roberts, 4–6. N.p.: Society for Pentecostal Studies, 2001.

Ford, George L. *Like a Tree Planted: The Life Story of Leslie Ray Marston.*

Winona Lake, IN: Light and Life Press, 1985.

Frank, Douglas. *Less Than Conquerors: How Evangelicals Entered the Twentieth Century*. Grand Rapids, MI: Eerdmans, 1986.

Gause, R. Hollis. "Issues in Pentecostalism." In *Perspectives on the New Pentecostalism*, edited by Russel P. Spittler, 106–16. Grand Rapids, MI: Baker, 1976.

———. *Living in the Spirit: The Way of Salvation*. Rev. ed. Cleveland, TN: CPT Press, 2009. First published 1980.

———. "Worldliness." Paper and panel discussion presented at "Seminar on Holiness," Mount Paran Church of God, Atlanta, GA, November 16, 1970. Dixon Pentecostal Research Center, Cleveland, TN.

Goff, James R., Jr. *Fields White unto Harvest: Charles F. Parham and the Missionary Origins of Pentecostalism*. Fayetteville: University of Arkansas Press, 1988.

Grosclaude, Jérôme. *Le Méthodisme: Un tison tiré du feu*, préface de Bernard Cottret. N.p.: Éditions Ampelos, 2017.

Hatch, Nathan O. *The Democratization of American Christianity*. New Haven: Yale University Press, 1989.

Hocken, P. D. "Charismatic Movement." In *The New International Dictionary of Pentecostal and Charismatic Movements*, edited by Stanley M. Burgess and Eduard M. van der Maas, 477–519. Grand Rapids, MI: Zondervan, 2002.

Hollenweger, Walter J. "Handbuch der Pfingstbewegung." PhD diss., Universitat Zurich, 1965. https://archive.org/details/pts_handbuchderpfings_1422_1.

———. *New Wine in Old Wineskins: Protestant and Catholic Neo-Pentecostalism*. Gloucester: Fellowship Press, 1973.

Howard, Victor B. *Religion and the Radical Republican Movement, 1860–1870*. Lexington: University Press of Kentucky, 1990.

Jones, Charles E. *Black Holiness: A Guide to the Study of Black Participation in Wesleyan Perfectionist and Glossolalic Pentecostal Movements*. ATLA Bibliography Series 18. Metuchen, NJ: Scarecrow Press, 1987.

———. *The Charismatic Movement: A Guide to the Study of Neo-Pentecostalism with Emphasis on Anglo-American Sources*. ATLA Bibliography Series 30. Metuchen, NJ: Scarecrow Press, 1995.

———. *A Guide to the Study of the Pentecostal Movement*. ATLA Bibliography Series 6. Metuchen, NJ: Scarecrow Press, 1983.

———. *The Holiness-Pentecostal Movement: A Comprehensive Guide*. ATLA Bibliography Series 54. Lanham, MD: Scarecrow Press, 2008.

———. *The Keswick Movement: A Comprehensive Guide*. ATLA Bibliography Series 52. Lanham, MD: Scarecrow Press, 2007.

———. *The Wesleyan Holiness Movement: A Comprehensive Guide*. ATLA Bibliography Series 50. Lanham, MD: Scarecrow Press, 2005.

Knight, Henry H., III. *Anticipating Heaven Below: Optimism of Grace from Wesley to the Pentecostals*. Eugene, OR: Cascade, 2014.

———, ed. *From Aldersgate to Azusa Street: Wesleyan, Holiness, and Pentecostal Visions of the New Creation*. Eugene, OR: Pickwick Publications, 2010.

Kostlevy, William, ed. *The A to Z of the Holiness Movement*. A–Z Guide Series 164. Lanham, MD: Scarecrow Press, 2010.

———. *Holy Jumpers: Evangelicals and Radicals in Progressive Era America*. Oxford: Oxford University Press, 2010.

Kuosmanen, Juhani. *Herätyksen Historia*. Tikkurila, Finland: Ristin Voitto, 1979.

Laborie, Lionel. *Enlightening Enthusiasm: Prophecy and Religious Experience in Early Eighteenth-Century England*. Manchester: Manchester University Press, 2015.

Land, Steven J. "A Passion for the Kingdom: An Analysis and Revision of Pentecostal Spirituality." PhD diss., Emory University, 1991.

———. *Pentecostal Spirituality: A Passion for the Kingdom*. Sheffield: Sheffield Academic Press, 1993.

Little, James Amasa. "Biography of Lorenzo Dow Young." *Utah Historical Quarterly* 14 (1946): 118–21.

Marks, Marilla, ed. *Memoirs of the Life of David Marks, Minister of the Gospel*. Dover, NH: Free-Will Baptist Publishing, 1846.

McCracken T., and Robert B. Blodgett. *Holy Rollers: Murder and Madness in Oregon's Love Cult*. Caldwell, ID: Caxton Press, 2002.

McGonigle, Herbert. "Pneumatological Nomenclature in Early Methodism." *Wesleyan Theological Journal* 8 (1973): 61–72.

Murdock, Norman H. *Origins of the Salvation Army*. Knoxville: University of Tennessee Press, 1994.

Nelson, Rudolph. "Fundamentalists at Harvard: The Case of Edward J. Carnell." *Quarterly Review* 2, no. 2 (1982): 79–98.

Phillips, Jim, and Rosemary Gartner. *Murdering Holiness: The Trials of Franz Creffield and George Mitchell*. Vancouver: UBC Press, 2003.

Robeck, Cecil M., Jr. *The Azusa Street Mission and Revival: The Birth of the Global Pentecostal Movement*. Nashville: Thomas Nelson, 2006.

Roberts, Mark E., ed. *The Society for Pentecostal Studies: Commemorating Thirty Years of Annual Meetings, 1971–2001*. N.p.: Society for Pentecostal Studies, 2001.

Rosell, Garth M. *Surprising Work of God: Harold John Ockenga, Billy Graham, and the Rebirth of Evangelicalism*. Grand Rapids, MI: Baker Academic, 2008.

Schwartz, Hillel. *The French Prophets: The History of a Millenarian Group in Eighteenth-Century England*. Berkeley: University of California Press, 1980.

Smith, Timothy L. "The Doctrine of the Sanctifying Spirit: Charles G. Finney's Synthesis of Wesleyan and Covenant Theology." *Wesleyan Theological Journal* 13 (1978): 92–113.

———. "How John Fletcher Became the Theologian of Wesleyan Perfectionism, 1770–1776." *Wesleyan Theological Journal* 15, no. 1 (1980): 77–87.

———. *Revivalism and Social Reform in Mid-Nineteenth-Century America*. Nashville: Abingdon Press, 1957.

Spittler, Russell P. "Society for Pentecostal Studies." In *The New International Dictionary of Pentecostal and Charismatic Movements*, edited by Stanley Burgess and Eduard M. van der Maas, 1079–80. Grand Rapids, MI: Zondervan, 2002.

Stranger, Frank Bateman. "A Tribute to Dr. Susan A. Schultz." *Asbury Seminarian* 33, no. 3 (1978): 3–5.

Strong, Douglas M. *Perfectionist Politics: Abolitionism and the Religious Tensions of American Democracy*. Syracuse: Syracuse University Press, 1999.

Synan, Vinson, ed. *Aspects of Pentecostal-Charismatic Origins*. Plainfield, NJ: Logos International, 1975.

———. "Beginnings of the Society for Pentecostal Studies." http://storage.cloversites.com/societyforpentecostalstudies/documents/synan_sps_beginnings.pdf.

———. *The Holiness-Pentecostal Movement in the United States*. Grand Rapids, MI: Eerdmans, 1971.

Taiz, Lillian. *Hallelujah Lads and Lassies: Remaking the Salvation Army in America, 1880–1930*. Chapel Hill: University of North Carolina Press, 2001.

Vuilleumier, Henri. *L'histoire de l'Église Réformée du Pays de Vaud sous le Régime Bernois*. 4 vols. Lausanne: Éditions La Concorde, 1927–33.

Wacker, Grant. "Travail of a Broken Family: Evangelical Responses to Pentecostalism in America, 1906–1916." *Journal of Ecclesiastical History* 47, no. 3 (1996): 505–28.

Ward, W. R. *The Protestant Evangelical Awakening*. Cambridge: Cambridge University Press, 1992.

Woolley, Tim. "'Have Our People Been Sufficiently Cautious?' Wesleyan Responses to Lorenzo Dow in England and Ireland, 1799–1819." *Wesley and Methodist Studies* 9, no. 2 (2017): 141–62.

AT THE BEGINNING

CHAPTER 1

The Preachers and Their Students
God's Bible School as a Seedbed of Radical
Holiness and Pentecostal Leaders, 1892–1910

David Bundy

Populism and the Progressive Era in the United States (ca. 1890–ca. 1920) spawned many populisms and progressivisms during the transition from the excesses of the Gilded Age (ca. 1870–ca. 1900). Historians have identified major concerns of the Progressives: the reform of the power structures of society by overthrowing the elites, antitrust measures, desire for direct democracy, temperance/prohibition, and rights for women. The arguments and investigations of those in power were often led by the editors and reporters of the "muckraking" periodical publications and newspapers.[1] The Radical Holiness and Pentecostal networks evolved during this period.[2] They shared many of the concerns of the more secular Progressives but also can be understood as populist; they had less faith in both humanity and government than many Progressives did. Many of the Radical Holiness periodicals shared the methods and the temperaments of the "muckraking" periodicals of Populists and Progressives. One such node in the Radical Holiness Networks was God's Bible School (GBS).

GBS is perched on the edge of a hill overlooking downtown Cincinnati; neat, small, functional brick buildings sit close together. It was once arguably a center of a religious reformation; now it seems less than revolutionary—indeed, conservative. It is not pretentious as educational institutions go. It never has been. Initially it was the fulfillment of the dream of one man, Martin Wells Knapp (1853–1901), who died just as GBS was becoming a somewhat classically structured educational institution.³ In protest against the practice of donors giving money to have their names on the facades of buildings/institutions, he named it "God's Bible School." He willed it to God, who he claimed all along was the owner; Knapp was merely the chief steward. It took decades for the courts to determine that God could not own property in Ohio.⁴

Not only was the ownership ambiguous; so, too, was the date of its establishment. First there were, from 1882, prayer, worship, and training sessions for workers to which prospective workers appear to have been invited. Then there were "Chapel Classes," mostly taught by Knapp, visiting evangelists, and periodical ministry staff from the mid-1890s, perhaps earlier. All of this occurred before the official opening of GBS in 1900.⁵ The project was known by the title of its very successful religious periodical publication, the *Revivalist*, later renamed *God's Revivalist and Bible Advocate*; it sustained and promoted Knapp, the *Revivalist* ministries, and from 1900 God's Bible School.⁶

Faculty (teaching staff) is also a problematic category. The distinctions among visiting preachers, *Revivalist* staff, students, and teaching faculty were often ambiguous. For example, Beatrice M. Finney, a Southern Methodist from Kentucky, was on the "original" faculty (English language) of 1900. However, she was also on an early list as one of the "original" students.⁷ It is probable that she was both student and faculty, a testimony to equality. Nettie Peabody arrived as a student in 1901 but joined the faculty a year later, becoming a widely published scholar.⁸ The faculty/preachers, as well as the students, were diverse in their backgrounds. Among them, all Radical Holiness advocates, were varieties of Methodists, Congregationalists, Baptists, Quakers, and Presbyterians, among others.

Despite or perhaps because of these ambiguities, GBS became an important institution for both the Pentecostal and the Radical Holiness movements of the early twentieth century. GBS provided a generation of leaders for both movements. When these future leaders attended GBS, they were not yet divided into separate religious traditions. They were merely Radical Holiness "Pentecost" students. In the modest halls and chapel, a revolution was fomented that continues to shape World Christianities.

This chapter argues that the theological, liturgical, and social framework of the Radical Holiness "Pentecostal" approach to Christian life taught and learned at GBS, variously presented, articulated, and defined, stood in the background as key leaders of the Radical Holiness and post-1906 Pentecostal movements differentiated over religious experience, theological definitions, and personal/group expectations of those experiences. The *Revivalist* ministry and GBS shared values with populism and the Progressive Movement but were also their critics.

Fig. 1.1 Interior and exterior of God's Tabernacle and Men's Dormitory, God's Bible School and College, Cincinnati, Ohio, early twentieth century. Courtesy of God's Bible School and College.

Four disclaimers are essential. First, no claim is made of "firstness" for either GBS or Knapp. In a diffuse global network, ideas and relationships ebbed and flowed easily, were often contentious, and were subject to political as well as theological redefinition. Second, no claim is made that the Radical Holiness Networks node developed by Knapp at GBS was the only node in those global networks that formed future Pentecostal and Radical Holiness leaders, or even necessarily the most important node. Third, the Radical Holiness Movements or Networks are referred to in the plural, signifying their diversity. There was no magisterium and GBS did not pretend to provide one. Fourth, this chapter should not be read either as a critique or endorsement of existing theories for understanding the origins of Pentecostalism.[9]

Because of its lack of pretension, and perhaps because of the quirkiness of its luminaries, GBS has been generally ignored by historians of American religion. Moody Bible Institute and Northfield are frequently discussed, but GBS hardly at all. However, an institution that arguably trained or otherwise influenced many of the first generation of post-1906 Pentecostal leadership and many of the same generation's Radical Holiness leaders deserves attention.

PENTECOST: THE THEOLOGICAL AND SOCIAL FRAMEWORK OF THE RADICAL HOLINESS MOVEMENTS

The crucial historiographical questions related to Holiness Movements and the origins of Pentecostalism at the turn of the twentieth century are generally dealt with in one of three ways. The first is the tendency to simplistically lump together the diversity of those phenomena into a singularly identified phenomenon, usually articulated through the prism of Methodism and of a version of Methodist theology. The second is to categorize everything as "evangelical" as if that explains the characters in the drama. Third, there is a tendency to look at denominational backgrounds of participants and take those as the primary hermeneutical keys. Thus, Quakers are always Quakers; Baptists and Presbyterians are viewed as Reformed, and Methodists are viewed as a group. The reality was ever so much more complex. All of the actors in our drama, before 1906, were part of a worldwide, initially nondenominational series of networks, the Radical Holiness Movements.

The Radical Holiness Movements were those outside or on the margins of Methodism, which accepted various versions of sanctification (holiness, baptism of the Holy Spirit, Christian perfection). Both conversion and sanctification/baptism with the Holy Spirit were to be instantaneous, expedited by the faith of the individual. The "ideal" process of both included personal and cosmic struggle reflecting the biblical Pentecost narratives.

Radical Holiness people who were Methodist usually found themselves at odds with the Methodist leadership, as did Knapp. Those not already Methodist normally did not become Methodist or express interest in the larger Methodist identity but remained loosely related to their denominations or became independent nodes of the Radical Holiness Networks. Their primary ecclesial and theological identity was usually the new networks, even as diverse church memberships and aspects of earlier theological frameworks enabled them to work and have conversations across defined religious borders. The new networks in some instances came to function as new movements or denominations. The Radical Holiness Networks understood the baptism with the Holy Spirit (sanctification, Christian perfection), generally not distinguishing among the three terms, to constitute the basis for transcending the limitations and boundaries of the theologies based in debates from the fourth to the nineteenth century. Importantly, they were open to innovation in theology, governance, and practice in ways not yet part of the larger Christian traditions. There was no magisterium or creed to enforce uniformity. People were free to change their opinions, expressions of those opinions, and networks. There was nothing more than the court of public opinion to keep them from doing so. That court was rarely a restraint, unless sexuality, financial malfeasance, or accusations related to these were involved.

The self-perception of the Radical Holiness Movements, at GBS and elsewhere, was that they were creating community on the model of the Pentecost events described in the narrative of the Acts of the Apostles. The Pentecost narratives were the essential and exclusive model for Christian experience, community, and mission. It was anticipated that this Pentecost community would unite all people "Baptized with the Holy Ghost and with Fire," bringing them into the "Promised Land."[10] Faith healing and premillennialism were crucial, contested, and diversely understood parts of the Pentecost paradigm. Shaped by the international quartet of Charles Cullis, William Boardman, Otto Stockmayer, and Andrew Murray, faith healing became central to the Radical Holiness Movements.[11] Premillennialism came through various avenues from the (British) Brethren.

Mission (both domestic and foreign) was central to the identity of the Radical Holiness Movements. The key figures were William Taylor and Georg Müller.[12] The initial discussion of foreign mission in the *Revivalist* included a tribute to Bishop William Taylor and support for Taylor's plea for 100,000

Fig. 1.2 Martin Wells Knapp. Frontispiece of A. M. Hills, *A Hero of Faith and Prayer; Or, Life of Rev. Martin Wells Knapp* (Cincinnati: Mrs. M. W. Knapp, 1902).

Holiness Christians to go to Africa as self-supporting missionaries. Knapp applied to become a Taylor missionary, but he was turned down because of health reasons.¹³ Articles on mission frequently included references to Taylor.¹⁴ When Knapp was searching for faculty for the Beulah Bible School in Kentucky, he called for a person who was sanctified, able to lead and teach singing, able to deny self, and "willing like Bishop Taylor's missionaries, to launch out on faith alone."¹⁵

There were important social components to this "Pentecost" vision, beyond the already radical egalitarian vision of Spirit baptism. Individuals were not to be valued based on gender, class, race, wealth, or education. It was a vision of a new humanity without borders, not even ecclesiastical borders.¹⁶ This theological and social paradigm gave the movement intellectual, praxis, and social coherence as well as cross-situational coherence. The common "Pentecost" language and values enabled them to respond to both correlational evidence and experiential evidence and to develop group-accepted praxis, theory, and relationships.¹⁷ However, it must be noted that for all the mutual interest and commonly held values, there was competition to attract crowds, to sell publications, and to achieve recognition. Therefore, scholars looking for total uniformity of language, ideas, or methods—or consistency of networks—will be frustrated and/or misled.

MARTIN WELLS KNAPP AND GOD'S BIBLE SCHOOL: A LOCAL EXPRESSION OF THE RADICAL HOLINESS MOVEMENTS

GBS became one of the major nodes in the Radical Holiness Networks arguably because of Knapp's publishing acumen. The periodical publication, the *Revivalist*, provided network connectivity. The Revivalist Press published large quantities of books, pamphlets, and tracts that shaped the theology of the Radical Holiness Networks. Knapp was the central defining figure for the GBS node in the Radical Holiness Networks in our period. Those who taught or studied at GBS shared and participated in the promulgation of the Radical Holiness faith and praxis.

Many scholars of revivalistic religion have seen the participants as antiurban, anti-industrialization, and antimodern, and as promoters of primitivism seeking to replicate an ideal world in the past that did not exist. This has been the case at least since the publication of William Warren Sweet's *Religion on the American Frontier* (1931).[18] However, the reality was much more complex.[19] Knapp is a case in point.

Modernization

When Knapp moved to Cincinnati (1892), he located his publishing and mission project as close to the nexus of communication and transportation as possible.[20] He sought the urban and celebrated modernity even as he criticized its brutality and exploitation of the poor and immigrants to the city.[21] Examples of his use of technology as a positive metaphor can be seen in "Revival Electricity," a cartoon entitled "Two Railroads" that used the choices offered by railroad junctions as a type of religious choices leading to heaven or hell, songs such as "Powerhouse in the Sky," and his railroad songs.[22] The transcontinental railroads and the widening network of telegraph lines were exciting to Knapp and his audiences; these, and publishing technologies, enhanced the strength of the *Revivalist* network. Knapp and his Radical Holiness Movements colleagues were not Luddites!

Although celebrating new technologies, Knapp contested them as they made the powerful more powerful and enabled the purveyors of addictive materials (alcohol, tobacco, drugs) to more easily reach and expand their market. He did not attack the systems (trains) that made the low-cost distribution possible, but the purveyors of death, and insisted the Christian be neither a consumer nor purveyor of addictive agents.[23] Christians were urged to "live long" by resisting "strong drink," narcotics, gluttony, licentiousness, and other sins.[24] Knapp opined that even coffee might become a substitute addiction for alcohol.[25] Bruno Latour denominated the phenomena as "actants." That is, these substances act independently of the person to control the minds and bodies of those who adopt them as companions in life's way.[26]

Power

The question of "power" was central for Knapp. There were two kinds of power: positive and negative. Positive power had its source in God. Negative satanic power was exhibited in human exploiters (the state, political parties, industry, secret societies, church). These institutions conspired together and separately to limit the power of God for their own purposes. The churches were more evil than the others because they were not what they claimed to be, excluding from power those who promoted the transforming power of God, accepting support from exploiters in exchange for ignoring the effects of their exploitation, and not working to transform people and their context as the Bible demands. Knapp insisted that power was not to be centralized in any individual in the church, society, or social group. Power was to be dispersed throughout the society. Sanctified people were able to actualize positive power better than others.[27]

In his social, religious, and cultural situation, Knapp could not imagine organizing the larger society to fight for social justice and transformation. He was experiencing the social backlash against the Holiness Movement resulting from growing Northern racism and racist anger against migrating African Americans from the South. Like the agendas of the Populists and the Progressive Party, his faced determined opposition. Knapp developed projects to transform the lives of the people he and his colaborers could afford to reach. He anticipated that individualist transformation would have social consequences. He wrote: "God, who in nature transforms rot and refuse into roses, fruits and fragrances, in the realms of grace, surprises still more startling transformations."[28]

Knapp did speak out on macro social issues. He insisted that the large industries were evil when they promoted goods appealing to human greed or fostered addictions that take away the health and free will of the individual. He opposed exploitation, selfishness, and secrecy of decisions affecting social life. He spoke against the "worldliness" of Christians and their churches:

> Worldliness is one of the most fatal worms that saps the life of spirituality. Wherever it gnaws, leaves wither and die. Its presence on every hand may be seen by the following outward marks:
>
> *Conformity to worldly fashions;*
> *Sacrificing to worldly political parties;*
> *Popularity of worldly churches;*
> *Affiliation with worldly fraternities;*
> *Adoption of worldly methods of business;*
> *Promotion of worldly advertisements in religious papers;*
> *Insertion of unseemly cuts in such advertisements;*
> *Worldly people as leaders of choirs, Sunday schools, on official boards;*
> *The discussion of worldly themes in the pulpit and by the religious press.*[29]

The issue at each point was the abuse of power and the subsequent damaging of the lives and spirituality of those encountering such power. The older churches claimed to be different from the world but were not. Knapp observed that these, with their mind-numbing rituals, were sustained and presided over by egotistical men. They sought to control people and control access to God so that they could acquire money, titles, and power for themselves. Women and the poor were excluded from positions and ministry in the churches.[30] He insisted that "The societies of God's church should be governed by New Testament principles and practices."[31] Abuses by the older churches, especially by the Methodist Episcopal Church, were recurring themes in the *Revivalist* and Knapp's other publications. In support of his position, he published an article by Newton Wray asserting that the Methodist Episcopal Church bragged about its statistics but was in a state of famine of the Spirit, encouraging nominal rather than transformative faith.[32] He reprinted a text by A. T. Pierson, who argued that the "The ideal church ... is one that is working for the conversion of souls, an educational church, and a democratic church; but it must be in my judgment, a free church."[33] More pointed were the articles by I. Reid, "Protestant Popery," and E. H. Dashiel, "Ecclesiasticism Versus Jesus."[34] Knapp insisted that he was not against organizations or against the churches but "against the prostitution of the organization in the interests of the world."[35] Knapp published a detailed analysis of the power issues that forced him to resign from the Methodist Episcopal Church.[36]

The Methodist-dominated National Holiness Association (NHA) was criticized for having nondemocratic values similar to those of the Methodist Episcopal Church or Freemasons. They were elitist and worked to exclude the Radical Holiness Movements not in total agreement with them from the National Holiness Association. Knapp understood the NHA as endeavoring to maintain a Methodist monopoly on "holiness" and to make it socially acceptable in order to support their upward social aspirations.[37] Knapp argued that government, business, church, and the NHA were designed by the powerful for their benefit, rather than for the common people. He reminded readers that the Radical Holiness Movements must inform people that all resources belong to God, and that the church and individual Christians must struggle for personal and social transformation and social justice. Corruption and abuse of the poor by governments and businesses will not last: "What a transition from poverty to plenty. . . . This earth belongs to Jesus Christ, and he will not always allow His brothers and sisters to be treated as they are today."[38] This has striking parallels with the 1905 Preamble to the *Constitution* of the Industrial Workers of the World (Wobblies): "There can be no peace so long as hunger and want are found among millions of the working people and the few, who make up the employing class, have all the good things of life."[39]

Quality of Life and Equality

The last half of the nineteenth century was a time of expanding aspirations for the improvement of the quality of life, democracy, as well as empowerment for women, the working classes, and the poor. The Salvation Army (and derivatives) were strong. Radical Holiness missions were a prominent part of the urban landscape. The "Social Gospel" movement led by Walter Rauschenbusch made nearly the same arguments.[40]

Knapp was in some ways more comprehensive in his arguments, framed in the mid-American context, than many other radicals. He argued that humans have rights that are given by God but taken away by the negative powers. He was against war.[41] He insisted that the Christian was to care for the poor,[42] minister to prisoners,[43] heal the sick,[44] and lift up the downtrodden: "fallen women,"[45] orphans,[46] uneducated people,[47] African Americans,[48] and Appalachian poor.[49] Healing for Knapp was a complicated concept: inclusive, liberating, transformational, including physical healing, with or without doctors. He did not blame those who were ill for their lack of faith for healing or for having sin as a background to their sicknesses. After all, his beloved saintly first wife, Lucy Glenn Knapp, became ill and died; he himself was continuously ill.[50]

Knapp was committed to struggling against destructive uses of power, injustice, human division, and poverty but negatively assessed the chances for success. He and most of the Radical Holiness Movement adopted pessimistic premillennialism rather than the more optimistic postmillennialism of the more affluent, upwardly mobile, and socially integrated members of the National Holiness Association and the Methodist Episcopal Church. Life was improving only superficially, and they believed any large-scale transformation would require divine intervention through the second coming of Christ.

Women in Ministry and Culture

The attitude of the Radical Holiness Movements to women in ministry was normally positive. William Baxter Godbey, the famous Kentucky evangelist and later God's Bible School professor, began his volume *Women Preachers* with the question "Shall Women Preach?" The next word is "Yes," and then he argued on the basis of biblical texts and William Taylor that women had the right and responsibility to serve as preachers and missionaries.[51] This book was recommended by Knapp, who insisted "Women may be Pentecostal Preachers." A woman may be "the most effective of Pentecostal preachers."[52] Knapp's first wife, Lucy Glenn Knapp, was active in the *Revivalist* ministry in Michigan; his second wife, Minnie Ferle Knapp, was a leader in Cincinnati. His mother, Octavia N. Knapp, directed ministries in both cities. Knapp willed GBS to God, leaving three women in charge: Minnie Knapp (his widow), Bessie Queen (his assistant), and fiery Irish immigrant advocate and educator of women for ministry, Mary Storey.[53]

At God's Bible School women served, from the beginning, as leaders, administrators, teachers, and published theologians. Original faculty member, Beatrice M. Finney, became a regular contributor of articles on spirituality and theology to the *Revivalist* and, in 1901, a missionary to South Africa.[54] Nettie Peabody became a frequent contributor to the *Revivalist*, popular Bible teacher, and theologian.[55] Abbie Clemens Morrow, editor of the (Sunday school) *Illustrator*[56] and *Arnold's Practical Sunday-school Commentary*,[57] published books with Martin Wells Knapp and became a weekly contributor to the *Revivalist* as an exegetical specialist. She later married A. C. M. Brown and became Pentecostal. She served as editor of the *Revivalist* magazine for youth: *Sparkling Water from Bible Fountains* from January 1902. Although she never joined the

GBS faculty full-time, she was a prominent woman in the GBS and other Radical Holiness Networks.[58] Administrator Mary Storey early supported Knapp's ministries, especially those to the poor. She became a prominent evangelist and an important public representative of GBS in the region. Storey developed a robust "warfare" language to describe the struggles to evangelize and the problems related to conversion and sanctification experiences.[59]

Thus, at a time when women were struggling for political, social, religious, and legal rights in the United States, the Radical Holiness Networks, including the node at Cincinnati represented by GBS, provided opportunities of leadership for women in all aspects of its ministry and educational projects. The appointment of the three women to lead the organization after Knapp's death demonstrates the commitment was broader than to women in ministry. As noted, they published that commitment to gender equality. Women represented and spoke for the ministry.

Mission

Knapp's *Revivalist* gave missionaries free publicity, prayer supporters, and potential speaking engagements when in the United States, as well as financial support. The missionary network included North American mission organizations such as the Vanguard Mission (St. Louis and India),[60] the Free Methodist Ward family (India),[61] the Hirst family,[62] Juji Nakada and the Cowmans (Japan),[63] among others.

Knapp and his associates believed that if all missionaries scattered around the world would accept the theology and experience of the Radical Holiness Movements, they would be more effective missionaries, as William Taylor and others had demonstrated. In an effort to increase the number of "baptized in the Holy Spirit" missionaries, Quaker Radical Holiness evangelists Charles H. Stalker and Byron J. Rees undertook (1901) to visit mission fields around the world, not to establish new missions, but to encourage missionaries and indigenous leaders to experience baptism of the Holy Spirit.[64] This mission was supported and reported on by Knapp and the *Revivalist* and became paradigmatic for later Radical Holiness and Pentecostal evangelists.[65]

PREACHERS, TEACHERS, AND STUDENTS

GBS was a school for Bible study, religious experience, reflection, and action. Knapp had no intention of starting a seminary or university.[66] GBS was one of many institutions of the Radical Holiness Networks influenced by but different from W. E. Boardman's project (1877) restructured as Mary Boardman's and Elizabeth Baxter's Bethshan (London, 1882), A. B. Simpson's Missionary Training Home (New York, 1882), and Moody Bible Institute (1886). The preachers/teachers and students at GBS were there at the invitation of Knapp and his successors. They shared the "Pentecost" vision, biblical hermeneutic, as well as the social, cultural, and mission goals of the Radical Holiness Networks. The "Pentecost" experience of baptism with the Holy Spirit was central.

The liturgical values of the "Pentecost" community at GBS had two facets: supporting the faith of believers and evangelism of unbelievers. It was experiential, participatory, lively, and noisy. Worship offended neighbors in Cincinnati, and Knapp was convicted of causing social "disorder" and "excessive noise."[67] The liturgy facilitated expression of "Pentecost" social and theological values; it was adaptable and transportable. It was not limited to the inside of the church but was also used in public places as both community worship and evangelism. It facilitated participation of people of diverse ethnic and racial identities. Preachers/teachers were invited who could function well within that liturgical structure while reinforcing, or sometimes modestly reinterpreting, the "Pentecost" understanding of Christianity. As Knapp expressed it:

> The opening up of Pentecostal dispensation was signaled by a 'sound from heaven' which filled the house, aroused the city, and heralded the incoming of the Holy Ghost which transforms believers into such a joyous, noisy, shouting band of revival workers as to create the criticism that they were on a drunken spree. What a contrast to the cold cemeteries that a dying and dead ecclesiasticism would palm off on people as the Church of God! A live Church is a noisy Church. A Pentecostal revival will be accompanied by Pentecostal manifestations. Its sounds are not those that are gotten up to order, manufactured for the occasion, which have the sound of a cracked bell; but they have the characteristics of their Pentecostal precedent. It is a celestial noise. It came from heaven. No amount of human racket can be substituted for it. It was a penetrating noise. It filled the whole house and was heard.[68]

Preachers/teachers and students were expected to fit into the life of the "Pentecost" community. It was disciplined, ascetic, communal, socially activist, featuring ministry to the poor. It reflected the egalitarian, inclusive, and multi-ethnic social vision of the "Pentecost" paradigm. Experiments in "Pentecost" communalism were undertaken. Knapp insisted that "*accumulation of property for self is absolutely prohibited.*"[69] Oswald Chambers, who taught at GBS for six months in 1907, reflected: "This is truly Holiness socialism."[70] Most, if not all, shared Knapp's enthusiasm for modernization, technology, sharing of power, ministry of women, and racial equality. Most were involved in mission, either domestic or foreign. Students, believing this vision, chose to attend GBS, a choice that normally made them too religiously and socially radical and therefore marginally welcome in the older churches.

Early women faculty have been mentioned above. Male faculty included Methodist Episcopal pastor and evangelist G. D. Watson (1845–1924), Quaker evangelist Seth Cook Rees (1854–1933), Methodist Episcopal Church, South, minister and evangelist William B. Godbey (1833–1920), Quaker Charles H. Stalker (1875–1963), Oberlin- and Yale-educated Congregationalist A. M. Hills (1848–1935), and British Baptist Oswald Chambers (1874–1917). These figures were well known in the global Radical Holiness Networks. All published influential work. All shared and helped articulate Knapp's Radical Holiness vision. All of them contributed to the *Revivalist*. They passed this vision on to prospective students around the world and developed it in students studying at GBS.

WHAT THE STUDENTS LEARNED, ACCEPTED, OR REJECTED

The ideas, values, and actions of Knapp, GBS, and the Radical Holiness Movements were both paralleled in the Progressive movements of ca. 1900 to ca. 1920 and contested by larger society, both secular and religious. Knapp and GBS and other Radical Holiness Networks were far more committed to gender and racial equality than the Progressive movements or the established churches.[71] African Americans were included in classes, ministries, and worship events.[72] It was socially alienating to promote Radical Holiness social and racial values as the Gilded Age, KKK, and Jim Crow laws loomed large in society. The status accorded women and racial equality came under immense social pressure. During the first decade of Pentecostalism in, for example, Indianapolis, Pentecostals were not persecuted because they spoke in tongues, but because of interracial relationships and services, which sometimes were banned or segregated by the police.[73] Former GBS student Seymour barely escaped with his life after baptizing well-to-do white women in Indianapolis's Fall Creek. The women were divorced by their husbands.[74] Because of these pressures, many Holiness and Pentecostal networks and denominations scaled back the ordinations of women and their visible roles. Preachers/teachers and students of GBS lived with these tensions as did their audiences throughout the United States.

Success in the United States and in foreign mission was not as the Radical Holiness theory anticipated. Many Radical Holiness believers saw the limitations and marginal successes of the proponents of the Radical Holiness "Pentecost" paradigm. Where was the power of God for transformation and mission promised by the baptism of the Holy Spirit? The question was frequently asked in later Radical Holiness and early Pentecostal literature: Why have the historic mission programs, even the "Pentecost"-oriented missions, been generally unsuccessful? Why were there not more missionaries like William Taylor? Looking again at the biblical Pentecost paradigm, the question of glossolalia became central. It was the only part of the biblical Pentecost narratives that had not been taken seriously by most of the nodes of the Radical Holiness Movements. It was a small intellectual step to argue that if God could save, sanctify, heal, and come again to restore the world to God, surely God could give utilitarian languages to missionaries.

As one examines the lives and teaching of the students of GBS, there appears to be only two significant differences between students who later identified with the Radical Holiness "Pentecost" and those who became post-1906 Pentecostals. These are, first, the accessibility of unlearned languages for missionary work and, second, the development of baptism in the Holy Spirit as indicative of personal spirituality; that is, the *necessity* of speaking in tongues, glossolalia, as evidence (later, especially in the United States, the initial evidence) of baptism of the Holy Spirit. After failures to receive actual human languages, glossolalia developed from being considered the instant acquisition of foreign languages to a liturgical/religious experiential moment. This had the side effect of bringing into doubt the conviction that there were two spiritual events in the process of salvation and ministry. Some innovative theologians decided there were three or more stages. Some decided that perhaps the ethical transformation promised or required by sanctification was not so important after all or it was subsumed as an aspect of conversion. The religious politics of the period being what they were, there was no room for the live and let-live solution of A. B. Simpson between the advocates and opponents of the new interpretations of glossolalia.[75]

Among the hundreds of students at GBS before 1906 were some who evolved from Radical Holiness "Pentecost" students to prominent post-1906 Pentecostal leaders. These included: William Seymour (1870–1922), a founder of Azusa Street Mission; A. J. Tomlinson (1865–1943), founder of the Church of God (Cleveland) and Church of God of Prophecy, Quaker Radical Holiness friend of Seth Cook Rees; Robert Edward McAlister (1880–1953), a founder of the Pentecostal Assemblies of Canada; and Lillian Hunt Trasher (1887–1961), orphanage worker, and later missionary to Egypt.[76]

Most students remained part of the Radical Holiness "Pentecost" Networks. Prominent leaders who were students during this period included Charles (1868–1924) and Lettie Cowman (1870–1960), cofounders with Juji Nakada of the Oriental Missionary Society and world-renowned Quaker evangelist Charles L. Slater (1884–1950). Students who later became prominent Church of the Nazarene leaders included: Lula Glatzel Schmelzenbach (1886–1960) of Lutheran background, who with her husband Harmon F. Schmelzenbach (1882–1929) were missionaries in Swaziland (now Eswatini); religious educator Charles Brenton Widmeyer (1884–1974); and the originally Free Methodist U. E. Harding (1883–1958), "one of the most influential folk evangelists of the early 20th century Holiness movement."[77]

CONCLUSION: IMPLICATIONS FOR THE PROBLEM OF "HOLINESS AND PENTECOSTAL"

The theology, liturgy, and social perspectives of GBS and the Radical Holiness Movements, variously presented, articulated, and understood, stood in the background as the Radical Holiness "Pentecost" Movements and the post-1906 Pentecostal Movements differentiated over religious experience, the theological definitions, and personal/group expectations of those experiences. Ironically, the point of division became the biblical narrative of "Pentecost," which people in both networks expected to unite them. The arguments of the new "Apostolic Faith" that became known as Pentecostalism were most forcefully and persuasively stated by former GBS student William Seymour from 1906 to 1908 in Los Angeles in his periodical, the *Apostolic Faith*. George Soltau, British Brethren Radical Holiness evangelist, reported on the situation in Los Angeles observed on an early 1908 visit: "in Los Angeles there are twenty different schools of Holiness teaching, all of them split-offs from the Churches, some of them claiming with loud voice the gift of Tongues, and others with as loud a voice disclaiming and denouncing."[78]

The commonality of identity observed by Soltau and evidenced by the contributions of Martin Wells Knapp and GBS is less visible now, generally not appreciated or even remembered. A careful nonideological analysis of the intersections of the Radical Holiness "Pentecost" Movements and the Pentecostal

Movements worldwide would reveal other nodes and radiating networks that differentiated, or did not, as in the United States. For historians of American culture, there is still the task of working to incorporate more fully American radical religious activism of the Radical Holiness "Pentecost" Networks and post-1906 Pentecostal Movements into the understandings of populism and progressivism. This study demonstrates the commonalities of the GBS networks with those broader movements in American life. For World Christian Studies there is the same issue: Radical Holiness and Pentecostal preachers/teachers and students of GBS (1892–1910), fulfilling the vision of Martin Wells Knapp, were one node of networks that provoked new transformative processes still at work in World Christianity. These are today, for better or worse, the largest face of Protestant Christianity and have had a large impact on Catholic Christianity as well.

NOTES

1. On these periods, see Michael McGerr, *A Fierce Discontent: The Rise and Fall of the Progressive Movement in America* (New York: Free Press, 2003); Maureen Flanagan, *America Reformed: Progressives and Progressivisms* (Oxford: Oxford University Press, 2007); Lawrence Goodwyn, *Democratic Promise: The Populist Movement in America* (New York: Oxford University Press, 1976); Michael Kazin, *The Populist Persuasion: An American History* (New York: Basic Books, 1995).

2. Radical Holiness Networks are only beginning to be discussed. See William Kostlevy, *Holy Jumpers: Evangelicals and Radicals in Progressive Era America* (Oxford: Oxford University Press, 2010), 17–36; David Bundy and Masaya Fujii, "Barclay Fowell Buxton, Japanese Christians, and the Japan Evangelistic Band," *Journal of World Christianity* 8, no. 1 (2018): 48–50; David Bundy "Sophia Chambers, Founder of the Holiness Church: A Case Study of Victorian Entrepreneurial Religious Leadership," *Wesley and Methodist Studies* 11, no. 1 (2019): 24–49.

3. On Knapp and God's Bible School, see Lloyd Raymond Day, "A History of God's Bible School in Cincinnati, 1900–1949" (Ed.M. thesis, University of Cincinnati, 1949); Kostlevy, *Holy Jumpers*; Wallace Thornton Jr., *When the Fire Fell: Martin Wells Knapp's Vision of Pentecost and the Beginnings of God's Bible School* (Lexington, KY: Emeth Press, 2014); David Bundy, "Religion for Modernity: Martin Wells Knapp and the Radical Holiness Network of the American Progressive Era," *World Christianity and the Fourfold Gospel* 1, no. 1 (2015): 43–79.

4. Thornton, *When the Fire Fell*, 244–50.

5. The evolution of the program needs to be considered when adjudicating dates claimed by people to have attended. See the discussion of the fragmentary evidence in ibid., 51–55. The name of the periodical was the name of the ministry: *Revivalist*.

6. The *Revivalist* (1888–1900) was founded in Albion, Michigan. Knapp moved to Cincinnati in 1892, bringing the periodical with him. The title changed in 1901 to *God's Revivalist and Bible Advocate*. Cited as *Revivalist*. Volume and

issue numbers are not provided because of printing or editorial errors and changes in publication frequency. The dates of the fascicles were systematically provided, often as running page headers, and have been found reliable.

7. Larry D. Smith, *A Century on the Mount of Blessings: The Story of God's Bible School* (Cincinnati: Revivalist Press, 2016), 66, 78, 140.

8. William Kostlevy, "Peabody, Nettie," in *The A to Z of the Holiness Movement*, ed. William Kostlevy, A–Z Guide Series 164 (Lanham, MD: Scarecrow Press, 2010), 232.

9. See the brief discussion of the existing theories for understanding the origins of Pentecostalism in the introduction of this book.

10. Martin Wells Knapp, *Out of Egypt into Canaan: Lessons in Spiritual Geography* (Cincinnati: Cranston & Stowe for the Author, 1888). See Bundy, "Religion for Modernity," 50, 60.

11. Many of the citations of Andrew Murray and Otto Stockmayer in American Radical Holiness periodicals appear to be taken without attribution from *Thy Healer*. After the publication of Andrew Murray, *Divine Healing: A Series of Addresses* (New York: Alliance Press, 1900), *Revivalist* serialized much of it; for example, "Persevering Prayer and Healing," *Revivalist* (October 17, 1901): 10; "Sickness and Death," *Revivalist* (October 24, 1901): 10. Most of this volume was published as articles in *Thy Healer* and its successor title, *Jungle Help and Home Need*, at Bethshan, London, during the 1890s. It appears not to have been otherwise published in England until 1943 by the (Pentecostal) Victory Press. Knapp highly recommended H. T. Davis, *Modern Miracles* (Cincinnati: God's Revivalist Office, 1901), and A. J. Gordon, *The Ministry of Healing: Miracles of Cure in All Ages* (Chicago: F. H. Revell, 1882); for example, "Books on Healing," *Revivalist* (October 17, 1901): 10, and "Modern Miracles," *Revivalist* (October 31, 1901): 10.

12. On Taylor, see David Bundy, "Bishop William Taylor and Methodist Mission: A Study in Nineteenth Century Social History. Part I: From Campmeeting Convert to International Evangelist," *Methodist History* 27, no. 4 (1989): 197–210; Bundy, "Bishop William Taylor and Methodist Mission: A Study in Nineteenth Century Social History. Part II: Social Structures in Collision," *Methodist History* 28, no. 1 (1989): 3–21; Bundy, "William Taylor (1821–1902): Entrepreneurial Maverick for the Indigenous Church," in *Mission Legacies: Biographical Studies of Leaders of the Modern Missionary Movement*, ed. Gerald H. Anderson et al. (Maryknoll, NY: Orbis, 1995), 461–68. On Müller, see Darin Duane Lenz, "'Strengthening the Faith of the Children of God': Pietism, Print, and Prayer in the Making of a World Evangelical Hero, George Müller of Bristol (1805–1898)" (PhD diss., Kansas State University, 2010); Timothy C. F. Stunt, *The Elusive Quest of the Spiritual Malcontent: Some Early Nineteenth-Century Mavericks* (Eugene, OR: Wipf & Stock, 2015).

13. Martin Wells Knapp, "Bishop Taylor," *Revivalist* (February 1890): 1.

14. Martin Wells Knapp, "Motives for Engagement in Missionary Work," *Revivalist* (January 1893): 2; "Prayer Answered," *Revivalist* (January 1893): 2; Minnie Ferle Knapp, "Samuel Morris," *Revivalist* (November 1897): 3.

15. Martin Wells Knapp, "Wanted, A Teacher," *Revivalist* (July 1895): 6.

16. See Bundy, "Sophia Chambers."

17. Daniel Cervone, "Socio-Cognitive Mechanisms and Personality Coherence: Self-Knowledge, Situational Beliefs, and Cross-Situational Coherence in Perceived Self-Efficacy," *Psychological Science* 8, no. 1 (1997): 43–50; Albert Bandura, *Social Foundations of Thought and Action: A*

Social Cognitive Theory (Englewood Cliffs, NJ: Prentice-Hall, 1986).

18. William Warren Sweet, *Religion on the American Frontier* (Chicago: University of Chicago Press, 1931).

19. David Bundy, "Blaming the Victim: The Wesleyan/Holiness Movement in American Culture," *Wesleyan Theological Journal* 32, no. 1 (1997): 161–78.

20. On the move to the YMCA building, see *Revivalist* (November 1895): 5.

21. See, for example, Martin Wells Knapp, "Revival Success in Cities," *Revivalist* (March 14, 1901): 1.

22. Martin Wells Knapp, "Revival Electricity," *Revivalist* (February 22, 1910): 1; Knapp, "Two Railroads," 7; [Knapp], "The 'By Faith and Now Line' to Beulah Land," *Revivalist* (April 1894): 2. The entire fascicle of *Revivalist* 10 (April 1896) featured railroad imagery. L. Pickett, J. R. Bryant, and Martin Wells Knapp, eds., *Tears and Triumphs Combined for Revivals, Sunday Schools and the Home*, 2nd ed. (Cincinnati: Martin Wells Knapp, YMCA Building, 1899; 1st ed., 1894). By 1898, more than 200,000 copies had been sold. *Pentecostal Messengers* (Cincinnati: M. W. Knapp, 1898), 66.

23. Anonymous, Washington, North Carolina, "The Tobacco Devil Cast Out," *Revivalist* (December 1894): 3: "learned . . . from *The Revivalist* that it must be wrong to sell it as well as use it. . . . I desire to be made perfect in love."

24. [Martin Wells Knapp], "How to Live Long," *Revivalist* (January 1894): 4.

25. Martin Wells Knapp, "Coffee Drunkards," *Revivalist* (October 25, 1900): 9.

26. Bruno Latour, *La science en action: Introduction à la sociologie des sciences* (Paris: La Découverte, 1989); Latour, *Aramis ou l'amour des techniques* (Paris: La Découverte, 1992); Latour, *Enquête sur les modes d'existence: Une anthropologie des modernes* (Paris: La Découverte, 2012).

27. For example, Martin Wells Knapp, "Bigotry a Hindrance to Revival," *Revivalist* (December 1893): 1; Knapp, "Wrecked Humanity and Hirelings," *Revivalist* (February 28, 1901): 1; Knapp, *Lightning Bolts from Pentecostal Skies; or Devices of the Devil Unmasked* (Cincinnati: Office of the Revivalist, 1898), 164–88, 264–307. This argument was presented in quite other intellectual categories and contexts by Michel Foucault and others influenced by him: Michel Foucault, *L'archéologie du savoir* (Paris: Gallimard, 1969); Foucault, *Surveiller et punir: naissance de la prison* (Paris: Gallimard, 1975); Foucault, *Histoire de la sexualité* (Paris: Gallimard, 1976–84); Foucault, *Sécurité, territoire, population: Cours au Collège de France, 1977–1978* (Paris: Seuil, Gallimard, 2004).

28. Martin Wells Knapp, "A Glorious Transformation," *Revivalist* (November 22, 1900): 1.

29. Martin Wells Knapp, "Worldliness," *Revivalist* (April 13, 1899): 5.

30. Jacob Knapp, "Honorary Doctors," *Revivalist* (June 1897): 5; Martin Wells Knapp, "The New Testament Church," *Revivalist* (September 1897): 1; Knapp, "Hirlings," *Revivalist* (June 8, 1899): 8; Knapp, "Anti-Revival Churches," *Revivalist* (December 20, 1900): 1; Knapp, "The New Testament Church," *Revivalist* (December 27, 1900): 1; Knapp, "Societies of God's Church vs. Worldly Societies and Denominations," *Revivalist* (February 14, 1901): 8; Knapp, "Wrecked Humanity and Hirelings," *Revivalist* (February 28, 1901): 1, accompanied by a cartoon, "The Salary Seeking Minister," which shows the clergy getting fat and rich at the expense of the poor.

31. Martin Wells Knapp, "Come-outerism and Revivals," *Revivalist* (April 4, 1901): 1.

32. Newton Wray, "Church Statistics and Spiritual Famine," *Revivalist* (December 20, 1900): 9.

33. A. T. Pierson, "The Ideal Church," *Revivalist* (January 24, 1901): 4.

34. I. Reid, "Protestant Popery," *Revivalist* (February 9, 1899): 8; E. H. Dashiel, "Ecclesiasticism Versus Jesus," *Revivalist* (February 9, 1899): 8.

35. Martin Wells Knapp, "The Revivalist and the Church," *Revivalist* (June 29, 1899): 1.

36. Martin Wells Knapp, *Pentecostal Aggressiveness; or, Why I Conducted the Meetings of the Chesapeake Holiness Union at Bowens, Maryland* (Cincinnati: M. W. Knapp, 1899).

37. "Sectarian Narrowness," *Revivalist* (January 3, 1901): 1. On the struggle with the NHA, see "Chicago Holiness Convention, March 1–10, 1901," *Revivalist* (February 14, 1901): 8; Martin Wells Knapp, "Full Orbed Holiness," *Revivalist* (May 2, 1901): 2; and the important analysis of Kostlevy, *Holy Jumpers*.

38. Martin Wells Knapp, "Governmental Positions," *Revivalist* (August 10, 1889): 7; Knapp, "In Union There Is Strength," *Revivalist* (March 1893): 1 [quote].

39. Industrial Workers of the World, "Constitution," http://www.IWW.org.

40. Christopher H. Evans, *The Kingdom Is Always but Coming: A Life of Walter Rauschenbusch* (Grand Rapids, MI: Eerdmans, 2004).

41. See, for example, Martin Wells Knapp, "There Shall Be No More War," *Revivalist* (December 1894): 3; Knapp, "Kindness More Effective Than Weapons," *Revivalist* (October 1894): 2; Knapp, "The War in South Africa," *Revivalist* (March 1, 1900): 9, disapproved of attitudes of governments toward war.

42. See, for example, Martin Wells Knapp, "Around the World," *Revivalist* (February 9, 1899): 9: "Pentecostal holiness is not selfish. It acts the good Samaritan to the bruised and wounded who are dying without the Gospel." See also, Knapp, "Holiness in the Sermon on the Mount," *Revivalist* (June 1896): 2; Knapp, "Governmental Positions," *Revivalist* (August 10, 1899): 7.

43. See, for example, Martin Wells Knapp, "Stewards of God, Attention!," *Revivalist* (June 1894): 3, which called for ministry to the poor and to prisoners; Martin Wells Knapp with Minnie Knapp, "In Prison and Ye Visited Me," *Revivalist* (October 1897): 8.

44. Martin Wells Knapp, "Divine Healing," *Revivalist* (October 19, 1899): 10; Knapp, "Healing Magnified," *Revivalist* (January 1899): 10.

45. Beatrice M. Finney, "A Plea for Fallen Girls," *Revivalist* (April 18, 1901): 16; Anonymous [Martin Wells Knapp?], "Rescue Home in Sight," *Revivalist* (July 18, 1901): 15. See also Mrs. Martin Wells Knapp [Minnie Ferle Knapp], "Glimpses of Darkest Cincinnati," *Revivalist* (March 1, 1899): 13. "The False Employment Snare," *Revivalist* (June 8, 1899): 8, warned against sex slavery.

46. Finney, "A Plea for Fallen Girls"; Martin Wells Knapp, "Our Cincinnati Center," *Revivalist* (March 7, 1901): 9; F. W. Messenger, "Slum Work in Cincinnati," *Revivalist* (March 21, 1901): 14.

47. Martin Wells Knapp, "Beulah Heights Bible School," *Revivalist* (August 1894): 1, expressed hope that the school would alleviate suffering in Appalachia, much of which Knapp attributed to lack of education. Cf. Knapp's "A Training School for Christian Workers," *Revivalist* (May 10, 1900): 3.

48. Knapp published an essay by Charles C. Cook, "Is the World Getting Better or Worse," *Revivalist* (February 16, 1899): 6, claiming increased numbers of lynchings and violence against African Americans demonstrated the world was getting worse; it was an argument for premillennialism.

49. Martin Wells Knapp, "Beulah Heights Holiness Campmeeting," *Revivalist* (August 1894): 1; Knapp, "Beulah Heights Bible School," 1. Both

were intended to provide healing bridges between North and South.

50. See Martin Wells Knapp, "The 'by Faith and Now' Line," *Revivalist* (April 1894): 2; Compare W. B. Godbey, "Drugs and Divine Healing," *Revivalist* (May 10, 1900): 10.

51. W. B. Godbey, *Women Preachers* (Louisville, KY: Pentecostal Publishing, 1891), 3.

52. Knapp, *Lightning Bolts*, 231. See Thornton, *When the Fire Fell*, 177.

53. Thornton, *When the Fire Fell*, 178–82.

54. Among Beatrice M. Finney's contributions: "Heart Disease," *Revivalist* (January 31, 1901): 10; "Ten Scheduled Events Which Will Occur During the Millennium," *Revivalist* (February 14, 1901): 7; "The Little Preacher," *Revivalist* (February 21, 1901): 6; "Telegrams from Heaven," *Revivalist* (March 7, 1901): 13; "Hid With Christ in God," *Revivalist* (March 14, 1901): 3; "A Plea for Fallen Girls," *Revivalist* (April 18, 1901): 16; "Unmeasured Blessings," *Revivalist* (April 25, 1901): 4; "Rest in the Lord (Psalm xxxvii, 7)," *Revivalist* (May 2, 1901): 2–3; "Be Still and Know That I Am God," *Revivalist* (June 20, 1901): 2–3; "Jesus Is All," *Revivalist* (July 18, 1901): 4.

55. Nettie Peabody, *Outline for Bible Study* (Cincinnati: N.p., 1942); Peabody, *The Glory of the Son of God* (Cincinnati: God's Bible School and College, 1960).

56. Title varies; no copies located. Published in Minneapolis by T. J. Morrow (husband). It was widely advertised, for example: *Sunday School Times* 31 (April 13, 1889): 240.

57. *Arnold's Practical Sunday-School Commentary*. Mrs. Abbie Clemens Morrow was frequently listed as an editor. No complete file has been discovered. It was published by Fleming Revell in Chicago, New York, and London from at least 1897.

58. "Mrs. Knapp's Letter," *Revivalist* (December 19, 1901): 7. See A. C. Morrow Brown, *The Autobiography of Abbie C. Morrow Brown* (Dayton, OH: J. J. Scruby, 1932).

59. "She Is Not Here," *Revivalist* (April 5, 1906): 2; "A 'Warrior' Crowned," *Revivalist* (April 5, 1906): 8; Thornton, *When the Fire Fell*, 180–81.

60. David Bundy, "Pauline Missions: The Wesleyan Holiness Vision," in *The Global Impact of the Wesleyan Traditions and Their Related Movements*, ed. Charles Yrigoyen Jr., Pietist and Wesleyan Studies 14 (Lanham, MD: Scarecrow Press, 2002), 13–26.

61. See, for example, Ethel Ward, "Voices from India," *Revivalist* (May 31, 1900): 6; C. B. Ward, "Good News from India," *Revivalist* (August 30, 1900): 9.

62. See, for example, William. N. Hirst, "World Wide Missionary Conference," *Revivalist* (May 10, 1900): 2; William N. and Mabel Hirst, "Announcement—Good News," *Revivalist* (September 27, 1900): 7, regarding sailing from New York to South Africa as *Revivalist* missionaries.

63. Numerous articles mention Nakada or are by Nakada in the *Revivalist*. See especially [Martin Wells Knapp], "Ho! For Japan," *Revivalist* (November 8, 1900): 9; Knapp, "From Japan," *Revivalist* (February 21, 1901): 9. See Meesaeng Lee Choi, *The Rise of the Korean Holiness Church in Relation to the American Holiness Movement: Wesley's Scriptural Holiness and the Fourfold Gospel*, Pietist and Wesleyan Studies 28 (Lanham, MD: Scarecrow Press, 2008), 59–86; Bundy and Fujii, "Barclay Fowell Buxton."

64. Charles H. Stalker, *Twice Around the World with the Holy Ghost; or, The Impressions and Convictions of the Mission Field* (Columbus, OH: Author, n.d.), 13–125.

65. See, for example, the reports of Byron J. Rees, "The Journey Begins," *Revivalist* (February 7, 1901): 3; "From Brother Stalker," *Revivalist* (July 4, 1901): 9; Charles H. Stalker, "From 'Round the World," *Revivalist* (July 18, 1901): 9;

"From Brother Stalker," *Revivalist* (July 25, 1901): 9; "From Brother Stalker," *Revivalist* (November 21, 1901): 9. This became a pattern in the Radical Holiness and Pentecostal movements. See, for example, Luther J. Oconer, *Spirit-Filled Protestantism: Holiness-Pentecostal Revivals and the Making of Filipino Methodist Identity*, foreword by David Bundy (Eugene, OR: Wipf & Stock, 2017); Myung Soo Park, "Roots of the Korea Evangelical Holiness Church with Special Reference to the Doctrine of Holiness" (STM thesis, Boston University, 1992).

66. Thornton, *When the Fire Fell*, 51–95.

67. A neighbor sued Knapp for the disruption to "peace" occasioned by the camp meeting at GBS. An account, transcript, and analysis were published: "Revival Persecution," *Revivalist* (August 1, 1901): 1–12, quotes on p. 10.

68. [Martin Wells Knapp], "Revival Noise," *Revivalist* (August 22, 1901): 1.

69. Knapp, *Lightning Bolts*, 91; emphasis in original.

70. Oswald Chambers, "A Great and Blessed Season," *Revivalist* (January 17, 1907): 4. See Thornton, *When the Fire Fell*, 237; David McCasland, *Oswald Chambers: Abandoned to God. The Life Story of the Author of My Utmost for His Highest* (Grand Rapids, MI: Discovery House Publishers, 1993), 105.

71. Susie C. Stanley, *Holy Boldness: Women Preachers' Autobiographies and the Sanctified Self* (Knoxville: University of Tennessee Press, 2002).

72. Thornton, *When the Fire Fell*, 145–46, 167–68.

73. David Bundy, "G. T. Haywood: Religion for Urban Realities," in *Portraits of a Generation: Early Pentecostal Leaders*, ed. James R. Goff Jr. and Grant Wacker (Fayetteville: University of Arkansas Press, 2002), 237–53.

74. Ibid., 241–43.

75. Charles W. Nienkirchen, *A. B. Simpson and the Pentecostal Movement: A Study in Continuity, Crisis, and Change* (Eugene, OR: Wipf and Stock, 2010).

76. Articles on these individuals can be found in Stanley M. Burgess and Eduard M. van der Maas, eds., *The New International Dictionary of Pentecostal and Charismatic Movements* (Grand Rapids, MI: Zondervan, 2002).

77. Kostlevy, *A to Z of the Holiness Movement*, 140. Kostlevy, *A to Z of the Holiness Movement*, includes articles on the Cowmans (80–81) and Nakada (212). On L. G. Schmelzenbach, see Harmon Schmelzenbach III, *Schmelzenbach of Africa* (Kansas City, MO: Nazarene Publishing, 1937); Mary Schmelzenbach, *Memories of Africa: Stories from a Pioneer Missionary* (Kansas City, MO: Nazarene Publishing, 1993). On C. L. Slater, see Maude L. Slater, *Missionary Evangelist: A Biography of Charles L. Slater* ([Pasadena, CA]: N.p., 1951). On Widmeyer, see C. B. Widmeyer, *A Story of Religious Education* (Pasadena, CA: Evangel Press, [1935]). On Harding, see also Thornton, *When the Fire Fell*, 280–81.

78. George Soltau, "Divine Healing: The Power of Faith and Prayer," *Eleventh Hour and Jungle Need: A Monthly Paper for the Present Day* 6, no. 2 (February 1908): 46.

BIBLIOGRAPHY

Bandura, Albert. *Social Foundations of Thought and Action: A Social Cognitive Theory*. Englewood Cliffs, NJ: Prentice-Hall, 1986.

Brown, A. C. Morrow. *The Autobiography of Abbie C. Morrow Brown*. Dayton, OH: J. J. Scruby, 1932.

Bundy, David. "Bishop William Taylor and Methodist Mission: A Study in

Nineteenth Century Social History; Part I: From Campmeeting Convert to International Evangelist." *Methodist History* 27, no. 4 (1989): 197–210.
———. "Bishop William Taylor and Methodist Mission: A Study in Nineteenth Century Social History; Part II: Social Structures in Collision." *Methodist History* 28, no. 1 (1989): 3–21.
———. "Blaming the Victim: The Wesleyan/Holiness Movement in American Culture." *Wesleyan Theological Journal* 32, no. 1 (1997): 161–78.
———. "G. T. Haywood: Religion for Urban Realities." In *Portraits of a Generation: Early Pentecostal Leaders*, edited by James R. Goff Jr. and Grant Wacker, 237–53. Fayetteville: University of Arkansas Press, 2002.
———. "Pauline Missions: The Wesleyan Holiness Vision." In *The Global Impact of the Wesleyan Traditions and Their Related Movements*, edited by Charles Yrigoyen Jr., 13–26. Pietist and Wesleyan Studies 14. Lanham, MD: Scarecrow Press, 2002.
———. "Religion for Modernity: Martin Wells Knapp and the Radical Holiness Network of the American Progressive Era." *World Christianity and the Fourfold Gospel* 1, no. 1 (2015): 43–79.
———. "Sophia Chambers, Founder of the Holiness Church: A Case Study of Victorian Entrepreneurial Religious Leadership." *Wesley and Methodist Studies* 11, no. 1 (2019): 24–49.
———. "William Taylor (1821–1902): Entrepreneurial Maverick for the Indigenous Church." In *Mission Legacies: Biographical Studies of Leaders of the Modern Missionary Movement*, edited by Gerald H. Anderson, Robert T. Coote, Norman A. Horner, and James M. Phillips, 461–68. Maryknoll, NY: Orbis, 1995.
Bundy, David, and Masaya Fujii. "Barclay Fowell Buxton, Japanese Christians, and the Japan Evangelistic Band." *Journal of World Christianity* 8, no. 1 (2018): 47–74.
Burgess, Stanley M., and Eduard M. van der Maas, eds. *The New International Dictionary of Pentecostal and Charismatic Movements*. Grand Rapids, MI: Zondervan, 2002.
Cervone, Daniel. "Socio-Cognitive Mechanisms and Personality Coherence: Self-Knowledge, Situational Beliefs, and Cross-Situational Coherence in Perceived Self-Efficacy." *Psychological Science* 8, no. 1 (1997): 43–50.
Choi, Meesaeng Lee. *The Rise of the Korean Holiness Church in Relation to the American Holiness Movement: Wesley's Scriptural Holiness and the Fourfold Gospel*. Pietist and Wesleyan Studies 28. Lanham, MD: Scarecrow Press, 2008.
Davis, H. T. *Modern Miracles*. Cincinnati: God's Revivalist Office, 1901.
Day, Lloyd Raymond. "A History of God's Bible School in Cincinnati, 1900–1949." MEd thesis, University of Cincinnati, 1949.
Eleventh Hour and Jungle Need: A Monthly Paper for the Present Day. London, 1903–10.
Evans, Christopher H. *The Kingdom Is Always but Coming: A Life of Walter Rauschenbusch*. Grand Rapids, MI: Eerdmans, 2004.
Flanagan, Maureen. *America Reformed: Progressives and Progressivisms*. Oxford: Oxford University Press, 2007.
Foucault, Michel. *L'archéologie du savoir*. Paris: Gallimard, 1969.
———. *Histoire de la sexualité*. Paris: Gallimard, 1976–84.
———. *Sécurité, territoire, population: Cours au Collège de France,*

1977–1978. Paris: Seuil, Gallimard, 2004.

———. *Surveiller et punir: Naissance de la prison*. Paris: Gallimard, 1975.

Godbey, W. B. *Women Preachers*. Louisville, KY: Pentecostal Publishing, 1891.

Goodwyn, Lawrence. *Democratic Promise: The Populist Movement in America*. New York: Oxford University Press, 1976.

Gordon, A. J. *The Ministry of Healing: Miracles of Cure in All Ages*. Chicago: F. H. Revell, 1882.

Industrial Workers of the World. "Constitution." http://www.IWW.org.

Kazin, Michael. *The Populist Persuasion: An American History*. New York: Basic Books, 1995.

Knapp, Martin Wells. *Lightning Bolts from Pentecostal Skies*. Cincinnati: Revivalist, 1898.

———. *Out of Egypt into Canaan: Lessons in Spiritual Geography*. Cincinnati: Cranston & Stowe for the Author, 1888.

———. *Pentecostal Aggressiveness; or, Why I Conducted the Meetings of the Chesapeake Holiness Union at Bowens, Maryland*. Cincinnati: M. W. Knapp, 1899.

Kostlevy, William, ed. *The A to Z of the Holiness Movement*. A–Z Guide Series 164. Lanham, MD: Scarecrow Press, 2010.

———. *Holy Jumpers: Evangelicals and Radicals in Progressive Era America*. Oxford: Oxford University Press, 2010.

Latour, Bruno. *Aramis ou l'amour des techniques*. Paris: La Découverte, 1992.

———. *Enquête sur les modes d'existence: une anthropologie des modernes*. Paris: La Découverte, 2012.

———. *La science en action: Introduction à la sociologie des sciences*. Paris: La Découverte, 1989.

Lenz, Darin Duane. "'Strengthening the Faith of the Children of God': Pietism, Print, and Prayer in the Making of a World Evangelical Hero, George Müller of Bristol (1805–1898)." PhD diss., Kansas State University, 2010.

McCasland, David. *Oswald Chambers: Abandoned to God. The Life Story of the Author of My Utmost for His Highest*. Grand Rapids, MI: Discovery House Publishers, 1993.

McGerr, Michael. *A Fierce Discontent: The Rise and Fall of the Progressive Movement in America*. New York: The Free Press, 2003.

Nienkirchen, Charles W. *A. B. Simpson and the Pentecostal Movement: A Study in Continuity, Crisis, and Change*. Eugene, OR: Wipf and Stock, 2010.

Oconer, Luther J. *Spirit-Filled Protestantism: Holiness-Pentecostal Revivals and the Making of Filipino Methodist Identity*. Foreword by David Bundy. Eugene, OR: Wipf & Stock, 2017.

Park, Myung Soo. "Roots of the Korea Evangelical Holiness Church with Special Reference to the Doctrine of Holiness." STM thesis, Boston University, 1992.

Peabody, Nettie. *The Glory of the Son of God*. Cincinnati: God's Bible School and College, 1960.

———. *Outline for Bible Study*. Cincinnati: N.p., 1942.

Pentecostal Messengers. Cincinnati: M. W. Knapp, 1898.

Pickett, L., J. R. Bryant, and Martin Wells Knapp, eds. *Tears and Triumphs Combined for Revivals, Sunday Schools and the Home*. 2nd ed. Cincinnati: Martin Wells Knapp, YMCA Building, 1899; 1st ed., 1894.

Revivalist (1888–91, Albion, MI; 1892–1900, Cincinnati), *God's Revivalist and Bible Advocate* (1901–present, Cincinnati).

Schmelzenbach, Harmon, III. *Schmelzenbach of Africa*. Kansas City, MO: Nazarene Publishing, 1937.

Schmelzenbach, Mary. *Memories of Africa: Stories from a Pioneer Missionary*. Kansas City, MO: Nazarene Publishing, 1993.

Slater, Maude L. *Missionary Evangelist: A Biography of Charles L. Slater*. [Pasadena, CA]: N.p., 1951.

Smith, Larry D. *A Century on the Mount of Blessings: The Story of God's Bible School*. Cincinnati: Revivalist Press, 2016.

Soltau, George. "Divine Healing: The Power of Faith and Prayer." *Eleventh Hour and Jungle Need: A Monthly Paper for the Present Day* 6, no. 2 (February 1908): 45–48.

Stalker, Charles H. *Twice Around the World with the Holy Ghost; or, The Impressions and Convictions of the Mission Field*. Columbus, OH: Author, n.d.

Stanley, Susie C. *Holy Boldness: Women Preachers' Autobiographies and the Sanctified Self*. Knoxville: University of Tennessee Press, 2002.

Stunt, Timothy C. F. *The Elusive Quest of the Spiritual Malcontent: Some Early Nineteenth-Century Mavericks*. Eugene, OR: Wipf & Stock, 2015.

Sweet, William Warren. *Religion on the American Frontier*. Chicago: University of Chicago Press, 1931.

Thornton, Wallace, Jr. *When the Fire Fell: Martin Wells Knapp's Vision of Pentecost and the Beginnings of God's Bible School*. Lexington, KY: Emeth Press, 2014.

Widmeyer, C. B. *A Story of Religious Education*. Pasadena, CA: Evangel Press, [1935].

CHAPTER 2

Pandita Ramabai, the Holiness Movement, and the Mukti Revival of 1905

Robert A. Danielson

This chapter explores the Holiness network that surrounded Pandita Ramabai and the Mukti Mission in the years leading up to the Mukti Revival. The presence of this network is examined in three ways: first, through an analysis of Ramabai's personal library; second, through the connection with Albert Norton, who worked closely with her at the Mukti Mission; and third, through looking at lesser-known connections with Radical Holiness missionaries, including E. F. Ward and Phebe Ward, the Pentecost Bands, and William Godbey. Taken as a whole, this evidence indicates important interaction between Ramabai and European and American Holiness leaders, both inside and outside of India.

In June 1905, a group of about 550 girls from the Mukti Mission in Kedgaon, India (near Pune outside present-day Mumbai) had been gathering in prayer for revival in India. They were doing so at the instruction of the founder of the Mukti Mission, Pandita Ramabai (1858–1922), since word had been received of a revival in the Khassia (Khasi) Hills as a result of the Welsh Revival. Ramabai called for volunteers to leave the mission and preach in the surrounding villages, and thirty girls volunteered. While this smaller group was meeting in prayer, the Holy Spirit fell and revival broke out in the Mukti Mission and began to spread. By 1907, word of the revival reached the Azusa Street Revival, which began in 1906. The Mukti Revival was of interest to those at the Azusa Street Revival because the accounts of the Mukti Revival included speaking in tongues.

One of the most commonly noted Holiness connections is Minnie Abrams, a Methodist who worked with Ramabai in the Mukti Mission.[1] The level of her influence is questionable, since most of her involvement was self-reported and occurred as she became closely connected to Pentecostalism after the revival. Ramabai recorded the account of her own experience of sanctification from the 1895 preaching of Rev. Joseph Gelson Gregson (1835–1909) at the Lanouli (Lonaula) camp meeting in India.[2] Gregson was a Baptist missionary in India but spoke at Keswick in 1886 and is most often connected with that branch of the Holiness Movement.[3]

Scholars of Pentecostalism are familiar with the Mukti Revival of 1905.[4] Some accounts have tried to explain the revival by connecting it to the Holiness revival inspired by the Welsh Revival in the Khasi Hills, over 3,000 miles from the Mukti Mission,[5] but Ramabai was seeking revival in India from before that time, even sending her daughter and Miss Abrams to Australia in 1903 after reports of a revival there.[6] Others explained the Mukti Revival as a spontaneous outpouring of the Holy Spirit, and still others attributed it directly to the influence of Pandita Ramabai, as if there was little or no external influence.[7] What is frequently absent from the academic discussion is the presence of a Holiness mission partner thirteen miles away in Daund and Radical Holiness orphanages experiencing revivals among children just 600 miles away on the main railroad route, both of which were connected by common links in a relational network prior to 1905 and even prior to the Welsh Revival itself. While this is primarily circumstantial evidence, it deserves as much attention for its potential influence on the Mukti Revival as the Welsh Revival influence in the Khasi Hills. The aim of this chapter is to provide documentation for some of Pandita Ramabai's contacts with Holiness Networks, the significance of which has often been overlooked in the accounts of the Mukti Revival.[8] The intention here is not to underestimate the work of Ramabai or dispute the significance of the Welsh Revival for her and the Mukti Revival. Yan Suarsana observed that the Pentecostal Movement was not aware of the Mukti Revival until it was reported to the Azusa Street Revival in 1907. In fact, Suarsana also noted how early Pentecostalism attempted to make the Mukti Revival appear to be a consequence of Azusa instead of a separate outpouring of the Holy Spirit on the Indian subcontinent.[9] What we describe as "Pentecostalism" is really an institutionalization of a part of the Holiness Movement that was not defined as a separate entity until the 1910s. Pandita Ramabai would not have self-identified as "Pentecostal" at the time of the Mukti Revival but rather would have seen herself as clearly within the Holiness Movement.[10] Ramabai's interaction with

Fig. 2.1 Image of Pandita Ramabai from *Frank Leslie's Illustrated Newspaper* (New York), April 7, 1888, 120–21.

MME. PUNDITA RAMABAI SARASVATI, FROM CHRISTIAN WOMEN OF INDIA.

British and American Holiness Movement leaders, especially in the immediate vicinity of the Mukti Mission before the 1905 revival, suggests that the factors contributing to the Mukti Revival were more complex than normally presented in the historiography.

PANDITA RAMABAI'S PRIVATE LIBRARY

The first stream of evidence to be examined, although not a conclusive way of looking at influences on Ramabai, is to study the list of 249 books found in her library at the Mukti Mission in 2001.[11] If we remove titles by unknown authors and books written by Ramabai herself, and look at which authors are most represented,[12] we are left with an intriguing list:

- Alfred S. Dyer (eight books)
- Jesse Penn-Lewis (five books)
- Mrs. M. Baxter (four books)
- Helen S. Dyer (four books, one repeated)

Mrs. Marcus B. Fuller (four books, one repeated)
Rev. Nehemiah Goreh (three books)
Rev. W. Haslam (three books)
J. Gregory Mantle (three books)
B. T. Roberts (three books, one repeated)
Catherine Booth (two books)
Mary Carpenter (two books)
J. R. Miller (two books)
Rev. R. Newton (two books)
Baba Padmanji (two books)
John Paton (two books)
Frances E. Willard (two books)
Mrs. M. B. Woodworth-Etter (two books)
A. S. Worrell (two books)

These books represent 22 percent of the entire collection (fifty-five of 249 volumes), and women wrote 44 percent of these fifty-five volumes. While the themes of the books often overlap into several categories, I am primarily interested in the authors themselves. From my breakdown of this list, I see four general categories of authors: Holiness-related authors, social reformers, Brahmin Christian converts/theologians, and authors of unclear backgrounds.

Social reformers include Alfred S. Dyer, Mary Carpenter, and Frances E. Willard. (I will deal later with Alfred Dyer, who represents a social reform agenda but also was a Holiness advocate.) Mary Carpenter (1807–1877) was a British Unitarian, who was committed to antislavery movements. She was also influenced by the philosophy of Hindu reformer, Ram Mohan Roy (in one of her books in Ramabai's library he is the principal subject). Frances E. Willard (1839–1898) was a Methodist social reformer primarily known for her leadership of the Women's Christian Temperance Union. Besides Willard's two volumes, a third volume is labeled as a personal gift from Willard. Social reform was a major interest of Ramabai, who fought against child marriage and worked with child widows and orphans.

In the category of Brahmin Christian converts and theologians are the works of Rev. Nehemiah (Nilakanth) Goreh (1825–1895)[13] and Baba Padmanji (1831–1906).[14] Both were prolific writers and would have appealed to Ramabai, who was herself a Brahmin Christian convert and a theologian. Goreh worked to understand Christianity within a Hindu cultural framework, while Padmanji was known as a social reformer who espoused women's education.

Authors whose positions are less clear include: J. R. Miller (1840–1912),[15] a Presbyterian pastor and author, Richard Newton (1813–1887), an Episcopalian pastor and author known for his books of sermons for children, and John H. Paton (1843–1922),[16] a writer who was born in Scotland but immigrated to Almont, Michigan. He became Advent Christian as the result of a heresy trial and would befriend Charles T. Russell, later the founder of the Jehovah's Witnesses. While Newton's books may be of interest for Ramabai's work with girls and their spiritual education, the positions of the other two writers are not well defined at this point to understand their potential influence.

The majority of the authors found in this list have connections to the Holiness Movement in the United States or the Higher Life Movement in Britain. They represent 61 percent of the books in the list. Some of these writers are well known: B. T. Roberts (1823–1893), founder of the Free Methodist Church, Catherine Booth (1829–1890), cofounder of the Salvation Army, and Maria Woodworth-Etter (1844–1924), an independent Holiness evangelist and healer who would ultimately join the Pentecostal Movement in 1912. Others are less well known, including Adolphus Spaulding Worrell (1831–1908), a Baptist professor, educator, and evangelist who focused on divine healing and is mentioned in one obituary as having "taught earnestly constantly what he termed the 'Spirit-filled Life.'"[17] J. Gregory Mantle (1853–1925) was a pastor and educator who was involved with both Keswick and the Christian and Missionary Alliance.[18] Rev. William Haslam (1818–1905) was a Church of England revivalist who taught sanctification. Haslam was also a major influence on Canon Hartford-Battersby, one of the principal founders of Keswick.[19] Haslam was also noted by Ramabai in her own account of her sanctification experience as an influence on her spiritual development.[20]

The top five authors in Ramabai's library reveal additional Holiness connections. Alfred Stace Dyer (1849–1926)[21] and his wife Helen S. Dyer (1851–1919) were clearly prominent and important. Alfred Dyer came from a Quaker background and was very early on interested in social reform. He was involved in a number of social reform efforts against sex trafficking of women and the opium trade. Dyer traveled to India as part of his concern for social reforms as they were applied to the colonies.

In 1888, while traveling to India with his wife, Dyer was presented with the opportunity to purchase and edit the *Bombay Guardian*, a religious paper earlier operated by Methodist missionary George Bowen from 1851 until his death in 1888.[22] With the support of the Friends' Association for the Abolition of the State Regulation of Vice, the Dyers maintained a strong stance against vice of all types. In 1898, the Dyers left India due to Alfred's poor health, and the *Bombay Guardian* fell to new leadership.²³ While the writings of the Dyers seem to lean toward a Holiness viewpoint, it is not clear whether this attitude came with them to India or was a result of their experiences in Bombay.²⁴

Helen S. Dyer in her own right became a major conduit for spreading the work of Pandita Ramabai to the West. Her books, such as: *Pandita Ramabai: Her Vision, Her Mission and Triumph of Faith*, *Revival in India*, and *Pandita Ramabai: The Story of Her Life* helped promote the Mukti Revival, especially as influenced by the Welsh Revival. However, she wrote another work, *A Life for God in India: Memorials of Mrs. Jennie Fuller of Akola and Bombay*. This book has an introduction written by Ramabai and is about the life of Mrs. Marcus B. Fuller, one of the other top five authors in Ramabai's library.

Before discussing Jennie Fuller in greater detail, it is useful to note the other top five authors. Jesse Penn-Lewis (1861–1927) was a friend of Evan Roberts and involved with the Welsh Revival. She also spoke at the Keswick Convention of 1902 prior to the Welsh Revival.²⁵ Mrs. M. Baxter (Elizabeth Foster Baxter) (1837–1926) was from a Quaker background. Her husband, Michael Baxter (1834–1910), founded the *Christian Herald* in July 1874 to report on the Moody and Sankey revivals.²⁶ Both husband and wife were actively involved with Keswick and the Higher Life Movement, which included opening a Faith Healing Home in London. Most of Baxter's books were published through the Christian Herald Office and are tied to Holiness ideas.

Jennie Frow Fuller (1851–1900) is a particularly interesting link between many of the people in this chapter and Pandita Ramabai. Jennie Frow was a classmate of Mary Norton at Oberlin College and was influenced by Charles Finney. She spent several years helping Albert and Mary Norton in their mission work in India and also assisting Ernest and Phebe Ward in their work. She returned to Rochester, New York, where she worked with B. T. Roberts in his college in North Chili, New York (where Ramabai sent her only daughter for education),²⁷ and at that time married Marcus Fuller. They became involved with A. B. Simpson and the Christian and Missionary Alliance and returned to India as Alliance missionaries, where they set up an orphanage at Akola, geographically located between the Wards' orphanage work and Ramabai's. Jennie Fuller wrote articles for Dyer in the *Bombay Guardian* and authored a book entitled *The Wrongs of Indian Womanhood*, which is a collection of these published articles.

While an analysis of her library is not conclusive of Ramabai's involvement with the Holiness Movement, it is certainly a good indication that she encountered and likely read the works of these influential Holiness writers.

It is important to note that almost all the books predate the Mukti Revival, with the exception of most of the Dyers' books (indicating possibly a stronger relationship after the revival) and Penn-Lewis's *War on the Saints* (1912), and Woodworth-Etter's *Acts of the Holy Ghost* (1912). Both books could indicate a swing toward the Pentecostal Movement after the revival. But to gain a greater appreciation for Ramabai's interaction with Holiness Movement figures, it is necessary to move beyond the library.

ALBERT NORTON

A second stream of evidence that supports the argument for a Holiness network around the Mukti Mission is rooted in Ramabai's partnership with an independent faith missionary, Albert Benjamin Norton (1847–1923).[28] Norton arrived in India in December 1872 at the call of Methodist bishop and Holiness advocate William Taylor.[29] Norton was raised in Genesee County, New York, shortly after the Holiness teachings of B. T. Roberts in the same region led to the split that created the Free Methodist Church. Norton remained in the Methodist Episcopal Church and trained for ministry in Evanston, Illinois. As a student in Northwestern University and Garrett Biblical Seminary, his life was transformed by a Holiness camp meeting in Dalton, Illinois, and by George Müller's ideas on faith missions. When Bishop Taylor called young men to go to India, Norton left on faith and established an independent mission in central India.

After extensive work among the Korku people of central India, the Nortons returned to the United States in 1889. Norton settled in Rochester, New York, and began a paper called *India's Millions* to promote mission work in India. He also was involved with A. B. Simpson and the Christian and Missionary Alliance through Jennie Frow Fuller.

In 1898 Pandita Ramabai visited Rochester, New York, where Albert Norton had publicized her work with widows in his paper. She was invited to visit Albert and Mary Norton and there she asked them to return to India and help build the Mukti Mission.[30] The Nortons agreed and November 25, 1898, they arrived in Kedgaon, then ravaged by the famine of 1897.[31] There, Albert Norton and Pandita Ramabai together laid the cornerstone for the Mukti Mission.

With Albert Norton's assistance, Ramabai built a number of buildings for the new Mukti Mission, while the Nortons lived and worked with Ramabai to establish the mission work. Then in early 1899 another famine hit Gujerat. At this time, Ramabai took in both boys and girls and assigned the boys to Norton to care for at the Mukti Mission. Soon the numbers were so large that Norton moved the boys to a new site thirteen miles away in Daund.³² This orphanage became the Boy's Christian Home in Dhond, where Norton spent the rest of his life in mission. It later became the Boy's and Girl's Christian Home and is still in operation today.

Norton was present for the early part of the Mukti Revival, and it was Albert Norton who wrote the letter in the April 1907 issue of the *Apostolic Faith*, which introduced the Mukti Revival to the Azusa Street Revival in Los Angeles. Norton continued to work with Ramabai to help with a famine in Bahraich, and a group of missionaries from Azusa Street joined him in December 1908. Norton had his own experience of speaking in tongues at this time.³³

Albert Norton continued the work at the Dhond Boy's Home as an independent Pentecostal missionary until his death in 1923. It was through Norton that other more Radical Holiness missionaries, such as the Wards, became part of the Holiness network in the surrounding areas of Mumbai and central India and were introduced to Ramabai.

RADICAL HOLINESS NETWORKS

The third stream of evidence for a Holiness network around Pandita Ramabai is more speculative and consists of more circumstantial evidence. But evidence does exist for a network of Holiness missionaries going back to the work of Bishop Taylor at work in the area around Mumbai. Connecting this network with the work of the Mukti Mission is more challenging.

Ernest and Phebe Ward

Ernest and Phebe Ward represent a network of Holiness leaders in the United States connected to Free Methodism, including the Pentecost Bands and the Vanguard Mission, who had contact with Ramabai. These relationships encouraged visits from other Holiness leaders, such as William Godbey. In Godbey's account of his visit to India, he clearly perceived Ramabai as being within this Indian network of Holiness missions.

In 1879, while on furlough, Albert Norton met Ernest Freemont Ward at an unidentified Illinois camp meeting. He encouraged the young man to come to India as a faith missionary and marry Phebe Cox. Ward followed his suggestions and the couple soon became the Free Methodist Church's first missionaries.³⁴ In January 1881, the Wards arrived in Bombay and made their way to Ellichpur (Achalpur) near Norton's mission to the Korku people.

Fig. 2.2 Ward family. Frontispiece of Ernest F. Ward, *Echoes from Bharatkhand* (Chicago: Free Methodist Publishing House, 1913).

The Wards were part of a branch of the Holiness Movement that considered itself "radical." Howard Snyder defines this position as, "Though maintaining some irenic contact with the broader Holiness Movement, its leaders and writers often warned against too low a standard of holiness: an experience that did not go deep enough, was not sufficiently world-denying, and compromised particularly with the amusements and ostentations of the age."[35] The Wards were fully aligned with this way of thinking. Ernest would ultimately become the founding president of the Indian Holiness Association in 1910.[36]

In 1892 the Wards returned to the United States on furlough. Just before this time, Ethel Ward recorded the Wards' first known visit to Ramabai as they looked to place an Anglo-Indian girl they were caring for before they left.[37] While they waited to leave Bombay, the Wards encountered two young women representatives of the Pentecost Bands.[38] One was Bessie Sherman, daughter of Holiness leader C. W. Sherman of the Vanguard Mission of St. Louis, Missouri. It is unclear when the Wards joined the Pentecost Bands but by 1894 they are listed in the *Pentecost Herald*, the official publication of the Pentecost Bands, with Ernest Ward and Phebe Ward listed as band leaders.[39]

Upon returning to India, the Wards found a new location in central India at Raj Nandgaon and resumed mission work. However, the famine of 1897 radically altered their plans. The Wards performed the exhausting work of caring for orphaned children and feeding those dying of starvation with little help or outside resources. Finally, the Pentecost Bands sent a small group to form the first Indian Band and help with the work already established by the Wards. By this time the Pentecost Bands had become independent from the Free Methodist Church,[40] and unfortunately, Ward found himself in conflict with the new leader, Frank Hotle.

In September 1898, the Wards again returned to the United States on furlough and there actively spoke about the work of Pandita Ramabai and wrote articles for the *Pentecost Herald*. Alongside a letter from Phebe about the famine appears the first report in the *Pentecost Herald* of Ramabai's work helping girls impacted by the crisis, written by Alfred S. Dyer of the *Bombay Guardian*.[41] Ward was closely connected to the work of the *Pentecost Herald* during this furlough and published numerous reports on the work in India. An article about one of the Wards' speaking engagements concludes with a plug to "Send 5 cents for the illustrated sketch of the life of Pandita Ramabi [sic]."[42] Clearly the Wards and the Pentecost Bands were aware of Ramabai well before the Mukti Revival.

On the Wards' second return, the conflict with Hotle increased until in October 1901, Ernest and Phebe withdrew from the Pentecost Bands. Because their mission work at Raj Nandgaon was now under the administration of the Pentecost Bands, the Wards were forced out of their own work, and from December 1901 to April 1902 their old friend Albert Norton took them in.

Ernest took Methodist missionary C. B. Ward to visit Ramabai in February 1902, and on March 28, 1902, well before the 1905 revival, we know Phebe and her daughters visited Ramabai along with C. W. Sherman.[43] Despite the close connections with both Norton and Ramabai, for Ernest Ward, both missions did not seem significantly instilled with Holiness teachings. From Daund, he wrote to Phebe on April 7, 1902, about the possibility of working with either Norton or Ramabai:

> I have very little hope of a permanent affiliation with this work. Both sides of the house are neither in harmony with our teaching nor our practice on thorough holiness lines <u>if we are at all aggressive</u>, and until they radically change will continue to head us off in our work among the orphans. I think it should be exactly the same at Khedgaon if they had invited us there and I don't see why Bro. Sherman has any hope in that direction. I don't see a bit for true holiness with the advisors P.R. [probably Pandita Ramabai] has about her now (or) P. herself, unless she shows a desire to shake loose of everybody unspiritual who have a controlling voice at home or abroad.

While they were seen as potential Holiness allies by C. W. Sherman, apparently Ramabai and Norton did not seem radical enough by E. F. Ward's Holiness standards. The Wards went on to Sanjan to join the work of Sherman's Vanguard Mission,[44] until they ultimately returned to the Free Methodist Church and its work in Yeotmal in June 1904.

Ernest and Phebe Ward were in Yeotmal by the time of the Mukti Revival in June 1905. According to Helen Dyer's account, the revival began in late June 1905 and quickly spread to other areas of Pune, including Soonderbai Powar's Zenana Training Home and the Methodist Boy's School in Pune, then the Boy's Christian Home in Dhond (run by Norton), then it spread, not to Bombay but to the Free Methodist Mission at Yeotmal, where the Wards were located.[45] Only *after* the revival spread to Yeotmal did Dyer point out that the revival was then taken to Bombay and other areas.[46]

While such evidence is not conclusive, the early days of the Mukti Revival seem to indicate a spread through networks of people close to Ramabai and the Mukti Mission. The fact that this revival spread to Yeotmal while Ernest and Phebe Ward were there, just one month after the revival started, indicates some level of relationship, even if that connection is primarily through Albert Norton and the brief time the Wards lived and worked in Daund in 1902. How the Wards may have personally impacted Ramabai with their Radical Holiness views may never be determined.

The Pentecost Bands and the Vanguard Mission

The Pentecost Bands in India had their own interactions with the Mukti Mission. Hotle sent a letter dated April 5, 1899, from Poona (Pune) to the *Pentecost Herald*: "We go to Kedgaon tonight, a village thirty miles east of here where we wish to visit the high caste "Widows' Home" conducted by the notable woman, Pandita Ramabia [*sic*]. We are praying and hope to obtain some special and valuable information as to principles and management of this wonderful work."[47] The Pentecost Band journal indicated that Sister Tucker, on her way home for furlough on April 20, 1903, "will go to Dardar, Bombay, and Pandita Ramabai's" before sailing.[48] Members of the Pentecost Bands in India visited Ramabai and were willing to learn from her work. Given their views on holiness, they likely felt her views were at least compatible with their own. More importantly, both Ramabai and the Pentecost Bands were involved in caring for orphans and both had a concern for revival. During these visits, it is possible these topics were discussed.

The journal for the Pentecost Band in Raj Nandgaon contains accounts of spiritual revivals that occurred among the orphans. Accounts such as these were not uncommon in the period, especially in the radical branches of the Holiness Movement. However, a few examples can convey the way in which the Pentecost Band combined their evangelistic work with their orphanage work. An account from November 25, 1900, is typical of the language used to describe these Holiness revivals.

> Sunday- A Sabbath day indeed. All nature is keeping it holy. In the early morning most of the workers went to a village to hold services. The Spirit came down in our midst as the workers began telling of a savior for the Heathen. Some of the workers jumped, danced, and shouted while the natives looked on in wonderment. Praise the Lord! At eleven o'clock a Hindi service was held in the chapel. In the bazaar meeting again the Spirit was poured out in blessing. The English service at seven p.m. was a time of heart searching as the truths of the Bible and how to be a soul winner was pressed home to the workers. O Hallelujah for the blood and fire track!

A similar account is found from May 12, 1901:

> Sunday- Hindi morning meeting led by Sis. Wiley and Alcorn and Sumerit and Rukhumin. It was followed by a rousing prayer meeting with the children in their school house where a number of them got saved. The evening meeting showed the results of it. We had a blessed time and all seemed so free, as the children were in readiness and gave their testimonies with such speed. Many testified to being saved from shame, which they manifested in the morning meeting by not taking up their crosses. The fire fell at the first of the services and many ran around, shouting, and praising God. Hallelujah! We can live free and cut loose in Hindi as well as English. Praise the Lord.

These accounts are all prior to the Mukti Revival of 1905 and yet strikingly similar to the early accounts recorded by Ramabai:

> the Spirit of God [falling] on those praying people with such power, that it was impossible to keep them silent. They burst out in tears; loud cries, were heard in all parts of the Church building, and we were awe-struck.... Little children, middle sized girls and young women wept bitterly and confessed their sins. Some saw visions and experienced the Power of God, and things

that are too deep to describe. Two little girls had the spirit of prayer poured on them in such great torrents, that they continued to pray for hours. They were transformed with heavenly light shining on their faces.⁴⁹

Such similarities suggest the sharing of a common understanding of a Holiness revival among orphans, and at least show the presence of similar concepts and language to describe such a revival was present in central India among groups like the Pentecost Bands before the Mukti Revival.⁵⁰

There may have been other interactions between the Radical Holiness Movement and Ramabai, albeit with far less evidence to support any direct influence. C. W. Sherman and the Vanguard Mission has already been mentioned. He visited the Mukti Mission in 1902 and his daughter was active in the Pentecost Bands as well. When the Wards went to Sanjan, they worked with Bessie Sherman Ashton and her husband (who had also left the Pentecost Bands) as part of the Vanguard Mission. According to Phebe Ward's diary, she wrote articles for the *India Vanguard* and did the proofing of the *India Vanguard* at the end of October 1902 and prepared it for publication.⁵¹ Phebe Ward oversaw the copy, editing, and distribution of the *India Vanguard* at least through the end of 1903. If copies can be located, access to the *India Vanguard* might provide further evidence of a Holiness network that incorporated the Mukti Mission.

William B. Godbey

Another Radical Holiness figure is William B. Godbey (1833–1920), who toured around the world and spent a good part of a book published in 1907 discussing Holiness missions around Bombay.⁵² He clearly included Ramabai within the sphere of Holiness missions in this region. He discussed Ernest Ward and the Free Methodists at Yeotmal, Albert Norton at Dhond, the Vanguard Mission at Sanjan, the Pentecost Bands at Raj Nandgaon, as well as the Southern Pentecostal Mission at Vasind, the Peniel Mission at Dharangaon, the Christian Alliance Mission at Bhusawal, the Eastern Pentecostal Mission at Buldana Berar, and the American Mennonite Mission at Sunderganz. He visited all these places from 1905 to 1906. However, in the middle of his reports, he focused on the work of Ramabai in Kedgaon more than all the others.

Godbey noted, "She [Ramabai] is never content with the superficial, but is constantly going for the deeper things of God, i.e., radical sanctification and the copious infilling and abiding of the Holy Ghost."⁵³ He went on to report that she asked him to speak on entire sanctification. He also noted that he visited Ramabai with a certain degree of skepticism:

> When I was preaching in India, before I had gone to Ramabai's great work which I had heard so much about, I feared they had gone into fanaticism, and that I would realize on arrival my painful duty to put my foot on some things, by the help of God endeavoring to separate the vile from the pure. When I got there and diagnosed the situation, recognized my environments, and inhaled copiously the spiritual atmosphere, asking the Holy Spirit to put me in perfect harmony with His work in that place, soon the critic's cap fell off, or rather got burnt up by the fires of the Holy Ghost.[54]

Godbey would become an outspoken opponent of the gift of tongues within the Holiness Movement, so it is possible to speculate that he did not encounter it at the time of his visit to the Mukti Mission. It could be argued that Godbey accurately outlined the Holiness network as it existed in central India at the time of the Mukti Revival.[55]

CONCLUSION

The Mukti Revival was clearly not a spontaneous event, or an isolated occurrence with a simple relationship to the Welsh Revival. There was an entire network of people connected to the Holiness Movement in the United States, or the Higher Life Movement in Britain who were interwoven into the spiritual life of Pandita Ramabai. Some were connected through the literature she read, while others were more physically connected, such as the Nortons and perhaps the Wards. The Pentecost Bands demonstrate that Radical Holiness revivals among children in orphanages, similar to the Mukti Mission, were not unknown in the area, and their descriptions were similar to those of the Mukti Revival. Christian papers, such as the *Bombay Guardian*, the *India Vanguard*, and others, probably served to promote Ramabai and inform her of Holiness views and social concerns in the broader Christian world.

Based on Godbey's testimony, Ramabai fit into this network and participated in it. She would most likely have seen herself as being part of the Holiness Movement at the time of the Mukti Revival. While she may have aligned herself to Pentecostalism as it emerged in its early history, it would be in error to take this event out of its immediate context. More analysis of the context of the Mukti Revival is likely to reveal further evidence of Holiness influences in the immediate sphere of Ramabai's network. While the influence of the Welsh Revival will remain important in the study of the Indian revivals, it is also critical to examine other interactions and influences within those regions around Mumbai and the Mukti Mission.

NOTES

1. Minnie Abrams, *The Baptism of the Holy Ghost and Fire: Matt. 3.11* (Kedgaon, India: Mukti Mission Press, 1906); Minnie Abrams, "How the Recent Revival Was Brought About in India: The Power of Intercession," *Latter Rain Evangel* 1, no. 10 (July 1909): 6–13. See also Gary B. McGee, "'Baptism of the Holy Ghost & Fire!' The Mission Legacy of Minnie F. Abrams," *Missiology* 27, no. 4 (October 1999): 515–22.

2. See Helen S. Dyer's work, *A Great Life in Indian Missions: Pandita Ramabai: Her Vision, Her Mission and Triumph of Faith* (London: Pickering and Inglis, 1923), 44.

3. This camp meeting was founded by Methodists, but had a strong Christian Missionary Alliance influence, as evidenced by a report in the *India Alliance* 1, no. 4 (May 1894): 45, in which Marcus and Jennie Fuller were present. Retrieved from https://www.cmalliance.org/resources/archives/downloads/indiapdf/IA-1894-05.pdf.

4. For one overview of the history, see Allan Anderson, "Pandita Ramabai, the Mukti Revival and Global Pentecostalism," *Transformation* 23, no. 1 (2006): 37–48.

5. See Helen S. Dyer, *Revival in India: "Years of the Right Hand of the Most High"* (London: Morgan and Scott, 1907).

6. H. Dyer, *Pandita Ramabai*, 99.

7. Some minimalizing of the role of Pandita Ramabai is due to a colonial revisionist reading of the historical events, which tends to simplify the situation. For more discussion, see Yan Suarsana, "Inventing Pentecostalism: Pandita Ramabai and the Mukti Revival from a Post-Colonial Perspective," *PentecoStudies* 13, no. 2 (2014): 173–96. See also Yan Suarsana, *Pandita Ramabai und die Erfindung der Pfingstbewegung: Postkoloniale Religionsgeschichtsschreibung am Beispiel des "Mukti Revival,"* Studies in the History of Christianity in the Non-Western World 23 (Wiesbaden: Harrassowitz Verlag, 2013).

8. This is not to suggest that these interactions were primary drivers of the revival, or to suggest that they were the only interactions. Stanley M. Burgess, "Pentecostalism in India: An Overview," *Asian Journal of Pentecostal Studies* 4, no. 1 (2001): 85–98, demonstrates that there are many contenders for Pentecostal influence in India, both before and after the Mukti Revival.

9. Suarsana, "Inventing Pentecostalism," 189.

10. Besides Suarsana's work, see also Michael Bergunder, *The South Indian Pentecostal Movement in the Twentieth Century*, Studies in the History of Christian Mission (Grand Rapids, MI: Eerdmans, 2008), especially his discussion of the importance of the Mukti Mission in forming a Pentecostal network (23–26) and his discussion of pre-Pentecostal Holiness Networks as a foundation for the Pentecostal revivals (2–14).

11. These are available online in a finding aid for a microfiche collection made in 2001 by James Lutzweiler, Schnappsburg University Press, and available at the Yale University Library at http://divinity-adhoc.library.yale.edu/FindingAids/Pandita%20Ramabai%20Papers.pdf.

This library may have changed or had books removed since the death of Ramabai, but its current state provides a glimpse into writers whom Ramabai may have interacted with personally or through their written ideas.

12. I am focusing on authors represented by at least two books on the assumption that single volumes could have entered Ramabai's library as gifts, but multiple authors are more likely to represent active collecting by Ramabai. Authors represented by single volumes are not necessarily insignificant, and a deeper study of the library should be done. However, by excluding these volumes, we are more likely to narrow down the possibly significant influences on Ramabai's thought. Nevertheless, the evidence is more suggestive than representative of definite relationships.

13. Goreh was converted by the Church Missionary Society and appears to have remained connected with the Anglican tradition. See Richard Fox Young, "Enabling Encounters: The Case of Nilakanth-Nehemiah Goreh, Brahmin Convert," *International Bulletin of Missionary Research* 29, no. 1 (2005), 14–20.

14. Padmanji was converted by attending a mission school of the Free Church of Scotland. See Baba Padmanji, *Once Hindu, Now Christian: The Early Life of Baba Padmanji; An Autobiography*, ed. J. Murray Mitchell (New York: Fleming H. Revell, ca. 1900).

15. Some papers of Miller's are held at the Presbyterian Historical Society in Philadelphia, but the finding aid does not provide enough information to assess any involvement with the Holiness Movement.

16. An autobiography for Paton is available at: https://watchtowerdocuments.org/documents/1915_John_H_Paton_Autobiography.pdf, although it is difficult to discern any connection to the Holiness Movement.

17. *Louisville Courier-Journal* (August 1, 1908): 4. Worrell also wrote *Full Gospel Teachings* (Louisville, KY: Charles T. Dearing, 1900), which is clearly Holiness in nature.

18. Information from Path2Prayer website, "J. Gregory Mantle: Writer on Victory," https://www.path2prayer.com/holiness-and-spirituality-writers/j-gregory-mantle-writer-on-victory.

19. See John Charles Pollock with Ian Randall, *The Keswick Story: The Authorized History of the Keswick Convention—Updated!* (Ft. Washington, PA: CLC Publications, 2006), 28–29.

20. H. Dyer, *Pandita Ramabai*, 44.

21. Dyer can be confused with Rev. Alfred Saunders Dyer (1853–1906), an Anglican religious author who served as the canon of St. Paul's Cathedral in Calcutta. Library records frequently confuse the two men. See Katherine Mullin, "Dyer, Alfred Stace (1849–1926)," *Oxford Dictionary of National Biography*, October 4, 2008, https://doi.org/10.1093/refodnb/94647.

22. George Bowen is an interesting person with Holiness connections. While covering the revivals of Bishop William Taylor in India, he so related to Taylor's Holiness teachings that he joined the Methodists from the American Board of Foreign Missions. He then became an independent self-supporting missionary while editing the *Bombay Guardian*.

23. See Robert E. Speer, *George Bowen of Bombay: Missionary, Scholar, Mystic, Saint* (New York: The Missionary Review of the World, 1938), 245–46.

24. Works of Alfred S. Dyer, such as *Remember His Marvellous Works: A Record of Remarkable Providences and Answers to Prayer* (London: Morgan and Scott, 1915), and *A Christian Daughter of India* (London: Christian Workers' Depot, n.d.), contain chapters and references to Ramabai and seem clearly aimed toward a Holiness readership. A.

S. Dyer's book, *The Master and the Book* (N.p., 1912), relays Dyer's decision to leave the Society of Friends over issues that are decidedly Holiness in nature.

25. Pollock with Randall, *Keswick Story*, 162–65.

26. For a brief biography, see A. F. Munden, "Baxter [née Foster], Elizabeth [Lizzie] (1837–1926)," *Oxford Dictionary of National Biography*, September 23, 2004, https://doi.org/10.1093/refodnb/47105.

27. For more detail, along with other aspects of Ramabai's connection with Roberts and the Free Methodist Church, see Howard A. Snyder, "Holiness Heritage: The Case of Pandita Ramabai," *Wesleyan Theological Journal* 40, no. 2 (Fall 2005): 30–51.

28. Much of the material on Norton used here comes from Hubert Cooper and Ruth Norton, *The Triumph of Faith: The True Story of Albert and Mary Norton*, 2nd ed., ed. Charles Norton Shepard (Maharashtra, India: Boys and Girls Christian Home, 2017). See also Robert Danielson, "Albert B. Norton and the Mukti Revival: From Faith Missions to Pentecostal Advocate," *Pneuma* 42, no. 1 (2020): 5–24.

29. Bishop William Taylor was a Holiness leader in the Methodist Episcopal Church known for his work in Africa. He spent four years in Bombay and is probably the one most responsible for establishing a Holiness network in this area. See William Taylor, *Four Years' Campaign in India* (New York: Philips and Hunt, 1880).

30. H. Dyer, *Pandita Ramabai*, 66.

31. Cooper and Norton, *Triumph of Faith*, 90–91.

32. Ibid., 96–97.

33. Albert Norton, "Rain in the Time of the Latter Rain—A Testimony," *Bridegroom's Messenger* 2, no. 39 (June 1, 1909): 3.

34. Ethel Ellen Ward, *Ordered Steps, or, the Wards of India* (Winona Lake, IN: Light and Life Press, 1951), 23–28. See also Sherrill Yardy, "Going Out: Ernest and Phebe Ward," *Free Methodist World Mission People* (July–September 2011): 23.

35. Howard A. Snyder, "Radical Holiness Evangelism: Vivian Dake and the Pentecost Bands," in *The Radical Holiness Movement in the Christian Tradition: A Festschrift for Larry D. Smith*, ed. William Kostlevy and Wallace Thornton Jr. (Lexington, KY: Emeth Press, 2016), 70.

36. E. A. Seamands, "Holiness Association History," *The More Excellent Way* (May–June 1950): 4.

37. Ward, *Ordered Steps*, 69–71.

38. For details on the Pentecost Bands, see Ida Dake Parsons, *Kindling Watch-Fires: Being a Brief Sketch of the Life of Rev. Vivian A. Dake* (Chicago: Free Methodist Publishing, 1915); Thomas H. Nelson, *Life and Labours of Rev. Vivian A. Dake, Organizer and Leader of Pentecost Bands* (Chicago: T. B. Arnold, 1894).

39. *Pentecost Herald* 1, no. 2 (May 1894): 4.

40. The account of the Wards' work and the travel of the Pentecost Band to assist them can be read in almost every issue of the *Pentecost Herald* from this time period.

41. *Pentecost Herald* 4, no. 16 (whole no. 71) (November 15, 1897): 3.

42. *Pentecost Herald* 5, no. 16 (whole no. 95) (November 15, 1898): 8.

43. Phebe E. Ward's journal, "Papers of Ernest F. Ward," Archives and Special Collections, B. L. Fisher Library, Asbury Theological Seminary, Wilmore, KY, box 1, folder 5. For the account of this, see Robert Danielson, "From the Archives: Ernest F. Ward: The First Free Methodist Foreign Missionary," *Asbury Journal* 70, no. 1 (2015): 172–80, https://place.asbury seminary.edu/asburyjournal/vol70/iss1/11.

44. For the Vanguard Mission work in Sanjan, see Albert E. and Bessie Sherman Ashton, *From Famine to Famine: An Account of Famine Experience and Mission Work in India* (St. Louis, MO: Vanguard

Mission, ca. 1908), https://archive.org/details/ashtonfamine1908.

45. H. Dyer, *Revival in India*, 61.

46. See also Carrie T. Burritt, *The Story of Fifty Years* (Winona Lake, IN: Light and Life Press, ca. 1935), 71.

47. *Pentecost Herald* 6, no. 6 (whole no. 109) (June 15, 1899): 6.

48. References and quotations from the Pentecost Bands of India come from the "Records of Pentecost Bands in India," microfilm at Asbury Theological Seminary, ARC1010 1989-006 reel 1.

49. Pandita Ramabai Sarasvati, "More Surprises," *Mukti Prayer Bell* (October 1905): 7.

50. Edith Blumhofer wrote, "Three notable features seemed ubiquitous in this Indian revival: fire (felt and unseen), intense joy, and public confession of sin." Edith L. Blumhofer, "Consuming Fire: Pandita Ramabai and the Early Pentecostal Impulse," in *Indian and Christian: The Life and Legacy of Pandita Ramabai*, ed. Roger E. Hedlund, Sebastian Kim, and Rajkumar Boaz Johnson (Chennai: MIIS/CMS/SPCK, 2011), 141. These characteristics are also seen in the accounts of the Pentecost Bands in India.

51. Copies of the *India Vanguard* have not been located to date. Most likely the only copies to make it to the United States were stored in the Vanguard offices and then destroyed in the Pentecostal takeover of the mission. See John William Harris, *Tears and Triumphs: The Life Story of a Pastor-Evangelist* (Louisville, KY: Pentecostal Publishing, 1948), 334–35.

52. William Godbey, *Around the World, Garden of Eden, Latter Day Prophecies and Missions* (Cincinnati, OH: God's Revivalist Office, 1907), 432–78.

53. Ibid., 447.

54. Ibid., 453.

55. While Godbey's evidence is interesting, it is the account of a temporary visitor and his impressions at that moment. Godbey was a prolific writer, yet none of his books are in Ramabai's library. It remains unclear how much regular contact he had with the Holiness missionaries in India.

BIBLIOGRAPHY

Abrams, Minnie. *The Baptism of the Holy Ghost and Fire: Matt. 3.11*. Kedgaon, India: Mukti Mission Press, 1906.

———. "How the Recent Revival was Brought About in India: The Power of Intercession." *Latter Rain Evangel* 1, no. 10 (July 1909): 6–13.

Anderson, Allan. "Pandita Ramabai, the Mukti Revival and Global Pentecostalism." *Transformation* 23, no. 1 (2006): 37–48.

Anonymous. *India Alliance* 1, no. 4 (May 1894): 45.

Anonymous. *Louisville Courier-Journal*, August 1, 1908, 4.

Ashton, Albert E., and Bessie Sherman Ashton. *From Famine to Famine: An Account of Famine Experience and Mission Work in India*. St. Louis, MO: Vanguard Mission, ca. 1908.

Bergunder, Michael. *The South Indian Pentecostal Movement in the Twentieth Century*. Studies in the History of Christian Mission. Grand Rapids, MI: Eerdmans, 2008.

Blumhofer, Edith L. "Consuming Fire: Pandita Ramabai and the Early Pentecostal Impulse." In *Indian and Christian: The Life and Legacy of Pandita Ramabai*, edited by Roger E. Hedlund, Sebastian Kim, and Rajkumar Boaz Johnson, 127–54. Chennai, India: MIIS/CMS/SPCK, 2011.

Burgess, Stanley M. "Pentecostalism in India: An Overview." *Asian Journal of Pentecostal Studies* 4, no. 1 (2001): 85–98.

Burritt, Carrie T. *The Story of Fifty Years*. Winona Lake, IN: Light and Life Press, ca. 1935.

Cooper, Hubert, and Ruth Norton. *The Triumph of Faith: The True Story of Albert and Mary Norton*. 2nd ed., edited by Charles Norton Shepard. Maharashtra, India: Boys and Girls Christian Home, 2017.

Danielson, Robert. "Albert B. Norton and the Mukti Revival: From Faith Missions to Pentecostal Advocate." *Pneuma* 42, no. 1 (2020): 5–24.

———. "From the Archives: Ernest F. Ward: The First Free Methodist Foreign Missionary." *Asbury Journal* 70, no. 1 (2015): 172–80, https://place.asburyseminary.edu/asburyjournal/vol70/iss1/11.

Dyer, Alfred S. *A Christian Daughter of India*. London: Christian Workers' Depot, n.d.

———. *The Master and the Book: A Protest and Warning Addressed to Members of the Society of Friends Concerning the Modern Quaker Theology by Which the Son of God Is Dishonoured, and the Holy Scriptures Robbed of Their Authority*. N.p., 1912.

———. *Remember His Marvellous Works: A Record of Remarkable Providences and Answers to Prayer*. London: Morgan and Scott, 1915.

Dyer, Helen S. *A Great Life in Indian Missions: Pandita Ramabai: Her Vision, Her Mission and Triumph of Faith*. London: Pickering and Inglis, 1923.

———. *Revival in India: "Years of the Right Hand of the Most High."* London: Morgan and Scott, 1907.

Godbey, William. *Around the World, Garden of Eden, Latter Day Prophecies and Missions*. Cincinnati, OH: God's Revivalist Office, 1907.

Harris, John William. *Tears and Triumphs: The Life Story of a Pastor-Evangelist*. Louisville, KY: Pentecostal Publishing, 1948.

McGee, Gary B. "'Baptism of the Holy Ghost & Fire!' The Mission Legacy of Minnie F. Abrams." *Missiology* 27, no. 4 (October 1999): 515–22.

Mullin, Katherine. "Dyer, Alfred Stace (1849–1926)." *Oxford Dictionary of National Biography*, October 4, 2008. https://doi.org/10.1093/refodnb/94647.

Munden, A. F. "Baxter [née Foster], Elizabeth [Lizzie] (1837–1926)." *Oxford Dictionary of National Biography*, September 23, 2004. https://doi.org/10.1093/refodnb/47105.

Nelson, Thomas H. *Life and Labours of Rev. Vivian A. Dake, Organizer and Leader of Pentecost Bands*. Chicago: T. B. Arnold, 1894.

Norton, Albert. "Rain in the Time of the Latter Rain—A Testimony." *Bridegroom's Messenger* 2, no. 39 (June 1, 1909): 3.

Padmanji, Baba. *Once Hindu, Now Christian: The Early Life of Baba Padmanji; An Autobiography*. Edited by J. Murray Mitchell. New York: Fleming H. Revell, ca. 1900.

Parsons, Ida Dake. *Kindling Watch-Fires: Being a Brief Sketch of the Life of Rev. Vivian A. Dake*. Chicago: Free Methodist Publishing, 1915.

Path2Prayer Website. "J. Gregory Mantle: Writer on Victory." https://www.path2prayer.com/holiness-and-spirituality-writers/j-gregory-mantle-writer-on-victory.

Paton, John H. "John H. Paton (1843–1922)." http://www.watchtowerdocuments.org/documents/1915_John_H_Paton_Autobiography.pdf.

Pentecost Bands of India. "Records of Pentecost Bands in India." Microfilm at Asbury Theological Seminary, ARC1010 1989–006 reel 1: Band #1 at Raj Nandgaon (1897–1905), Band

#2 at Gondia (1899–1905), and Band #3 at Dondi Lohara (1899–1949).

Pentecost Herald 4, no. 16 (whole no. 71) (November 15, 1897).

Pentecost Herald 5, no. 16 (whole no. 95) (November 15, 1898).

Pentecost Herald 6, no. 6 (whole no. 109) (June 15, 1899).

Pollock, John Charles, with Ian Randall. *The Keswick Story: The Authorized History of the Keswick Convention—Updated!* Ft. Washington, PA: CLC Publications, 2006.

Sarasvati, Pandita Ramabai. "More Surprises." *Mukti Prayer Bell* (October 1905): 7.

Seamands, E. A. "Holiness Association History." *The More Excellent Way* (May–June 1950): 4.

Snyder, Howard A. "Holiness Heritage: The Case of Pandita Ramabai." *Wesleyan Theological Journal* 40, no. 2 (Fall 2005): 30–51.

———. "Radical Holiness Evangelism: Vivian Dake and the Pentecost Bands." In *The Radical Holiness Movement in the Christian Tradition: A Festschrift for Larry D. Smith*, edited by William Kostlevy and Wallace Thornton Jr., 69–84. Lexington, KY: Emeth Press, 2016.

Speer, Robert E. *George Bowen of Bombay: Missionary, Scholar, Mystic, Saint.* New York: The Missionary Review of the World, 1938.

Suarsana, Yan. "Inventing Pentecostalism: Pandita Ramabai and the Mukti Revival from a Post-Colonial Perspective." *PentecoStudies* 13, no. 2 (2014): 173–96.

———. *Pandita Ramabai und die Erfindung der Pfingstbewegung: Postkoloniale Religionsgeschichtsschreibung am Beispiel des "Mukti Revival."* Studies in the History of Christianity in the Non-Western World 23. Wiesbaden: Harrassowitz Verlag, 2013.

Taylor, William. *Four Years' Campaign in India.* New York: Philips and Hunt, 1880.

Ward, Ethel Ellen. *Ordered Steps, or, the Wards of India.* Winona Lake, IN: Light and Life Press, 1951.

Worrell, Aldophus Spaulding. *Full Gospel Teachings.* Louisville, KY: Charles T. Dearing, 1900.

Yardy, Sherrill. "Going Out: Ernest and Phebe Ward." *Free Methodist World Mission People* (July–September 2011): 23.

Young, Richard Fox. "Enabling Encounters: The Case of Nilakanth-Nehemiah Goreh, Brahmin Convert." *International Bulletin of Missionary Research* 29, no. 1 (2005): 14–20.

CHAPTER 3

Alexander A. Boddy, the Pentecostal League of Prayer, and the Wesleyan Roots of British Pentecostalism

Kimberly Ervin Alexander

Thomas Ball Barratt (1862–1940), an English-born Methodist minister from Norway, visited the United States after hearing of the Pentecostal revival at Azusa Street in Los Angeles and in New York City attended a prayer meeting, after which he testified to receiving a Pentecostal experience of Spirit baptism.[1] He left New York City, returned to Christiana (now Oslo) and began preaching the Pentecostal message there. When Rev. Alexander A. Boddy (1854–1930), vicar of All Saints Church, Sunderland, England, visited the Christiana Revival, he urged Barratt to come to England. Barratt obliged in the late summer of 1907. In those meetings, Boddy's wife, Mary, an able teacher known for her prayers of healing for the sick, and their two daughters, Mary and Jane, received the Pentecostal experience. Boddy's Spirit baptism would follow in December. The Boddys became leaders of the movement in England, with influence in Scotland, some influence on the Continent and in the United States as a result of their annual meetings and monthly periodical, *Confidence*.[2]

While the Wesleyan roots of Pentecostalism have been established by scholars, historians have assumed a Keswick influence on the Boddys and early British Pentecostalism.[3] Ian Randall suggested that there is a "striking" difference between American and British Pentecostalism, maintaining there is an "absence of strong Wesleyan roots in England." Further, he claims, "More powerful influences came through Keswick and Brethrenism."[4] While this argument may be made of British Pentecostalism as a whole, especially as it developed and

Fig. 3.1 A. A. Boddy family portrait outside their home, ca. 1913. Back: Jane and Mary Boddy. Front: Dorothy Kerin (seated), Mrs. Mary Boddy, and A. A. Boddy. Courtesy of Flower Pentecostal Heritage Center.

organized, the evidence where Boddy is concerned is scant.[5] Mark Cartledge challenges Randall's claim, maintaining a more Wesleyan influence upon early British Pentecostalism.[6] The significance of the influences of Richard Reader Harris, Mary Harris, and their Pentecostal League of Prayer (PLP) has been examined by Timothy Walsh, who notes especially the similarities in what today might be termed its mission and vision: "the spreading of 'Scriptural holiness by unsectarian methods.'"[7] A deeper exploration of the influences on Alexander Boddy's theological and spiritual development reveals not only the Wesleyan-Holiness influence of the PLP but also affinities with John Wesley and Methodism. British Pentecostalism, like its Scandinavian and American antecedents, can lay claim to a Wesleyan root.

Fig. 3.2 Reader Harris. Frontispiece of his *Daniel the Prophet* (London: S. W. Partridge, 1909).

THE LIMITS OF KESWICK'S IMPACT

There are previous studies of Boddy that have situated him as an Anglican vicar largely influenced by the Keswick Movement.[8] Neil Hudson introduces Boddy with the assumption, "He had long been a keen supporter and visitor to the Keswick Convention in the late nineteenth century, embracing their promise that one's Christian life could be more than a dour duty offered to a God who was almost impossible to please."[9] In the same volume, in a discussion of European Pentecostalism, Jean-Daniel Plüss maintains that Boddy had become "deeply influenced" by Keswick.[10] That Boddy attended Keswick is not in doubt, but the claim of its impact on him is perhaps overstated. Gavin Wakefield, Boddy's primary biographer, relies on the words of Jane Vazeille Boddy's brief memoir of her parents, as did Martin Robinson.[11] Jane Boddy's account simply noted, "He had been a nominal Christian in his youth but a change came when he went to a convention at Keswick. Then he decided to prepare for ordination, but his parents could not afford to send him to Cambridge, as they had done for Herbert [his brother], so my father saved up enough [for him] to go to Durham University for 2 years and take his L.Th."[12] She also claimed that her mother had attended the Keswick Convention but offers no detail as to when this occurred.[13] Wakefield goes on to trace "echoes" of Keswick in Boddy's life, which include faith, "peacefulness," "sin being controlled by the Holy Spirit," the imminence of Christ's return, and a "general dislike of dogma."[14]

American historian Edith Blumhofer refers to Boddy's "Keswickian emphases," but offers no real evidence of what that actually entailed.[15] However, she describes more fully the impact of the Welsh Revival on Boddy, especially given Evan Roberts's advice to Boddy to "'Fight heaven down.'"[16]

Boddy did attend the Keswick Convention in 1876, though it is not prominent in his own reflections. In Boddy's recounting of his spiritual journey, published in *Confidence* in 1914, he noted that he had been "converted, that is 'turned to God,'" but does not mention the specifics of time or place.[17] Unlike his daughter, he did not specifically connect Keswick to this event, nor to his seeking of ordination. Boddy's account had been published earlier in tract form as *A Vicar's Testimony: Pentecost at Sunderland*. In a section of that tract, "Part 2: Earlier Experiences," he gives a sweeping overview of his spiritual journey up to his baptism in the Spirit. He wrote, "It was not until the summer of 1892 that I could praise Him for fully saving me, 'Keswick,' had been a great help and especially had the visit to my Vicarage of a missionary friend."[18] This may refer to the 1876 meeting but it is not clear; nor is it clear that "a great help" refers to a conversion; finally, it seems that the visit of the unnamed friend had been a more significant "help." He did, however, reflect with much specificity about an experience in which "the Holy Spirit in infinite love came upon" him on September 21, 1892, "at about 8:40 in the morning" while participating in a Communion service at All Saints Church in Sunderland.[19] In the 1907 account, he called this experience "a Baptism or Anointing of His Holy Spirit," which was "a witness to my New Birth." Boddy elaborated, "It was after a time of great longing, when I realized the greatness of my need. He graciously came to me in my 'Church of all Saints,' Monkwearmouth, at a quiet weekday service in the early morning. He met me there within the Communion Rails. He came suddenly and unexpectedly." He continued, "He came to life [*sic*] me to a different life and to give me a love that enabled me to effect at once a reconciliation with enemies."[20] Since the details of the "help" provided by Keswick are not explained specifically by Boddy, it is difficult to assess it as a major influence. Additionally, any connection between the obviously important 1892 event and Keswick was not made specific.

If Keswick had been an important source of spirituality in his life, it is curious that Boddy did not visit the convention more often, given his penchant for travel.²¹ One critique of the Keswick Convention was that it was essentially the domain of the Anglican upper classes, given the expense of travel to the Lake District of England, much less the luxury of being able to stay for a week.²² The working classes, among whom the Boddys had always labored, simply could not have been a part of such an endeavor. Boddy did not choose to make the trek to Keswick again—at least not until *after* he encountered the Pentecostal Movement in Christiana in March 1907.

Early in 1907, Boddy wrote a letter published in the *Apostolic Faith* describing the revival in Christiana. He wrote, "Some of us ask ourselves the question, how will this affect the Keswick Convention meetings and other gatherings this year? Those who have 'Tongues' will be present, and unable and unwilling to control them when moved by the Spirit."²³ That summer, in July, Boddy made his second trip to Keswick, this time with the specific intent of distributing thousands of copies of his tract *Pentecost for England*, even though he had not yet experienced what he now understood as a Pentecostal experience of Spirit baptism. The following year, after he and his family were experiential Pentecostals, Boddy returned to Keswick, this time pleased to see folk who had attended his convention at Sunderland carrying copies of *Confidence* "ready for enquirers." Boddy did report that they "heard a message on the power of the Christ Life," but then described visiting the lake with "a happy Pentecostal party." He further detailed seeing Mr. Mogridge there with his "outspoken pamphlet 'Pentecost, and the need of Keswick for 1908.'"²⁴ He concluded the report of his visit: "Many of us thank God for Keswick in the past. We feel that the Lord is calling to His people to 'go forward.' He is calling His people to an experimental Pentecost, their Birthright because of the shed blood of Calvary. The 'Reproach' referred to in the letter of the Leaders, can be rolled away by the Lord. A real Pentecost is certainly the solution the Lord offers."²⁵

It seems that no matter how much Boddy may have revered the Keswick Convention, his one visit prior to the Pentecostal Movement did not make a significant enough impact on him to specifically mark it in his own biography, nor to attend it again in the thirty-one-year interval. Further, the two visits after the beginning of the Pentecostal Movement seem to have had a didactic purpose: the Pentecostal experience was much needed by England, even by Keswick folk.

BODDY'S TIES TO JOHN WESLEY AND AFFINITIES WITH METHODISM

To begin this exploration, it should be noted that Boddy was a direct descendant of Mary Vazeille, whose second husband was John Wesley. In other words, A. A.

Boddy's great-great-great-step-grandfather was a founder of the Methodist movement. The family name was apparently important to Boddy given that he gave all three of his children "Vazeille" as their middle name, as was the family tradition.[26] At a bicentenary celebration of John Wesley, convened at the Durham Road Wesleyan Church in Sunderland, Boddy was chosen to speak because of his direct connection to the Wesley family line. He referred both to his genealogical connection to Wesley's "much maligned wife" and "much loved" stepdaughter, Boddy's antecedent, and of having "much sympathy with the Methodists," saying he felt "at home" there.[27]

Further, the parishes with which Boddy was most familiar and in which he spent his life and ministry—Manchester, where he grew up, and northeast England, specifically Sunderland, the site of the revival—were proudly working-class areas. In those cities and the surrounding areas, among these laborers and trade unionists, Methodist enthusiasm and revivalism had flourished. It was in these regions that Lorenzo Dow preached in camp meetings and the Primitive Methodist Connexion was born in the earlier part of the nineteenth century.[28] As Wakefield has shown, where the national average of "worshippers attending the variety of Methodist chapels" was about 25 percent, in Sunderland that average was over 40 percent and Primitive Methodists outnumbered Wesleyan Methodists there.[29] It was also in Sunderland, in 1875, that a schism occurred in Primitive Methodism with over 300 members—known as the "Runaway Ranters"—breaking away to form the "Christian Lay Churches."[30] Wakefield observes and speculates that "The episode is an indication of the continuing independence of thinking in Sunderland in a denomination which was becoming more established and respectable. Such thinking played its part in helping to create a pool of people ready to respond to Boddy's meetings in September 1907, for the 'Prims' were still strong in the area at the centenary celebrations of May 1907."[31] British Pentecostal leader William Oliver Hutchinson, who was baptized in the Spirit at Sunderland in 1907 and later founded the Apostolic Faith Church in England, was born into a Primitive Methodist family in County Durham.[32]

In 1892, during a strike, Boddy advocated for miners and their families and especially those in related industries who were impacted.[33] The recognition of Boddy's work with the YMCA during this crisis is noted by Robinson, who cites the *YMCA Magazine*'s description of Boddy as a "friend to the working man," and as exhibiting a "catholicity of spirit," stating, "'His sympathies are broad, and in his common transactions with men of varying theological beliefs he is perfectly untrammeled by either sect or creeds. In Mr. Boddy, all men—whether Episcopalian or Methodist—may find a brother.'"[34]

Boddy recollected his work in his parish during the period of the revival in Wales, just prior to the Pentecostal Movement's beginnings: "Though a vicar of the Established Church, the Writer was lovingly welcomed in Methodist Chapels, Mission Halls, and many other meetings, as he told the hungry ones how God was working in Wales. Each meeting ended in revival on a small scale." He continued by quoting an account in a local paper: "'A remarkable meeting was held in the school room Behind Ewesley Road, Wesleyan Church, on Saturday night.'" He cites another article, which described "United Saturday Night Meetings"[35] and "Northside Midnight Marches": "'Methodists and Churchpeople work shoulder to shoulder, and pitmen come in on Saturday night from Castletown to support this movement.'"[36] Clearly, Boddy's upbringing in a vicarage in working-class Manchester had impacted his understanding of parish ministry and his successful ministry in Sunderland was marked by revival but also by his fellowship with Methodists.

BODDY AND THE PENTECOSTAL LEAGUE OF PRAYER

By 1901, Boddy had become a member of Reader Harris's (1847–1909) PLP, a movement with the purpose of promoting prayer but also an experience of entire sanctification, identified by Harris as baptism of the Holy Spirit. Boddy was not the only early British Pentecostal to have been so engaged. Given the association with the PLP of Boddy and other early British Pentecostal leaders, including Cecil Polhill, Smith Wigglesworth, and potentially William Oliver Hutchinson, it can be argued that the early British Pentecostal Movement was influenced both by the League's theology and practices.[37]

Though Bebbington classifies the PLP as a part of the "fringe sectaries," Randall writes, "The strand of Wesleyan thinking represented by Harris was present within mainstream denominational Methodism."[38] Further, Randall identifies the PLP as one of the groups that were "repositories of Wesleyan holiness." The aim of these groups was to offer "a radical alternative to existing ecclesiastical organisations."[39] Walsh argues that Harris would have resisted this description, seeing his organization as "'an undenominational society that labours equally in cathedral, church, chapel, or mission hall.'"[40] In January 1905, Harris made a bold claim of his purpose: "The Pentecostal League desires to help the Churches if they will only let us. We believe that God has given us a message to Christendom."[41]

To this end, the League had begun publication of a periodical, *Tongues of Fire*, in 1891. The masthead indicated that this was "A Journal for the Promotion and Extension of Spiritual Life, Purity and Power" and was edited by Harris. By the end of the nineteenth century, the PLP boasted a membership of 17,000 with 150 chapters in Great Britain.[42] Walsh notes the significance of the periodical's moniker, linking it to the 1856 publication of William Arthur's *The Tongue of Fire*, an important development in the identification of sanctification with baptism in the Spirit.[43]

Boddy became a regional secretary for the movement, which held monthly meetings in Sunderland, meeting at All Saints Church occasionally. The Sunderland chapter was one of the leading centers for the League.[44] Monthly reports of the chapter meetings are included in each issue of *Tongues of Fire*, and Sunderland led the PLP for numbers of subscriptions of its official publication, with seventy-eight subscriptions being "disposed of" on a monthly basis in Sunderland, nearly twice the number reported by the chapter reporting the next highest figure.[45]

Boddy was a keynote speaker at the annual meeting in London in May 1905 and in this address can be seen the first aspect of the PLP with which Boddy resonated and later attempted to duplicate in British and European Pentecostalism. Having expressed some reservation about some of the methods of the League's leadership to his bishop in 1901, by 1905, Boddy expressed no such reservation.[46] In his address, he expressed his gradual acceptance and ringing endorsement: "I was prejudiced, as a Church clergyman, against the League and its methods. Many will have passed and many others will pass through the same experience. First, prejudice, and then gradually a secret longing to join, but a little bit of fear as to the consequences. And then, led on by some motive or other, joining whole-heartedly with our dear friends of the Pentecostal League. And lastly, thanking God for the fellowship, thanking God for the teaching, and especially thanking God for the blessing in one's own Church and parish."[47] Boddy continued to describe how his church had become a place where the presence of God is experienced, citing specifically the words of a working woman in the congregation. In a service completely dedicated to praise, he said, "beautiful music is frequently heard, but it comes from those who love the Lord, and the praise is almost entirely congregational." He expressed his gratitude for the fellowship he experienced in the League and, importantly, noted that he had found that fellowship "a larger world of Spirit-filled brothers and sisters beyond, whose fellowship, whose sympathy, and whose prayers I am grateful for." Finally, he related what they were experiencing in League meetings to the work he witnessed under Evan Roberts in Wales.[48]

Though she does not discuss her father's association with the PLP, the important place of these meetings in her parents' life is alluded to in Jane Boddy's memoir: "About 1906 my parents began to feel that a revival was needed in the parish and a group of young men volunteered to meet together to pray for this. They and my parents met once a week in the vicarage and I still remember the fervor of their extemporary prayers."[49] This understanding seems to be corroborated in Alexander Boddy's 1910 account of the beginnings of the Pentecostal Movement, where he recalled this period of his ministry, referring to newspaper accounts of citywide meetings and marches, in which he shared with ministers and laypeople from various churches in the area about the Welsh Revival.[50]

With its "transdenominational" identity and goals, PLP centers were located in Anglican, Methodist, Baptist, and Congregational churches, incorporating leaders from these traditions. Randall summarized Harris's vision: "The League's perspective was that ecclesiastical distinctions were relatively unimportant: all denominations required the renewal which Wesleyan experience offered."[51] To this end, the PLP published its periodical, established regional chapters, and held annual conferences.

The similarity in vision with Boddy is apparent in the reports on his first Whitsuntide Conference, held at Sunderland in June 1908.[52] The theme was set in a preliminary meeting when Boddy's wife, Mary, addressed those gathered, speaking on "'No divisions' or unnecessary criticisms: 'The Body must be *one*—that the spiritual Unity may not be hindered.'"[53] It is this "transcending vision" that Robinson noted in his comparison of the Anglican Pentecostal vicar with later Anglican Charismatic Renewal leader Michael Harper.[54]

In the following years, when the Anglican Cecil Polhill, a member of the Cambridge Seven as well as the PLP and a missionary with the China Inland Mission, embraced Pentecostalism and, with Boddy, established the Pentecostal Missionary Union, Boddy commented again on his desire for unity: "The Writer has felt strongly that it is a mistake to form another home organization, which soon may become another 'church,' and follow the fate of so many before it. Union for the purpose of sending out and helping and advising Pentecostal Missionaries in the dark places of Heathenism, is to his mind, the great need today."[55] On this point, though having a similar vision as the Harrises'—renewal of the churches—Boddy differed from the PLP for fear that a "home organization" would evolve into a Pentecostal denomination; therefore, he urged that organization should focus on "foreign" missions.[56]

The second area of resonance between the PLP's ethos and Boddy's early Pentecostalism is in its Holiness orientation. Walsh notes that the promotion of "an experience of sanctification distinct from, and subsequent to, conversion" was integral to the PLP.[57] Throughout the pages of *Tongues of Fire*, the overt Holiness theology is apparent, as is the rejection of Keswick theology. Randall opens his examination of the PLP with a recounting of Harris's very public 1895 denouncement of Keswick Anglican H. W. Webb-Peploe's insistence that sin in the believer could only be counteracted and not eradicated.[58] Harris, in response, vowed to award £100 to anyone who could prove this from scripture.[59] His polemic, "Sin and Its Remedy," was printed in *Tongues of Fire* just under his challenge.[60] News of this "bet," as it was referred to by journalists, was picked up by the secular press in Great Britain.[61] Succeeding discussions and rebuttals of Keswick teaching in *Tongues of Fire* clearly expressed Harris's identity with Wesley. An article reprinted from the *Methodist Times* by Rev. Hugh Price Hughes retorted, "We need only say here that the doctrine which Mr. Reader Harris propounds in 'Sin and its Remedy' is precisely the doctrine which John Wesley taught, and which is believed by the most numerous and wide-spread Protestant Church in the world."[62] The point is Boddy embraced Harris and the PLP with this clear Wesleyan-Holiness stance fully in view. The next month, Harris continued the discussion and challenge on the front page, declaring, "The question has attracted the attention of many of the deepest Christian thinkers, who see in it a remarkable repetition of the controversy on almost identical lines which took place between **John Wesley** [emphasis in original] and his opposers more than a century ago." He went on to quote Hughes's article in the *Methodist Times*.[63] Harris reported at length on the coverage by others in both the secular and Christian press in a column titled "Is Sin A Necessity?"[64] This coverage became a regular column in the next three issues. In the March column, Harris defended his position as that of Wesley. In this apologetic, he cited numerous letters and articles printed in other Christian publications defending his position as congruent with Wesley and Fletcher.[65] Harris's self-understanding of his position as congruent with Wesley, at least as he understood Wesley's theology, was no secret.[66]

Boddy's commitment to the PLP, Harris, and that movement's Wesleyan-Holiness identity is also noteworthy given the Keswick leadership role of his bishop, Handley Moule. Moule addressed the convention for the first time in 1886.[67] He became bishop of Durham, the bishop to whom Boddy reported, in 1901, the same year in which Boddy became a member of the PLP.[68] Given Moule's oversight of Boddy's ministry, it is significant that the vicar would become so involved in a movement clear in its opposition to aspects of Keswick theology.

That Boddy subscribed to this Wesleyan-Holiness understanding of sanctification during this period is evident. In his testimony, printed in tract form,

A Vicar's Testimony, Boddy referred to times of anointing he experienced in the prayer meetings leading up to the Pentecostal revival at Sunderland. He described one of these meetings in which he received "a special witness of the Lord of my Sanctification."[69] He closed the tract with "Scriptural Prayer Steps to Pentecost," including prayers for justification, sanctification, and baptism of the Spirit.[70]

As Cartledge has demonstrated, the Boddys and *Confidence* fit solidly in the fivefold gospel stream of Pentecostalism until 1914.[71] He points to a statement that appeared in *Confidence* beginning in April 1911 and continuing through January/February 1917; the paper maintained: "'Confidence' advocates an unlimited Salvation for Spirit, Soul, and Body; the Honouring of the Precious Blood: Identification with Christ in Death and Resurrection, etc.; Regeneration, Sanctification; the Baptism of the Holy Ghost; the Soon-Coming of the Lord in the air (1 Thess. iv., 14); Divine Healing and Health (Acts iv., 13)."[72] His analysis of *Confidence* demonstrates a preference for Wesleyan-Holiness language such as "entire sanctification," "clean heart," and even "purging." He notes that when asked about sanctification as a prerequisite for Pentecostal experience, Boddy was emphatic in his affirmation of the order of justification, sanctification, and Spirit baptism.[73]

A third area in which the PLP's influence on the Sunderland form of early Pentecostalism may be seen is in its endorsement of women in ministry. Both Randall and Priscilla Pope-Levison have demonstrated that Harris, influenced especially by the work of Catherine Booth and the Salvation Army, fully endorsed women as preachers, promoting their work in *Tongues of Fire*. Women addressed the League's annual and regional meetings.[74] Indeed, women were leaders in the PLP, with up to 42 percent of the regional secretaries being female. As early as 1893, Harris defended "Female Ministry" in *Tongues of Fire*.[75] In 1903, *Tongues of Fire* published another defense of women preachers at a time, as Randall points out, when Keswick leaders were still debating the role of women.[76] For those who are familiar with Boddy's work in the Pentecostal Movement in Great Britain, the resonance, even duplication of method, will be rather obvious. During the week-long inaugural Sunderland Convention, numerous women preached, including Mary Boddy, Elizabeth Sisson (America), as well as Dagmar Gregersen and Agnes Thelle (Norway); other women are mentioned as testifying and taking part in discussions. Both Wakefield and Diana Chapman have discussed this prevalence of women as preachers and teachers at the Sunderland Conventions.[77] That women were active and engaging in public preaching and ministry is evidenced in the numerous sermons and articles printed throughout the pages of *Confidence*. Wakefield estimated that between 1908 and 1914, approximately one-third of the sixty-five leaders attending and participating in the annual meetings were women. However, a major discussion of women's "place," occurred at the 1914 meeting, the last one convened in Sunderland. Boddy opened the discussion on "Women's Place in the Church" with a reading of several Pauline texts. The meeting was dominated by male leaders with only one female voice being heard and that a seemingly compliant one. "'Mrs. Polman," wife of the Dutch Pentecostal, Gerritt Polman, argued for deference to male leadership.[78] No British Pentecostal women are recorded as having contributed to the discussion. Boddy offered a comment about there being no issue when husbands and wives worked "in harmony" and provided some clarification about the separation of women and men in Palestinian worship settings.[79] Chapman concluded that Boddy remained supportive of women in ministry and argued, "Without such a charismatic figure as Boddy leading the Pentecostal Movement in its early years in Britain, one wonders whether women would have had such freedom."[80]

FOLLOWING DIFFERENT PENTECOSTAL LINES

Harris and Boddy parted ways in the wake of the Pentecostal revival. In an interview with Boddy published in the Darlington *North Star* and reprinted in the June 1915 edition of *Confidence*, when asked to differentiate between the Pentecostal Movement and his conventions and the work of the PLP, Boddy simply said, "Mr. Harris didn't endorse the line I took."[81] Again, even before his own Pentecostal experience, Boddy became vocal about Pentecostalism, visiting Keswick with the intent of spreading the Pentecostal message. When the Pentecostal revival with Barratt began in Sunderland, the meetings, complete with "spontaneous prayer and hymn singing," "paroxysm of weeping," as well as "gabble" and "unintelligible sounds," were covered in the press.[82] The *Manchester Courier* described the "hysterical convulsions" of those who had thrown themselves to the floor.[83] Two months later, the meetings were still being discussed and denounced as "The Devil's Revival at Monkwearmouth."[84]

No doubt contributing to the schism with the PLP was the fact that Harris was leading his regional convention in Sunderland during this same period of time.[85] According to Desmond Cartwright, Barratt recorded in his diary that "'Mr Reader Harris delivered two lectures in the Victoria Hall in this city last week. The first on 'Tongues' and the second on 'Spiritism' in which he denounced the movement in terms far from Christian at times.'"[86] Barratt responded by combating those arguments in his address at the parish hall. In

November, Harris published a summary of his remarks and reported that the "extraordinary goings-on in Monkwearmouth and Devonshire" exhibited the marks of a "counterfeit."[87]

During this earliest period of the Pentecostal Movement in Great Britain, *Tongues of Fire* published articles and editorials questioning the validity of the "'Tongues movement.'"[88] In the same month as the competing conventions in Sunderland, an article by Rev. Oswald Chambers, titled "Gift of Tongues," was published. Chambers urged caution: "To-day, when this *gift of tongues* is being overrated, we do well to remember two things. (1) Don't underrate, and (2) Don't overrate." Chambers did go on, however, to see the insistence on speaking in tongues as a sign of Spirit baptism as occasion for the devil to "multiply his imitation of the gift of tongues." The "'new man'" is manifested "in *holiness*, not in *hysterics*." Still, he urged the PLP readers to "Keep every avenue of the nature open towards God. Be suspicious of nobody that has tongues unless they want to teach something that is a private interpretation of the Word of God."[89]

Reader Harris, however, was not so charitable or long-suffering. In November 1907, he wrote, "What has been lately taking place under the auspices of what is known as the 'Tongues Movement' is an evidence that to-day, as in St. Paul's day, there are persons in the Church who believe that a condition of spiritual excitement absolves them from the necessity of consulting their reason, or from those considerations and rules of decency which govern respectable people." He continued,

> Two very grave errors accompany the present so-called "Tongues Movement." One is that all Christians ought to speak in tongues; and the other is that speaking in tongues is *the* great evidence of the Pentecostal blessing. Both are unsupported by the Scriptures when compared with Scriptures, and the history of the Church.... The second error,—that speaking in tongues is the evidence of the Pentecostal blessing—is almost too absurd to warrant denial. But strange to say not a few of God's people, and sometimes even those who have experienced the Baptism with the Holy Spirit, have been led into darkness, error and soul loss, by this false teaching.[90]

Harris labeled the experience a "Satanic counterfeit."[91] In these polemics, following the Barratt Revival at Sunderland, Harris was no doubt referring to Pentecostal teaching in general but perhaps also to Boddy's writings specifically. In his tract distributed at Keswick earlier in 1907 and doubtlessly elsewhere, Boddy had indeed maintained that "As a rule it is those who believe that 'speaking in tongues' is an evidence of Pentecost who thus are blessed."[92]

The next month, on December 2, 1907, Harris's former colleague, PLP leader and keynote speaker, Alexander Boddy, while praying at the All Saints' vestry, spoke in tongues. He testified of his experience:

> So on that Monday night as I lay before the Lord He took my tongue as I yielded and obeyed. First speaking quickly but quietly and then more powerfully. The whole meeting at this point was adoring and praising the Spirit with great joy. The Lord was raising His hands in blessing above the meeting and we were conscious of His presence.
> How they sang—
> "*O come let us adore Him; Christ the Lord.*"
> My voice in tongues rose with theirs as a torrent of words poured out, asking the Lord for an interpretation (in accordance with 1 Corinthians 14:13), I understood Him to tell me that I had been repeating Psalm 107 down to the verses: "So He bringeth them into the haven where they would be. Oh that men would therefore praise him for His goodness and for His wonderful works toward the children of men."
> So far it had been between me and the Lord (1 Cor. 14:2) and I was indeed grateful that after nine months the sign I had hoped for had come at last. Hallelujah to the Lamb!⁹³

Boddy went on to describe the "open opposition" used by Satan to "terrorize" him, including "lectures with sensational titles" and "condemnation through the press (secular and religious)." Though disavowed by Harris, Boddy maintained his Holiness sensibilities, now formulated as the fivefold gospel.

Still to be fully examined, it is noteworthy that the orientation of *Confidence* and early British Pentecostalism as a whole shifted away from its Wesleyan-Holiness, fivefold gospel orientation at the time when Boddy's influence and leadership of the movement began to wane, owing to his support of the war effort, over and against many of the major Pentecostal leaders in Europe who remained pacifists.⁹⁴ The Sunderland congregation's hall became a hospital and the annual Pentecostal conferences moved south to London. Boddy remained in the north, continuing his role as "evangelical Anglican slum priest."⁹⁵

CONCLUSION

The earliest and most influential published expression of Pentecostalism in England may be categorized as Wesleyan-Holiness-Pentecostal, as much as many of the American expressions may be so categorized.[96] It is also likely that much of this can be attributed to Alexander Boddy's association with Reader Harris and the Pentecostal League of Prayer and perhaps his affinity with Wesley and Methodists. Boddy's vision for Pentecostalism was for a movement that brought spiritual vitality to the larger Christian church, convening yearly conventions in his Anglican parish and publishing a monthly periodical with an aim of "being a means of grace and of mutual encouragement ... to lonely ones and to scattered bands, to those who are attacked by doubt and difficulty, but longing to be loyal to the Almighty Deliverer."[97] Like Mary and Reader Harris, Mary and Alexander Boddy envisioned a Pentecostal Movement where women and men, in Pentecostal power, preached and taught a full salvation and holiness of heart and life, "a larger world of Spirit-filled brothers and sisters."

NOTES

The research for this chapter was done in 2018 while the author was a Visiting Research Fellow at the Manchester Wesley Research Centre.

1. For studies of Barratt's background in Methodism, see David Bundy, "Thomas Ball Barratt: From Methodist to Pentecostal," *EPTA Bulletin—Journal of the European Pentecostal Theological Association* 13, no. 1 (1994): 19–49; David Bundy, *Visions of Apostolic Mission: Scandinavian Pentecostal Mission to 1935*, Studia Historico-Ecclesiastica Upsaliensia 45 (Uppsala: Uppsala Universitet, 2009); Rakel Ystebø Alegre, "The Pentecostal Apologetics of T. B. Barratt: Defining and Defending the Faith 1906–1909" (PhD diss., Regent University, 2019).

2. The extent of Boddy's influence beyond the British Isles is a matter of some discussion among scholars. Jean-Daniel Plüss and Allan Anderson cite his influence as extensive on the Continent. Jean-Daniel Plüss, "Pentecostalism in Europe and the Former Soviet Union," in *The Cambridge Companion to Pentecostalism*, ed. Cecil M. Robeck Jr. and Amos Yong (New York: Cambridge University Press, 2014), 96; Allan Anderson, *An Introduction to Pentecostalism* (Cambridge: Cambridge University Press, 2004), 91–92. Cornelius van der Laan has argued for Boddy's influence on Dutch Pentecostalism. Cornelius van der Laan, "Alexander Boddy: Anglican Father of Dutch Pentecostalism," *Journal of the European Pentecostal Theological Association* 31, no. 1 (2011): 93–110. The earliest scholarly investigation of Boddy, a comparison of Boddy and later Anglican renewal leader, Michael Harper, limits Boddy's influence to the British Isles. Martin Robinson, "The Charismatic Anglican—Historical and Contemporary: A Comparison of the Life and Work of Alexander Boddy (1854–1930) and Michael C. Harper" (MLitt thesis, University of Birmingham, 1976), 4–5. However, he does call Sunderland an "International Centre for Pentecost" in the title of his third chapter (51). David Bundy, however, has argued for minimal long-term continental influence owing to his commitment to the Church of England, British nationalism, and support of World War I. Bundy, *Visions of Apostolic Mission*, 231–32.

3. See Vinson Synan, *The Holiness-Pentecostal Movement in the United States* (Grand Rapids, MI: Eerdmans, 1971);

Donald W. Dayton, *Theological Roots of Pentecostalism* (Metuchen, NJ: Scarecrow Press, 1987); Walter J. Hollenweger, *The Pentecostals* (Peabody, MA: Hendrickson, 1988). See William K. Kay, "Pentecostal Eschatology," in *Pentecostal and Charismatic Studies: A Reader*, ed. William K. Kay and Anne E. Dyer (London: SCM Press, 2004), 26; Anderson, *Introduction to Pentecostalism*, 91.

4. Ian M. Randall, *Evangelical Experiences: A Study in the Spirituality of English Evangelicalism, 1918–1939* (Carlisle: Paternoster Press, 1999), 207. See also Ian M. Randall, "Old Time Power: Relationships between Pentecostalism and Evangelical Spirituality in England," *Pneuma* 19, no. 1 (1997): 59. In an early history of British Pentecostalism, Donald Gee discussed the Keswick influence, but placed it alongside the rise of the Holiness Movement's influence. Donald Gee, *Wind and Flame: Incorporating the Former Book 'The Pentecostal Movement' with Additional Chapters* (Croydon: Heath Press, 1967), 3.

5. Robinson concludes that the Keswick influence is "difficult to assess." He does note similarities in some of Boddy's writings with those of Andrew Murray. Robinson, "Charismatic Anglican," 36.

6. Mark J. Cartledge, "The Early Pentecostal Theology of *Confidence* Magazine (1908–1926): A Version of the Five-Fold Gospel?," *Journal of the European Pentecostal Theological Association* 28, no. 2 (2008): 117–30.

7. Mary Howard Hooker, *Adventures of An Agnostic: Life and Letters of Reader Harris, Q.C.* (London: Marshall, Morgan & Scott, 1959), 111, cited by Timothy B. Walsh, *To Meet and Satisfy a Very Hungry People: The Origins and Fortunes of English Pentecostalism, 1907–1925*, Studies in Evangelical History and Thought (Milton Keynes: Paternoster Press, 2012), 38. Robinson notes a Holiness influence on Boddy, but does not examine the connection at length. Robinson, "Charismatic Anglican," 35–36.

8. See Gavin Wakefield, *Alexander Boddy: Pentecostal Anglican Pioneer*, Studies in Pentecostal and Charismatic Issues (London: Paternoster Press, 2007), 23; see also Wakefield, "The Human Face of Pentecostalism: Why the British Pentecostal Movement Began in the Sunderland Parish of the Church of England Vicar Alexander Boddy," *Journal of the European Pentecostal Theological Association* 28, no. 2 (2008): 163–64.

9. Neil Hudson, "The Development of British Pentecostalism," in *European Pentecostalism*, ed. William K. Kay and Anne E. Dyer, Global Pentecostal and Charismatic Studies 7 (Leiden: Brill, 2011), 43.

10. Jean-Daniel Plüss, "Pentecostal Theology and Protestant Europe," in *European Pentecostalism*, ed. William K. Kay and Anne E. Dyer, Global Pentecostal and Charismatic Studies 7 (Leiden: Brill, 2011), 294.

11. Wakefield, *Alexander Boddy*, 20; Robinson, "Charismatic Anglican," 15.

12. Jane Vazeille Boddy (Mother Joanna), "Alexander Alfred Boddy 1854–1930," unpublished manuscript, Community of the Resurrection of Our Lord, Grahamstown [South Africa], n.d.; copy held at Flower Pentecostal Heritage Center, Springfield, MO, 1. Taylor gives the date for this document as 1969. Malcolm John Taylor, "Publish and Be Blessed: A Case Study in Early Pentecostal Publishing History 1906–1926" (PhD thesis, University of Birmingham, 1994), 67n86. Robinson notes that it was originally an interview conducted by Charles Clarke for an article published in *Renewal*, a magazine published by the Fountain Trust and edited by Anglican Charismatic Renewal leader Michael Harper. See Charles Clarke, "When the Fire Fell in Sunderland," Pioneers of Revival (8), *Renewal*, no. 29 (October/November 1970): 20–21, 23–25. Robinson,

"Charismatic Anglican," 13n17, 258. He does say that Jane, then known as Mother Joanna, reviewed his work, making "careful comments and criticism" (12). The bibliography lists the date of her letter reviewing his work as September 19, 1975 (258).

13. J. V. Boddy, "Alexander Alfred Boddy," 2.

14. Wakefield, *Alexander Boddy*, 23.

15. Edith Blumhofer, "Transatlantic Currents in North Atlantic Pentecostalism," in *Evangelicalism: Comparative Studies of Popular Protestantism in North America, the British Isles, and Beyond 1700–1990*, ed. Mark A. Noll, David W. Bebbington, and George A. Rawlyk (Oxford: Oxford University Press, 1994), 358. To his credit, Pugh noted the seeming exaggeration of this claim when he commented, "While there is no evidence of any subsequent visits to Keswick until 1907, there is a broad though not rigorously substantiated consensus that Keswick theology was very influential upon him." B. A. Pugh, "Power in the Blood: The Significance of the Blood of Jesus to the Spirituality of Early British Pentecostalism and Its Precursors" (PhD thesis, University of Bangor, 2009), 195n701.

16. See "Evan Roberts's Message to Sunderland," *Sunderland Daily Echo and Shipping Gazette* (December 24, 1904): 3; Blumhofer, "Transatlantic Currents in North Atlantic Pentecostalism," 355.

17. A. A. Boddy, "Some Sacred Memories," *Confidence* 7, no. 2 (February 1914): 24.

18. Alexander A. Boddy, *A Vicar's Testimony: "Pentecost at Sunderland"* (Sunderland, UK: N.p., 1907), 4.

19. Boddy, "Some Sacred Memories," 24.

20. Boddy, *Vicar's Testimony*, 4–5.

21. Boddy was an avid traveler, author of travel memoirs, and member of several prestigious geographic societies. See Wakefield, *Alexander Boddy*, 34–54.

See also "Pentecostal Conventions at Sunderland: Interview with the Rev. A. A. Boddy," *Confidence* 8, no. 6 (June 1915), reprinted from the *North Star* (Darlington) (May 24, 1915): 107.

22. Bebbington discusses the appeal of Keswick to the educated, the wealthy, and the upper-middle classes. He concludes, "Although Keswick teaching was later to spread to a wider public, its initial constituency was drawn from the well-to-do." David Bebbington, *Victorian Religious Revivals: Culture and Piety in Local and Global Contexts* (Oxford: Oxford University Press, 2012), 326. See also Randall, "Old Time Power," 55.

23. A. A. Boddy, "New Scandinavian Revival—The Witness of 'Tongues' Manifested in Christiana," *Apostolic Faith* 1, no. 6 (February–March 1907): 1.

24. Unsigned article, "Brief Items," *Confidence* [1], no. 5 (August 15, 1908): 13. Mr. Mogridge was listed as having a Pentecostal center in Northlands, Lythum, in the July 15, 1908, issue of *Confidence* ([1], no. 4): 2. Numerous accounts of this center meeting in his home follow. See "Brief Items," *Confidence* 2, no. 9 (February 1909): 39; "Brief Notes," *Confidence* 3, no. 4 (April 1910): 86–87; "Pentecostal Items," *Confidence* 3, no. 12 (December 1910): 278.

25. "Brief Items," [1], no. 5 (August 15, 1908): 14. Wakefield assumed that this visit was intended "to show his continuing debt to this tradition, even as he sought to share his newest spiritual experiences and desires" (*Alexander Boddy*, 23). However, there is no real evidence to support this claim. Clarke characterized it as a "plea" that the Pentecostal revival would be "accepted and encouraged and promoted." He adds, "His plea fell on deaf ears. The leaders of the church generally made no response at all." Clarke, "When the Fire Fell in Sunderland," 21.

26. "Appendix Two: Boddy Family Tree," in Wakefield, *Alexander Boddy*, 233.

27. "Wesley Bi-Centenary—Celebration in Sunderland," *Sunderland Echo and Shipping Gazette* (June 18, 1903): 3.

28. See Julia Stewart Werner, *The Primitive Methodist Connexion: Its Background and Early History* (Madison: University of Wisconsin Press, 1984). See also Geoffrey E. Milburn, "Tensions in Primitive Methodism in the Eighteen-Seventies and the Origins of the Christian Lay Churches in the North-East," *Proceedings of the Wesley Historical Society* 40, no. 4 (February 1976): 96.

29. Wakefield, "Human Face of Pentecostalism," 161.

30. Ibid., 161–62.

31. Ibid. A testimony of the healing of a Primitive Methodist evangelist, Albert Shakesby, at this centennial celebration at Mow Cap was reprinted in the *Bridegroom's Messenger* in 1912. "The Healing of Mr. Albert Shakesby," *Bridegroom's Messenger* 5, no. 115 (August 1, 1912): 3. This healing had been referred to in a 1910 reprint of an article from the *Christian and Missionary Alliance*. "O Lord Thou Canst Heal Me," *Bridegroom's Messenger* 3, no. 67 (August 1, 1910): 2.

32. Walsh, *To Meet and Satisfy*, 68.

33. Wakefield, *Alexander Boddy*, 59–60.

34. Robinson, "Charismatic Anglican," 18, 19. Robinson here cites "Rev. Alex. A. Boddy. F.R.G.S.," *YMCA Flashes* 11, no. 8 (April 1895): 86. Taylor also cites this article as evidence for Boddy's "cordial relationships with Nonconformist ministers." Taylor, "Publish and Be Blessed," 54.

35. These may have been meetings sponsored by the United Temperance Council. A "United Saturday Night Meeting" is documented in a neighboring area in the northeast: West Hartlepool, "Temperance Council," *Northern Daily Mail* (March 20, 1896): 4.

36. A. A. Boddy, "The Pentecostal Movement: The Story of Its Beginnings in Sunderland and Its Present Position in Great Britain," *Confidence* 3, no. 8 (August 1910): 193, 194.

37. John Martin Usher, "'For China and Tibet, and for World-Wide Revival': Cecil Henry Polhill (1860–1938) and His Significance for Early Pentecostalism" (PhD thesis, University of Birmingham, 2015), 145, 201; Walsh, *To Meet and Satisfy*, 59–64, 68–69; see ibid., 177.

38. D. W. Bebbington, *Evangelicalism in Modern Britain: A History from the 1730s to the 1980s* (1989; repr., London: Routledge, 2005), 319; Ian M. Randall, "The Pentecostal League of Prayer: A Transdenominational British Wesleyan-Holiness Movement," *Wesleyan Theological Journal* 33, no. 1 (Spring 1998): 185.

39. Randall, *Evangelical Experiences*, 86.

40. Reader Harris, "Opposers and Their Objections," *Tongues of Fire* 15, no. 174 (May 1905): 6, cited in Walsh, *To Meet and Satisfy*, 39.

41. Reader Harris, "Revival—The Church Question," *Tongues of Fire* 15, no. 169 (January 1905): 1.

42. Randall, "Pentecostal League of Prayer," 187.

43. Walsh, *To Meet and Satisfy*, 40.

44. PLP meetings in Sunderland were reported on in the *Sunderland Daily Echo and Shipping Gazette* in the "Sunderland Day by Day" column. At the November 1900 meeting, Boddy was reported to have addressed the meeting (December 1, 1900): 5; other meetings were reported regularly; see *Sunderland Daily Echo and Shipping Gazette* (July 27, 1901): 3; (October 26, 1901): 6; (July 31, 1903): 4; (November 28, 1903): 4. At the March 1904 meeting, Boddy spoke on "The Fulness of Life in Christ" (March 5, 1904): 3.

45. "Tongues of Fire Sales," *Tongues of Fire* 15, no. 169 (January 1905): 10. Sunderland at this point had a population of approximately 146,077; the parish of All Saints included 5,500 of those; see http://englandsnortheast.co.uk/1901to1919

.html. See Wakefield, *Alexander Boddy*, 31; Walsh, *To Meet and Satisfy*, 41.

46. "Letter to Bishop Moule, 10 December 1901," University of Durham archive, All Saints Monkwearmouth file, cited in Wakefield, *Alexander Boddy*, 91.

47. "The Annual Meetings," *Tongues of Fire* 15, no. 174 (June 1905): 3. See Walsh's analysis of this address in *To Meet and Satisfy*, 41–42.

48. "The Annual Meetings," *Tongues of Fire* 15, no. 174 (June 1905): 3.

49. J. V. Boddy, "Alexander Alfred Boddy," 5. Boddy's recollection of dates is problematic because she goes on to say, "Not long afterwards my father heard of Evan Roberts and a revival that was going on in Wales, so, of course, he had to go and see it for himself!" A. A. Boddy visited Wales and met Evan Roberts in 1904. As his address at the PLP indicates, he was comparing the PLP meetings in Sunderland to what he had witnessed in Wales by 1905.

50. Boddy, "Pentecostal Movement," 193. Boddy journeyed to Wales to observe the revival and brought back a charge from revival leader Evan Roberts to the people of Sunderland: "'Tell them to believe the promises. Tell them to fight to bring Heaven down now and here. They must be in earnest.'" "Evan Roberts Message to Sunderland," 3. Further meetings were being conducted in various churches, beginning with the Newcastle Wesleyan Mission, in 1904–5, led by the Welsh evangelist Annie May Rees. See "The Religious Movement—Impressive Gatherings in Newcastle," *Newcastle Evening Chronicle* (March 17, 1905): 7; "Westgate Road Baptist Church—Yesterday's Services," *Newcastle Daily Chronicle* (March 20, 1905): 12; "Men and Women," *Newcastle Daily Chronicle* (April 20, 1905): 6.

51. Randall, "Pentecostal League of Prayer," 188.

52. Walsh discusses this desire on the part of both Harris and Boddy to cultivate "'revival in the churches.'" Walsh, *To Meet and Satisfy*, 110.

53. "Preliminary Meetings," *Confidence* [1], no. 3 (June 30, 1908): 5.

54. Robinson, "Charismatic Anglican," 6. Robinson noted that Harper called him "a prophet." Harper made this claim in the context of a discussion of how neither Boddy nor Polhill ever left Anglicanism. Michael Harper, *As at the Beginning* (1965; repr., Altadena, CA: Society of Stephen, 1994), 41. Robinson elaborated on this inclusive vision in his discussion of Boddy's world travels. Robinson, "Charismatic Anglican," 25–28.

55. A. A. Boddy, "Across the Atlantic," *Confidence* 2, no. 8 (August 1909): 175. See Bundy for a discussion of the issues surrounding the organization of the Pentecostal Missionary Union and the leaders on the Continent where he discusses the vision of the Pentecostal Missionary Union as originating with Barratt. Bundy, *Visions of Apostolic Mission*, 230–31. For further discussion on the Union's development, see Usher, "'For China and Tibet,'" 197–219.

56. Robinson describes this vision as eschatological in "Charismatic Anglican," 227–28.

57. Tim Walsh, "'Signs and Wonders That Lie': Unlikely Polemical Outbursts Against the Early Pentecostal Movement in Britain," in *Signs, Wonders, Miracles: Representations of Divine Power in the Life of the Church*, ed. Kate Cooper and Jeremy Gregory, Studies in Church History 41 (Woodbridge: Boydell Press, 2005), 410. For a discussion of the resonance between Harris's eschatology and that of the early Pentecostals, including Boddy, see Walsh, *To Meet and Satisfy*, 127.

58. See H. W. Webb-Peploe, "Sin," in *Keswick's Authentic Voice: Sixty-Five Dynamic Addresses at the Keswick Convention, 1875–1957*, ed. Herbert F. Stevenson (Grand Rapids, MI: Zondervan, 1959), 31–40. This sermon was preached in 1885 at Keswick.

59. "An Offer to Keswick Platform," *Tongues of Fire* 5, no. 59 (November 1895): 1. See Randall, "Pentecostal League of Prayer," 185.

60. Reader Harris, "Sin and Its Remedy," *Tongues of Fire* 5, no. 59 (November 1895): 1–3.

61. See "Facts and Gossip of the Week—Leaves from the Northerners' Notebook," *Penrith Observer* (November 5, 1895): 4; "Echoes of the Day," *Lincolnshire Echo* (November 1, 1895): 2; "Keswick," *Carlisle Journal* (November 5, 1895): 2.

62. Hugh Price Hughes, "A Reply to 'The Christian,'" *Tongues of Fire* 5, no. 60 (December 1, 1895): 2. Reader Harris, "The 'Is Sin a Necessity' Discussion," *Tongues of Fire* 6, no. 63 (March 1896): 1–3.

63. Reader Harris, "One More Offer to Keswick," *Tongues of Fire* 6, no. 61 (January 1896): 1.

64. Reader Harris, "The 'Is Sin a Necessity?' Discussion," *Tongues of Fire* 6, no. 61 (January 1896): 2–3.

65. Reader Harris, "The 'Is Sin a Necessity?' Discussion," *Tongues of Fire* 6, no. 63 (March 1896): 2, 3.

66. Walsh identified Harris as "an influential proponent of Wesleyan-Holiness views." Walsh, *To Meet and Satisfy*, 177.

67. Stevenson, *Keswick's Authentic Voice*, 27.

68. Wakefield, *Alexander Boddy*, 225.

69. A. A. Boddy, *Vicar's Testimony*, 10.

70. Ibid., 17, 18.

71. Cartledge, "Early Pentecostal Theology."

72. *Confidence* 4, no. 4 (April 1911): 75, cited in ibid., 118.

73. Ibid., 121, 122. See Walsh, "'Signs and Wonders,'" 420.

74. See Priscilla Pope-Levison, "Pentecost in the Churches: Women in the Pentecostal League of Prayer," *Wesley and Methodist Studies* 10, no. 1 (2018): 46–65; Priscilla Pope-Levison, "Five Women in Ministry Articles Transcribed from *Tongues of Fire*," *Wesley and Methodist Studies* 11, no. 1 (2019): 61–91.

75. Pope-Levison, "Pentecost in the Churches," 59, 51.

76. Randall, "Pentecostal League of Prayer," 192.

77. Wakefield, *Alexander Boddy*, 115; Diana Chapman, "The Rise and Demise of Women's Ministry in the Origins and Early Years of Pentecostalism in Britain," *Journal of Pentecostal Theology* 12, no. 2 (2004): 217–46; Diana Chapman, "The Role of Women in Early Pentecostalism 1907–1914," *Journal of the European Pentecostal Theological Association* 28, no. 2 (2008): 131–44. Walsh challenges Chapman's "anachronistic" reading of this material and concludes that this discussion was attempting to "accord women a more dynamic and pneumatic role than was typically the case in their respective traditions." Walsh, *To Meet and Satisfy*, 88–89n19. His interpretation of the debate seems quite generous.

78. "Women's Place in the Church," *Confidence* 11, no. 7 (November 1914): 208. Also absent was the voice of Cecil Polhill, who had appointed Eleanor Crisp as principal of the women's missionary training school for the Pentecostal Missionary Union in 1913. She, unlike the male principal of the school for men, served on the Pentecostal Missionary Union's executive council. See Usher, "'For China and Tibet,'" 232.

79. "Women's Place in the Church," 212–13.

80. Chapman, "Rise and Demise," 236.

81. "Pentecostal Conventions at Sunderland," 107.

82. "Speaking in Tongues," *Newcastle Evening Chronicle* (October 4, 1907): 6.

83. "Revival Scenes," *Manchester Courier* (October 2, 1907): 3.

84. "The Devil's Revival at Monkwearmouth," *Newcastle Evening Chronicle* (December 2, 1907): 8.

85. See Randall, "Pentecostal League of Prayer," 189.

86. Desmond Cartwright, "Everywhere Spoken Against: Opposition to Pentecostalism 1907–1930," http://www.smithwigglesworth.com/index.php/smith-wigglesworth-pensketches/miscellaneous/everywhere-spoken-against.

87. Reader Harris, "The Gift of Tongues," *Tongues of Fire* 17, no. 203 (November 1907): 2. See Walsh, *To Meet and Satisfy*, 44, 45.

88. See Cartwright "Everywhere Spoken Against," for a discussion of these articles as well as other polemical pamphlets circulated during the time of the early revival. See also Walsh, "'Signs and Wonders,'" 410–22.

89. Oswald Chambers, "Gift of Tongues," *Tongues of Fire* 17, no. 201 (September 1907): 9.

90. Reader Harris, "Editorials," *Tongues of Fire* 17, no. 203 (November 1907): 6.

91. Harris, "Gift of Tongues," 2.

92. Alexander A. Boddy, *Pentecost for England (and Other Lands) with Signs Following* (Sunderland, UK: N.p., 1907), 3; underlining in original.

93. Boddy, *Vicar's Testimony*, 14.

94. Cartledge raises the need for an exploration of the progression of the theology of British Pentecostalism in the Boddy era to the faith statements in the later developing denominations. Cartledge, "Early Pentecostal Theology," 129. See William K. Kay, "Visions on the Battlefield: Alexander A. Boddy, Early British Pentecostalism, and the First World War, 1914–1918," *Journal of Religious Studies* 32, no. 3 (September 2008): 281–302. Hollenweger attributes "the failure of Boddy's ecumenical vision" to the perception that he was "an aristocrat" and "a patriot." Walter J. Hollenweger, *Pentecostalism: Origins and Developments Worldwide* (Grand Rapids, MI: Baker Academic, 1997), 344.

95. Wakefield, "Human Face of Pentecostalism," 161.

96. See the chart of "Pentecostal Denominations in America," in Henry H. Knight III, ed., *From Aldersgate to Azusa Street: Wesleyan, Holiness, and Pentecostal Visions of the New Creation* (Eugene, OR: Pickwick Publications, 2010), 368.

97. "Confidence—Our First Number," *Confidence* [1], no. 1 (April 1908): 3.

BIBLIOGRAPHY

Periodicals
The following were accessed via digitized copies archived by the Consortium of Pentecostal Archives (https://pentecostalarchives.org/index.cfm):
Apostolic Faith (Los Angeles, CA, 1906–8)
Bridegroom's Messenger (Atlanta, GA, 1907–96)
Confidence (Sunderland, England, 1908–26)
The following was accessed at the archives of Nazarene Theological College, Manchester, United Kingdom:
Tongues of Fire (London, 1891–1915)
The following were accessed via digitized copies archived by The British Newspaper Archive: (https://www.britishnewspaperarchive.co.uk):

Newcastle Daily Chronicle
Newcastle Evening Chronicle
Northern Daily Mail
Sunderland Echo and Shipping Gazette
The following were accessed via digitized copies archived at Newspapers.com (https://www.newspapers.com):
Carlisle Journal
Lincolnshire Echo
Manchester Courier
Penrith Observer
Times (London)

Published Sources
Alegre, Rakel Ystebø. "The Pentecostal Apologetics of T. B. Barratt: Defining and Defending the Faith

1906–1909." PhD diss., Regent University, 2019.
Anderson, Allan. *An Introduction to Pentecostalism*. Cambridge: Cambridge University Press, 2004.
Bebbington, David W. *Evangelicalism in Modern Britain: A History from the 1730s to the 1980s*. Reprint, London: Routledge, 2005.
———. *Victorian Religious Revivals: Culture and Piety in Local and Global Contexts*. Oxford: Oxford University Press, 2012.
Blumhofer, Edith. "Transatlantic Currents in North Atlantic Pentecostalism." In *Evangelicalism: Comparative Studies of Popular Protestantism in North America, the British Isles, and Beyond, 1700–1990*, edited by Mark A. Noll, David W. Bebbington, and George A. Rawlyk, 251–64. Oxford: Oxford University Press, 1994.
Boddy, Alexander A. *Pentecost for England (and Other Lands) with Signs Following*. Sunderland, UK: N.p., 1907.
———. *A Vicar's Testimony: "Pentecost at Sunderland."* Sunderland, UK: N.p., 1907.
Boddy, Jane Vazeille. "Alexander Alfred Boddy, 1854–1930." Unpublished manuscript. Community of the Resurrection of Our Lord, Grahamstown, n.d. Copy held at Flower Pentecostal Heritage Center, Springfield, MO.
Bundy, David. "Thomas Ball Barratt: From Methodist to Pentecostal." *EPTA Bulletin—Journal of the European Pentecostal Theological Association* 13, no. 1 (1994): 19–49.
———. *Visions of Apostolic Mission: Scandinavian Pentecostal Mission to 1935*. Studia Historico-Ecclesiastica Upsaliensia 45. Uppsala: Uppsala Universitet, 2009.
Cartledge, Mark J. "The Early Pentecostal Theology of Confidence Magazine (1908–1926): A Version of the Five-Fold Gospel?" *Journal of the European Pentecostal Theological Association* 28, no. 2 (2008): 117–30.
Cartwright, Desmond. "Everywhere Spoken Against: Opposition to Pentecostalism 1907–1930." http://www.smithwigglesworth.com/index.php/smith-wigglesworth-pensketches/miscellaneous/everywhere-spoken-against.
Chapman, Diana. "The Rise and Demise of Women's Ministry in the Origins and Early Years of Pentecostalism in Britain." *Journal of Pentecostal Theology* 12, no. 2 (2004): 217–46.
———. "The Role of Women in Early Pentecostalism 1907–1914." *Journal of the European Pentecostal Theological Association* 28, no. 2 (2008): 131–44.
Clarke, Charles. "When the Fire Fell in Sunderland." Pioneers of Revival (8). *Renewal*, no. 29 (October/November 1970): 20–21, 23–25.
Dayton, Donald W. *Theological Roots of Pentecostalism*. Metuchen, NJ: Scarecrow Press, 1987.
Gee, Donald. *Wind and Flame: Incorporating the Former Book 'The Pentecostal Movement' with Additional Chapters*. Croydon: Heath Press, 1967.
Harper, Michael. *As at the Beginning*. 1965. Reprint, Altadena, CA: Society of Stephen, 1994.
Hollenweger, Walter J. *Pentecostalism: Origins and Developments Worldwide*. Grand Rapids, MI: Baker Academic, 1997.
———. *The Pentecostals*. Peabody, MA: Hendrickson, 1988.
Hudson, Neil. "The Development of British Pentecostalism." In *European Pentecostalism*, edited by William K. Kay and Anne E. Dyer, 41–60. Global Pentecostal and Charismatic Studies 7. Leiden: Brill, 2011.
Kay, William K. "Pentecostal Eschatology." In *Pentecostal and Charismatic Studies: A Reader*, edited by William

K. Kay and Anne E. Dyer, 25–46. London: SCM Press, 2004.

———. "Visions on the Battlefield: Alexander A. Boddy, Early British Pentecostalism, and the First World War, 1914–1918." *Journal of Religious Studies* 32, no. 3 (September 2008): 281–302.

Knight, Henry H., III, ed. *From Aldersgate to Azusa Street: Wesleyan, Holiness, and Pentecostal Visions of the New Creation.* Eugene, OR: Pickwick Publications, 2010.

Laan, Cornelius van der. "Alexander Boddy: Anglican Father of Dutch Pentecostalism." *Journal of the European Pentecostal Theological Association* 31, no. 1 (2011): 93–110.

Milburn, Geoffrey E. "Tensions in Primitive Methodism in the Eighteen-Seventies and the Origins of the Christian Lay Churches in the North-East." *Proceedings of the Wesley Historical Society* 40, no. 4 (February 1976): 93–101.

Plüss, Jean-Daniel. "Pentecostalism in Europe and the Former Soviet Union." In *The Cambridge Companion to Pentecostalism*, edited by Cecil M. Robeck Jr. and Amos Yong, 93–111. New York: Cambridge University Press, 2014.

———. "Pentecostal Theology and Protestant Europe." In *European Pentecostalism*, edited by William K. Kay and Anne E. Dyer, 293–311. Leiden: Brill, 2011.

Pope-Levison, Priscilla, "Five Women in Ministry Articles Transcribed from Tongues of Fire." *Wesley and Methodist Studies* 11, no. 1 (2019): 61–91.

———. "Pentecost in the Churches: Women in the Pentecostal League of Prayer." *Wesley and Methodist Studies* 10, no. 1 (2018): 46–65.

Pugh, B. A. "Power in the Blood: The Significance of the Blood of Jesus to the Spirituality of Early British Pentecostalism and Its Precursors." PhD thesis, University of Bangor, 2009.

Randall, Ian M. *Evangelical Experiences: A Study in the Spirituality of English Evangelicalism, 1918–1939.* Carlisle: Paternoster Press, 1999.

———. "Old Time Power: Relationships Between Pentecostalism and Evangelical Spirituality in England." *Pneuma* 19, no. 1 (1997): 53–80.

———. "The Pentecostal League of Prayer: A Transdenominational British Wesleyan-Holiness Movement." *Wesleyan Theological Journal* 33, no. 1 (Spring 1998): 185–200.

Robinson, Martin. "The Charismatic Anglican—Historical and Contemporary: A Comparison of the Life and Work of Alexander Boddy (1854–1930) and Michael C. Harper." MLitt thesis, University of Birmingham, 1976.

Synan, Vinson. *The Holiness-Pentecostal Movement in the United States.* Grand Rapids, MI: Eerdmans, 1971.

Taylor, Malcolm John. "Publish and Be Blessed: A Case Study in Early Pentecostal Publishing History, 1906–1926." PhD thesis, University of Birmingham, 1994.

Usher, John Martin. "'For China and Tibet and For World-Wide Revival': Cecil Henry Polhill (1860–1938) and His Significance for Early Pentecostalism." PhD thesis, University of Birmingham, 2015.

Wakefield, Gavin. *Alexander Boddy: Pentecostal Anglican Pioneer.* Studies in Pentecostal and Charismatic Issues. London: Paternoster Press, 2007.

———. "The Human Face of Pentecostalism: Why the British Pentecostal Movement Began in the Sunderland Parish of the Church of England Vicar Alexander Boddy." *Journal of the European Pentecostal Theological Association* 28, no. 2 (2008): 158–68.

Walsh, Tim. "'Signs and Wonders that Lie': Unlikely Polemical Outbursts Against the Early Pentecostal Movement in Britain." In *Signs, Wonders, Miracles: Representations of Divine Power in the Life of the Church*, edited by Kate Cooper and Jeremy Gregory, 410–22. Studies in Church History 41. Woodbridge: Boydell Press, 2005.

Walsh, Timothy B. *To Meet and Satisfy a Very Hungry People: The Origins and Fortunes of English Pentecostalism, 1907–1925*. Studies in Evangelical History and Thought. Milton Keynes: Paternoster Press, 2012.

Webb-Peploe, H. W. "Sin." In *Keswick's Authentic Voice: Sixty-Five Dynamic Addresses at the Keswick Convention, 1875–1957*, edited by Herbert F. Stevenson, 31–40. Grand Rapids, MI: Zondervan, 1959.

Werner, Julia Stewart. *The Primitive Methodist Connexion: Its Background and Early History*. Madison: University of Wisconsin Press, 1984.

CHAPTER 4

A World Tour of Evangelism
Henry Clay Morrison's Radical Holiness
Meets "Global Holiness," 1909–10

Luther Oconer

It was on the morning of July 19, 1909, when famed Southern Holiness evangelist Henry Clay Morrison (1857–1942) left his home in Wilmore, Kentucky, to begin his eleven-month "tour of evangelism." Morrison, the soon-to-be president of Asbury College and founder of Asbury Theological Seminary, kept his supporters abreast of his activities through a series of articles titled "Our World Tour of Evangelism" in the editorial section of the *Pentecostal Herald*, of which he was also the editor. These accounts, which were published in the *Herald* from 1909 to 1911, were later slightly revised and abridged in the book *World Tour of Evangelism* (1911).[1]

Morrison's evangelistic trip, however, was not by any means a "world tour" since much of his preaching activities took place in Asia, particularly India, Korea, and Japan. His narrative nonetheless provides an interesting snapshot not only of his successful evangelistic career but also of the brand of Radical Holiness revivalism he promoted. David Bundy argues that Radical Holiness is a "self-designation and a self-identifying code for the radicalized Holiness movements that grew out of Methodism and other denominations in the post–Civil War period." Radical Holiness advocates took the Book of Acts seriously as a "normative and ideal vision for spirituality, church life, and mission." Therefore, aside from their deep commitment to the Methodist doctrine of sanctification, they also promoted faith healing and premillennialism.[2] As a result, many

Holiness radicals separated from Methodism to form independent denominations. However, there were a few, like Morrison, who stayed and continued to thrive in Methodism while keeping their Radical Holiness message intact.[3]

Morrison's tour thus provides an opportunity to examine closely his brand of Radical Holiness and its encounter with preexisting manifestations of holiness spirituality that developed in the mission field or what Bundy calls "global holiness."[4] Hence, this chapter is divided into three parts. First, it provides some essential background surrounding Morrison's trip. Second, it establishes Morrison's Radical Holiness commitments and the ways in which he promoted them. Finally, it examines the contours of the "global holiness" encountered by Morrison and the factors that allowed them to intersect with his brand of Radical Holiness revivalism.

THE SCOPE OF MORRISON'S TOUR

Morrison's tour was initially conceived by the Board of Missions of the Holiness Union, which appointed him in the fall of 1908. His mission was to "make an evangelistic tour around the world preaching full salvation, assisting missionaries in revival meetings, making careful note of the spiritual state of the church," and to gather useful information for the board for future evangelistic efforts to "promote the doctrine and experience of entire sanctification in the various mission fields of the world."[5] The Holiness Union (later renamed Southern Holiness Association) was a regional Holiness organization established by individuals from various denominations in the south, primarily Methodists, in the fall of 1904.[6] Four years later, it established its Board of Missions, as Morrison outlined in *World Tour*, with the following objectives:

> It was the unanimous decision of this Board of Missions that we should not undertake the organization of churches, or the establishment of independent missions or schools in any of the foreign fields, but that our work should be evangelistic and that we should send out evangelists to travel in the various mission fields, assisting the missionaries of existing churches in promoting revivals of religion. It would be the special work of such evangelists to seek to bring missionaries and native Christians into the experience of entire sanctification. The great desire and purpose of the Holiness Union is to assist in promoting a world-wide revival of full salvation, to help, so far as in them lies, to carry to the ends of the earth the glad news that Christ Jesus is able to save all men from all sin.[7]

Interestingly, while the board used the word "evangelistic" to describe its goal, its primary mission was not the evangelization of non-Christians but rather the promotion of the Wesleyan doctrine of entire sanctification to "missionaries and native Christians." Simply put, its primary aim was to convert the already-Christian toward a deeper level of experience of God through Holiness revivals. Accordingly, while Morrison always invited his audiences to seek justification by faith in Christ, he gave more weight to the promotion of sanctification as a second work of grace subsequent to justification in his revival gatherings. Hence, as we will see later, Morrison also called these gatherings "Pentecostal meetings" since he equated the experience of entire sanctification with the baptism of the Holy Spirit or, in his preferred words, "baptism *with* the Holy Ghost."[8] Morrison's use of the word "Pentecostal" effectively illustrates the fact that by this time, many Holiness advocates in American Methodism had shifted their articulation of Methodism's "grand depositum" in Pentecostal terms and this peaked in the 1890s.[9] It was also during the same period, in 1897, that Morrison changed the name of his periodical from the *Methodist and the Way of Life* to the *Pentecostal Herald*.[10] Popular among Holiness advocates who also manifested this shift was northern Methodist Samuel A. Keen, a presiding elder from Ohio, who conducted Pentecostal meetings in seventy-six Methodist Episcopal Church (MEC) annual conferences beginning in 1891. Keen was succeeded by Joseph Smith, who emerged as the foremost Holiness evangelist among northern Methodists at the beginning of the twentieth century. Morrison conducted Pentecostal meetings with Smith in connection with the 1904 and 1908 General Conferences of the MEC.[11]

In addition to the Holiness Union's Board of Mission's mandate to reach missionaries and native Christians with the message of holiness, the board also made it clear that the work of its evangelists must be done within the confines of "existing churches" on the field. There were many independent Holiness "faith missions" that emerged during the period and operated outside the more traditional missionary boards and were a source of concern for other missionaries. These independent missions were mostly connected with the emergence of "come-outer" Radical Holiness groups, which left their mother denominations during the period.[12] For example, Morrison, an ordained minister in the Methodist Episcopal Church, South (MECS), was no stranger to such persecution as he was tried and defrocked in 1896 for his Holiness revival work. However, his credentials were quickly restored a year later, but to spare himself from further heartaches, he eventually resigned from the ordained ministry in 1891 and became a lay member of the denomination.[13] Furthermore, within the Holiness Movement itself, further

Fig. 4.1 Holiness evangelist Henry Clay Morrison (front row, center) with members of the Philippine Islands Annual Conference of the MEC, Knox Memorial MEC, Manila, March 2–8, 1910. For six days, Morrison conducted Pentecostal meetings during the conference, where "the altar was filled every morning with people seeking the Lord for pardon, restoration or full salvation." From *The Official Journal of the Third Session of the Philippine Islands Annual Conference of the Methodist Episcopal Church* (Manila: Methodist Publishing House, 1910), 10.

radicalization of its teachings resulted in the rise of new independent Pentecostal factions that arose as a result of a powerful yet controversial revival at Azusa Street in Los Angeles three years earlier. Hence, given this backdrop, it is understandable that the Holiness Union, through its missionary board, wanted to allay fears about its mission by projecting a more mainstream-friendly image that would enable it to maintain cordial ties with established denominations. Nevertheless, while this appears to establish Morrison in the "mainline Holiness" camp of the Holiness Movement,[14] this did not prevent him from working with the Radical Holiness Oriental Missionary Society (OMS) in Tokyo.

Morrison began his tour in the fall of 1909, just before he was to assume the presidency of Asbury College. He first stopped to minister at the Holiness camp meetings in Des Plaines near Chicago and Mooers in upstate New York and then on August 19, boarded a train to Montreal, Canada, with his traveling companion, Jehu L. Piercy, an Asbury student from Ames, Iowa.[15] From Montreal, they boarded a steamer that would take them to Liverpool, England. They toured Methodist historical sites in the country and eventually continued to Scotland, France, Italy, and Palestine.[16] After a quick pilgrimage of the Holy Land, the two proceeded to India, staying there for more than three months from October 19, 1909, to February 1, 1910. In fact, about half of the accounts Morrison recorded took place in this vast South Asian country, preaching and conducting Pentecostal meetings in several gatherings held mostly in MEC churches in Lucknow, Lanowli (now Lonavla), Bombay (now Mumbai), Jabalpur, Bangalore (now Bengaluru), Baroda (now Vadodara), Bareilly, Muttra (now Mathura), and Calcutta (now Kolkata).[17] After India, he and Piercy embarked on a five-week revival tour of major MEC stations in Southeast Asia, particularly Rangoon (now Yangon in Myanmar), Singapore (then part of Malaysia), and Manila (in the Philippines), preaching primarily during the annual conferences and conducting Pentecostal meetings in MEC local churches. The duo left Manila for China on March 8,[18] reaching Soochow (now Suzhou), a significant center for the MECS mission, more than a week later and where they began work under the auspices of the MECS mission. Morrison also preached in MECS locations in Sungkiang and Shanghai and worked with the MEC mission in Nanking (now Nanjing).[19]

Following China, Morrison, together with Piercy, took a quick detour to Nagasaki and Fukuoka in Japan, where he preached at a Young Men's Christian Association (YMCA) convention and meetings organized by the MEC mission.[20] From Fukuoka, they proceeded to Seoul (now in South Korea), ministering in MEC, MECS, and YMCA gatherings.[21] On April 25, they took the train for Songdo (now Kaesong in North Korea), where they conducted revivals with the MECS mission.[22] From there, they ventured further north to Pyongyang, the site of a powerful revival three years earlier known as the "Korean Pentecost."[23] Morrison preached in both Presbyterian and MEC churches there.[24] After Pyongyang, the pair returned to Seoul for one final meeting among missionaries at the MEC Girls' School to complete their twenty-two-day mission in the country.[25] From Korea, they returned to Japan but this time to the northeast of the country in Kobe, where Morrison preached in the Japan Methodist Church sanctuary several times and in other gatherings organized for him by the MECS mission.[26] The pair then proceeded to nearby Osaka, where they ministered with the Free Methodist Church (FMC), and following this traveled more than 300 miles east to Tokyo, where they were hosted by the OMS mission. Morrison preached among Baptists, Methodists, and students at the OMS mission school.[27] From Japan, they made their way back to the United States, arriving in San Francisco on June 17, thereby concluding their tour, which took almost eleven months to complete.[28]

MORRISON, THE "RADICAL" HOLINESS REVIVALIST

Morrison's ability to convince and compel his audiences to press toward the altar marked much of his work as a professional revivalist during the tour. For example, a summary of his altar ministry during the annual *Dasehra* meeting in Lucknow, a gathering for the promotion of holiness among MEC workers,[29] his first revival work during the tour, summarized this best:

> We had preaching every morning at 8:30 and evening at 5:30. It was my privilege to preach at all of these morning and evening services. The congregations were large and responsive and the altar well filled at the close of every service; sometimes all the space about the altar was filled and many souls were blessed. Missionaries, Indians, and broad-shouldered artillerymen from a British battery and a man in the red coat and plaid pants of a Scotch regiment, were all crowding about one common mercy seat. Some were converted, some reclaimed, some sanctified, and others greatly renewed in grace and refreshed in love.[30]

It is clear from the above description that Morrison compelled his audiences to primarily seek justification or sanctification at the altar. However, he also provided Christians who had backslided into sin the opportunity to be "reclaimed" by encouraging them to rededicate their lives to God.

Accordingly, Morrison described similar accounts that showed occurrences of justification and sanctification or even rededication in other locations that he and Piercy visited. At the Pentecostal meetings he held during the Bombay Annual Conference of the MEC, Morrison recalled, "Preachers, both white and Indian, were at the altar; members of other churches and a number of soldiers from the Royal Artillery were among those calling upon the Lord. A number claimed pardon and a number sanctification."[31] In Jubblepur (now Jabalpur), "one of the pastors, a fine young Englishman, was sanctified at the altar and gave a clear testimony. Later on one of the most experienced missionaries in the conference who once enjoyed full salvation, but had let it leak out, received it back again."[32] In Singapore, "Every night during the meetings there were from thirty to forty young men, Chinese, Japanese and Malays, in the meetings, who could understand the gospel in English, and from ten to fifteen of them were at the altar seeking pardon or purity at each evening service, conversing with an intelligence and praying with an earnestness that was truly encouraging."[33] In Manila, "The altar was filled every morning with people seeking the Lord for pardon, restoration or full salvation. Missionaries and natives flocked together to the mercy seat, and prayed and sobbed out their heart longings into the ear of our compassionate God, and he blessed them."[34] In Nanking (now Nanjing), "The blessing of the Lord was upon us. Many persons came to the altar, and there was deep conviction and strong crying out to God for salvation and some souls were blessed. There were a number of Bible women present, who received the word of full salvation with eager hearts; I learned later that several of them received the blessing of sanctification."[35] In Nagasaki, "On Sabbath morning I preached at the Methodist Church to a large audience, made an altar call and many came; several strong-looking men sobbed out most earnest prayers. Of course I could not understand their, language, but their whole manner spoke deep earnestness. They tell me it is a rare thing for Japanese to weep, but these men wept."[36] In Tokyo, Lettie Cowman and Ernest A. Kilbourne of the OMS reported in the *Pentecostal Herald*: "Every day was a day of soul-satisfying interests. Many Christians attended the day services morning and evening and plunged into the fountain of cleansing opened in the house of David for sin and uncleanness. What praying through! What groans and struggles! What victory!"[37]

Despite the noted earnest praying, weeping, sobbing, groans, and struggles, Morrison's descriptions, while short on details, seem tame in comparison with written accounts of powerful revivals like those found in early British and American Methodism or in other revival movements in Protestant Christianity. Nevertheless, what these descriptions do, in addition to confirming Morrison's evangelistic success, is to highlight the prominence of holiness motifs in his sermons. As MEC missionary A. L. Grey of India confirmed, "He has preached against all kinds of sins and waged a relentless warfare against the 'old man of sin.' He has hewed the line, put the sword of the Spirit in and down the farthest end of the root of bitterness, and turned the light upon uncleanness and held it there until people wept their way to the cross and prayed through victory."[38] Grey alluded to Morrison's twofold understanding of sin—one prior to conversion and one subsequent to conversion. Morrison affirmed the former while reflecting on the best way to propagate revivals in the countries they visited. He believed that such can be accomplished if they "preach earnestly against sinning, to call sins by name, and point out the ruin in them, offer Christ as a Savior, explain how God so loved the world that he gave his Son, and exhort the people to come to the altar; when there, instruct and pray with them, trusting the Holy Ghost to enlighten, convict and save."[39] Simply put, preaching against sins, warning against the "ruin" they bring, and pointing people to the saving work of Christ is the best way to awaken unbelievers and compel them to repentance until they experience justification at the altar through the help of ministers who will "instruct and pray with them."

However, Morrison's relentless assault on sin was certainly not limited to nonbelievers. In his record of a Pentecostal meeting he held in Muttra (now Mathura) among Indian ministers of the Northwest India Conference, Morrison briefly summarized the sermon he preached regarding the remains of sin among the regenerated:

> When I spoke to the native ministers alone I made the doctrine of the remains of sin in the regenerated and its cleansing away by an act of God's grace as clear as I could possibly put the truth; then I appealed to their personal experience in the matter: "You well remember the time when your sins were forgiven; you know you love God and would not turn back from his service, but you often feel something within your breasts, a war within your members, the flesh lusting against the Spirit. Your intelligence and conscience condemn all of these unholy uprisings; you deeply lament their presence and oft have longed for freedom from them. This deliverance may be had in the cleansing blood of Christ; it is received by faith." Almost the entire body of ministers would come to the altar and mightily cry out to God for freedom from all sin, and a number of them claimed the witness that the blessed work was done.[40]

After acknowledging the existence of the sinful nature that causes "the flesh to lust against the Spirit" among believers, Morrison encouraged his already-justified hearers to seek "freedom from all sin" "by faith," which was very much in keeping with the Wesleyan understanding that faith is the only requirement for entire sanctification.[41] Nevertheless, what made his message so distinctive, particularly to his overseas audiences, was his unrelenting and unequivocal view of the possibility of "freedom from all sin" or the total eradication of sin, a central feature of the Radical Holiness vision of the Christian life. Hence, it was no accident that the Radical Holiness OMS periodical *Electric Message*, of which Ernest A. Kilbourne was the editor, pointed out the Radical Holiness character of Morrison's preaching in its report on the seventh annual conference of the OMS held in Tokyo:

> Bro. Morrison's messages were not only full of love and unction but carried no uncertain sound of doctrine, and there was no room given for the suppression of old carnality. Radical, Pauline holiness, (as taught also by

Wesley) was the theme, and God honored it, as he always does, by definite results. There is a great deal of indefinite "holiness" work these days which never lands a fish, but when the blood of Jesus is exalted in its power and efficacy to cleanse from all sin, and destroy the root of inbred sin definite results follow. When death to carnality, [sic] is preached, folks go down, die out and pray through to victory; whereas if suppression is taught, the struggle with inbred sin is simply, [sic] continued and no deliverance and joy ever come.[42]

The writer, presumably Kilbourne, seemed to certify Morrison's Radical Holiness credentials even though Morrison remained loyal to Methodism.[43] His "Radical, Pauline holiness" message, the writer observed, stood diametrically opposite to "indefinite" holiness teaching, commonly called the "suppression" doctrine of the Keswick Movement, which, the writer maintained, "never lands a fish."

While there is no evidence that Morrison spoke against suppression during his tour, he did express surprise regarding his frequent encounters with the popular Keswick teaching in the countries he visited. Hence, in the very first editorial he wrote after he had returned to Kentucky, he lamented:

I frequently came in contact on my journey with the Keswick teachings of suppression of indwelling sin, and was profoundly impressed with the wide difference between this and Mr. Wesley's clear teaching of the eradication of sin. This suppression doctrine is a dangerous, unscriptural and unMethodist heresy, and has no place and should be shown no quarters in our great holiness movement. Jesus Christ was not manifest in the flesh to suppress the works of the devil, but to destroy them.... Take that, [sic] famous text of the holiness movement, "If we walk in the light, as he is in the light, we have fellowship one with another, and the blood of Jesus Christ his Son cleanseth us from all sin." Hark! not suppresseth, but cleanseth us from all sin. There is a great gulf fixed between the unscriptural teaching of suppression and the precious Bible doctrine of eradication or cleansing from sin.

I have been informed that some students have gone out from Asbury College, [sic] with pitiful notions in their heads of a sanctification which is simply a suppression of indwelling sin. I wonder if they will hold meetings and call believers to come forward to the altar and have their carnal nature suppressed.... The secret of the success of this school, with its students scattered broadcast about the world preaching with so much power and fruitfulness, arises out of the fact that the Rev. John W. Hughes, the founder of the institution, was and is a *radical*, when it comes to the great doctrines of the new birth and entire sanctification; he insisted that his theological students should experience these works of grace, and he hammered these great Bible truths into their heads and taught them how to preach and defend them, and sent them out with hearts on fire, and no uncertain sound.[44]

Among the places where Morrison encountered suppression teachings was India where Keswick expressions of holiness had become ubiquitous in many evangelical circles, including the MEC mission.[45] Furthermore, it is also worth noting that Morrison's complaint about some Asbury students' "pitiful notions" on suppression led him to remind them of the "radical" Holiness roots of the school through the teachings of John Wesley Hughes, its founder. This, in essence, suggests that, just like Kilbourne's assessment of his preaching as we have previously pointed out, Morrison saw himself as a preacher of radical holiness.

What seems to be more at stake for Morrison, however, was not merely the need to stay faithful to the Wesleyan articulation of holiness doctrine, but rather his understanding of the role of the Holy Spirit in sanctification. His prescription for the MEC mission in India made this abundantly clear:

> We need power. We want to put life and spirit into our services. We want the heat and action produced by the Holy Ghost. The masses of the people care but little for the mere human forms of religion; they would like to see the unmistakable evidences of the *supernatural power* of salvation among men. Let Methodism separate 'herself from all worldliness, be filled with the Spirit, sing and shout and preach a free and full salvation from all sin. Then she will have to enlarge the seating capacity of her places of worship the world over. . . . Men are eager to hear of a Christ who is able to save all men from all sin.[46]

Morrison believed that salvation "from all sin" is a testament to the "supernatural power" of the Holy Spirit, which nonbelievers were yearning to see and would, therefore, lead them to flock to Methodist churches. This is also why he, along with other Radical Holiness advocates, equated instantaneous sanctification to the "baptism with the Holy Ghost," distinct and subsequent to regeneration, as he had preached on a number of occasions during his tour.[47]

Correspondingly, the belief in the supernatural work of the Spirit to bring about Christian perfection was very much consistent with the supernaturalism found among proponents of Radical Holiness, which also enabled them to find miraculous accounts in the Book of Acts, like divine healing, as normative for Christian practice.[48] Nevertheless, Morrison did not engage in any form of faith healing during his tour and, at least based on his autobiography, there are no indications he did so prior or subsequent to it.[49] Nonetheless, it is safe to assume that he did not reject the practice given the presence of reports on events, articles, and advertisements that mention it, even though few, in the *Herald* during the time of his tour.[50] Furthermore, there were also letters from subscribers that contained testimonies of miraculous healings.[51] Perhaps the closest Morrison ever came to some direct experience of "signs and wonders" type of supernaturalism during the tour was when he recalled battling "some evil spirit" and when he experienced partial healing. The former took place shortly after his arrival in India, when one night he "awoke and it seemed that the devil or some evil spirit" was in his room near his bed. "The cold chills ran over me and I prayed aloud to the Holy Spirit for protection and was comforted," he recalled.[52] The latter was on a ship en route to China when he had a vision in his room of Jesus confronting Satan, which resulted in his partial healing from the dysentery he contracted while in India.[53] Additionally, Morrison noted stories of the deliverance of Korean converts from demon possession, although was seemingly cautious to give his readers the impression that he believed them.[54] Nevertheless, he enthusiastically retold accounts from the Pyongyang Revival of 1907, which included people falling over "stiff" or "dead" after confessing their sins.[55] Still, these do not establish a likelihood that he engaged in divine healing practices.

Nevertheless, one of the most tangible manifestations of Radical Holiness spirituality in Morrison was his premillennial eschatology, or his firm belief in the imminent return of Christ. For example, a survey of articles in the *Herald* during the time of the tour indicates that this was a theme that it actively promulgated.[56] Also, it was about the same time that the periodical advertised Morrison's book, *The Second Coming of Christ*, along with other books on the Second Coming published by his Pentecostal Publishing Company from authors like L. L. Pickett. W. B. Godbey, J. O. McClurkan, and others.[57] Morrison also published other follow-ups to *Second Coming*, increasingly embracing dispensational premillennialism in the years following World War I: *The World War in Prophecy: The Downfall of the Kaiser and the End of the Dispensation* (1917), *The Optimism of Pre-Millennialism* (1927), *Is the World Growing Better; or, Is the World Growing Worse?* (1932), among others.[58] Nevertheless, even though Morrison's publishing endeavors point to premillennialism as a subject he was passionate about, it was barely a theme he talked about during his tour. For example, there was at least only one recorded instance when he preached on the topic, which was at a gathering of missionaries at the Methodist Girls' School in Seoul, where he spoke on "The Coming of the Lord and the Wedding Garment."[59] In India, he also commended T. Walker, a "low church" Episcopalian priest who preached at the Keswick-styled interdenominational Lanowli (or Lanovla) Convention, where Morrison also preached, for being "clear on the second coming of Christ."[60]

RADICAL HOLINESS MEETS "GLOBAL HOLINESS"

Various missionary organizations in the field hosted Morrison and Piercy and opened their churches to them. In India, Rangoon, Singapore, and Manila, it was MEC missionaries who facilitated much of Morrison's meetings. In China, he ministered primarily with the MECS mission. In Korea, he preached in MECS, MEC, YMCA, and Presbyterian gatherings. In Japan, he ministered in MEC, MECS, FMC, OMS, and YMCA settings. The fact that the majority of these places were Methodist mission stations points to the persistence of Holiness values in American Methodism. While the Holiness Movement was increasingly attacked and relegated to the fringes back home, although in varying degrees within the MEC and MECS, this was not the case in the mission field as the warm reception to Morrison's message illustrates. He essentially confirmed such disparity between ministers back home and those who were overseas, at least among Southern Methodists, when he bluntly remarked, "In all my travels in China, Korea and Japan, I have not found a Southern Methodist preacher who uses the filthy weed!"[61] Simply put, for Morrison, an indication that the MECS missionaries he encountered were Holiness people was that they did not smoke tobacco, unlike their counterparts in the United States.

Additionally, the trip reveals the existence of an informal network of Methodist missionaries whose spirituality had been shaped by various manifestations of Holiness-type revivalism either in America or in the mission field or both. To illustrate this best, let us first turn our attention to William F. Oldham (1854–1937), missionary bishop of the MEC for Southern Asia, who was mostly responsible for Morrison's visit to India, Rangoon, Singapore, and Manila. Born in Bangalore, India, and a son of a British military officer, Oldham was among the many Anglo-Indian converts of William Taylor's famous revival work in south India, having been converted in Poona in 1873 through the preaching of Daniel O. Fox, one of Taylor's self-supporting associates. After devoting some years to study in the United States and pioneer MEC work in Singapore, Oldham returned to the United States in 1895 to accept a teaching position at Ohio Wesleyan University. He was elected missionary bishop in 1904 and three years later experienced entire sanctification after lecturing on the "Higher Christian Life" at the interdenominational "Tuesday meetings" in Singapore. After confessing before his audience that he was "void of the experience," he invited them to join him in seeking sanctification through "yielding consent and in earnest supplication." Oldham recalled falling unconscious on the floor as people came forward to pray for "complete deliverance from the belittling and harassing power of sin."[62] This experience led him to promote holiness vigorously and launched revival campaigns in south India, Malaysia, and the Philippines afterward. Hence, when Morrison came to the *Desahra* meeting in Lucknow, the bishop was already functioning as a Holiness revivalist:

> One afternoon I heard Bishop Oldham preach to the native Christians on the *Canaan life*. . . . He preached to the three hundred native preachers and the great audience a plain, powerful sermon on entire sanctification and the blessed fruits of perfect love. While Bishop Oldham preached, Bishop Warne slipped out of his chair and got upon his knees in prayer and remained there through most of the sermon. As I looked upon this scene, the one Bishop preaching full salvation, the other Bishop on his knees in prayer, and three hundred native preachers still as death giving rapt attention to the truth, I got a hopeful outlook for the future of Methodism in India.[63]

Morrison was not in unchartered waters but as he would later find out, preexisting holiness or postconversion teachings in the Methodist missions he visited did not necessarily match Wesleyan-Holiness doctrine. Such manifestations of Holiness teachings overseas, which Bundy terms "global holiness," a loose category that encompasses the variety of Holiness Movements that developed outside the United States, including in the United Kingdom and Europe, were largely shaped by the contexts from which they emerged.[64] Again, a case in point would be the MEC mission in India. While it appears that Oldham's message was more compatible with the eradicationist sensibilities of Morrison, his predecessor James Thoburn, and colleague Francis Warne, the other bishops named in the above account expressed misgivings about Wesleyan perfectionist articulations of holiness by adopting a more "Keswickfied" or suppressionist understanding of holiness.[65] Their revised theological views on holiness were part of a much bigger shift in Indian Methodism, which emerged from its interactions with Keswick-inspired "Holy Ghost" evangelicals in the years prior to the Great Indian Revival of 1905–7. This revival first broke out in the Welsh Calvinistic Methodist mission in Khasi Hills, Assam Province, and later in Pandita Ramabai's Mukti mission in Kedgaon.[66] Indian Methodists experienced powerful revivals as well in their stations during the same period as a result of these connections.[67] We can, therefore, argue that it was the Great Indian Revival that shaped much of holiness articulations among Methodists in India. Given the MEC mission's experience surrounding the revival, a different form of holiness expression developed, one that was distinct from the one advocated by most holiness advocates in the United States. Hence, it was no accident that the difference between these two forms of holiness manifested during Morrison's tour. For instance, when he preached on the eradication of the sinful nature during the *Dasehra* meeting, it was quickly seen as a novelty by his hearers, as one attendee had observed: "Holiness, the desire of God for his people, was held before us as something attainable in life. Though brought up a Methodist, we have never listened to such a careful and earnest presentation of these doctrines which concern the higher life of the Christian."[68]

In addition to Oldham, we now turn our attention to Robert A. Hardie (1865–1949), a MECS missionary who hosted and assisted Morrison in Seoul. Hardie, who was teaching at Union Seminary in Seoul at that time, also served as Morrison's interpreter for much of his revival work in the city. Although raised Methodist in Canada, Hardie first came to Korea in 1890 as a missionary with the YMCA. He joined the MECS mission eight years later, becoming its first missionary doctor in the country.[69] He was a central figure in the Wonsan Revival of 1903 that culminated in the Pyongyang Revival three years later, a watershed moment in the history of Korean Christianity.[70] The revival in Wonsan (now in North Korea) began in November 1903, when an outpouring of the Holy Spirit took place during a one-week study on prayer led by Hardie and attended by six other missionaries, five from the MECS and one Presbyterian. Hardie shared that while preparing for his lecture, he was baptized in the Holy Spirit after confessing his lack of faith in "cleansing from all sin," the absence of an "abiding life," and "unwillingness to confess his need of the infilling of the Holy Spirit." Deeply convicted by his testimony, the others took turns confessing their sins as the "Holy Spirit came" among them.

Not long after, Hardie shared the same testimony with his congregation at First Church Wonsan and a similar awakening occurred. The revival spread further as Hardie held other meetings in Kangwon province, Songdo (now Kaesong), Seoul, Pyongyang, and other places, spurring spontaneous mass confessions and outpourings of the Spirit. In Pyongyang, for instance, Hardie preached in both Presbyterian and MEC congregations in 1904, thereby helping set the stage for what was to become the Pyongyang Revival of 1907.[71] Morrison visited these places in 1910 as mentioned earlier in this chapter. Hardie's testimony and the ensuing mass confessions that followed show that the central motifs of the revivals in Korea were repentance, holiness, and Spirit baptism, familiar themes in Morrison's Pentecostal meetings, which help account for his successful meetings there.

Morrison's tour brings to the fore the roles that revivals played in shaping "global holiness" in the areas he visited. Aside from the revivals in India (1905–7) and Korea (1903–7), similar revivals in China (1906–9) and Japan (1906–9) also preceded Morrison's tour. Therefore, Oldham's sanctification and Hardie's Spirit baptism need to be seen in light of what we can call a "trans-Asian revival," which was interlinked via a complex web of relationships involving holiness-influenced missionaries, native evangelists, visiting revivalists, and literature, including reports, devotionals, and books that crossed the seas surrounding South Asia and East Asia and the Pacific Ocean. Since Oldham and Hardie's experiences took place in the mission field, we also cannot ignore the unique contextual and cultural or indigenous forces at play that made them distinct from each other. Their experiences, therefore, help illustrate the forms of global holiness that developed in these countries. However, despite the varied global holiness experiences of the two missionaries, both found in Morrison a partner in their desire to see revival in their respective stations. While Morrison was fixated on perpetuating the intricacies of the Radical Holiness doctrine he professed, these missionaries found something in his revivalism—his message and methods—that they felt would resonate in the field. Since the revivals in most of these areas were at their tail end (like in China and Japan) or deemed to have subsided (like in India and Korea), perhaps they found in Morrison's revivalism the potential of extending or resuscitating these revivals.

Thus, Morrison's tour illuminates one of the ways Radical Holiness Movements intertwined with global holiness, which consequently helped create the conditions for the rise of global Pentecostalism.[72] While the legacy of Morrison's tour in India, Korea, and Japan is subject to further investigation, its impact in the Philippines has been a focus in a recent study by this author.[73] Morrison's six-day Pentecostal meetings in Manila was far from being a temporary blip on the radar screen, as Oldham confirmed shortly after the evangelist's visit:

> When I cabled you, I did not know how marked a step forward your coming would bring. I called the mission together yesterday to discuss especially

the matter of revival and I found the men's hearts are all aglow, but they all feel that we must organize Revival bands in which Americans and Filipinos shall go together all over our territory to call the people to repentance and the Christians to a deeper life of holiness. Your coming has practically fixed the holiness idea as the birthright of every man in the Methodist Church, and I desire these revival bands to move through the country not only for the sake of sinners, but that we might have sincere saints.[74]

Bishop Dionisio Alejandro, one of the two Filipino students recruited by Morrison to study at Asbury after his tour, later substantiated this. Morrison's visit, he wrote, had made the term *culto Pentecostal* (Pentecostal meeting) the "watchword" in early Philippine Methodist life and culture as these services lasted "from one week to ten days and continued until the outbreak of World War II."[75] However, as this author suggests, the impact of Morrison's visit was much more. The Holiness-Pentecostal revival culture it helped create also contributed to the shaping of Filipino Methodist identity in the decades that followed, which included, among others, the prominent role played by Filipino Methodists in the Manila Healing Revival in the 1950s and the rise of Pentecostalism in the country.[76]

CONCLUSION

Morrison reinforced his status as a "mainline Holiness" figure when he did his "world tour of evangelism," mainly among Methodist mission stations in Asia. However, the fact that it was the OMS that hosted and organized his visit in Tokyo illustrates his ambiguous position among the nonradicals and radicals in the Holiness Movement. Accordingly, he was one of the few Methodist loyalists who defied conventions by promoting Radical Holiness teachings that were mainly attributed to separatist Holiness radicals. Despite the increasing popularity of Keswick suppression teachings in most of the places he visited, his unrelenting and unequivocal adherence to the eradication of the sinful nature figured prominently in his preaching. But what made his message deeply radical was his recognition that the eradication of "all sin" is a supernatural work made possible through Holy Spirit baptism. Morrison's linking of entire sanctification with the miraculous was very much consistent with the supernaturalism found among proponents of Radical Holiness, which also enabled them to find miraculous accounts in the Book of Acts, like divine healing, as normative for Christian practice. While Radical Holiness has always been defined to include the practice of faith healing, Morrison neither practiced it during his tour, nor was it a theme in his writings and ministry. Nevertheless, premillennialism, which was another marker for the radical wing of the Holiness Movement, figured prominently in his teachings and publications, although it was a subject that he rarely preached about during his tour.

However, the tour not only showcased the contours and nuances of Morrison's Radical Holiness values, it also brought to the fore the varied manifestations of global holiness spirituality that developed in the places he visited. In the case of Asia, global holiness has been largely shaped by the interrelated series of simultaneous revivals, preceding Morrison's coming, during the first decade of the twentieth century. Hence, the warm reception given to his revivalism was one of the means that missionaries employed to resuscitate or continue the revivals in their stations. Thus, Morrison's tour illuminates one of the ways Radical Holiness Movements coalesced with global holiness. This coalescing eventually helped create the conditions for the rise of global Pentecostalism, as visiting Radical Holiness revivalists and missionaries began introducing teachings, like divine healing and premillennialism, overseas. Although Morrison did not include a faith healing message and barely taught premillennialism among the repertoire of teachings during his tour, the impact of his brand of Radical Holiness, though tempered, cannot be ignored. Given its contributions to the development of Methodism and eventually Pentecostalism in the Philippines, further research into the legacy of Morrison's tour in other countries he visited may yet surprise us.

NOTES

1. See Henry Clay Morrison, *World Tour of Evangelism* (Louisville, KY: Pentecostal Publishing, 1911).

2. David Bundy, Foreword to *Spirit-Filled Protestantism: Holiness-Pentecostal Revivals and the Making of Filipino Methodist Identity*, by Luther J. Oconer (Eugene, OR: Pickwick Publications, 2017), xii. Jay R. Case argued that these Radical Holiness commitments arose largely from its antimodern impulse. See Jay R. Case, "And Ever the Twain Shall Meet: The Holiness Missionary Movement and the Birth of World Pentecostalism, 1870–1920," *Religion and American Culture* 16, no. 2 (2006): 128–29, 141–47.

3. Myung Soo Park, "The 20th Century Holiness Movement and Korean Holiness Groups," *Asbury Journal* 62, no. 2 (2007): 84, 87; Wallace Thornton Jr., *When the Fire Fell: Martin Wells Knapp's Vision of Pentecost and the Beginning of God's Bible School* (Lexington, KY: Emeth Press, 2014), 25, 43.

4. Bundy, Foreword to *Spirit-Filled Protestantism*, xiii.

5. Morrison, *World Tour*, 8–9.

6. Ibid., 8; Henry Clay Morrison, *Some Chapters of My Life Story* (Louisville, KY: Pentecostal Publishing, 1941), 195–98.

7. Morrison, *World Tour*, 8.

8. See Henry Clay Morrison, *Baptism with the Holy Ghost* (Louisville, KY: Pentecostal Publishing, 1900), p. 1 and throughout the book; emphasis added.

9. Donald W. Dayton, *Theological Roots of Pentecostalism* (Metuchen, NJ: Scarecrow Press, 1987), 91–92.

10. Percival A. Wesche, *Henry Clay Morrison "Crusader Saint"* (Wilmore, KY: Seminary Press, 1963), 59–60.

11. Delbert R. Rose, *Vital Holiness: A Theology of Christian Experience; Interpreting the Historic Wesleyan Message* (Salem, OH: Schmul Publishing 2000), 95–96; Timothy L. Smith, *Called Unto Holiness: The Story of the Nazarenes, the Formative Years* (Kansas City, MO: Nazarene Publishing, 1962), 53.

12. For more on independent Holiness missions, see Dana L. Robert, *American Women in Mission: The Modern Mission Era, 1792–1992* (Macon: Mercer University Press, 1997), 189–254.

13. Wesche, *"Crusader Saint,"* 82–92; William Kostlevy, "Morrison, Henry Clay," in *The A to Z of the Holiness Movement*, ed. William Kostlevy, A–Z Guide Series 164 (Lanham, MD: Scarecrow Press, 2010), 207.

14. Myung Soo Park classifies holiness advocates who maintained connections with the National Holiness Association as "traditional holiness" or "mainline holiness." See Park, "20th Century Holiness Movement," 84, 87.

15. Morrison, *World Tour*, 11–12; Morrison, *Some Chapters*, 202–3.

16. Morrison, *World Tour*, 18–77.

17. Ibid., 77–194.

18. *Pentecostal Herald* (May 18, 1910): 8. Hereinafter designated as *PH*.

19. See *PH* (May 25, 1910): 1, 8; *PH* (June 1, 1910): 1, 8; *PH* (June 8, 1910): 1, 8; *PH* (June 15, 1910): 1, 8; Morrison, *World Tour*, 226.

20. *PH* (June 22, 1910): 1, 8.

21. *PH* (July 13, 1910): 1, 8; *PH* (July 20, 1910): 1, 8.

22. *PH* (July 27, 1910): 1, 8; *PH* (August 3, 1910): 1, 8.

23. For eyewitness accounts, see, for example, William N. Blair, *The Korea Pentecost and Other Experiences on the Mission Field* (New York: The Board of Foreign Missions of the Presbyterian Church of the USA, 1910); Jonathan Goforth, *When the Spirit's Fire Swept Korea* (Grand Rapids, MI: Zondervan, 1943).

24. *PH* (August 10, 1910): 1, 8.

25. *PH* (August 17, 1910): 1, 8–9.

26. *PH* (August 24, 1910): 1, 8.

27. *PH* (August 31, 1910): 1, 8; *PH* (September 14, 1910): 1, 8.

28. *PH* (August 17, 1910): 1.

29. For more on the *Dasehra* meetings, see Luther J. Oconer, "'Keswickfied' Methodism Holiness Revivalism and The Methodist Episcopal Church Mission in India, 1870–1910," *Wesleyan Theological Journal* 49, no. 2 (2014): 127–28.

30. *PH* (January 12, 1910): 8.

31. *PH* (February 16, 1910): 1.

32. *PH* (February 16, 1910): 8.

33. *PH* (April 27, 1910): 8.

34. *PH* (May 4, 1910): 8.

35. *PH* (June 15, 1910): 1.

36. *PH* (June 29, 1910): 1.

37. *PH* (September 28, 1910): 10.

38. *PH* (March 2, 1910): 5. See also report from the *Bombay Methodist Monthly Visitor* in *PH* (February 23, 1910): 4.

39. *PH* (June 29, 1910): 1.

40. *PH* (March 23, 1910): 1; cf. Morrison, *World Tour*, 160.

41. See, for example, Sermon 43 in John Wesley, "The Scripture Way of Salvation," in *Sermons II*, vol. 2 of *The Works of John Wesley*, ed. Albert C. Outler (Nashville: Abingdon Press, 1985), 167–69.

42. *PH* (July 27, 1910): 8; emphasis added; cf. *PH* (September 28, 1910): 10.

43. See Thornton, *When the Fire Fell*, 25, 43.

44. *PH* (August 17, 1910): 1; emphasis added.

45. For a detailed study on this, see Oconer, "'Keswickfied Methodism.'"

46. *PH* (February 9, 1910): 8; emphasis added.

47. See, for example, *PH* (May 4, 1910): 8; *PH* (August 17, 1910): 1; *PH* (August 24, 1910): 1. See also Morrison, *Baptism with the Holy Ghost*, 22–29.

48. Bundy, Foreword to *Spirit-Filled Protestantism*, xiii; Case, "And Ever the Twain Shall Meet," 128.

49. See Morrison, *Some Chapters*, 69–200.

50. See, for example, *PH* (July 27, 1910): 12; *PH* (August 31, 1910): 10; *PH* (November 2, 1910): 10.

51. See *PH* (January 26, 1910): 6; *PH* (February 23, 1910): 5; *PH* (September 28, 1910): 15; *PH* (November 9, 1910): 10.

52. *PH* (January 5, 1910): 11.

53. Wesche, *"Crusader Saint,"* 80–81. For the term "signs and wonders," see, for example, Acts 5:12, NRSV.

54. *PH* (August 3, 1910): 1.

55. *PH* (August 10, 1910): 8. For more on the Korean Revival, see, for example, Myung Soo Park, "'The Korea Pentecost' A Study of the Great Revival of 1903–1910 in Relationship to Contemporary Worldwide Holiness Revival Movements," in *The Global Impact of the Wesleyan Traditions and Their Related Movements*, ed. Charles Yrigoyen Jr., Pietist and Wesleyan Studies 14 (Lanham, MD Scarecrow Press, 2002).

56. See, for example, *PH* (January 26, 1910): 2; *PH* (May 4, 1910): 5; *PH* (May 11, 1910): 5; *PH* (August 31, 1910): 7.

57. See, for example, *PH* (January 12, 1910): 4; *PH* (February 2, 1910): 6; *PH* (March 9, 1910): 4; *PH* (April 20, 1910): 6; *PH* (August 17, 1910): 6. A later edition of *The Second Coming of Christ* was published in 1914. See Henry Clay Morrison, *The Second Coming of Christ* (Louisville, KY: Pentecostal Publishing, 1914).

58. Each of these books was published by Pentecostal Publishing, in Louisville, KY.

59. *PH* (August 17, 1910): 8.

60. *PH* (August 26, 1910): 1.

61. *PH* (August 17, 1910): 8.

62. Oconer, *Spirit-Filled Protestantism*, 76–77; Theodore R. Doraisamy, *Oldham, Called of God: Profile of a Pioneer, Bishop William Fitzjames Oldham* (Singapore: The Methodist Book Room, 1979), 57–58. *Christian Advocate* (November 29, 1917): 1266.

63. *PH* (January 12, 1910): 8.

64. Bundy, Foreword to *Spirit-Filled Protestantism*, xiii.

65. Oconer, "Keswickfied Methodism," 130–39.

66. Ibid., 136, 140–43; Gary B. McGee, "'Baptism of the Holy Ghost & Fire!' The Mission Legacy of Minnie F. Abrams," *Missiology: An International Review* 27, no. 4 (1999): 517–19; Gary B. McGee, "'Latter Rain' Falling in the East: Early-Twentieth-Century Pentecostalism in India and the Debate over Speaking in Tongues," *Church History* 68, no. 3 (1999): 651–53.

67. For accounts of revivals in the MEC mission in India, see Francis W. Warne, *The Revival in the Indian Church* (New York Board of Foreign Missions Methodist Episcopal Church, 1907).

68. *The Indian Witness* (November 11, 1909): 5.

69. Chil-Sung Kim, "The Role of Robert Alexander Hardie in the Korean Great Revival and the Subsequent Development of Korean Protestant Christianity" (PhD diss., Asbury Theological Seminary, 2012), 41–48.

70. A recent study argues that the Wonsan and Pyongyang revivals are related and therefore should be seen as one Korean Revival of 1903–7. See ibid., 179–84.

71. Ibid., 143–47.

72. For a definition of "global Pentecostalism" and its complexities, see Allan Anderson, "Varieties, Taxonomies, and

Definitions," in *Studying Global Pentecostalism: Theories and Methods*, ed. Allan Anderson et al. (Berkeley: University of California Press, 2010), 13–27.

73. See Oconer, *Spirit-Filled Protestantism*.

74. Quoted in Morrison, *World Tour*, 213.

75. Dionisio D. Alejandro, *From Darkness to Light: A Brief Chronicle of the Beginnings and Spread of Methodism in the Philippines* (Quezon City, Philippines: United Methodist Church Philippines Central Conference Board of Communications and Publications, 1974), 106–7; Oconer, *Spirit-Filled Protestantism*, 84–87.

76. See Oconer, *Spirit-Filled Protestantism*.

BIBLIOGRAPHY

Alejandro, Dionisio D. *From Darkness to Light: A Brief Chronicle of the Beginnings and Spread of Methodism in the Philippines*. Quezon City, Philippines: United Methodist Church Philippines Central Conference Board of Communications and Publications, 1974.

Anderson, Allan. "Varieties, Taxonomies, and Definitions." In *Studying Global Pentecostalism: Theories and Methods*, edited by Allan Anderson, Michael Bergunder, André Droogers, and Cornelis van der Laan, 13–29. Berkeley: University of California Press, 2010.

Blair, William N. *The Korea Pentecost and Other Experiences on the Mission Field*. New York: The Board of Foreign Missions of the Presbyterian Church of the USA, 1910.

Bundy, David. Foreword to *Spirit-Filled Protestantism: Holiness-Pentecostal Revivals and the Making of Filipino Methodist Identity*, by Luther J. Oconer, xi–xiii. Eugene, OR: Pickwick Publications, 2017.

Case, Jay R. "And Ever the Twain Shall Meet: The Holiness Missionary Movement and the Birth of World Pentecostalism, 1870–1920." *Religion and American Culture* 16, no. 2 (2006): 125–59.

Dayton, Donald W. *Theological Roots of Pentecostalism*. Metuchen, NJ: Scarecrow Press, 1987.

Doraisamy, Theodore R. *Oldham, Called of God: Profile of a Pioneer, Bishop William Fitzjames Oldham*. Singapore: The Methodist Book Room, 1979.

Goforth, Jonathan. *When the Spirit's Fire Swept Korea*. Grand Rapids, MI: Zondervan, 1943.

Kim, Chil-Sung. "The Role of Robert Alexander Hardie in the Korean Great Revival and the Subsequent Development of Korean Protestant Christianity." PhD diss., Asbury Theological Seminary, 2012.

Kostlevy, William. "Morrison, Henry Clay." In *The A to Z of the Holiness Movement*. A–Z Guide Series 164, edited by William Kostlevy, 207–8. Lanham, MD: Scarecrow Press, 2010.

McGee, Gary B. "'Baptism of the Holy Ghost & Fire!' The Mission Legacy of Minnie F. Abrams." *Missiology: An International Review* 27, no. 4 (1999): 515–22.

———. "'Latter Rain' Falling in the East: Early-Twentieth-Century Pentecostalism in India and the Debate over Speaking in Tongues." *Church History* 68, no. 3 (1999): 648–65.

Morrison, Henry Clay. *Baptism with the Holy Ghost*. Louisville, KY: Pentecostal Publishing, 1900.

———. *Is the World Growing Better; or, Is the World Growing Worse?* Louisville, KY: Pentecostal Publishing, 1932.

———. *The Optimism of Pre-Millennialism*. Louisville, KY: Pentecostal Publishing, 1927.

———. "Our World Tour of Evangelism." *Pentecostal Herald*, January 5, 1910–November 9, 1910.

———. *The Second Coming of Christ*. Louisville, KY: Pentecostal Publishing, 1914.

———. *Some Chapters of My Life Story*. Louisville, KY: Pentecostal Publishing, 1941.

———. *World Tour of Evangelism*. Louisville, KY: Pentecostal Publishing, 1911.

———. *The World War in Prophecy: The Downfall of the Kaiser and the End of the Dispensation*. Louisville, KY: Pentecostal Publishing, 1917.

Oconer, Luther J. "'Keswickfied' Methodism: Holiness Revivalism and The Methodist Episcopal Church Mission in India, 1870–1910." *Wesleyan Theological Journal* 49, no. 2 (2014): 122–43.

———. *Spirit-Filled Protestantism: Holiness-Pentecostal Revivals and the Making of Filipino Methodist Identity*. Eugene, OR: Pickwick Publications, 2017.

Park, Myung Soo. "'The Korea Pentecost': A Study of the Great Revival of 1903–1910 in Relationship to Contemporary Worldwide Holiness Revival Movements." In *The Global Impact of the Wesleyan Traditions and Their Related Movements*, edited by Charles Yrigoyen Jr., 201–16. Pietist and Wesleyan Studies 14. Lanham, MD: Scarecrow Press, 2002.

———. "The 20th Century Holiness Movement and Korean Holiness Groups." *Asbury Journal* 62, no. 2 (2007): 81–108.

Robert, Dana L. *American Women in Mission: The Modern Mission Era, 1792–1992*. Macon: Mercer University Press, 1997.

Rose, Delbert R. *Vital Holiness: A Theology of Christian Experience; Interpreting the Historic Wesleyan Message*. Salem, OH: Schmul Publishing, 2000.

Smith, Timothy L. *Called Unto Holiness: The Story of the Nazarenes, the Formative Years*. Kansas City, MO: Nazarene Publishing, 1962.

Thornton, Wallace, Jr. *When the Fire Fell: Martin Wells Knapp's Vision of Pentecost and the Beginning of God's Bible School*. Lexington, KY: Emeth Press, 2014.

Warne, Francis W. *The Revival in the Indian Church*. New York: Board of Foreign Missions Methodist Episcopal Church, 1907.

Wesche, Percival A. *Henry Clay Morrison "Crusader Saint."* Wilmore, KY: Seminary Press, 1963.

Wesley, John. "The Scripture Way of Salvation." In *Sermons II*, vol. 2 of *The Works of John Wesley*, ed. Albert C. Outler, 155–69. Nashville: Abingdon Press, 1985.

UNITY AND DIVERSITY

CHAPTER 5

"Spiritual Railroading"
Trains as Metaphor and Reality in the Holiness
and Pentecostal Movements, ca. 1880–ca. 1920

Daniel Woods

As the year 1899 drew to a close, Cincinnati-based evangelist and Holiness entrepreneur Martin Wells Knapp chose to spend the holiday season in Greensboro, North Carolina, "a pleasant and growing city of about fifteen thousand." He traveled there to organize a band of sixty-five "Spirit-baptized saints" from several denominations into a Pentecostal Holiness Union. Knapp began his report to the *Revivalist* with glowing comments about the people's friendliness, their facilities, and God's manifest presence in the meetings but he soon turned his attention to the train ride south. "As is our custom," he told his readers, "in going east from Cincinnati we took the Chesapeake & Ohio Railroad, which for accommodations, comfort, beauty, and variety of scenery and object lessons along the way, from which valuable spiritual lessons may be learned, we prefer above all other roads." In passionate words, Knapp described his "sudden transition from the smoke and dust and soot of the city to the rushing rivers, wonderful cascades, forest-crowned mountains, and electrical atmosphere" of Appalachia. He found this familiar route a "forceful illustration of the change from the life of sin to the spiritual fountains and rivers and mountains which delight all who travel on the Great Celestial Railroad from earth to heaven."[1] Like most other Holiness preachers, Knapp found much to rail against in the modern world—everything from worldly fashions to worldly sermons—but clearly, he liked the railroad. It provided an unprecedented opportunity for

Fig. 5.1 "Lost, Saved, Sanctified." From Martin Wells Knapp, *Lightning Bolts from Pentecostal Skies* (Cincinnati: Revivalist, 1898), 32.

LOST, SAVED, SANCTIFIED

him to run from one spiritual battle to another and to do so in comfort and as the Lord spoke to him through the windows. Seth Rees, cofounder with Knapp of the Pilgrim Holiness Church, aptly described this mix of practical and inspirational benefits as "spiritual railroading."[2]

Such "spiritual railroading" is evident in both the Holiness Movement of the late nineteenth century and its daughter, the Pentecostal Movement, which emerged in the first decade of the twentieth century. Despite a great deal of mutual suspicion and even antagonism, both camps shared a common evangelistic zeal, eschatological urgency, and aversion to emerging consumer culture.[3] And the dynamic expansion of both movements was deeply entwined with the concurrent explosive growth in transportation, which historians refer to as the "Golden Age of the Railroad."[4] A focus on "spiritual railroading" illuminates the power of widespread technological innovation to create new paths for the flow of religious ideas and witness, increasing the exchange not only of information but also of spiritual anointings that, under the proper circumstances, lead to the formation of new religious movements and institutions. Because of the nature of rail expansion, such religious innovations tended to move from areas of rapid economic and population growth to more traditional communities less directly impacted by the railroad. In addition, new technologies, like rail travel, often provide the faithful with fresh ways of thinking about the interplay between the material and spiritual worlds—between the visible and the invisible—providing new words and images for testifying to religious rapture. Hence, the Holiness and Pentecostal movements can be viewed as doubly entwined, first with each other as related expressions of Wesleyan evangelicalism but also with the railroad as an expander of the ways these witnessing people interacted with their times. In both relationships, we see presuppositional commonalities alongside pronounced wariness.

RAILROADS AND ESCHATOLOGICAL VISION

Martin Wells Knapp thought well on trains; he also thought well with them. One of many in the 1890s who stretched the definition of sanctification to include supernatural power for effective service, Knapp drew on developments in contemporary American life to find apt metaphors for his understanding of the "pentecostal holiness" that the last days required. He blended familiar allusions to tornadoes and lightning bolts with such new metaphors as dynamite, electricity, and the "revival train." Railroad references became so common in his writings that one supporter found it natural to describe his favorite Knapp books this way: "'Out of Egypt' may be likened to the instructions for making a steam engine. 'Christ Crowned Within' to the engine putting on steam, and 'Tornadoes' to the engine at full steam."[5] Knapp even published several "Railroad Editions" of the *Revivalist* that laid out a dizzying variety of creative—if not always consistent—lessons drawn from both the experiences of the traveler and from the mechanical and business principles involved in the efficient operation of a railroad. For example, Knapp likened pastors to "station agents," whose job was to stay in one community issuing tickets for the "Redemption Railroad Company." Evangelists, on the other hand, were like "conductors," riding the rails to make sure that every passenger possessed a properly stamped ticket and followed the "straight and narrow" rules of the road. Knapp compared local pastors to nearly every other railroad job, including "brakesman," "baggageman," and engineer. But the engineer could also be Jesus or denominational officials or the lay Christian. Regardless of who was at the throttle, though, it took

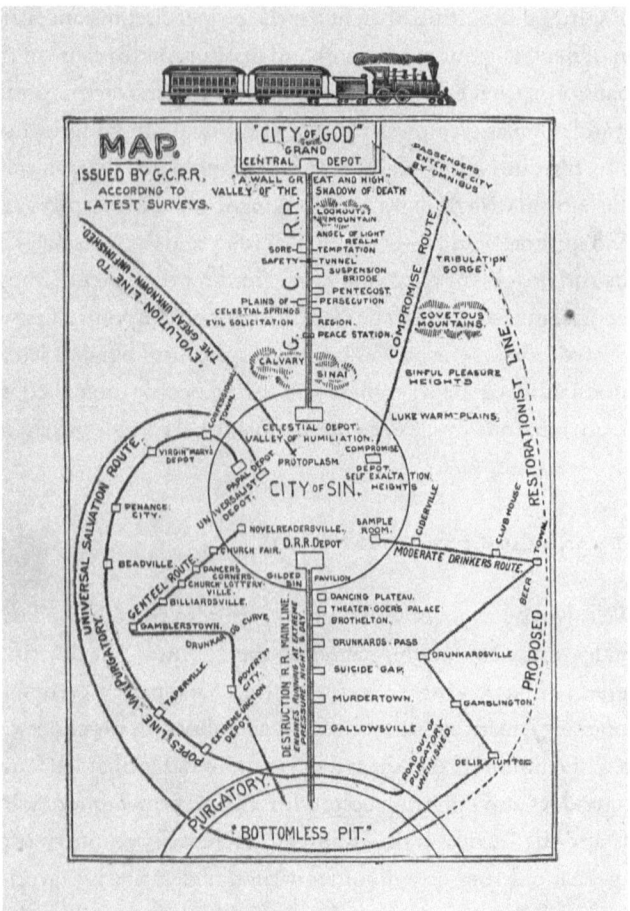

Fig. 5.2 Frontispiece of Olin Marvin Owen, *The Great Celestial Railroad . . .* (Syracuse, NY: A. W. Hall, 1893).

"two blessings to run the train: a. Water; b. Fire." Without "both the water of redemption and the fire of the indwelling Holy Ghost," Knapp explained, "there will be no steam and no motion." The truth of "two blessings" found figurative expression in other ways. Passengers, for instance, had the option of riding in the "common coach" of regeneration or moving up to the "parlor car" of entire sanctification. Knapp was so committed to this "second blessing" that his visual images of "The Two Railroads" often presented the "Holiness Railroad to Heaven," and not the "Redemption Railroad," as the only alternative to the "Lost Souls Line." The choice, in other words, was really "Holiness or Hell."[6]

Like many of his contemporaries, Knapp drew heavily on two complementary books on "spiritual railroading" by Holiness authors: Olin Marvin Owen's *The Great Celestial Railroad*, an allegory about the competing lines offering passage away from "the City of Sin," and Aaron W. Orwig's *All Aboard*, a practical guide for "taking our religion along when we travel."[7] Owen (1847–1918) served for many years as a Free Methodist pastor in upstate New York.[8] He had earlier authored several other books, including sensational warnings about the evils of rum, Roman Catholic education, and Robert Green Ingersoll.[9] Orwig (1838–1931) grew up in northeastern Ohio as part of the Evangelical Alliance. His father, Bishop William W. Orwig, edited their paper *Die Heils Fuelle* (Full salvation).[10] As a minister, Aaron Orwig followed his father's Holiness leanings and later embraced the inchoate Pentecostal Movement, moving to Los Angeles either just before or during the Azusa Revival of 1906–9.[11] While Orwig explained how Holiness people could benefit from a savvy engagement with railroads, Owen turned nearly every aspect of train travel into exciting illustrations of the pardon, purity, and power available to believers.

Owen's update of *Pilgrim's Progress* struck a responsive chord with his peers.[12] His rich symbolic language is easily traced in subsequent publications of the Holiness Movement (and in those of its offspring, the Pentecostal revival) well into the twentieth century. Owen drew his title from Nathaniel Hawthorne's 1843 story in which a pilgrim foolishly eschews the well-worn footpath to heaven to save time and effort on "The Celestial Railroad," a deceptive new line that takes its passengers only as far as Vanity Fair.[13] In Owen's allegory, however, there are no footpaths, and his Great Celestial Railroad goes all the way to the City of God. As Charles Edwin Jones has shown in his study of the railroad metaphor in Holiness hymnody, the positive image of a "Heavenly Railroad" dates at least to the 1850s.[14] Owen fused this hopeful popular image with Hawthorne's wariness by creating a variety of competing lines, most of which terminated in the Bottomless Pit.

Owen begins by having his pilgrim, Transgressor, compare his options for leaving the increasingly wretched City of Sin.[15] Giving no thought to the fast track to Hell called Destruction Railroad, Transgressor briefly considers the merits of boarding the Evolution Line at Protoplasm Station, the Purgatory Line at Papal Depot, and the Genteel Route at Novelreadersville, as well as the Universalist and Moderate Drinker's Routes. Finally, he is torn between the Celestial and Compromise depots, located in the Valley of Humiliation and on Self-Exaltation Heights, respectively. Transgressor chooses the Great Celestial line and steams straight between Sinai and Calvary on his way to the City of

God. Along the way, he must fend off fear, persecution, and "sore temptation," but the most critical juncture of the trip is Pentecost Station, where many passengers return to the City of Sin after rejecting the need for a second blessing, and others get lost in the surrounding wilderness after switching off on unidentified "sidetracks."[16] Transgressor chooses to go forward and receives a fiery baptism that purifies and empowers him for the rest of his journey. His acquaintances who choose the Compromise Route are not as blessed. For a while, they enjoy their ride because the Compromise Railroad features an unusually large baggage car and a unique gearing mechanism that allows its trains to adjust their gauge to ride on all the other routes, except the extremely narrow gauge of the Great Celestial Railroad. On Sundays, the gauge is narrowed so the passengers can enjoy the appearance of religious rectitude, and then on Mondays widened to allow for a little greed, "light wine," and "theatre-going."[17] The problem is that this line crashes at midnight into Tribulation Gorge. Many respectable Christians are killed, but God mercifully dispatches an omnibus for any of the survivors who are willing to leave all their worldly possessions behind.

By the mid-1890s, railroad metaphors became commonplace in Holiness periodicals. In a letter to Henry Clay Morrison's *Pentecostal Herald*, for example, a pastor's wife described her experience of sanctification as being expressed "from the depot of Regeneration . . . into the Land of Canaan" by "the train of Faith, which is touched off by the electricity of Jesus Christ's fire of love."[18] In addition to updated pilgrimage analogies, some writers created strikingly new metaphors. For example, E. A. Ferguson, widely known among Methodists in the Ohio Valley as the "Fire-Baptized Railroad Evangelist," explained victory over self-centeredness by comparing the believer to a "small railroad" that "merges itself into a larger one, loses its identity, and goes under the name of the larger corporation."[19] While both familiar and novel railroad images abound, Holiness spokesmen fixed their attention on two particular points Owen raised in his description of "Pentecost Station." One was his brief depiction of the American church as a powerless "locomotive standing on the track." Owen lamented that efforts to spruce up the old engine had failed because "new drive wheels, a silver bell, and new paint cannot take the place of fire and steam. So it is in carrying on church work. We may have everything else, but if we lack the power of the Holy Spirit, we fail at the most essential point."[20] As early as 1896, Martin Wells Knapp reprinted Owen's discussion in the *Revivalist*.[21] The following year Beverly Carradine personalized the metaphor by pointing out that "the great Adversary" has "no alarm and concerns himself but little over the multitude of Christians who spend most of their time in the Round House receiving or waiting for repairs. But let one of them obtain the Baptism of the Holy Ghost and fire and be transformed in a flash from a condition of helplessness into a great spiritual locomotive full of divine life and power, heading for heaven, and carrying a long train of souls with them; and then full of fury he plots and endeavors from that moment the ruin of that same useful life."[22] This was one Holiness image the subsequent Pentecostal revival would have no trouble perpetuating.

Owen's even briefer mention of unnamed "sidetracks" leading from Pentecost Station also resonated with many Holiness leaders and they soon made efforts to identify these dangerous routes in print. Archie B. Adams saw the substitution of human effort for simple faith as the main sidetrack.[23] Clement C. Cary got more specific. Sidetracks were any distraction from "the main line on which early Methodists ran," especially teachings on "'divine healing,' 'the second coming,' [and] 'fire baptism'" that were not "necessary to holiness or salvation."[24] Others singled out radical "come-outer" advocates and exponents of "marital purity" (who in turn described their willingness to live without sex as "going the death route").[25] A decade later, opponents of the new Pentecostal teaching—that Spirit baptism was experienced after the second blessing of sanctification and accompanied by tongues speech—were quick to label their brethren as "switched off the line." W. B. Godbey warned that Pentecostals would "side track you from the Grand Trunk Line of Holiness," and John F. Knapp maligned the "expression used by some of their teachers and preachers, 'put your heart on the express and the Lord will send your head by freight.'"[26] Yet the Pentecostal Movement survived, and with it the Holiness obsession with sidetracks. As early as 1908, Frank Bartleman, the "apostle of Azusa Street," warned his fellow Pentecostals that every previous "work God has started by divine life has been sidetracked . . . short of its real object by the enemy." Our main task is to let God "keep us sanely, soberly balanced by the Spirit, on the main line."[27] And in 1921 G. F. Taylor, writing about some members of the Pentecostal Holiness Church who at prophetic urging had changed their names and destroyed their photographs and fine china, characterized them as good Christians who somewhere "got switched off the line."[28]

RAILROADS AND EVANGELISTIC OPPORTUNITY

If Owen's *Great Celestial Railroad* enriched and accelerated the use of train imagery, Orwig's *All Aboard* offered practical suggestions for Christian travelers in an effort to make them comfortable with depots, dining cars, and other railroad spaces. Reassurance was clearly needed in the 1890s and for decades to come.[29] The growing presence of the railroads in national and local life caused many Holiness folks considerable anxiety over such things as the efficacy of Sunday travel for preachers and membership in labor unions (most of which were organized as fraternal orders) for sanctified railroad workers. They also worried about the dangers of greed and speed. Frequent news reports about manipulative "trusts" and deadly train wrecks carried personal as well as prophetic implications: Railroads could cheat or kill you, and their growing centralization and incessant "running to and fro" probably foreshadowed the rise of the Antichrist.[30] Furthermore, like sailors, railroad men developed the same unsavory reputation as gamblers, drunkards, and lechers.[31] And depots, as unregulated public spaces where young women could experience "familiarity between the sexes" and learn "coarse slangy language," were virtual training grounds for the "Red Light districts."[32]

In response to these anxieties, Orwig compiled more than 250 pages of instructive stories, inspirational poems, and impressive "railroad facts" in an effort to convince his readers that trains offered unprecedented opportunities for prosperity, safe travel, and effective evangelism.[33] "We cannot estimate the blessings resulting from the railroad," he told them. Foods from "temperate zones" and "colder regions," for example, are now "common affairs," and "our mail is laid upon our desk sometimes before we have finished our morning meal." To emphasize safety, a number of Orwig's selections depicted a member of the Godhead boarding a train to guide, protect, or anoint some traveling believer. And most railroad workers, though too often unchurched and given to alcohol, were dedicated professionals willing to risk their lives for the protection of their passengers. For Orwig, these railroad men became symbols of a vast, mobile harvest field steaming its way across America. Who would tell them—and the crude businessmen and careless youths they served—about "full salvation"? Orwig challenged his readers with stories of saints who battled the enemy for the soul of the rail system. Some were innocent children; others were bold "railroad evangelists" like Jennie Smith, popular representative of both the Women's Christian Temperance Union and the National Railroad YMCA, and F. W. Henck, founder of the East Tennessee Holiness Association best known for preaching in crowded depots and singing hymns of assurance whenever the train entered a long, dark tunnel.[34] Orwig's principle burden was to convince every reader to enter the battle for this contested space with a heartfelt prayer, a kind smile, or a timely word. He had a ready answer for any excuse: If one did not possess the courage or self-assurance to talk to sinners, at least one could scatter through trains and depots some of the many "salvation tracts" Orwig published. "Surely, it is a blessed work in which we can all engage. As it requires neither talent nor education, no one can plead inability."[35]

Orwig hoped that believers would come to see rail travel, for all its dangers, as a potential aid to effective Christian living. There is considerable evidence to suggest that Holiness proponents and their Pentecostal brethren learned this lesson well. Veteran and upstart evangelists alike left footpaths and horses behind at the first opportunity to ride the train. In an extreme example, W. B. Godbey reported traveling more than 10,000 miles in seven months during 1904, nearly all of it by rail, in pursuit of his "long cherished hopes for the conquest of the world for Christ."[36] Two years later, L. L. Pickett moved even faster, covering 6,500 miles in just ten weeks.[37] Such extensive travel required major investments of time and money. Thurman Cary, a young minister in the Fire-Baptized Holiness Church, recorded in his diary receiving a total of $188.28 in 1904, of which he gave $21.45 away and spent $83.40 on rail fare.[38] Heroic tales of walking home long distances from meetings abound in Holiness and Pentecostal narratives but this generally occurred when the evangelist failed to collect an offering sufficient to cover the return fare. Daniel Awrey, for instance, rode the train whenever he could but sometimes he received as little as twenty cents for several days of hard preaching. On one "missionary trip" early in his ministry, Awrey traveled "four hundred miles, all of which I walked with the exception of forty miles."[39] In 1895, he did walk over 1,000 miles from southeastern Tennessee to Texas but only because he heard the Lord say, "I have many people on the way who need the truth, and I want you to walk." Awrey obediently worked his way across the South on foot but upon crossing the Texas line he immediately boarded a fast train for the Marshall Camp Meeting.[40]

The Holiness press did its part to integrate railroading into every saint's worldview. Convention announcements and revival reports often combined the ring of boosterism with the flavor of alphabet soup. Consider H. G. Turner's 1894 description of the proposed camp meeting site at Asbury College: "I know of no other place in Kentucky better suited for a meeting. Wilmore is five miles from Nicholasville, the junction of the C. S. and R. N. I. & B. R. R's. It is twenty-five miles from Junction City, the crossing of the C. S. & L. & N. R. R's, about ten miles from Burgin the terminus of the L. S. It is only seventeen miles from Lexington and less than 100 miles from Cincinnati. It is easy access in every direction."[41] Other meeting places were selected with the railroad in mind. The Southern Illinois Holiness Association, for example, located their "Bonnie Camp" on "twenty acres of beautiful land" adjacent to the "Chicago & Eastern R. R.," and M. L. Yeakley chose to hold Holiness meetings in Martinsburg, West Virginia, so that "any one passing through on the main of the B. & O. can stop over and enjoy a 'feast of fat things.'"[42] Not to be left behind, the promoters of older camp meetings were careful to point out the distance to the nearest depot and the fact that "conveyance can be had."[43] In 1898, T. L. Adams suggested calling "a great central holiness convention. Fix the time and place at some railroad center, secure good rates for thirty days... and let's have Pentecost reenacted that the holiness movement may be so accelerated that it will speedily 'girdle the globe with salvation.'"[44] To help these world-changers on their way, many papers carried train schedules and the latest railroad news.[45]

By the turn of the century, few sanctified saints could deny that the virtual omnipresence of the railroad had created wonderful new opportunities for God's people, including easy access to Holiness conventions, camp meetings, colleges, and—best of all—whole communities where the message of "full salvation" had yet to take root. An advertisement for Meridian Women's College made the point visually by picturing six well-dressed young women on the rear platform of a luxury passenger car under a sign reading "Meridian—325 Miles."[46] Because of rail service, Lula Dudley was able to scatter her children from central Alabama to Holiness schools across the South during the late 1890s: "One of my boys entered Asbury College, Wilmore, Ky. The next school year, God opened the way, and another one entered the Holiness school at Meridian, Mississippi and the next year following, two of my boys with four of the boys and girls of our village, went to Ruskin Cave College, in Tennessee; and best of all," she added, "every one of them got saved."[47] Not only did the rails carry young people from sleepy villages to schools in neighboring states, they facilitated the close cooperation of veteran Holiness promoters in far-flung cities, like Martin Wells Knapp in Cincinnati and Seth Rees in Providence, and gave them access to the most remote landscapes and communities. For example, when Rees first traveled with Knapp into Kentucky's Bluegrass region, he found the "scenery at High Bridge" so "grand and majestic" that he had to remind himself it did "not compare with that of the country 'beyond Jordan.'"[48] Further along, he was thrilled to find himself with the opportunity to preach Holiness to "sturdy mountaineers" willing to leave their "one-roomed houses" in southern Kentucky and journey "in big wagons, on horseback, [and] afoot" up to forty miles to experience sanctification. Estimating that nearly three million more "unschooled and practically un-Christianized mountain people live in Tennessee, the Carolinas, and Virginia," Rees called on "Holiness idlers, gathered in self-preservative squads in New England," to "come here, buy land at $2.50 an acre and light up these old peaks with full salvation."[49]

Even more exciting was the rail system's ability to hurl evangelical publications and evangelists alike across the country at unprecedented speed. In 1918, Pentecostal preacher L. Howard Juillerat, a member of the Church of God (Cleveland, Tennessee), rejoiced that "six great transcontinental lines ... hurry over the plains, snort up the mountain passes and slide down the other side with their long trains of freight and human souls behind them." "Even the holiness preacher," he explained, "derives many benefits from rapid locomotion." While these included access to a shrinking world—like reading the "latest news from the ends of the earth" and eating "foods gathered from earth's remotest bounds"— Juillerat was more impressed by the fact that he could "hold a ten days meeting in Florida, close on Sunday night, get on the 'Dixie Flyer' and by Thursday night be ready to fight the devil in Milwaukee, the home of beer, or lay siege to Boston, the home of Christian Science." Just as the Roman highways "were a great aid to the spread of Christianity" in the first century, the "titanic force" of the railroads would help spread the gospel at a lightning pace as Christ's return drew near.[50]

The prominence of railroads in the Holiness and Pentecostal press raises serious doubts about persistent images of the movements as rural and countermodern.[51] In fact, a closer examination of both revivals suggests that they generally followed the rails from city to town to countryside.[52] In the hilly terrain of western Virginia and southern West Virginia, for example, Holiness missions first appeared in the Roanoke-Salem area, headquarters of the Norfolk & Western and Virginian railroads. Then they found their way to outlying boomtowns, like Pulaski and Bluefield, which connected Roanoke to the rich iron and coal fields in the mountains and ultimately to the mining camps themselves. A 1900 report from Salem evangelist J. W. Hypes illustrates this flow. Writing to the *Revivalist* from Bluefield, he was glad to report that he had moved beyond the city to take Holiness directly into the coal camps. Preaching three times a day, including "two miles underground" during the miners' lunch hour, Hypes found obvious delight "looking into the faces of Greeks, Jews, Africans, Hungarians, Italians, and Americans, as they sit in rows, faces all black alike, listening to this glorious truth."[53] The Holiness Movement first reached Galax, a mountaintop Virginia town at the end of a branchline from Pulaski, in 1906 when the local rail agent, who had embraced "full salvation" at a Beverly Carradine meeting in his native Salem, arranged for E. A. Ferguson to hold meetings at the Methodist church.[54] Once the Pentecostal revival moved through the area three years later, it followed the same tracks west from Roanoke. The key proponents were Edward D. Reeves, a Holiness preacher and railroad machinist, and several of his N & W coworkers. They found considerable success in industrial towns like

Radford and Pulaski in Virginia and Princeton and Bluefield in West Virginia, moderate success in the outlying mining camps and mill villages, and almost no success (except among a few kith and kin) in the farming communities where they were born. Consequently, one could expect to hear two distinctive sounds at most early Pentecostal meetings in the area: the thrilling shouts of victory and the shrill blasts of a nearby train whistle.[55]

COUNTING THE COSTS OF SPIRITUAL RAILROADING

Even in the afterglow of such glorious meetings, preachers still had to count the costs, which included the high cost of train tickets. Railroad companies helped spread the "red-hot gospel" into the hinterlands through the distribution of passes. Generally half fare, these special rates were administered through regional clergy bureaus and went only to ordained ministers (including pastors, evangelists, and missionaries) who devoted their "entire time to religious work" and depended "entirely upon the Lord" for their support.[56] Such requirements worked against preachers still dependent on secular employment to make ends meet, and against the many women belonging to organizations whose leaders could not bring themselves to ordain females but only grant them "preaching licenses" or "home missions credentials." Soon after the formation of the Assemblies of God, for example, Howard A. Goss broke the bad news that credentialed women evangelists "need not make applications for clergy rates over the railroads" because "the Clergy Bureau has definitely decided that" they do not qualify "on the grounds that they do not receive a guaranteed income." Goss stressed that "this does not apply to men who are properly ordained nor to foreign women missionaries," and that "the Railroads make these rules and not we ourselves." He could only advise female preachers "to trust God for full fare."[57]

Holiness and Pentecostal advocates who failed to qualify for half-price clergy passes, including women evangelists, could get help from the railroads when traveling to one of the increasingly frequent conventions, conferences, and assemblies. But it took considerable care and effort. The railroads' regulations, especially after the passage of the Hepburn Act in 1906, read much like instructions for filing a modern tax return—with multiple opportunities for mistakes and subtle changes in the requirements almost every year. Throughout most of the era, travelers to large Holiness and Pentecostal gatherings could expect to receive a significant discount on their return fares (anywhere from a one-third to a two-third rate) but only if they followed the procedures of the "certificate plan" to the letter. Therefore, editors of religious papers regularly devoted several columns of valuable space to these rules and gave them such headlines as "The Louisville Convention: Instructions in Regards to Rates," "Study This If You Are Coming," and even "Cut This Out and Paste It In Your Hat."[58] Despite the frequent warnings, misunderstandings created a constant source of headaches for the organizers of these gatherings.[59]

For most convention-goers and organizers, though, railroad discounts were worth the trouble. They afforded sanctified believers opportunities to mingle with like-minded brethren across an ever-widening territory—and sometimes "the power fell" before the meetings even started as godly companionship transformed trains into sacred spaces. For instance, having arrived in Louisville a day early for the 1905 Pentecostal Convention, C. F. Wimberly took "a trip over the Pewee Valley Suburban railroad, in company with Bro. Paul, to the home of Bro. Morrison." Wimberly noted the "scenery and accommodations" but what he enjoyed most was the spiritually charged fellowship: "We shall never forget the pleasures of that day. We sang, prayed, and counciled. *It was an Upper Room to us all.* The 'sound of the going in the mulberries' could be heard twenty-four hours before the first sermon was preached."[60]

Yet for all the railroad's ability to enrich the imagination and expand the experiences of the saints, a nagging ambivalence about all this "running to and fro" persisted. A 1914 letter from Harry V. Clarke, a member of the newly formed Assemblies of God, offered a sobering counterpoint to testimonies like Wimberly's. After reminding readers of the many missionaries who had "left every pleasure of the natural" to take Pentecost around the world, Clarke trained his sights on the "many saints in the home land" who are "spending thousands of God's dollars in attending conventions and camp-meetings and in traveling from place to place." Going from "one large assembly to another," they bypass many harvest fields in order to enjoy gatherings "where there are already so many workers that they are in each others' [sic] way." Suggesting that Pentecostals probably spent more each year traveling to meetings than they did reaching out to the lost, Clarke posed a troublesome question for all who enjoyed the many benefits of train travel: "Are the railroad companies getting the money the missionaries should have?"[61] As Harry Clarke's letter warns, the very innovation that could help reach a lost world in the "eleventh hour" before Christ's return also had the potential to deceive saints into steaming right past sinners on their way to enjoy a shouting good time with other believers. Apparently, spiritual railroading—like every other good thing in the Holiness-Pentecostal world—required constant vigilance against overindulgence to keep it on track.

CONCLUSION

Despite their wariness of the railroad—and of each other—Holiness and Pentecostal leaders mutually benefited from rail expansion and modeled fruitful engagement with the opportunities train travel offered to accelerate evangelism of the world. Many of them also appropriated technological innovations of the rail age to help people grasp the theological distinctions of their movements. Martin Wells Knapp was not the only evangelist to ride out to battle the world, flesh, and devil aboard the world's latest and most pervasive engineering accomplishment. Nor was he the only one to allow train imagery to enrich his preaching and writing in creatively relevant ways. Examples of these two sides of what Seth Rees dubbed "spiritual railroading" abound in the sermons, testimonies, ministry reports, fiction, and autobiographies produced by the presses of both movements, giving their publications a simultaneously countercultural and contemporary feel. Highly visible men and women in the Holiness Movement and its Pentecostal offspring counted the costs of "spiritual railroading" and found them favorable. For all its worldly dangers, train travel offered irresistible practical and inspiration value.

NOTES

The author thanks Glenn Gohr, Cheryl Hundley, Charles E. Jones, William Kostlevy, George Loveland, Louis Morgan, Erica Rutland, Randall Stephens, and H. Stanley York for help in securing some of the sources used in this chapter.

1. *Revivalist* (December 28, 1899): 12.

2. Quoted in A. M. Hills, *A Hero of Faith and Prayer; or, Life of Rev. Martin Wells Knapp* (Cincinnati: Mrs. M. W. Knapp, 1902), 137.

3. For an excellent survey of the late nineteenth-century Holiness Movement and its shaping of the subsequent Pentecostal Movement, see Vinson Synan, *The Holiness-Pentecostal Tradition: Charismatic Movements in the Twentieth Century* (Grand Rapids, MI: Eerdmans, 1997), 22–149.

4. For succinct discussions of rail ascendency in the late nineteenth and early twentieth century, see Ruth Schwartz Cowan, *A Social History of American Technology* (New York: Oxford University Press, 1997), 149–56; Albro Martin, *Railroads Triumphant: The Growth, Rejection, and Rebirth of a Vital American Force* (New York: Oxford University Press, 1992), 56–109; D. W. Meinig, *Transcontinental America, 1850–1915*, vol. 3 of *The Shaping of America: A Geographical Perspective on 500 Years of History* (New Haven: Yale University Press, 1998), 245–65.

5. Quoted in R. G. Robins, *A. J. Tomlinson: Plainfolk Modernist* (New York: Oxford University Press, 2004), 241n25.

6. These examples come from the April 1896 issue of the *Revivalist*, the only surviving "Railroad Edition" of the paper; and from two of Knapp's visual representations of the train metaphor: "The Two

Railroads" (*Revivalist* [April 13, 1899]: 7), and "Lost, Saved, Sanctified" (*Lightning Bolts from Pentecostal Skies* [Cincinnati: Office of the Revivalist, 1898], 32).

7. Knapp built his special "Railroad Edition" of the *Revivalist* around extensive excerpts from these two books ([April 1896], 2–8).

8. *New York State Census, 1875*; *Utica City Directory, 1883*; *New York State Census, 1905*.

9. See, e.g., Olin Marvin Owen, *Rum! Rags! Ruin!* (Utica, NY: T. J. Griffiths, 1889); Olin Marvin Owen, *The School Plot Unmasked, or, The Papal Conspiracy Against American Institutions* (Syracuse, NY: A. W. Hall, 1893); and Olin Marvin Owen, *Ingersoll Answered from the Bible and Ingersoll Against Himself* (Saratoga Springs, NY: John Johnson, 1886).

10. A bulletin insert provided by the United Methodist Church General Commission on Archives and History describes him as the "bishop who restricted heaven to the sanctified." John G. McEllhenney, "William Orwig, 1810–1889," http://www.gcah.org/history/biographies/william-orwig.

11. For example, Orwig wrote these words to the upstart Pentecostal paper *Bridegroom's Messenger*: "Surely there can be no[thing] greater than heart purity and the baptism with the Holy Ghost. May this come upon all of us in Pentecostal fullness" (January 15, 1909): 3.

12. The discussion that follows draws on Olin Marvin Owen, *The Great Celestial Railroad from the City of Sin to the City of God, the Only Direct and Through Line: With a Description of the Cars, Persons, Places and Scenes on the Route, from Notes Taken on the Way; Containing also a Brief Description of Opposition Roads; An Allegory* (Syracuse, NY: A. W. Hall, 1893), especially chapters 1–5 and 17–18. This is the edition Martin Wells Knapp used in his writings. *The Great Celestial Railroad* was first published four years earlier by T. J. Griffiths in Utica, NY.

13. Nathaniel Hawthorne, "The Celestial Railroad," in *Mosses from an Old Manse* (New York: Modern Library, 2003), 144–60.

14. Charles Edwin Jones, "The Railroad to Heaven," *North Dakota Quarterly* 40, no. 4 (Autumn 1972): 69–76.

15. The various routes available to Transgressor are handily mapped in the frontispiece of Owen's book. Cornell University Library has made this illustration ("Map Issued by G.C.R.R. According to Latest Surveys") available at https://digital.library.cornell.edu/catalog/ss:19343185.

16. *Great Celestial Railroad*, 137.

17. Ibid., 47–48.

18. Mrs. Missouri E. Wilson, "A Trip of a Preacher's Wife," *Pentecostal Herald* [hereinafter cited as *PH*] (August 3, 1898): 5. After assuming the editorship of *Kentucky Methodist*, Henry Clay Morrison took the paper in a strongly Holiness direction. In 1897, he renamed it *Pentecostal Herald*, nearly a decade before the Azusa Revival launched the modern Pentecostal Movement, in order to highlight the enhanced evangelistic power he believed was being restored to the end-time church.

19. "Give All, Get All," *PH* (September 2, 1908): 3.

20. *Great Celestial Railroad*, 142–43.

21. See, e.g., *Revivalist* (April 1896): 2.

22. Rev. Beverly Carradine, *The Sanctified Life* (Cincinnati: Office of the Revivalist, 1897), 237.

23. "Two Side-Tracks," *PH* (June 14, 1899): 6.

24. "One Thing I Want to Say," *PH* (October 25, 1899): 2–3. It should be noted that what Cary considered "side tracks," many of his contemporary Holiness writers considered vital parts of the "main line."

25. Carradine, *The Sanctified Life*, chapter 17 entitled "Sidetracks"; Elder A. H. Kauffman, *Fanaticism Explained*:

Symptoms, Cause and Cure (Grand Rapids, MI: By the author, 1904), 82–91.

26. W. B. Godbey, *Try the Spirits* (Greensboro, NC: Apostolic Messenger Publishing, n.d.), 8–9; John F. Knapp, "Off the Track," *PH* (September 26, 1906): 8.

27. "Report of the Camp Meeting, Alliance, Ohio," *Bridegroom's Messenger* (July 15, 1908): 2.

28. "Our Church History, Chapter X," *Pentecostal Holiness Advocate* (March 31, 1921): 9.

29. On the prevalence of anxiety about the dangers associated with the new public spaces created by railroad expansion in the late nineteenth century, see Amy G. Richter, *Home on the Rails: Women, the Railroad, and the Rise of Public Domesticity* (Chapel Hill: University of North Carolina Press, 2005), 32–57. Discomfort with the potential "worldliness" of the railroad persisted into the twentieth century, even after the Azusa Revival so successfully exploited the rail system to speed enthusiastic advocates of the emerging Pentecostal message across North America both in print and in person. On the railroads' role in the Azusa Revival, see Cecil M. Robeck Jr., *The Azusa Street Mission and Revival* (Nashville: Thomas Nelson, 2006), 53–56, 64–65, 95–98, and 108–9.

30. See, e.g., H. C. Morrison, "Watchman, What of the Night, No. IV: God's Attitude Toward the Trusts," *PH* (September 30, 1908): 1; G. F. Taylor, *The Second Coming of Jesus* (1916; repr., Franklin Springs, GA: Publishing of the Pentecostal Holiness Church, 1950), 23–24.

31. See, e.g., *The Experience of Charles C. Waterman, Conductor* (Colorado Springs, CO: Gospel Stationary & Tract House, n.d.).

32. Mrs. Lula M. Dudley, *Christine's Meditations, and Other Heart Messages to the Young* (Louisville, KY: Pentecostal Herald Publishing, n.d.), 34–37. Dudley was a Holiness stalwart who embraced the Pentecostal message late in life.

33. The discussion that follows draws on A. W. Orwig's *All Aboard; or, Entertaining and Instructive Incidents of Travel, with Useful Hints About Traveling* (Cleveland, OH: By the author, 1895). While Orwig gives some consideration to travel by stage and steamer, his primary focus is railroading.

34. For more on these two, see Jennie Smith, *Incidents and Experiences of a Railroad Evangelist* (Washington, DC: By the author, 1920); John S. Keen, *Memoir of F. W. Henck, with Notes and Comments* (Highway, KY: Bible Advocate Printers, 1899).

35. For an advertisement of Orwig's tracts, see *PH* (January 4, 1899): 14. See also his letter to *PH*, "Souls Saved Through Tracts" (October 11, 1899): 9.

36. "Ten Thousand Miles in Seven Months," *PH* (July 13, 1904): 7; "Ten Thousand Miles in Seven Months—Concluded," *PH* (August 17, 1904): 3–4.

37. "Bro. Pickett's Report," *PH* (September 19, 1906): 3.

38. A. E. Robinson, ed., *Memoirs of Thurman Augustus Cary* (Royston, GA: Live Coals Press, n.d.), 4.

39. "Life Sketches," *Latter Rain Evangel* (March 1910): 22.

40. "Life Sketches: Beaten With Many Stripes," *Latter Rain Evangel* (April 1910): 16.

41. "The Camp Meeting," *Kentucky Methodist* (January 18, 1894): 1.

42. R. E. Hoskinson, "Campmeeting Notice," *PH* (April 13, 1898): 6; Yeakley, "West Virginia," *PH* (March 9, 1898): 5.

43. See, e.g., "Dixie Holiness Camp-Meeting," *Kentucky Methodist* (August 23, 1894): 6.

44. "Magdalena, N. M.," *PH* (September 21, 1898): 6.

45. For examples of schedules, see any issue of *Kentucky Methodist*, *Pentecostal Herald*, or *Way of Faith and Neglected*

Themes from the 1890s. For railroad news, see "Secular News," *Kentucky Methodist* (September 17, 1891): 6; "Pullman, Illinois," *Kentucky Methodist* (January 25, 1894): 7; and brief notices in *PH* about "the largest shipment of wire fencing ever made at one time over any railroad" ([December 21, 1898]: 16) and the new Cotton Belt Bridge across the Mississippi ([April 26, 1904]: 13).

46. *PH* (July 29, 1908): 11. The text of the ad describes the school's location as "surrounded by native pines and fields of the country, yet within twenty minutes trolley ride of the heart of the city."

47. Mrs. Lula M. Dudley, *In the Sweet Clover Fields: Real Events in the Life of the Author* (Louisville, KY: Pentecostal Publishing, n.d.), 103.

48. "A Camp Meeting Campaign," repr. in Hills, *A Hero of Faith and Prayer*, 136–38. Rees was one of many evangelists to find inspiration at High Bridge (see, e.g., Z. O. Avery, "Trip to Meridian, Mississippi," *PH* [January 3, 1906]: 15).

49. "Flat Rock, Ky.," *PH* (September 28, 1898): 7.

50. "Many Shall Run To and Fro," *Church of God Evangel* (August 24, 1918): 1–2.

51. For a critique of the "farm to city" interpretation, see Daniel Woods, "Living in the Presence of God: Enthusiasm, Authority, and Negotiation in the Practice of Pentecostal Holiness" (PhD diss., University of Mississippi, 1997), 139n13.

52. For example, Woods, "Living in the Presence of God"; Robins, *A. J. Tomlinson*; and several of the biographical sketches in James R. Goff Jr. and Grant Wacker, eds., *Portraits of a Generation: Early Pentecostal Leaders* (Fayetteville: University of Arkansas Press, 2002), especially Edith L. Blumhofer's study of William H. Durham and Goff's chapter on Thomas Hampton Gourley, who was decapitated when the *Dixie Flyer* crashed in the north Georgia mountains.

53. "Bluefield, W. Va.," *Revivalist* (June 7, 1900): 11.

54. E. A. Ferguson, "In the Field: Galax, Va.," *PH* (February 21, 1906): 6.

55. Woods, "Living in the Presence of God," 135–52.

56. [E. N. Bell], "To Preachers," *Word and Witness* (December 20, 1912): 1. Clergy passes are one of the few railroad favors that survived the various regulations imposed by the federal government between the creation of the Interstate Commerce Commission in 1887 and World War I (see John F. Stover, *American Railroads* [Chicago: University of Chicago Press, 1961], 123, 139). For a contemporary reflection on the ethical propriety of clergy passes, see Rev. C. W. Warlick, *The Christian Ministry, or the Problem of the Church* (Reading, PA: I. M. Beaver, 1909), 270–73.

57. "Notice to Women Missionaries," *Word and Witness* (June 1915): 5. More research is needed to give a fuller picture of discrimination against women by the various railroad companies' Clergy Bureaus.

58. Headlines from *PH* (September 25, 1907): 3; (October 9, 1907): 4; and (July 29, 1908): 16. Sponsors of large Pentecostal gatherings, like A. J. Tomlinson of the Church of God (Cleveland, TN), gave railroad discounts the same high level of attention. See, e.g., his labored explanation of changes in the certificate plan between 1920 and 1921, including a larger minimum number of participants before the reduced fare would be honored and a significant decrease in the discount itself ("Come to the Assembly," *Church of God Evangel* [October 8, 1921]: 1).

59. For example, John Paul, in a short notice "To Those Disappointed in the Rates to Birmingham," described returning home to find "a number of railroad certificates sent to me by those who had to pay full fare" on the way home because they missed a new wrinkle in the validating procedure. "I take it," Paul added in a clearly

frustrated tone, "that all who have sent me these certificates have first tried to have the matter adjusted through their local agents" (*PH*, [November 25, 1908]: 13).

60. "Pentecostal Convention," *PH* (June 7, 1905): 2; emphasis added.

61. "Make Good Use of God's Money," *Christian Evangel* (December 26, 1914): 3.

BIBLIOGRAPHY

Periodicals
Bridegroom's Messenger (1908–9)
Christian Evangel (1910)
Church of God Evangel (1918–21)
Kentucky Methodist (1891–94)
Latter Rain Evangel (1910)
Pentecostal Herald (1897–1908)
Pentecostal Holiness Advocate (1921)
Revivalist (1896–1900)
Way of Faith and Neglected Themes (1894–97)
Word and Witness (1912–15)

Published Sources
Carradine, Rev. Beverly. *The Sanctified Life*. Cincinnati: Office of the Revivalist, 1897.
Cowan, Ruth Schwartz. *A Social History of American Technology*. Oxford: Oxford University Press, 1997.
Dudley, Mrs. Lula M. *Christine's Meditations, and Other Heart Messages to the Young*. Louisville, KY: Pentecostal Herald Publishing, n.d.
———. *In the Sweet Clover Fields: Real Events in the Life of the Author*. Louisville, KY: Pentecostal Publishing, n.d.
The Experience of Charles C. Waterman, Conductor. Colorado Springs, CO: Gospel Stationary & Tract House, n.d.
Godbey, W. B. *Try the Spirits*. Greensboro, NC: Apostolic Messenger Publishing, n.d.
Goff, James R., Jr., and Grant Wacker, eds. *Portraits of a Generation: Early Pentecostal Leaders*. Fayetteville: University of Arkansas Press, 2002.

Hawthorne, Nathaniel. "The Celestial Railroad." In *Mosses from an Old Manse*, 144–60. New York: Modern Library, 2003.
Hills, A. M. *A Hero of Faith and Prayer; or, Life of Rev. Martin Wells Knapp*. Cincinnati: Mrs. M. W. Knapp, 1902.
Jones, Charles Edwin. "The Railroad to Heaven." *North Dakota Quarterly* 40, no. 4 (Fall 1972): 69–76.
Kauffman, Elder A. H. *Fanaticism Explained: Symptoms, Cause and Cure*. Grand Rapids, MI: By the author, 1904.
Keen, John S. *Memoir of F. W. Henck, with Notes and Comments*. Highway, KY: Bible Advocate Printers, 1899.
Knapp, Martin Wells. *Lightning Bolts from Pentecostal Skies*. Cincinnati: Office of the Revivalist, 1898.
Martin, Albro. *Railroads Triumphant: The Growth, Rejection, and Rebirth of a Vital American Force*. New York: Oxford University Press, 1992.
McEllhenney, John G. "William Orwig, 1810–1889." http://www.gcah.org/history/biographies/william-orwig.
Meinig, D. W. *Transcontinental America, 1850–1915*. Vol. 3 of *The Shaping of America: A Geographical Perspective on 500 Years of History*. New Haven: Yale University Press, 1998.
New York State Census, 1875.
New York State Census, 1905.
Orwig, A. W. *All Aboard; or, Entertaining and Instructive Incidents of Travel, with Useful Hints About Traveling*. Cleveland, OH: By the author, 1895.

Owen, Olin Marvin. *The Great Celestial Railroad from the City of Sin to the City of God, the Only Direct and Through Line: With a Description of the Cars, Persons, Places and Scenes on the Route, from Notes Taken on the Way; Containing also a Brief Description of Opposition Roads; An Allegory.* Syracuse, NY: A. W. Hall, 1893.

Richter, Amy G. *Home on Rails: Women, the Railroad, and the Rise of the Public Domesticity.* Chapel Hill: University of North Carolina Press, 2005.

Robeck, Cecil M., Jr. *The Azusa Street Mission and Revival.* Nashville: Thomas Nelson, 2006.

Robins, R. G. *A. J. Tomlinson: Plainfolk Modernist.* New York: Oxford University Press, 2004.

Robinson, A. E., ed. *Memoirs of Thurman Augustus Cary.* Royston, GA: Live Coals Press, n.d.

Smith, Jennie. *Incidents and Experiences of a Railroad Evangelist.* Washington, DC: By the author, 1920.

Stover, John F. *American Railroads.* Chicago: University of Chicago Press, 1961.

Synan, Vinson. *The Holiness-Pentecostal Tradition: Charismatic Movements in the Twentieth Century.* Grand Rapids, MI: Eerdmans, 1997.

Taylor, G. F. *The Second Coming of Jesus.* 1916. Reprint, Franklin Springs, GA: Publishing of the Pentecostal Holiness Church, 1950.

Utica City Directory, 1883.

Warlick, Rev. C. W. *The Christian Ministry, or the Problem of the Church.* Reading, PA: I. M. Beaver, 1909.

Woods, Daniel. "Living in the Presence of God: Enthusiasm, Authority, and Negotiation in the Practice of Pentecostal Holiness." PhD diss., University of Mississippi, 1997.

CHAPTER 6

Black Radical Holy Women at the Intersection of Christian Unity and Social Justice

Cheryl J. Sanders

This chapter explores the contributions of several black women leaders whose social witness influenced the emergence of two successive religious movements in the United States: the Radical Holiness Movement in the nineteenth century and Pentecostalism in the twentieth century. The women chosen for this study represent several denominational traditions. Evangelist Amanda Berry Smith was a member of the African Methodist Episcopal Church. The women who ministered alongside William J. Seymour during the Azusa Street Revival were from the Holiness or "sanctified" tradition. Lizzie Robinson and Lillian Brooks Coffey were two pioneering church mothers of the Church of God in Christ. Three models of Christian social witness are ascribed to these women to interpret how they operated under the rubric of exilic ecclesiology "in the world, but not of it" as they followed Jesus: (1) cosmopolitan evangelism, (2) egalitarian revivalism, and (3) sanctified civic engagement. Because of their race, sex, and social class, these women were uniquely positioned to confront and dismantle barriers to Christian unity and social transformation. Their efforts in this regard will be evaluated here from two distinct vantage points, the social ethics of H. Richard Niebuhr and the womanist thought of Alice Walker, with a view toward understanding how the Christian witness of these black female Holiness leaders evolved into an emergent Social Gospel. A preliminary step to begin this analysis is a brief historiographical overview of the Radical Holiness Movement and black women's participation in the Sanctified Churches.

RADICAL HOLINESS, EXILIC ECCLESIOLOGY, AND BLACK WOMEN IN THE SANCTIFIED CHURCHES

The term "Radical Holiness" is used here in reference to those Holiness groups whose commitment to the doctrine and experience of entire sanctification as a second work of grace set them apart from other denominations. These groups were comprised of those whose testimony of the baptism of the Holy Spirit caused them either to "come out" or be "put out" of their churches and communions. Donald Dayton noted that some of these movements were rooted in a call to the sanctification of people and society, embracing "both a greater 'piety' and a greater 'radicalism' than characterized the mainstream churches of their time."[1] This call to sanctification of both self and society caused them to place a moral value on everything from smoking, drinking, and card-playing to poverty, slavery, and war. The earliest social justice concern of the Holiness Movement was abolitionism, and agitation on the race issue led to concern for the equality of women. In fact, the first women's rights convention was held in the Wesleyan Methodist Church of Seneca Falls, New York. Priority was given in the Holiness churches to ministry among the poor and oppressed, and the rescue mission movement is largely the product of Holiness initiative. The Holiness and Pentecostal churches also assumed a pacifist stance in the early decades.[2]

Generally speaking, restorationism signifies a return to the doctrine and practices of the New Testament Church in pursuit of a purer and more ancient form of Christianity. Steven Ware's research on Radical Holiness as a restorationist movement has added the important insight that the wedding of restorationism to the experience of entire sanctification set the stage for the more explicit restorationism of Pentecostalism as it developed in the early twentieth century.[3] The sanctified restorationists believed that they had discovered the key to unlocking the door to Christian unity: "the experience of entire sanctification, through which all desires to do or be anything other than a follower of Jesus Christ were obliterated and replaced with the fullness of the Holy Spirit's presence."[4] In his book *Ye That Are Men Now Serve Him: Radical Holiness Theology and Gender in the South*, Colin Chapell described how Radical Holiness leaders claimed an identity rooted in a distinct process of sanctification that separated them from, and elevated them above, everyone else, not based upon socioeconomic class, biological sex, or even racial identity but rather a spiritual state that freed them from the restrictions of their culture.[5] The major ethical themes of the Radical Holiness Movement linked personal piety to social responsibility, fostered a renewed vision of Christian unity, and nullified race, class, and sex as markers of cultural identity and privilege.

The term "ecclesiology" indicates the nature, role, and function of the church in relation to the world. Holiness and Pentecostal movements can be characterized in terms of three predominant but distinctive ecclesiologies: (1) exilic—"in the world, but not of it"; (2) fluidic—signifying no separation between the sacred and secular; and (3) aesthetic—"of the church but not in it." The exilic ecclesiology originates with the marginalization of the Holiness ministers and movements who were drawn out of the Protestant mainstream because of their attraction to stricter articulations of the Methodist doctrine of sanctification and/or their rejection of aspects of the autonomous, congregational polity of the Baptist churches.[6] Adherents of exilic ecclesiology were free to conduct their worship and live their lives in a manner consistent with the hermeneutic they applied to the biblical mandate: "Love not the world, neither the things that are in the world." (1 John 2:15a) Fluidic ecclesiology, on the other hand, endorses the worldly identity and aspirations of the churches and their congregants, while aesthetic ecclesiology names the imprint of church-based spiritual formation as it finds expression in the perspectives and performance styles of artists and intellectuals who have left the church but retain its deep spiritual sensibilities in their work.[7]

The historiography of black participation in the Radical Holiness and Pentecostal movements begins with attention to the contributions of William J. Seymour, chief apostle of the Azusa Street Revival, and Charles Harrison Mason, bishop and founder of the Church of God in Christ (COGIC). However, there are several books that bring specific focus to the roles of black women in the Radical Holiness and Pentecostal movements. *The Sanctified Church* is a collection of essays by Zora Neale Hurston published in 1981 based on anthropological research she conducted earlier in the twentieth century.[8] She defined the Sanctified Church as "a protest against the high-brow tendency in Negro Protestant congregations as the Negroes gain more education and wealth." It is related to African religion, white "protest Protestantism" (her designation for the Holiness Movement), and Haitian *vaudou*. Hurston noted the existence of "strong sympathy" between the white and Negro "saints" and the predominance of women adherents. Cheryl Townsend Gilkes published several of her own sociological studies of women in the Sanctified Church tradition, and especially within the Church of God in Christ, in her 2001 anthology *If It Wasn't for the Women*. Anthea Butler's historical text *Women in the Church of God in Christ: Making a Sanctified World* (2007) provided an insightful analysis of the leadership, impact, and organization of COGIC women in the church and society. Susan Hill Lindley devoted significant attention to black women in the Holiness and Pentecostal churches in her general history of women and religion in America, *"You Have Stept out of Your Place"* (1996). Susie Stanley included Zilpha Elaw, Julia Foote, Jarena Lee, Amanda Berry Smith, and several other black women in *Holy Boldness*, her comprehensive analysis of the spiritual autobiographies of women preachers in the Wesleyan/Holiness tradition, published in 2002. Other useful sources on black women in the Holiness and Pentecostal movements include Adrienne M. Israel's biography of *Amanda Berry Smith* (1998), Estrelda Y. Alexander's biographical sketches of *The Women of Azusa Street* (2012), and Bettye Collier-Thomas's history of African American women and religion, *Jesus, Jobs, and Justice* (2010). Also of special interest here is Judith Casselberry's *The Labor of Faith* (2017), the first sustained ethnographic study of black Apostolic women in the Church of Our Lord Jesus Christ.

"IN THE WORLD, BUT NOT OF IT": MODELS OF BLACK WOMEN'S SANCTIFIED SOCIAL WITNESS

These and other studies of black women in the Holiness and Pentecostal movements offer data from which can be discerned three models of Christian social witness that operated under the general rubric of exilic ecclesiology, toward the end of illuminating our understanding of what it meant for these women to operate "in the world, but not of it" as they followed Jesus. Each of these models is associated with a black woman or group of women in the radical Holiness and/or Pentecostal tradition: the cosmopolitan evangelism of Amanda Berry Smith, the egalitarian revivalism of the Azusa Street washwomen, and the sanctified civic engagement of the COGIC church mothers, Lizzie Robinson and Lillian Brooks Coffey.

Amanda Berry Smith (1837–1915) was born to enslaved parents in Maryland. After her father was able to purchase his family's freedom, she moved with her family to Pennsylvania and later to New York. She became converted to Christianity in 1856 while kneeling in prayer in the basement of the Quaker family who employed her as a maid. Her testimony of sanctification occurred under the preaching of the Methodist Holiness leader John Inskip in 1868. Soon thereafter she became an evangelist who ministered at churches, camp meetings, and conventions of the Women's Christian Temperance Union in the United States and abroad.[9] She endured criticism and rejection on the basis of her race, sex, and social class. However, it was her experience of racism that gave her insight into the social ethical implications of sanctification: "But if you want to know and understand properly what Amanda Smith has to contend with, just

Fig. 6.1 Amanda Berry Smith. Frontispiece of her *An Autobiography: The Story of the Lord's Dealings with Mrs. Amanda Smith; The Colored Evangelist* (Chicago: Meter and Brother, 1893).

turn black and go about as I do. And I think some people would understand the quintessence of sanctifying grace if they could be black about twenty-four hours."[10] When Smith sought someone to receive her mantle of leadership, she chose a young woman, Mary McLeod Bethune (1875–1955), and consecrated her with a prayer: "I remember when dear Amanda Smith came to me one day and said: 'Mary McLeod Bethune, I have been to Africa three times; I have traveled around the world; I have been looking for someone upon whom to throw my mantle. As I talk with you, Mary Bethune, I believe you are the one to wear my mantle. Get down here child, and let us pray.'"[11]

Several black women were involved in the leadership of the Azusa Street Revival in Los Angeles, California, from 1906 to 1908, as documented by Estrelda Alexander in her book, *The Women of Azusa Street*.[12] Among them are Julia Hutchins, Neely Terry, Lucy Farrow, and Jennie Moore Seymour, the wife of the leader of the Revival, William J. Seymour. His testimony, published in the first edition of the *Apostolic Faith* newspaper, was that the Revival centered on the work of black Holiness washwomen who fostered the emergence of Christian unity by disregarding barriers of race, sex, and class: "The work began among the colored people. God baptized several sanctified wash women with the Holy Ghost, who have been much used of Him. The first white woman to receive the Pentecost and gift of tongues in Los Angeles was Mrs. Evans who is now in the work in Oakland. Since then multitudes have come. God makes no difference in nationality, Ethiopians, Chinese, Indians, Mexicans, and other nationalities worship together."[13] This egalitarian revivalism was further informed by Seymour's commitment to holiness and unity in keeping with his exposure to the teachings of the Evening Light Saints of the Church of God while living in Indianapolis, Indiana, and in Cincinnati, Ohio, at God's Bible School several years prior to the Revival.[14]

Anthea Butler's book provides detailed spiritual biographies of COGIC women leaders during the formative decades of the denomination after the Azusa Street Revival. Two of them, Lizzie Robinson and Lillian Brooks Coffey, were the first to hold the office of General Mother and Supervisor of the Women's Department. Both were cherished assistants to Bishop Mason. They made significant contributions to guide the growth and organization of the denomination through the first half of the twentieth century.

Mother Lizzie Robinson (1860–1945) was born to enslaved parents in rural Arkansas, where she spent her early childhood working in the fields and in the home of the white slaveowners. She became sanctified in 1901 after studying the *Hope* newspaper written and distributed by Joanna Moore, a Baptist home missionary to the South who promoted Holiness and sanctification through her newspaper and Bible Bands. In a letter written in 1908, Moore described the transition of Lizzie Robinson from washwoman to Bible teacher as a dramatic and transformative answer to Moore's prayer: "One day several years ago I visited her home in Pine Bluff; she was earning her living by washing; I knelt with her by the washtub and asked God to take her hands out of that tub and fill them with Bibles and send her from house to house to feed hungry souls with the Bread of Life. God has answered my prayer. Glory to his Name!"[15]

Mother Robinson sold subscriptions to *Hope*, distributed Bibles, and was trained as a home missionary worker at a Baptist training academy. When Bishop Mason preached at the Baptist training academy in 1911, she received the baptism of the Holy Spirit, speaking in tongues. Subsequently, she was disfellowshipped by the Baptists. She moved to Memphis, Tennessee, and in 1912 was appointed by Bishop Mason to establish the women's work in the Church of God in Christ. Under her thirty-three years of leadership, COGIC women established new congregations, started Bible studies and prayer groups, engaged in home and foreign missions work, and raised funds for building a national denominational headquarters in Memphis.[16] Mother Robinson died of cardiac arrest in 1945

Fig. 6.2 Mother Lizzie Robinson, ca. 1930s. Courtesy of Flower Pentecostal Heritage Center.

Fig. 6.3 Mother Lillian Brooks Coffey standing in front of her home, ca. 1960s. Courtesy of Flower Pentecostal Heritage Center.

at the age of eighty-five. Her funeral was held in the newly completed Mason Temple, and the eulogy was offered by Bishop Mason. Her assistant, Lillian Brooks Coffey, officiated at the service and was installed as her successor as General Mother.[17]

Mother Coffey was born in Paris, Tennessee, in 1891. Her grandfather was a Baptist minister and an acquaintance of Brother Mason before he was disfellowshipped by the Baptists. She was converted at an early age while attending a Sunday school established by Brother Mason. He chose her to be trained and mentored for future leadership of the COGIC women. Mother Coffey's leadership focus was distinctly different from Mother Robinson's because she placed a greater emphasis upon connecting with black women leaders, with women's organizations, and with elected officials to foster civic engagement. After her death in 1964, a telling acknowledgment of her legacy of leadership was published in the COGIC magazine, *The Evangelist Speaks*: "We sincerely regret the loss of Dr. Coffey as she was an outstanding patriarch." Butler's summary of Mother Coffey's impact charts a transition in sanctified approaches to ecclesiology and civic engagement: "Coffey was able to expand the visible and material definitions of sanctification to a more modern expression of sanctified womanhood to include civic engagement and black prosperity, helping to shed the image of sanctified church members as poor and otherworldly."[18]

CHRIST AND CULTURE: A SOCIAL ETHICAL ANALYSIS OF BLACK RADICAL HOLY WOMEN

H. Richard Niebuhr's classic text *Christ and Culture*, first published in 1951, has stayed in print for seven decades. His typology remains a useful and relevant tool for assessing the relationship between Christians and society.[19] The five types Niebuhr set forth to characterize Christ and culture will be used here to analyze the nuances of exilic ecclesiology represented among the black Radical Holiness and Pentecostal women in this study, with particular focus on their alternate modes of following Jesus in their own time and context. These types and corresponding designations identify the various ways that Christians follow Christ in society, namely:

- Christ against culture: Radicals who emphasize the opposition between Christ and culture, and whose allegiance to Christ obligates them to pursue holiness and reject worldliness.
- Christ of culture: Accommodationists who recognize the agreement between Christ and culture, and who identify Christ with its highest ideals and values.
- Christ above culture: Synthesists whose primary encounter with Christ occurs in the realm of the supernatural, both now and in the hereafter.
- Christ and culture in paradox: Dualists who acknowledge allegiance to two separate realms, "living precariously and sinfully in the hope of a justification which lies beyond history."[20]
- Christ transforming culture: Conversionists whose commitment to Christ empowers them with vision, mandates, and strategies for changing the world.

Niebuhr's typology and designations offer insight into the key inquiry of this study: How did these women follow Jesus in the church and society? In the case of Amanda Berry Smith, the cosmopolitan evangelist who followed Jesus by traveling internationally to disciple people in all nations, the type is Christ above culture. The Azusa washwomen, egalitarian revivalists, followed Jesus by performing miracles of healing and deliverance in his name across the barriers of race, sex, social class, and language, also in keeping with Christ above culture. The COGIC church mothers followed Jesus by organizing black women to sanctify the world. Especially when viewed in light of their participation with Mary McLeod Bethune and the National Council of Negro Women, the World Council of Churches, and other organizations beyond the scope of their denomination, their sanctified civic engagement exemplifies the type Christ transforming culture.

What correlation, if any, can be detected between the extreme types, Christ against culture and Christ of culture, and the Christian witness of black Holiness women? Briefly, a reading of Judith Casselberry's study of contemporary Church of Our Lord Jesus Christ (COOLJC) Apostolic women in Brooklyn, New York, suggests that these women follow Jesus by strict adherence to ethical practices of holiness, including tongues-speaking, highly restrictive dress codes, and intense involvement in emotional, intimate, and aesthetic work, that is, the labor of faith.[21] Their rigid restorationism resonates with the type Christ against culture. The opposite extreme, the Christ of culture type, may be exemplified by the modern COGIC wives whom Butler holds responsible for the demise of civic engagement in the women's work after the death of Mother Coffey. In Butler's view, the women whose leadership derived directly from their roles as wives of COGIC bishops became preoccupied with internal concerns such as fashionable hats and clothing "as beautifully dressed foils to the bishops and pastors of the denomination."[22] An ethos of regressive accommodationism encouraged these women to follow Jesus in compliance with a patriarchal politics of respectability that entailed a prosperity gospel aesthetic.

The remaining type from Niebuhr's scheme is Christ and culture in paradox. Who are the dualists among the black women of the Radical Holiness and Pentecostal movements? Following Donald Dayton's historiographical and theological interpretation of the relationship between the Holiness Movements and mainstream Protestantism, the best fit for Christ and culture in paradox in this analysis might be the antiblack Protestantism these holy black women encountered when they promoted cosmopolitan, egalitarian, and socially transformative sensibilities in their efforts to follow Jesus. Dayton noted how theological opposition to Holiness social ethics was grounded historically in Christian realism, especially that of nineteenth-century Princeton theologians, who "argued explicitly that slavery and political despotism were morally indifferent from the perspective of Christian faith," and who used the themes of "Christian realism" to undermine the impact of the Christian abolitionists—so much so that their writings were printed in volumes defending the institution of slavery.[23] After the Civil War and the end of slavery, antiblack Protestants in the South sometimes gave extremely crude and profane expression to dualist views of race and religion. In his study of black Holiness and Pentecostal movements, Clarence Hardy has documented the contempt expressed several years after the founding of the Church of God in Christ by a Baptist minister in southeastern Texas who used racist expletives to warn his Baptist colleagues about Mason's group: "You fellows better be careful if you go down there. Them damned niggers got the Bible cold, on everything they say. They're going exactly by it."[24] Pamela E. Klassen's 2004 study "The Robes of Womanhood: Dress and Authenticity among African American Methodist Women in the Nineteenth Century" gives a detailed account of how the AME women preachers used plain dress and educators used more fashionable wardrobe choices to signify spirituality and respectability, respectively. However, there were places in society where these nuanced messages of spirituality and status were obliterated by antiblack sentiment: "The plain dress of Amanda Berry Smith and Sojourner Truth and the respectable dress of Frances Harper and Ida B. Wells may have conveyed different religious messages, but their insistence on entering public, white-dominated space as ladies led to at least one similar ordeal—they were all driven from trains, streetcars, or churches because they were black, regardless of what they were wearing."[25] Klassen concludes that notwithstanding these blatant and frequent acts of racial discrimination, black Holiness women maintained discourses of authenticity that "were often remarkably critical, both of self-motivation and of cultural markers of class, race, and gender in a world that made a fetish of whiteness."[26]

WOMANIST PERSPECTIVES ON BLACK RADICAL HOLY WOMEN

One of the most significant intellectual influencers of black women's religious thought and theological discourse is Alice Walker. In the preface of her 1983 collection of prose essays, *In Search of Our Mothers' Gardens*, Walker set forth a detailed definition of black feminism to introduce the term "womanist". Since that time, womanist approaches to the study of religion and society have come into play with the emergence of black feminist theologians, ethicists, historians, and sociologists who have been influenced by her definition and insights in their collective body of work. Womanist scholars have devoted special attention to investigating the representation of black women and their experiences in both primary and secondary sources. Primary sources document black women's own spiritual autobiographies, letters, and interviews. Secondary sources include the work of black women scholars who have immersed themselves in these women's sacred spaces, perused their documents, and produced detailed historical, sociological, ethical, theological, and anthropological analyses of black women's lives and work. Their intent has not been to exclude or discount the importance of primary and secondary sources created by men or by white women but rather to assign priority to bringing the black woman's experience and vantage point to bear upon scholarship that examines the contributions of black women to religion and society.

Gilkes has observed that Walker's definition of womanist organizes and interprets the heroic historical experience of African American women with reference to their femaleness, their relationship to community, their strategies for change, and their cultural emphases. Walker's definition signifies a holistic and universalist commitment to the community's survival. Gilkes has argued that "given the pivotal place of African-American women in the racial-ethnic, class, and gender hierarchies of American culture, a ministry that concentrates on their empowerment should benefit the entire community."[27]

To label any of these black Radical Holiness women as womanists would be a misnomer, if not also an anachronism. No one among them may measure up in every way to the stringent, overarching egalitarian feminism inherent in Walker's articulation of womanism, but there are facets of this definition that resonate with key aspects of these women's lives and leadership. What follows, then, is a series of illustrations revealing significant points of convergence between the witness of sanctified black women and select trajectories of womanist thought as ordered in Walker's definition.[28] Five such trajectories are offered for consideration:

1. Responsible, in charge, serious;
2. Appreciates and prefers women's culture, emotional flexibility, strength;
3. Traditionally universalist (with respect to skin color diversity);
4. Traditionally capable; and
5. Loves struggle. Loves the Folk. Loves herself. Regardless.

Mother Lillian Brooks Coffey is an exemplar of the womanist ideal described as "responsible, in charge, serious." Butler's history of COGIC women includes photographs of Mother Coffey that depict her as a responsible, in charge, and serious personality, whether poised at her desk with pen in hand, presiding over an assembly from a podium, posing in front of the White House, or seated in the company of elected officials.[29] Her fashionable dress, hairstyles, and demeanor signified the advancement of sanctified women in culture and class sophistication. As a young woman she was chosen and authorized by Bishop Mason to lead the COGIC women. She excelled in public speaking, administration, and fund-raising. Coffey was an exceptional preacher and a prolific church founder, who established COGIC congregations throughout the Midwest, in Wisconsin, Ohio, Michigan, and Illinois. Her establishment of the National Women's Convention and the Lillian Brooks Coffey Rest Home in Detroit offer further evidence of the serious impact and effectiveness of her leadership.[30] Citing COGIC oral tradition, Gilkes noted that Mother Coffey was a militant leader of legendary proportions, a feminist, and an energetic supporter of the black women's club movement who "engineered the Women's Convention's participation in larger black women's movements through her close relationship to Mary McLeod Bethune."[31] Her reputation for responsible serious leadership extended far beyond her denominational work. She was featured in *Ebony* magazine as an exceptional leader among church women: "Women church leaders in most denominations are generally strong-minded enough to deal with God and a male hierarchy, but few can hold a candle to Lillian Brooks Coffey, indomitable General Supervisor of the Church of God in Christ's Women's Department." The *Ebony* article further described Coffey as "stern, authoritative, vigorous, and forceful."[32] This posture was attested by Coffey's own words: "I am a servant of the most high God. God gave me this appointment and no man can take it from me."[33]

Mother Coffey's noble predecessor, Mother Lizzie Robinson, exhibited a distinctly different facet of womanism: "appreciates and prefers women's culture, emotional flexibility, strength." Mother Robinson was the first church mother in the COGIC denomination, the official head of women's ministry appointed by Bishop Mason. As mentioned earlier, prior to her becoming a Pentecostal, Mother Robinson had been recruited and trained by Baptist home missionary Joanna Moore to teach and disciple poor black women in her home state of Arkansas in the aftermath of slavery. Her leadership focused on the roles and responsibilities of women to their families, blending the principles of motherhood, homemaking, and cleanliness into a doctrine of sanctification. According to Butler, "Robinson had influenced the temporal and spiritual lives of black women who were at the margins of American society and COGIC, organizing them through the office most revered by the black community: motherhood." This emphasis upon motherhood not only created a space for women's culture to flourish; it also changed the course of the denomination, transforming it from "merely a sanctified church" to a large woman's organization that conveyed and embodied the message of Holiness.[34] Mother Robinson was strict and austere in her approach to developing the spirituality of COGIC women while maintaining subjection to the exclusive leadership and authority of men to perform the tasks of ordained ministry. Her emphasis upon teaching, as distinct from preaching, made space for the instruction and empowerment of women to flourish without infringement upon the patriarchal privilege of men. Under Mother Robinson, women were required to dress based on traditional Victorian values and the holiness ethos of moderation and piety—ankle-length skirts, long sleeves, no makeup or facial cosmetics, natural (unstraightened) hair pulled back in a bun— as she herself is depicted in photographs published in Butler's text.[35] These images convey her deep commitment to a distinctive ethos of feminine spirituality that came to be associated with the sanctified tradition in general.

Traditionally universalist, as in: "Mama, why are we brown, pink, and yellow, and our cousins are white, beige, and black?" Ans. "Well, you know the colored race is like a flower garden, with every color flower represented."[36] Amanda Berry Smith self-identified as a colored washerwoman who became an evangelist. Her international experiences crossing boundaries of race, nationality, culture, and language gave her a universalist point of view. Smith held deep convictions linking her understanding of sin, salvation, and sanctification to the problem of antiblack color prejudice. In her view, salvation converted discriminatory attitudes and practices based on skin color, and sanctification cleansed away color prejudice. These perspectives are illustrated in her account of a newly converted white woman who instantaneously overcame her skin color prejudice:

> One dear woman that I met last fall at the Saturday night holiness meeting, told me she was converted at that meeting; also her husband and two children. She told me how she disliked me because I was a colored woman; how she went to church full of prejudice, but when God saved her He took it all out, and now she loves me as a sister and thinks I have a beautiful color! Of course, I call that a good conversion to begin with. Some people don't get enough of the blessing to take prejudice out of them, even after they are sanctified.

Smith regarded her own dark skin color as God's gift, signifying royalty rather than disdain: "we who are the royal black are very well satisfied with His gift to us in this substantial color. I, for one, praise Him for what He has given me, although at times it is very inconvenient." She gave sobering illustrations of this understated "inconvenience" of racial discrimination and exclusion based upon her travels to major cities such as Philadelphia, New York, Baltimore, and Austin, Texas, where she was barred from hotels and restaurants because of her color, despite her ability to pay, her proper behavior, and her elegant attire: "I could pay the price—yes, that is all right; I know how to behave—yes, that is alright; I may have on my very best dress so that I look elegant—yes, that is alright; I am known as a Christian lady—yes, that is alright; I will occupy but one chair; I will touch no person's plate or fork—yes, that is alright; but you are black!" Smith was resolved to put up with this "inconvenience" with prayerful anticipation of a future "where all these little things will be lost because of their absolute smallness! May the Lord send the future to meet us! Amen."[37]

Walker alluded directly to the leadership legacy of Harriet Tubman in the part of her definition that denoted the womanist concept of capability: "Traditionally capable, as in Mama, I'm walking to Canada and I'm taking you and a bunch of other slaves with me." Reply: "It wouldn't be the first time."[38] Sarah Bradford's *Harriet Tubman: The Moses of Her People* describes Tubman's rescue of her parents from slavery in Maryland to freedom in Canada, the specific event referenced in Walker's definition: "In 1857 she made her most venturesome journey, for she brought with her to the North her old parents, who were no longer able to walk such distances as she must go by night. Consequently she must hire a wagon for them, and it required all her ingenuity to get them through Maryland and Delaware safe. She accomplished it, however, and by the aid of her friends she brought them safe to Canada, where they spent the winter."[39] The traditional capability readily associated with Tubman's story includes courage, vision, and resourcefulness. As a young girl who had been born into slavery on the Eastern Shore of Maryland, Tubman suffered a cracked skull when a slaveowner hurled a weight at her. She survived the assault but the damage to her brain left her with several permanent impairments: a sleeping disorder, a predisposition to vibrant dreams and visions, and loss of certain inhibitions, including the inability to experience fear. However, these disabilities enhanced her leadership capabilities in ironic and uncanny ways. First, the neurological damage she suffered influenced the force and frequency of the visions of freedom that motivated her escape from slavery and her repeated efforts to rescue others. Second, her inability to sleep through the night enabled her to make optimal use of the cover of darkness the night provided to conduct her missions undetected. Third, her courage in the face of danger, threats, and uncertainty was directly related to her inability to process fear. Even Tubman's resourcefulness can be associated with her lack of inhibition when it came to appealing to others for money or assistance.[40]

Loves struggle. Loves the Folk. Loves herself. Regardless. This part of Walker's definition of womanism finds expression in the life and witness of Mary McLeod Bethune, the celebrated educator and clubwoman who served as a member of President Franklin Delano Roosevelt's Black Cabinet, was founder and president of Bethune-Cookman University in Daytona Beach, Florida, and headed the National Council of Negro Women. As a Christian she identified with the Presbyterian and Methodist churches but her affiliations with the Holiness Movement and Pentecostalism were substantive and significant. For example, Bethune was the first black student to enroll in Moody Bible Institute, where she was trained in evangelism and experienced the baptism of the Holy Spirit at a meeting led by Dwight L. Moody.[41] And as has been noted earlier, as a young woman Bethune was endowed with a mantle of spiritual leadership during a chance encounter with the aging evangelist Amanda Berry Smith. In later years Bethune worked collegially with Mother Coffey and other Holiness women leaders to organize black women for social change. Her empathy for black suffering and her vision of the ongoing struggle for freedom and equality were set forth in her "Last Will and Testament," a series of bequests that were circulated widely by the black press shortly before her death. Bethune's list of bequests began with love: "Loving your neighbor means being interracial, interreligious and international." Her final bequest exhorted black youth to continue to struggle for justice and freedom: "Our children must never lose their zeal for building a better world. They must not be discouraged from aspiring toward greatness, for they are to be the leaders of tomorrow. Nor must they forget that the masses of our people are still underprivileged, ill-housed, impoverished and victimized by discrimination. . . . The Freedom Gates are half ajar. We must pry them fully open."[42] Bethune's love for black people was underscored by her self-love as a dark-skinned, African-featured woman who took great pride in the pure Africanity of her family lineage, regardless of the reigning color elitism of her era.[43]

In summary, these selective convergences of Radical Holiness black women's experiences with womanist principles signify the social ethical character of their collective witness as serious, compassionate, capable women committed to universal ideals of justice, freedom, and love.

CONCLUSION: VISION AND VOICES OF A SANCTIFIED SOCIAL GOSPEL

In her 1990 study "'Neglected Voices' and 'Praxis' in the Social Gospel," Susan Lindley underscored the key factor that has distinguished the Social Gospel from traditional religious charity and reform, namely, "recognition of structural evil and corporate sin, salvation, and identity, along with emphasis on individual sin, faith, and conversion."[44] Her understanding of the Social Gospel was informed by devoting special attention to the voices of persons other than Washington Gladden, Walter Rauschenbusch, and other educated white males whose theoretical discourse and reflection are widely regarded as constitutive of the tradition. Lindley's article is focused on the contributions of Vida Scudder, Reverdy Ransom, and Nannie Helen Burroughs. Including the voices of women and black men requires an expanded understanding of the Social Gospel with primary emphasis on activities in addition to theory and reflection. Lindley concluded that these "neglected voices" added depth and eloquence to the message of the Social Gospel in several ways: (1) their attempt to apply the teachings of Jesus and message of salvation to society and institutions; (2) their view of racial equality as a divine demand with a willingness to protest injustice; (3) their focus on the specific needs (practical and political) of black women domestic workers; and (4) their attacks on racism, ultimately rooted in their understanding of God's will for human life in the created sphere.[45] These findings resonate with the activities and insights of black women in the Radical Holiness Movement. They applied the teachings of Jesus and the message of salvation to society and institutions, especially the institutions they organized and established to this end, such as congregations, black women's clubs and conventions, orphanages, and senior citizens' homes. All of them viewed racial equality as a divine demand, and their means of protest included personal speeches and testimonies, as well as concerted collective action. The focus on the specific needs of black women domestic workers was a given for the several women in this study who self-identified as "washwomen," as well as those whose key audiences and followers were comprised mostly of black women engaged in domestic work. These women attacked racism with a clear vision of its inherent incompatibility with God's will for the freedom and flourishing of black people. Their social gospel witness was informed by direct engagement of the relationship between spirituality and intersectionality, frank responses to antiblackness of white Christians, and a global vision of the thriving of all people made in the image of God. The challenge of sustaining an authentic and faithful Christian witness in a world that made a fetish of whiteness gave them good reason to see themselves as holy black women living "in the world but not of it."

The COGIC church mothers who organized black women to worship, pray, study the Bible, and support home and foreign missions played a pivotal role in crafting and implementing a practical Social Gospel serving the needs of black women, men, and children. Butler's interpretation of the evolution of sanctified social engagement in the COGIC under Mother Coffey's leadership brings to mind the expanded configurations of the Social Gospel proposed by Lindley in light of the contributions of Ransom and Burroughs, both of whom were Coffey's contemporaries: "Being a sanctified woman then, would have to be reconfigured from a woman who was dressed as becometh holiness, with little interest in political activity, to a smartly dressed, well coiffed and well versed church mother with a vocabulary steeped in scripture yet attuned to social realities on earth, rather than heaven. Instead of standing on the street corners to find converts, the new converts to COGIC would come through the engagement of the church mothers with the world in social and civic arenas." Partnerships made all the difference in the advocacy and advancement of this sanctified social gospel. Without exception, these black Radical Holiness women partnered with other churches, preachers, and teachers, including Baptists, Methodists, and others, to implement and sustain their social vision in the form of resolutions and other initiatives: "The women of COGIC were adamant for their equal rights, but they were mindful of the partnerships that needed to be created in order to achieve their goals for racial equality. The old ideal of holiness that was coupled with social concern for not just the Saint but for the world at large became a capstone of the resolutions that helped to connect COGIC women to those outside of their church communities."[46]

EPILOGUE: WASHWOMEN AND FISHERMEN

Most of the black Radical Holiness women leaders named in this study worked as washerwomen at some point in their lives. Even the COOLJC women of the twenty-first century, notwithstanding their diversity of secular occupations, voluntarily engaged in domestic labor when called upon to do bereavement ministry. Casselberry's text begins and ends with a dramatic description of church women cleaning the home of a deceased church member who was a single parent of teenaged children: "On the day Louise Franklin passed away, women gathered to hand material and spiritual tasks, to prepare themselves, the house, and soon the community of faith for the hours, days, and months ahead. At first glance, it might be easy to view the sweeping, scrubbing, polishing, washing, and folding as solely caring labor, the sometimes paid, sometimes unpaid work that so many women do all the time. But on closer examination we understand that the good women performed intimate, emotional, and aesthetic religious labor as well."[47] Black radical holy women have regarded domestic work as means of supporting their ministries, families, and communities. Their vision of following Jesus focused more on labor and education than on liberation, toward the end of promoting survival of black people in hostile environments and adverse circumstances.

By fostering their own empowerment, equality, and social ethics as authentic evidence of their sanctification, operating under various iterations of the overarching rubric of exilic ecclesiology "in the world but not of it," black Radical Holiness women of the late nineteenth and early twentieth century challenged barriers to Christian unity, including race, sex, class, and denomination. Their peculiar experiences of spiritual formation for leadership in a church and society plagued by racism, sexism, and poverty encompassed several arenas of ministry and mission: the cosmopolitan evangelism of Amanda Berry Smith and the Women's Christian Temperance Union; the egalitarian revivalism of the women of Azusa Street; and the sanctified civic engagement of the COGIC church mothers in alliance with Mary McLeod Bethune and the National Council of Negro Women. Under these circumstances, it was their abiding testimony that the Holy Spirit baptized and sanctified black female bodies that had been despised and exploited by the world, thus authorizing and equipping them to evangelize women and men of all nations, races, and classes with a compelling social gospel message of Christian unity. Among them were sanctified washwomen—Amanda Berry Smith, Lizzie Robinson, the women of Azusa Street—whose social witness reimagined the vocation of the Galilean fishermen whom Jesus called away from the work of their hands in water to become the fishers of men (Matt. 4:19). May their works follow them.

NOTES

1. Donald W. Dayton, "Yet Another Layer of the Onion: Or Opening the Ecumenical Door to Let the Riffraff In," *Ecumenical Review* 40, no. 1 (1988), 104.

2. See Donald W. Dayton, "The Holiness Churches: A Significant Ethical Tradition," *Christian Century* 92, no. 7 (February 26, 1975): 197–201.

3. Steven L. Ware, "Restoring the New Testament Church: Varieties of Restorationism in the Radical Holiness Movement of the Late Nineteenth and Early Twentieth Centuries," *Pneuma* 21, no. 2 (1999): 234.

4. Ibid., 243.

5. Colin B. Chapell, *Ye That Are Men Now Serve Him: Radical Holiness Theology and Gender in the South* (Tuscaloosa: University of Alabama Press, 2016), 100. See also Jay R. Case, "And Ever the Twain Shall Meet: The Holiness Missionary Movement and the Birth of World Pentecostalism, 1870–1920," *Religion and American Culture* 16, no. 2 (2006): 125–60.

6. Cheryl J. Sanders, *Saints in Exile: The Holiness-Pentecostal Experience in*

African American Religion and Culture (New York: Oxford University Press, 1996), 16.

7. For more on the theme of exile in black Holiness and Pentecostal thought, see Amos Yong, "Justice Deprived, Justice Demanded: Afropentecostalisms and the Task of World Pentecostal Theology Today," *Journal of Pentecostal Theology* 15, no. 1 (2006): 127–47; Clarence E. Hardy III, "From Exodus to Exile: Black Pentecostals, Migrating Pilgrims, and Imagined Internationalism," *American Quarterly* 59, no. 3 (2007): 737–57.

8. Full bibliographical details on all the sources mentioned in this paragraph can be found in the bibliography at the end of this chapter.

9. For a detailed account of the life and work of Amanda Berry Smith, see Adrienne M. Israel, *Amanda Berry Smith: From Washerwoman to Evangelist* (Lanham, MD: Scarecrow Press, 1998).

10. Carole Lynn Stewart "'The Quintessence of Sanctifying Grace': Amanda Smith's Religious Experience, Freedom, and a Temperate Cosmopolitanism," *Journal of Africana Religions* 1, no. 3 (2013), 354.

11. Anthea D. Butler, *Women in the Church of God in Christ: Making a Sanctified World* (Chapel Hill: University of North Carolina Press, 2007), 110.

12. Estrelda Y. Alexander, *The Women of Azusa Street* (Cleveland, OH: Pilgrim Press, 2005).

13. William J. Seymour, *Apostolic Faith* 1, no. 1 (1906).

14. Ithiel Clemmons, cited by Estrelda Y. Alexander in *Black Fire: One Hundred Years of African American Pentecostalism* (Downers Grove, IL: IVP Academic, 2011), 131.

15. Butler, *Women in the Church*, 23.

16. Alexander, *Black Fire*, 314.

17. Butler, *Women in the Church*, 132–33.

18. Ibid., 161, 155.

19. H. Richard Niebuhr, *Christ and Culture* (New York: HarperSanFrancisco, 1951).

20. Niebuhr, *Christ and Culture*, 43.

21. Judith Casselberry, *The Labor of Faith: Gender and Power in Black Apostolic Pentecostalism* (Durham: Duke University Press, 2017).

22. Butler, *Women in the Church*, 165.

23. Dayton, "Yet Another Layer of the Onion," 104–5.

24. Hardy, "From Exodus to Exile," 745.

25. Pamela E. Klassen, "The Robes of Womanhood: Dress and Authenticity among African American Methodist Women in the Nineteenth Century," *Religion and American Culture* 14, no. 1 (2004): 68–69.

26. Ibid., 81.

27. Cheryl Townsend Gilkes, *"If It Wasn't for the Women . . .": Black Women's Experience and Womanist Culture in Church and Community* (Maryknoll, NY: Orbis, 2001), 201–2.

28. Alice Walker, *In Search of Our Mothers' Gardens* (Orlando: Harcourt Brace Jovanovich, 1983), xi–xii.

29. Butler, *Women in the Church*, 59, 125, 140, 147, 148, 162.

30. Alexander, *Black Fire*, 315.

31. Gilkes, *"If It Wasn't for the Women,"* 124.

32. Lillian S. Calhoun, "Woman on the Go for God: Church of God in Christ's Woman Leader Has Overcome Illness, Adversity to Work for Faith," *Ebony* 18, no. 7 (May 1963): 78.

33. Gilkes, *"If It Wasn't for the Women,"* 86.

34. Butler, *Women in the Church*, 133.

35. Ibid., 36, 132.

36. Walker, *In Search of Our Mothers' Gardens*, xi.

37. Amanda Berry Smith, *An Autobiography. The Story of the Lord's Dealings with Mrs. Amanda Smith: The Colored Evangelist* (N.p.: CreateSpace Independent Publishing, 2013), 258, 132, 133.

38. Walker, *In Search of Our Mothers' Gardens*, xi.

39. Sarah Bradford, *Harriet Tubman: The Moses of Her People* (New York: Corinth Books, 1961), 115–16.

40. For a detailed account of Tubman's head injury and disabilities, see Kate Clifford Larson, *Bound for the Promised Land: Harriet Tubman: Portrait of an American Hero* (New York: One World / Ballantine Books, 2004), 42–45.

41. Butler, *Women in the Church*, 110.

42. Mary McLeod Bethune, "My Last Will and Testament," *Ebony*, special issue 18, no. 11 (September 1963), 156.

43. Butler, *Women in the Church*, 112. See also Barbara Dianne Savage, *Your Spirits Walk Beside Us: The Politics of Black Religion* (Cambridge: Belknap Press of Harvard University Press, 2008), 123.

44. Susan H. Lindley, "'Neglected Voices' and 'Praxis' in the Social Gospel," *Journal of Religious Ethics* 18, no. 1 (1990), 75.

45. Ibid., 96.

46. Butler, *Women in the Church*, 136, 152.

47. Casselberry, *The Labor of Faith*, 170.

BIBLIOGRAPHY

Alexander, Estrelda Y. *Black Fire: One Hundred Years of African American Pentecostalism*. Downers Grove, IL: IVP Academic, 2011.

———. *The Women of Azusa Street*. Cleveland, OH: Pilgrim Press, 2005.

Bethune, Mary McLeod. "My Last Will and Testament." *Ebony*, special issue 18, no. 11 (September 1963): 150–56.

Bradford, Sarah. *Harriet Tubman: The Moses of Her People*. New York: Corinth Books, 1961.

Butler, Anthea D. *Women in the Church of God in Christ: Making a Sanctified World*. Chapel Hill: University of North Carolina Press, 2007.

Calhoun, Lillian S. "Woman on the Go for God: Church of God in Christ's Woman Leader Has Overcome Illness, Adversity to Work for Faith." *Ebony* 18, no. 7 (May 1963): 78–81, 84, 86, 88.

Case, Jay R. "And Ever the Twain Shall Meet: The Holiness Missionary Movement and the Birth of World Pentecostalism, 1870–1920." *Religion and American Culture* 16, no. 2 (2006): 125–60.

Casselberry, Judith. *The Labor of Faith: Gender and Power in Black Apostolic Pentecostalism*. Durham: Duke University Press, 2017.

Chapell, Colin B. *Ye That Are Men Now Serve Him: Radical Holiness Theology and Gender in the South*. Tuscaloosa: University of Alabama Press, 2016.

Collier-Thomas, Bettye. *Jesus, Jobs, and Justice: African American Women and Religion*. New York: Alfred A. Knopf, 2010.

Dayton, Donald W. "The Holiness Churches: A Significant Ethical Tradition." *Christian Century* 92, no. 7 (February 26, 1975): 197–201.

———. "Yet Another Layer of the Onion: Or Opening the Ecumenical Door to Let the Riffraff In." *Ecumenical Review* 40, no. 1 (1988): 87–110.

Gilkes, Cheryl Townsend. *"If It Wasn't for the Women . . .": Black Women's Experience and Womanist Culture in Church and Community*. Maryknoll, NY: Orbis, 2001.

Hardy, Clarence E., III. "From Exodus to Exile: Black Pentecostals, Migrating Pilgrims, and Imagined

Internationalism." *American Quarterly* 59, no. 3 (2007): 737–57.

Hurston, Zora Neale. *The Sanctified Church*. Berkeley, CA: Turtle Island, 1981.

Israel, Adrienne M. *Amanda Berry Smith: From Washerwoman to Evangelist*. Lanham, MD: Scarecrow Press, 1998.

Klassen, Pamela E. "The Robes of Womanhood: Dress and Authenticity among African American Methodist Women in the Nineteenth Century." *Religion and American Culture* 14, no. 1 (2004): 39–82.

Larson, Kate Clifford. *Bound for the Promised Land: Harriet Tubman: Portrait of an American Hero*. New York: One World / Ballantine Books, 2004.

Lindley, Susan H. "'Neglected Voices' and 'Praxis' in the Social Gospel." *Journal of Religious Ethics* 18, no. 1 (1990): 75–102.

———. *"You Have Stept out of Your Place": A History of Women and Religion in America*. Louisville: Westminster John Knox, 1996.

Niebuhr, H. Richard. *Christ and Culture*. New York: HarperSanFrancisco, 1951.

Sanders, Cheryl J. *Saints in Exile: The Holiness-Pentecostal Experience in African American Religion and Culture*. New York: Oxford University Press, 1996.

Savage, Barbara Dianne. *Your Spirits Walk Beside Us: The Politics of Black Religion*. Cambridge: Belknap Press of Harvard University Press, 2008.

Seymour, William J. *Apostolic Faith* 1, no. 1 (1906).

Smith, Amanda Berry. *An Autobiography. The Story of the Lord's Dealings with Mrs. Amanda Smith; The Colored Evangelist*. N.p.: CreateSpace Independent Publishing, 2013.

Stanley, Susie C. *Holy Boldness: Women Preachers' Autobiographies and the Sanctified Self*. Knoxville: University of Tennessee Press, 2002.

Stewart, Carole Lynn. "'The Quintessence of Sanctifying Grace': Amanda Smith's Religious Experience, Freedom, and a Temperate Cosmopolitanism." *Journal of Africana Religions* 1, no. 3 (2013): 348–75.

Walker, Alice. *In Search of Our Mothers' Gardens*. Orlando: Harcourt Brace Jovanovich, 1983.

Ware, Steven L. "Restoring the New Testament Church: Varieties of Restorationism in the Radical Holiness Movement of the Late Nineteenth and Early Twentieth Centuries." *Pneuma* 21, no. 2 (1999): 233–50.

Yong, Amos. "Justice Deprived, Justice Demanded: Afropentecostalisms and the Task of World Pentecostal Theology Today." *Journal of Pentecostal Theology* 15, no. 1 (2006): 127–47.

CHAPTER 7

Pneumatology as a Basis for Ecumenical Dialogue Between the Korean Methodist, Holiness, and Pentecostal Traditions

Insik Choi

Pneumatology has been and remains a controversial theological subject among Korean Protestant churches. At the heart of the issue are the perspectives of the Reformed and Wesleyan traditions. Both traditions are engaging in lively debates on the Holy Spirit not only at the intellectual theological level but also within church life. The necessity of "integrated pneumatology" is under discussion.[1] However, concrete attempts to creatively integrate conflicting theological elements remain missing. The main task of this chapter will be to consider the characteristics attributed to the Holy Spirit in Korean Methodist, Holiness, and Pentecostal theology, all largely rooted in Wesleyan theology. Based on this analysis, a paradigm for integrating diverse approaches into a holistic, integral, "Wesleyan-Holiness-Pentecostal pneumatology" will be proposed.

THE HOLY SPIRIT IN KOREAN METHODIST THEOLOGY

The Methodist presence in Korea began with a visit by Robert Samuel Maclay, of the Methodist Episcopal Church in Japan in 1884. He obtained permission from King Gojong to do educational and medical work. On Easter Sunday, April 5, 1885, Rev. Henry G. Appenzeller, with Horace G. Underwood, a Presbyterian missionary, arrived. In October 1895, a visit by Bishop Eugene R. Hendrix and Dr. Clarence F. Reid of the Methodist Episcopal Church South was made possible by Korean scholar Yoon Chi-Ho, a Methodist Episcopal Church South convert in China. The Korean revivals (1903–7) led to rapid growth as well as creative theological reflection. In 1930 the Methodist Episcopal Church North and the Methodist Episcopal Church South of Korea merged to form the independent Korean Methodist Church. World War II and the Korean War brought extensive suffering, destruction, and division. Yet since the 1920s, Korean scholars have been working to make the Korean Methodist theological framework inherited from the American churches more congruent with Korean culture.[2]

The theological framework of John Wesley informs the pneumatology of Korean Methodist theology. There are two primary approaches to building on this heritage. First was the attempt by Hu-jeong Lee (1956–) and Hong-gi Kim (1950–) to describe the pneumatology of Wesley in light of important later Methodist theologians. The second was the effort of Jong-cheon Park (1954–) and Jeong-bae Lee (1955–) to develop a Korean pneumatology within the framework of Wesley's theology.

Seon-hwan Byun (1927–1995), who taught Jong-cheon Park and Jeong-bae Lee, wrote about Wesley's pneumatology. His study provided a new direction in the theological dialogue between Christianity and other religions. Byun suggested that Wesley's pneumatology could help solve the challenges of religious pluralism, particularly when Christianity had not yet taken root among indigenous religions. He introduced Wesley's pneumatology and argued that it "should shed light on the understanding of our context." He appraised the pneumatology of Wesley: "Wesley is convinced of the triune God who is immanently present in human life and completes salvation. The Holy Spirit is freely and directly engaged in its own activities. It is active universally, and responsible personally in cooperation with human beings. It is the driving force of the Christian life; it enables one to live in holiness, righteousness, and love, as did Jesus Christ. This is the essence of the work of the Holy Spirit in John Wesley's theology."[3] Some of Byun's disciples advocate adherence to Wesley's pneumatology, while others use it as a starting point for developing a theologically indigenous pneumatology.

Korean Methodist Understandings of Wesley's Views of the Holy Spirit

Korean Methodist church historian Hu-jeong Lee conceptualized Wesley's understanding of the Holy Spirit based on the work of Albert C. Outler.[4] Lee argued that the spirituality of the Syrian writer Macarius was important for Wesley's pneumatology. In addition, he explored the Wesleyan synergistic epistemology of "the spiritual sense," the experience of the Holy Spirit, and the relationship between the Holy Spirit and sanctification.

Lee suggested that Wesley's synergism can be established based on Macarius's pneumatology. According to Macarius, since the image of God remains part of fallen humanity, believers can ask for God's grace with their grace-enabled free will and resist sinful tendencies even if they cannot conquer them. To do this, they must "cooperate with the grace of the Holy Spirit in ourselves."[5] Therefore, it can be argued that Wesley's "synergism" constituted a partnership between the Holy Spirit and believers.[6] For Macarius, the goal of salvation is *apotheosis*, which is ultimately accomplished by being filled with the Holy Spirit.[7] In Macarius's sermons, "humans not only recover the first Adam's state due to the power of the Holy Spirit that makes them reborn, but also reach a better qualitative state. Humans are to be deified (*apotheoutai*)"[8]—an aspect of Macarius's theology with parallels in Wesley. Lee placed this within the philosophical framework of eighteenth-century British empiricism, especially the work of John Locke.[9]

Relying on Lycurgus Starkey's work, Lee asserted that Wesley's concept of sanctification is placed teleologically, as in Macarius; progress toward perfection is "gradual" and accompanied by a "social" dimension.[10] Lee argued that "the logical structure of Wesley's thought does not fully describe the mystical dimensions of the work of the Holy Spirit."[11] He opined that Wesley "greatly adored the spirituality of Macarius."[12]

While Hu-jeong Lee focused on one of Wesley's Eastern Christian sources, Hong-gi Kim, a Methodist historian, addressed aspects of the Western background of Wesley's thought. He argued that Wesley's understandings of justification and sanctification were deeply rooted in Augustine. Kim suggested that Reformation leaders, concerned about the concept of merit, took issue with both the practices related to merit and the advocacy of mystical experience by some medieval Scholastics while emphasizing Augustine's "imputation" of grace. Therefore, in theologies of the Reformation, faith through the words that come to us objectively from outside of us (*extra nos*) was emphasized rather than the subjective inner experience (*in nobis*). The work of the Holy Spirit was grace encountered "in the Word, through the Word, with the Word."[13]

Kim then argued that with the doctrine of justification restored during the Reformation, Wesley emphasized the doctrine of sanctification. To this end, he actively accepted "imparted" grace based on Augustine. However, Kim continued, Wesley sought to revive both justification by imputed grace and sanctification by imparted grace, which emphasized the actual (*in nobis*) change.[14]

Wesley understood that the Holy Spirit indwelling humans may sanctify them. The Holy Spirit changes lives in cooperation with believers and in believers.[15]

The Holy Spirit for Minjung *Cultural Realities*

While some Methodist historians were actively engaged in articulating the theological ideas of Wesley to enhance Methodist identity in Korea, others were seeking to develop indigenous Korean approaches to Methodist theology. The key scholars of the first and second generation were Byung-heon Choi (1858–1927), Seong-beom Yoon (1916–1980), Seon-hwan Byun, and Dong-sik Yoo (1922–). Here, however, the focus is on the indigenous pneumatology of third-generation scholars, especially Jong-cheon Park and Jeong-bae Lee, who have actively engaged with Korean culture while broadly interpreting the theology of Wesley in light of Korean cultural paradigms.

Jong-cheon Park presented his method and theological perspective in several books, including *Theology of Living Together* and *Crawl with God, Dance in the Spirit!*[16] In a lecture he suggested that theology should be communicated to the "contemporary" in order not to be a "theological dialect."[17] Park sought balance between traditional pneumatology, preserving the concept of the biblical Holy Spirit and the understanding of the Holy Spirit in contemporary theology, seeking to address the difficulties of modern people, such as human oppression and ecological crisis. In addition, Park observed religious and cultural distance between Western pneumatology and Korean spirituality, and insisted it is necessary to deal with such a difference carefully. If not, Western iconoclasm would be confused with Christian prophetism and, as a result, "the destruction of the traces of God's spiritual existence in the rich history of Korean religion" could be repeated.[18]

Concerned about this problem, Park criticized the position of Karl Barth from the perspective of Rosemary Reuther and Jürgen Moltmann.[19] For Park, Barth's interpretation of the confession of faith—"conceived by the Holy Spirit, born of the Virgin Mary"—in the Apostles' Creed was understood to be patriarchal, Jesus-oriented, and revelatory in ways that diminished the role of Mary. From this critical standpoint, Park presented an ecological pneumatology for the liberation of contemporary oppressed women.[20] He actively embraced Moltmann's thesis that "God in Creation is God in the Holy Spirit,"[21] and the statement of Macarius that "the Holy Spirit is mother,"[22] suggesting the Holy Spirit as the cosmic Spirit can include the traditions of other religions. He drew support from the work of Geoffrey Wainwright, who suggested understanding

Mary as the "active model" of the church.²³ He concluded that as Mary conceived through the Holy Spirit, "the Holy Spirit that indwells in all the people filled by the Holy Spirit is never inferior to the presence of God in Jesus."²⁴ The Holy Spirit is open to all people and acts as a free and universal God infusing prevenient grace in all people.

Based on an understanding of the Holy Spirit according to the "principle of universal grace," Park *r*epresented "Lady-Bear theology" as "a new pneumatology" for the "Korean *minjung*" (oppressed people).²⁵ Already in the 1960s, his teacher Seong-beom Yoon had proposed "Lady-Bear theology" as a Korean indigenous theology. However, Park argued that Yoon's theology cannot liberate oppressed Koreans because it is caught in the frameworks of Confucian patriarchy and the Barthian interpretation of Confucianism. Just as Reuther and Moltmann presented the theology of Marian *Theotokos* based on feminist liberation and universal cosmology, Park presented the "Lady-Bear mythology" as liberation for the Korean people in oppression.

In a different context from Jong-cheon Park, Methodist systematic theologian and religious philosopher Jeong-bae Lee developed a Methodist indigenous theology based on the "theology of religion" of his teacher Seon-hwan Byun. This contrasted with Park's critical reading of Seong-beom Yoon's "Korean theology" while strengthening the theological motif of *minjung*. Lee published a systematic theology, *The Korean Theology of Life*, in which he developed pneumatology as part of "the theoretical development of Korean life theology."²⁶ In this work, Lee discussed earlier approaches to pneumatology, opting for "process pneumatology." He correlated this with "theory of the Korean *zi-chi* (至氣 Ultimate Doing; cf. *zi-ri*: 至理, Ultimate Being)," arguing for the necessity of dealing with the "Christian Holy Spirit from the perspective of *chi* (lit. wind)" as did the Chinese theologian Chun-sen Jang.²⁷ Later, *Lee* explored *chi*-pneumatology in his book *The Life of Theology and the Spiritualization of Theology*.²⁸

Jeong-bae Lee argued for an "ecological pneumatology," proposing that the Holy Spirit is "the living truth that heals the social structure of violence that makes human beings a scapegoat." It is a "life-form" for "the spiritual challenge to the concept of western selfhood that was indifferent to nature."²⁹ According to Lee, the Holy Spirit is "the one who gives strength to those who do not have power" and the Spirit is a political and cultural divine agent that changes the structures of social power.³⁰ What the Holy Spirit does is "to comfort the powerless with those who work for radical social change." The Holy Spirit lives in the new community formed by those who give up fighting violence with violence. The Holy Spirit does not suppress differences, but rather is the founder of differences even in social structures of violence that would seek to turn the marginalized into scapegoats. In this respect, the Holy Spirit makes it possible to establish a multicultural community that celebrates diversity.[31]

Lee asserted that creation has traditionally been understood from the perspective of God and humans, but that this should be changed so that it can be understood as from the Holy Spirit.[32] Thus, theological problems between revelation and nature, or history and nature, could be resolved because the Holy Spirit would take on the intermediary role in various problems of theology. There would be no longer a separation between Spirit and nature, but rather they would be seen in an interdependent relationship, the definition of which is difficult to define. For when talking about the indwelling of the Holy Spirit in all things, one could be suspected of a pantheism-based identification of God and nature, since dual structures such as God and the world, or grace and nature remain. The plan to solve this dualistic structure led to the elimination of the differences between human beings and other creatures. The Holy Spirit played a crucial role.[33]

By understanding the Holy Spirit in close relation with nature, Lee argued that the conventional view of human beings, who have been understood as the administrators or stewards of nature, should be changed into a view of humans as friends, pilgrims, and residents in the universe. The understanding of the Holy Spirit based on nature, as opposed to human beings, demands a transformation of the traditional understanding of the Holy Spirit; this is because the Holy Spirit, who healed a created world suffering from violence, cannot be properly addressed in human-centered theology. Ultimately, the Holy Spirit is "the ecological Spirit as the healing God of power alive in the present reality where the full restoration of the entire creation is called for."[34]

PNEUMATOLOGY OF THE KOREAN HOLINESS AND PENTECOSTAL TRADITIONS

The primary perspectives on pneumatology within Holiness and Pentecostal theology are broadly in the Wesleyan tradition, but different from the Methodist theologies already discussed. The Holiness-Pentecostal Movement in Korea is largely dominated by two clusters of denominations: Holiness churches and Pentecostal churches. Common characteristics of both clusters include articulations of the fourfold gospel as the focus of theology and emphases on the personal experience of the Holy Spirit. The core of the spiritual experience is the Spirit baptism. Therefore, it is crucial to understand the Spirit baptism and its characteristics in the Korean Holiness and the Pentecostal churches. The Holiness churches often understand Spirit baptism as holiness, while the Pentecostal churches tend to see Spirit baptism as power.[35] The Korean Evangelical Holiness Church and the Full Gospel Churches are chosen as representative of the fragmented traditions because of their size and influence throughout Korea and around the world.

The Pneumatology of the Korean Evangelical Holiness Church (KEHC)

The KEHC began in 1907 with the establishment of the Mission Hall in Seoul by Bin Jeong (1873–?) and Sang-joon Kim (1881–1933). They were graduates of Tokyo Bible School of Nakada and the Cowman & Kilbourne Mission (later the Oriental Missionary Society [OMS]). The school was founded by Nakada Juji (1870–1939) and enhanced by Charles E. Cowman (1868–1924) and E. A. Kilbourne (1865–1928). From this institution other Korean leaders also graduated, including Myung-heon Lee (1876–1928) and Myung-jik Lee (1890–1973).[36]

After hearing Albert B. Simpson (1894) at the Moody Church in Chicago, Cowman began to struggle with a call to missionary work. With his convert Kilbourne, he founded the Telegrapher's Mission Band to evangelize telegraph works in the Chicago area. Having already attended classes at Moody Bible Institute and Garrett Theological Seminary, Cowman then studied briefly at God's Bible School and Missionary Training Home, led by Martin Wells Knapp. He was commissioned by Knapp and Seth C. Rees of the International Holiness Union in Cincinnati as a missionary to Japan. At God's Bible School, he was influenced by Knapp's Holiness-Pentecostal "full gospel" theology.[37] Cowman joined Nakada, whom he had befriended in Chicago, at the Tokyo Bible School, where they were later joined by Kilbourne.[38]

The Tokyo Bible School in Japan and the Seoul Bible School in Korea intentionally used the name "Bible School" on the model of God's Bible School and similar institutions. Both institutions established traditions prioritizing spiritual training for evangelism rather than intellectual theological reflection. The schools focused on the biblical text, thereby seeking to avoid doctrinal controversy or denominationalism. Nakada, Cowman, and Kilbourne were all part of Radical Holiness Networks, having been converted in Methodist churches, but having left those to lead new organizations. Because they relativized their denominational backgrounds, they attracted collaboration from others attracted to the Radical Holiness vision of Christianity.[39]

Many scholars of the Korean Holiness Church have promoted or written about Wesleyan theology.[40] Among these, Seong-yong Jeon (1959–) focused on pneumatology. While systematically dealing with traditional understandings of the Holy Spirit, Jeon dialogued with the pneumatologies of John Wesley and Karl Barth.[41] Jeon understood Wesley's pneumatology and his spiritual experience as a root of the nineteenth- and twentieth-century "Pentecostal" movements. According to Jeon, Wesley's religious experiences at Aldersgate (May 24, 1738) and Fetter Lane (January 1, 1739) were Pentecostal experiences of the Holy Spirit. Because of these immediate and instantaneous experiences of the Holy Spirit, Wesley's soteriology and pneumatology have characteristics that distinguish him from previous Reformers. Thereafter Wesley emphasized sanctification as the work of the Holy Spirit that comes after regeneration. Jeon argued that the concept of baptism with the Holy Spirit as the second blessing in the later Pentecostal Movements derives from Wesley's pneumatology and personal experience of the Holy Spirit.[42] He considered Barth's primary contribution to be "a strong claim to the public responsibility of believers, which was almost neglected in existing theories of sanctification." He suggested Barth's fight against social-political evil was parallel to a concept of social sanctification.[43]

The main contribution of Jeon's pneumatology has been the discussion of "the baptism of the Holy Spirit," a topic not usually discussed by contemporary Methodist systematic theologians. He surveyed the biblical understandings of Spirit baptism and concluded it to be different from the Reformed tradition of equating regeneration and Spirit baptism. Jeon argued that water baptism in the early church presupposed Spirit baptism. Since within the older churches, nominal Christianity became the norm, it became hard to argue that water baptism and Spirit baptism are closely related. Jeon exhorted those who received water baptism "to receive Spirit baptism."[44]

So, what is Spirit baptism? Tae-gu Kim, a leader of the KEHC, insisted that "Christ is in us as the Holy Spirit, and this Holy Spirit will lead us to live a life of joy and power. This is the baptism of the Holy Spirit."[45] He characterized the unique role of Spirit baptism: "When the Holy Spirit is already in me, not part of me, but when the Holy Spirit has taken over my heart and my whole body, and when the Holy Spirit is fully active in all aspects, we say that we have been baptized by the Holy Spirit."[46]

The most important shaper of the pneumatology of the KEHC was Seong-bong Lee (1900–1965), called "the Korean Moody" and "one of the great revival pastors in Korea."[47] He graduated from Seoul Bible School (now Seoul Theological University) in 1928, served as a pastor for thirteen years, and subsequently

Fig. 7.1 The Rev. Seong-bong Lee [이성봉]. Courtesy of the Korea Evangelical Holiness Church, Seoul, South Korea.

worked as a revivalist for seventeen years.[48] Yong-gi Cho, pastor of Yoido Full Gospel Church, Seoul, observed that Seong-bong Lee had a "beautiful ministry," reflecting that the key reason for Lee's successful ministry was his experience, at the age of thirty-eight, the "baptism of fire," the "hot baptism of the Holy Spirit."[49] Cho understood Seong-bong Lee's experience of Spirit baptism to have four characteristics: (1) being guided by the Holy Spirit, (2) having an amazing passion, (3) achieving the work of love, and (4) proclaiming the message of hope.[50] Cho insisted that Lee's message of hope was delivered in the power of "divine healing in which incurable diseases are treated."[51] Cho was greatly encouraged and challenged by Lee's message of hope. Others have recognized that Lee's ministry was characterized by his "resoluteness not only in his own life but also in the fighting against injustice in the church."[52]

Seong-bong Lee described the Holy Spirit as a "true shepherd" who wanted to make the holy church holy in God's way as an example of biblical holiness.[53] Lee's sermons have the themes of the fourfold gospel: regeneration, sanctification, divine healing, and the second coming.[54] His sermons are understood in the KEHC as extending, deepening, and subdividing these four themes. He was convinced that the fourfold gospel encompassed the most important aspects of the Christian faith. He stated, "I received the fourfold gospel of the Holiness church, relied on it, and experienced it."[55] Each "Four-Fold Gospel" theme depended upon, and communicated his practical experiential pneumatology.[56]

In a sermon entitled "Revival," Lee insisted that revival is "the work of the Holy Spirit (Joel 2:28). The Holy Spirit has the power to cause revival in each direction like fire, wind, oil, and water."[57] In another sermon, "Have You Received the Holy Spirit," he argued that by receiving the Holy Spirit, Jesus evidenced that he is the Son of God. According to Lee, believers have the same experience as Jesus, who was born of the Holy Spirit (Luke 1:35), baptized by the Holy Spirit (John 1:32), and filled with the Holy Spirit (John 3:34). "We must not only be regenerated through the Holy Spirit, but also baptized by the Holy Spirit" (John 7:38).[58]

The Understanding of the Holy Spirit of the Pentecostal Churches in Korea

The Korean Holiness and Pentecostal movements are heirs of the American Radical Holiness and Pentecostal movements. These movements emphasized baptism of the Holy Spirit.[59] The core values of this Korean Holiness-Pentecostal revival movement in the Korean churches were the power of prayer, made possible thorough confession of sin, and the presence of the power of the Holy Spirit.[60] These themes were already present in the Korean Revival (1907), which also emphasized the baptism of the Holy Spirit, distinguishing it from regeneration. Horace Underwood, a Presbyterian missionary, testified that "the Korean church was baptized by the Holy Spirit."[61]

Mary Rumsey (ca. 1885–?) was a participant in the Azusa Street Revival in Los Angeles. Formerly a Methodist, from 1932, as an American missionary, she worked with Huh Heong, a Salvation Army secretary, to establish the first Pentecostal congregation in Seoul. By 1937, Korean preachers and missionaries had established six Pentecostal congregations before the missionaries were forced to leave in the lead-up to World War II. The post–World War II preaching of Methodist Ra Woon Mong about Spirit baptism and healing sensitized people to Pentecostal ideas, creating the "prayer mountain movement," or "Holy Spirit movement." In 1948, Gui Im Park founded the Suncheon Pentecostal Church; in 1950 Korean ministers organized the Korean Pentecostal Church. Eight of these congregations became the Korean Assemblies of God under the leadership of United States military chaplain Arthur Chesnut. Huh Heong eventually became (1957) the first official Korean leader of the Korean Assemblies of God. Other missionaries arrived from different (primarily) United States Pentecostal denominations. Through mission efforts and post–Korean War migration and reverse migration, many independent and United States–related Pentecostal denominations were founded. The most important congregation, Yoido Church, became crucial to Pentecostal theological development in Korea and beyond, due largely to charismatic figure Yong-gi Cho. This congregation/denomination has been selected for analysis here.[62]

The importance of Yong-gi Cho (1936–2021) for the Korean Pentecostal traditions can hardly be overstated. His spiritual experience and understanding of the Holy Spirit are historically central to Korean Pentecostal theology. His significance in Korea has far exceeded that of Charles F. Parham and William J. Seymour in the United States. Cho has been well known and read globally for more than half a century in many languages. Both Parham and Seymour were marginal to Pentecostal development after 1908. Pentecostal pneumatology in Korea is based primarily on the work of Yong-gi Cho.[63]

After the Korean War, the Pentecostal Movement in Korea was enhanced by the ministry of Yong-gi Cho. He began with a tent church in Seoul on May 18, 1958; today the church is the largest in the world. The story of the Yoido Full Gospel Church has been described as "a record of the history of the Holy Spirit constantly working."[64] After its humble beginnings, Yoido experienced explosive growth. Central to this growth was the Pentecostal understanding of "baptism of the Holy Spirit," evidenced by *glossolalia*. When Cho asserted that every believer must be baptized with the Holy Spirit, conservative Presbyterian theologians began to criticize his pneumatology.[65] They insisted that every believer was already baptized with the Holy Spirit at the moment of conversion.[66]

Cho responded to his critics in a book entitled *The Fivefold Gospel and the Threefold Blessing*.[67] For him, the first two of five "Gospels" were regeneration and Spirit baptism. In regeneration, Cho asserted that a believer welcomes the Holy Spirit, but also prays to be filled with the power of the Holy Spirit.[68] Spirit baptism began with Pentecost, "the birthday of the church," which became crucial for the faith-life of the Pentecostal full gospel. The church was born through the coming of the Holy Spirit at Pentecost. It was the historical moment the Holy Spirit began working in earnest in the world.

Cho's threefold explanation of the significance of the biblical Pentecost reveals the central features of his pneumatology. First, at Pentecost, God acknowledged the salvific ministry of Jesus Christ. Therefore, the gospel of

Fig. 7.2 Yong-gi Cho [조용기] speaking at the World Assemblies of God Congress in Seoul, South Korea, October 1994. Courtesy of Flower Pentecostal Heritage Center.

Jesus could suddenly pour forth through the "work of the incomprehensible Holy Spirit" to spread throughout the world. The Pentecostal advent of the Holy Spirit demonstrated that Jesus of Nazareth is the Messiah for salvation.[69] Second, Pentecost speaks of Spirit baptism. The Holy Spirit works not only as "the spirit of salvation" but as "the spirit of power" given to those who have been baptized with the Holy Spirit.[70] Third, Pentecost made available holiness and the fruits of the Holy Spirit. Those who experienced the baptism of the Holy Spirit not only improved their spiritual abilities but also experienced "transformation in the personal and social environment."[71]

Spirit baptism can be understood theologically in various ways. Cho takes a different stance from both the Reformed and Holiness traditions. According to Cho, regeneration is the experience of accepting a new life by being attached to Christ's body, the church, with the Holy Spirit and the Word, while Spirit baptism is an experience of spiritual power for ministry. Therefore, regeneration and Spirit baptism cannot be the same experience.[72] Cho stated, "in order to achieve a successful life of faith, we must experience Spirit baptism after regeneration."[73]

Cho taught that the gospel of spiritual fullness should not only be the gospel of Spirit baptism (*charisma*), but also the gospel of holiness. He understands holiness in two ways: passive holiness that keeps one away from sin, and active holiness, which leads one to honor God. Moreover, he teaches that holiness is "the life that fits the image and will of God" and "the practice of love." In this context, the evidence of holiness is "the fruit of the Holy Spirit" (Gal. 5:22–23) and "the character of God" (2 Pet. 1:1–4). There are three kinds of evidence of holiness: (1) "fruit for God," which is love, joy, and peace; (2) "fruit for people," which is patience, mercy, and goodwill; and (3) "fruit for oneself," which is loyalty, gentleness, and temperance.[74] He also regarded those traits of the character of God as evidence of holiness that is achieved by the Holy Spirit in the life of believers, such as faith, virtue, knowledge, moderation, patience, piety, brotherly fellowship, and love.[75]

As has been argued, the most important subject of pneumatology for Cho has been Spirit baptism, but he always emphasized the Holy Spirit as personal.[76] He insisted that the personality of the Holy Spirit should not be missed in the experience of the Holy Spirit.[77] He averred that the Holy Spirit is the most important personal ally: "The Holy Spirit is the most important person to me. He is my most trusted spiritual teacher. He is also my partner in the ministry."[78] Myeong-seon Moon, Mun-seon Shin, and Jong-ik Park confirm that Yong-gi Cho's pneumatology is based on understanding the Holy Spirit as a personal or relational aspect of the Triune God.[79]

CONCLUSION: PNEUMATOLOGY AND METHODIST, HOLINESS, AND PENTECOSTAL ECUMENISM

Characteristics of pneumatologies of the Korean Methodist Church, the Korean Evangelical Holiness Church, and Pentecostal Full Gospel Church have been examined. Based on this analysis of the three traditions, a holistic, integral, pneumatology from an ecumenical perspective can be proposed. All three Korean ecclesiastical and theological traditions are part of the Wesleyan tradition, rooted in the pneumatology of John Wesley. This is a fruitful starting point for ecumenical discussion.

Five points regarding the Holy Spirit could be commonly accepted by the Methodist, Holiness, and Pentecostal traditions: (1) the Holy Spirit gives the inner conviction and assurance that one has been saved; (2) the Holy Spirit gives "the second blessing" of sanctification instantaneously; (3) the Holy Spirit works synergistically with believers for their sanctification; (4) the Holy Spirit gives the sanctified power for service; and (5) the Holy Spirit comes to each person personally.

If one uses the so-called Wesleyan quadrilateral (scripture, tradition, reason, and experience) one may assert that the Word of God precedes the Holy Spirit, and that the Holy Spirit precedes the experience of human beings.[80] Wesley valued testimony to empirically demonstrated conviction by the Holy Spirit, resulting in an emotional or physical response. His constant hope was to restore "biblical Christianity" and to become "a man of one book." He found congruence with some pneumatologies of Reformation theology rooted in Augustine, but also in the spirituality and "optimism of grace" of Macarius.[81] The pneumatology of the Methodist, Holiness, and Pentecostal churches may be able to open a path to a richer spiritual experience using Wesley's ecumenical spirituality.

In connection with such a broad pneumatology, "Lady-Bear pneumatology," "*Gi*-pneumatology," and "Ecological pneumatology" proposed by scholars of the Korean Methodist Church can be accepted as creative challenges to the traditions of the Holiness and Pentecostal movements. Since the active work of the Holy Spirit is not only in the personal dimension between God and people, but also in the folk-historical, sociocultural, and cosmic-natural dimensions, Methodist *minjung* indigenous theology of the Holy Spirit should be treated as an important part of pneumatology. All these traditions allow that the Holy Spirit should be related to creatively sharing the spiritual view of life that makes the entire ecosystem of nature alive, as well as connected to the internal change of the human soul.

On the other hand, the Holiness and Pentecostal churches, founded on the fourfold gospel—regeneration, holiness/Spirit baptism, divine healing, and second coming—are so similar in theology that it is difficult to find important differences. Unlike the Methodist tradition, Holiness and Pentecostal theology insist that Spirit baptism is a core doctrine of each denomination's theology, although even slight differences in expression of these ideas loom large. In the Holiness Church, the most important experience of the Holy Spirit is the believer's Spirit baptism, and in the Pentecostal theology, the Spirit baptism is a doctrine directly related to its identity. Therefore, it is necessary to understand such a baptism in every way, from the theoretical level to the sociological and empirical. While Methodists do not actively promote Spirit baptism, John Wesley and his colleague John Fletcher articulated a pneumatology of the Spirit baptism, which decisively influenced the American and Korean Methodist, Holiness, and Pentecostal movements.[82] Examining the importance of Spirit baptism in the three Korean theological traditions may provide a basis for mutual understanding as well as cooperation in practice, theology, and mission.

The pneumatologies of the three traditions may be understood using the "A-B-C" typology of Richard P. Gilbertson.[83] Type A emphasizes *power for holiness*, where the Pentecostal baptism of the Holy Spirit is a means of sanctification; the emphasis is on sanctification, whether it is achieved or not, rather than on the Spirit baptism itself. If Korean Methodists can connect sanctification to the Spirit baptism, this model could be applied more positively.[84] Type B focuses on *holiness and power*; when individuals are Spirit baptized, they receive the fruit of the Holy Spirit and the gifts of the Holy Spirit. Holiness is a personal dimension of the Holy Spirit, while the gifts are ministerial dimensions of the Holy Spirit. This is the position of the KEHC.[85] Type C centers on *holiness for power*; Spirit baptism is for the benefit of obtaining power, not holiness.[86] In Korean Pentecostal theology, unlike in the Holiness Church, holiness and the Spirit baptism tend to be separated. These three models can eventually interact within a paradigm of "holiness-power." The polarity of "holiness-power" need not be regarded as mutually exclusive, so that each tradition may find ways to understand and accept the others while maintaining its own character.

Korean Methodist pneumatology seeks to affirm the dynamism of the Holy Spirit, who works as the power of life to save nature, history, and culture by paying attention to the "being" of the Holy Spirit rather than the "way" of Spirit baptism. The Pentecostal Full Gospel Church insists that the believer can live a powerful life that overcomes difficult living conditions by receiving the power from above in the midst of poverty, disease, and the ruins of war or social discrimination. In this reality, Spirit baptism can be experienced as a gift and power above all. The pneumatology of the Korean Evangelical Holiness Church emphasizes that anyone can live a "life of joy and power" if the personality and power of the Holy Spirit is received in Spirit baptism, a theology supported by conversion and martyr narratives transmitted within the KEHC.[87] Thus, the concepts of holiness-power and Spirit baptism may provide the framework for a holistic, integral pneumatology based on discussions between leaders and scholars of the Korean Methodist, Holiness, and Pentecostal traditions.

NOTES

1. Myung-yong Kim [김명용], "Pneumatology of the Reformed Church and Pneumatology of the Pentecostal Church" [in Korean], *ChangShin NonDan* 15, no. 12 (1999): 238. Bon-cheol Bae [배본철], "History and Prospect of the Spirit Movement in Korean Pentecostalism: The Origins and Developments of Pneumatology Debates" [in Korean], *Youngsan Theological Journal* 29 (2013): 7–56. Unless otherwise noted, all translations and transliterations from Korean to English

are by the author of this chapter. Full bibliographical details, including Korean titles, are in the bibliography.

2. Hong-ki Kim, "An Interpretation of the Korean Church in the Wesleyan Perspective," in *The Global Impact of the Wesleyan Traditions and Their Related Movements*, ed. Charles Yrigoyen Jr., Pietist and Wesleyan Studies 14 (Lanham, MD: Scarecrow Press, 2002), 201–16; L. George Paik, *The History of Protestant Missions in Korea: 1832–1910* (Seoul: Christian Literature Society, 1972); Tŏk-chu Yi [이 덕주], *A History of the Methodist Church in Korea* [in Korean] (Seoul: KMC/Ch'op'an, 2017).

3. Seon-hwan Byun [변선환], "Lycurgus M. Starkey Jr. History of the Spirit: A Study of Wesley's Theology" [in Korean], *Theology and the World* 7 (1981): 438.

4. Hu-jeong Lee [이후정], "Pneumatology," in *Wesley and the Theology of the Methodist Church* [in Korean], ed. Wesleyan Theological Society of Korea (Seoul: MTS Publishing, 1999), 118; Albert C. Outler, "A Focus on the Holy Spirit: Spirit and Spirituality in John Wesley," *Quarterly Review* 8, no. 2 (1988): 3–7.

5. Macarius [마카리우스], *Spiritual Sermons* [in Korean], trans. Hu-jeong Lee [이후정 역] (Seoul: Eun-sung, 1993), 124 (XV.25).

6. Lee, "Pneumatology," 120.

7. Ibid., 121.

8. Macarius, *Spiritual Sermons*, 189 (XXVI.2); Lee, "Pneumatology," 123.

9. Lee, "Pneumatology," 130.

10. Lycurgus M. Starkey Jr. [김덕순, 역], *John Wesley's Theology of the Holy Spirit* [in Korean], trans. Deok-soon Kim [김덕순] (Seoul: Eun-seong, 1994), 270–71; Lee, "Pneumatology," 138.

11. Hu-jeong Lee [이후정], "The Spirit of New Creation: John Wesley's Pneumatological Theology" [in Korean], *Theology and the World* 29 (1994): 101.

12. Ibid., 102.

13. Hong-gi Kim [김홍기], "The Influence of St Augustine's Theology of Grace on Reformed Theology" [in Korean], *Theology and the World* 34 (1997): 73.

14. Ibid., 108.

15. Ibid., 111; John Wesley, "Justification, Assurance and Sanctification" ("Minutes of Some Late Conversations Between the Rev. Mr. Wesleys and Others"), in *The Works of John Wesley*, vol. 8 (Peabody, MA: Hendrickson Publishers, 1986); John Wesley, *A Plain Account of Christian Perfection* (London: Epworth Press, 1960), 33.

16. Jong-cheon Park [박종천], *Theology of Living Together* [in Korean] (Seoul: Korea Theological Research Institute, 1991); Jong-cheon Park [박종천], *Crawl with God, Dance in the Spirit! A Creative Formulation of Korean Theology of the Spirit* [in Korean] (Seoul: Taehan Kidokkyo Sŏhoe, 1998).

17. Jong-cheon Park, "Lady-Bear Theology: The Holy Spirit and the Integrity of Creation," paper presented at the World Methodist Evangelism Seminar (1989). Published as [박종천], *Theology of Living Together* [in Korean], 195–220.

18. J. Park, *Theology of Living Together*, 196.

19. Rosemary R. Ruether, *Mary: The Feminine Face of the Church* (Philadelphia: Westminster Press, 1977); Jürgen Moltmann, *God in Creation*, trans. M. Kohl (London: SCM, 1985); J. Park, *Theology of Living Together*, 202.

20. J. Park, *Theology of Living Together*, 198–205.

21. Moltmann, *God in Creation*, 14; J. Park, *Theology of Living Together*, 205: "The Creator of Heaven and Earth God exists in one of his creatures through his cosmic spirit, and exists in the friendship of creation shared by the creatures."

22. Elisabeth Moltmann-Wendel and Jürgen Moltmann, *Humanity in God* (London: SCM, 1983), 103; J. Park, *Theology of Living Together*, 206.

23. Geoffrey Wainwright, *The Ecumenical Movement: Crisis and Opportunity for the Church* (Grand Rapids, MI: Eerdmans, 1983); J. Park, *Theology of Living Together*, 207.

24. J. Park, *Theology of Living Together*, 208.

25. Ibid., 209.

26. Jeong-bae Lee [이정배], *Theology of Life in the Korean Context as Systematic Theology* [in Korean] (Seoul: Tosŏ Ch'ulp'an Kamsin, 1996), 332–88.

27. Ibid., 388.

28. Jeong-bae Lee [이정배], *The Life of Theology and the Spiritualization of Theology* [in Korean] (Seoul: Korean Christian Book Association, 1999).

29. J. Lee, *Theology of Life*, 110–11.

30. Ibid., 114–15.

31. Ibid., 116. Compare Leonardo Boff, *Trinity and Society*, trans. Paul Burns (Maryknoll, NY: Orbis, 1988), 195–96.

32. J. Lee, *Theology of Life*, 117. Lee accepted Moltmann's dealing with the Spirit of Creation, but criticized Moltmann's assertion that all activities of the Holy Spirit obtain relative value only in Christ. Such arguments result in the expansion of the horizon of institutionalized Christianity rather than the realm of the Holy Spirit. See Jürgen Moltmann, *Der Geist des Lebens: Eine ganzheitliche Pneumatologie* [The Spirit of Life: A Holistic Pneumatology] (Munich: Kaiser Verlag, 1992), 10.

33. J. Lee, *Theology of Life*, 120.

34. Ibid., 132.

35. Bon-cheol Bae [배본철], *History of Protestant Pneumatology* [in Korean] (Anyang: Sungkyul University Publishing Department, 2003); Myung-soo Park [박명수], *Research on the Revival Movement of the Korean Church* [in Korean] (Seoul: Korea Christian History Research Institute, 2003).

36. Meesaeng Lee Choi, *The Rise of the Korean Holiness Church in Relation to the American Holiness Movement: Wesley's Scriptural Holiness and the Fourfold Gospel*, Pietist and Wesleyan Studies 28 (Lanham, MD: Scarecrow Press, 2008), 35–86.

37. Insik Choi [최인식], "A Study of the Theological Significance of Spirit-Baptism: Focusing on Martin Knapp and William Godbey" [in Korean], *Journal of KSST* 33 (2012): 37–73; Sung-wook Oh [오성욱], "Understanding Spirit-Baptism in the Tradition of the International Holiness Union, 1897, Focusing on Martin W. Knapp and William B. Godbey" [in Korean], *Youngsan Theological Journal* 35 (2015): 41–76. See also Lettie B. Cowman, *Charles E. Cowman, Missionary Warrior* (Los Angeles: Oriental Missionary Society, 1928), 83–114; Choi, *Rise of the Korean Holiness Church*, 35–86; Wallace Thornton Jr., *When the Fire Fell: Martin Wells Knapp's Vision of Pentecost and the Beginnings of God's Bible School* (Lexington, KY: Emeth Press, 2014), 107–25; David Bundy, "Religion for Modernity: Martin Wells Knapp and the Radical Holiness Network of the American Progressive Era," *World Christianity and the Fourfold Gospel* 1, no. 1 (2015): 43–79.

38. M. L. Choi, *Rise of the Korean Holiness Church*, 59–74.

39. Bundy, "Religion for Modernity, 72–74; David Bundy, "Barclay F. Buxton, A. Paget Wilkes, and the Japan Evangelistic Band: The Origins, Networks, and Theology of a Radical Holiness Mission," *World Christianity and the Fourfold Gospel* 3, no. 1 (2017): 41–64; David Bundy and Masaya Fujii, "Barclay Fowell Buxton, Japanese Christians, and the Japan Evangelistic Band," *Journal of World Christianity* 8, no. 1 (2018): 47–74.

40. For example, Jong-nam Cho [조종남], *John Wesley's Theology* [in Korean] (Seoul: CLSK, 1994); Seong-joo Lee [이성주], *Theology of Wesley* [in Korean] (Seoul: Daniel Publishing, 1991); Young-tae Han [한영태], *Systematic Theology of Wesley* [in Korean] (Seoul: Sungkwang MunWhaSa, 1993).

41. Seong-yong Jeon [전성용], *Who Is the Holy Spirit? A Trinitarian Pneumatology* [in Korean] (Seoul: Sebok, 2007), 298–300.

42. Seoung-yong Jeon, "History of the Holy Spirit" [in Korean], *Theology and Mission* 31 (2005): 12.

43. Jeon, *Who Is the Holy Spirit?*, 301.

44. Ibid., 344.

45. Tae-gu Kim [김태구], "Holiness and Spirit Baptism," in *Holistic Salvation and Holy Life* [in Korean], ed. Publishing Committee for Pastor Tae-gu Kim's Sermons (Seoul: Sebok, 2009), 381.

46. Ibid., 382.

47. Gyeong-bae Min [민경배], "Reexamination of the Revival Movement of the Pastor Seong-bong Lee," in *Understanding Pastor Seong-bong Lee's Revival Movement* [in Korean], edited by the Committee for Pastor Seong-bong Lee's Centennial Anniversary Works Project (Seoul: Word of Life Publishing, 2000), 187.

48. In-gyo Jeong [정인교], *Pastor Seong-bong Lee's Life and Preaching: A Homiletical Analysis of His Revivalistic Preaching* [in Korean] (Bucheon: Institute for Holiness Theology, 1998), 37–69. In-gyo Jeong divided Seong-bong Lee's life into three periods: (1) struggle with the call (1900–24); (2) the pastor (1925–37); and (3) the pastor as revivalist (1947–65).

49. Yong-gi Cho (often Yonggi Cho in English and European literature) selected "Bible first names," initially Paul and then David. English translations were published under all four versions of the name. Most scholarly literature in Korea and beyond omits the variable Bible name. Here the style respects Korean name formatting and the practice of the National Library, Seoul, South Korea. Yong-gi Cho [조용기], "The Holy Spirit in the Ministry of Pastor Seong-bong Lee," in *Understanding Pastor Seong-bong Lee's Revival Movement* [in Korean], ed. the Committee for the 100th Anniversary of the Birth of Pastor Seong-bong Lee (Seoul: Word of Life Publishing, 2000), 423–24.

50. Ibid., 426–28.

51. Ibid., 428.

52. Ki-ho Seong [성기호], "The Fourfold Gospel and the Revival Movement of Pastor Seong-bong Lee," in *Understanding Pastor Seong-bong Lee's Revival Movement* [in Korean], ed. the Committee for the 100th Anniversary of the Birth of Pastor Seong-bong Lee (Seoul: Word of Life Publishing, 2000), 285; Seong-bong Lee [이성봉], *Not by Words, with Death* [in Korean] (Seoul: Word of Life, 1993), 90.

53. Seong, "Fourfold Gospel," 285.

54. M. Park, *Research on the Revival Movement*, 254.

55. Jeong, *Pastor Seong-bong Lee's Life*, 120.

56. Y. Cho, "Holy Spirit in the Ministry," 425.

57. Seong-bong Lee [이성봉], *The Heart of Revivalistic Preaching*, vol. 2 of *The Works of Pastor Seong-bong Lee* [in Korean] (Seoul: Word of Life, 1985), 2:29.

58. Ibid., 42.

59. Young-hoon Lee, *The Holy Spirit Movement in Korea: Its Historical and Doctrinal Development*, Regnum Studies in Mission (Eugene, OR: Wipf & Stock, 2009); Yung Hun Choi, "Yonggi Cho's Influence on Pentecostal Theology in Korea," in *Asia Pacific Pentecostalism*, ed. Denise A. Austin, Jacqueline Grey, and Paul W. Lewis, Global Pentecostal and Charismatic Studies 31 (Leiden: Brill, 2019), 38.

60. Arthur Judson Brown, *Mastery of the Far East: The Story of Korea's Transformation and Japan's Rise to Supremacy in the Orient* (New York: Fleming Revell, 1929), 528, cited from Bae, "History and Prospect," 19.

61. Horace G. Underwood, *The Call of Korea* (New York: Fleming Revell, 1908), 6, cited from Bae, "History and Prospect, 19.

62. Y. Lee, *Holy Spirit Movement in Korea*; Ig-Jin Kim [김익진], *History and Theology of Korean Pentecostalism: Sunbogeum (Pure Gospel) Pentecostalism; An Attempt to Research the History of the Largest Congregation in Church History and the Theology of Its Pastor Yonggi Cho* (Zoetermeer: Boekencentrum, 2003).

63. Seong-hoon Myung [명성훈], *Church Growth and Holy Spirit: Focused on the Work of the Holy Spirit for Yoido Full Gospel Church* [in Korean] (Seoul: Seoul Book, 1992), 36; Y. H. Choi, "Yonggi Cho's Influence on Pentecostal Theology in Korea," 37–60; Young-hoon Lee, "The Holy Spirit Movement in Korea: Its Historical and Doctrinal Development" (PhD diss., Temple University, 1996), 146; Bae, "History and Prospect," 9.

64. Myung, *Church Growth and Holy Spirit*, 36. Important research on Yoido Church and Cho has been published, including among others: Byung-Wook Park, *Illusion, Wirklichkeit und Ideologie im Gottesdienst: Das theologische Denken von Yonggi Cho unter besonderer Berücksichtigung seiner Theorie und Praxis vom Gottesdienst* [*Illusion, Reality and Ideology in the Church Service: The Theological Thought of Yonggi Cho with Special Consideration of His Theory and Practice of Worship*] (Frankfurt am Main: P. Lang, 1998); Sung-Hoon Myung and Young-Gi Hong, eds., *Charis and Charisma: David Yonggi Cho and the Growth of Yoido Full Gospel Church* (Oxford: Regnum, 2003); I. J. Kim, *History and Theology of Korean Pentecostalism*; William W. Menzies, Wonsuk Ma, and Hyon-song Pae, *David Yonggi Cho: A Close Look at His Theology and Ministry* (Baguio City, Philippines: APTS Press, 2004); Tong-gyu Kim [김동규], *Korean Pentecostal Understanding of the Holy Spirit: Focus on Rev. Dr. Yonggi Cho's Holy Spirit Movement* (Paju-si Geonggi-do: Korean Studies Information 2009).

65. Hyung-ryung Park [박형룡], "Holy Spirit" [in Korean], *Shinhag Jinam* 35, no. 2 (1968): 45–47; cf. Bon-cheol Bae [배본철], "Yong-gi Cho's Doctrine of Baptism of the Holy Spirit: Controversies in Pneumatological Debate Among the Korean Churches from the 1970s to the 1980s" [in Korean], *Youngsan Journal* 36 (2016): 27.

66. Hyung-ryung Park [박형룡], "Baptism in the Holy Spirit and Fullness of the Holy Spirit" [in Korean], *Shinhag Jinam* 38, no. 4 (1971): 6–13; Hyung-ryung Park [박형룡], *Dogmatics: Soteriology* [in Korean] (Seoul: Eun-sung Munwhasa, 1972), 51–54.

67. Yong-gi Cho [조용기], *The Fivefold Gospel and the Threefold Blessing* [in Korean] (Seoul: Youngsan Publishing, 1983), 92.

68. Ibid., 93.

69. Ibid., 98.

70. Ibid., 99.

71. Ibid.

72. Yong-gi Cho [조용기], *Pneumatology* [in Korean] (Seoul: Youngsan Publishing, 1976), 134–5.

73. Y. Cho, *Fivefold Gospel*, 117.

74. Ibid., 123.

75. Ibid., 126.

76. Ibid., 94–97. Y. Cho, *Pneumatology*, 49–51, discussed the Spirit of God, Spirit of Christ, and Spirit of the Comforter.

77. Yong-gi Cho, *The Holy Spirit, My Senior Partner: Understanding the Holy Spirit and His Gifts* (Altamonte Springs, FL: Creation House, 1989); Yong-gi Cho, "The Holy Spirit as Person," in *Yong-gi Cho's Sermons* [in Korean] (Seoul: Seoul-MalsmSa, 1996), 19:105–14; Y. Cho, "Life with the Holy Spirit," in *Yong-gi Cho's Sermons*, 4:295–310.

78. David Yong-gi Cho, *Dr. David Yong-gi Cho: Ministering Hope for 50 Years* (Alachua, FL: Bridge-Logos, 2008), 148, cited from Myeong-seon Moon, "Pastor Yong-gi Cho's Pneumatology of Pentecostal Life" [in Korean], *Youngsan Theological Journal* 26 (2012): 231.

79. Moon, "Pastor Yong-gi Cho's Pneumatology of Pentecostal Life," 223; Myeong-seon Moon [문명선], "Pastor Yong-gi Cho's Theology Interpreted as a Theology of a Personal Holy Spirit" [in Korean], in *Essays for the Commemoration of Professor Kwang-sik Kim's Seventieth Birthday*, ed. Heo Ho-ik [허호익] (Seoul: Gangnam Publishing, 2009), 302–15. Jong-ik Park [박종익], "A Study on the Trinitarian Pneumatology of Pastor Yong-gi Cho" [in Korean], *Hanse-Holiness Theology Discussion* 1 (2004): 51–113.

80. Donald A. D. Thorsen, *The Wesleyan Quadrilateral: Scripture, Tradition, Reason, and Experience as a Model of Evangelical Theology* (Nappanee, IN: Francis Asbury Press, 1990).

81. Hong-gi Kim, "Influence of St Augustine's Theology," 113.

82. Laurence W. Wood, *The Meaning of Pentecost in Early Methodism: Rediscovering John Fletcher as John Wesley's Vindicator and Designated Successor* (Lanham, MD: Scarecrow Press, 2002); Laurence W. Wood, *Pentecost and Sanctification in the Writings of John Wesley and Charles Wesley with a Proposal for Today* (Lexington, KY: Emeth Press, 2018).

83. Richard Paul Gilbertson, *Baptism of the Holy Spirit: The Views of A. B. Simpson and His Contemporaries* (Camp Hill, PA: Christian Publications, 2003); Hyung-geun Im [임형근], "The Historical Background of Spirit Baptism in Classical Pentecostalism" [in Korean], *Youngsan Theological Journal* 21 (2011): 95, where three types of Spirit baptism are examined in detail.

84. Gilbertson, *Baptism of the Holy Spirit*, 14–15; cf. Im, "Historical Background of Spirit Baptism," 96.

85. Gilbertson, *Baptism of the Holy Spirit*, 99; cf. Im, "Historical Background of Spirit Baptism," 97–98.

86. Gilbertson, *Baptism of the Holy Spirit*, 148; cf. Im, "Historical Background of Spirit Baptism," 100.

87. Seung-jun Yoo [유승준], *The Island That Swallowed the Sun: The Story of Martyrs Pan-il Lee and His Son In-jae and Those of Iland Im-ja* [in Korean] (Seoul: Hongseung-sa, 2017); Seung-min Chu [주승민], "The Korean War and the Holiness Church: A Study of the Martyr Narratives of Evangelist Joon-kyung Moon and Elder Pan-il Lee" [in Korean], *Theology and Mission* 33 (2007): 329–59; Myungsoo Park [박명수], "The Korean Holiness Church and Martyrs, and the Memorial Project for Martyrs" [in Korean], *Holiness Church and Theology* 17 (Spring 2007): 243–62; Ki-sik Song [송기식], *Biography of Martyr Pastor Bong-jin Park* [in Korean] (Seoul: Memorial Project Committee of the KEHC, 1996).

BIBLIOGRAPHY

Bae, Bon-cheol [배본철]. 「한국 오순절 성령운동의 역사와 전망: 성령론 논제들의 발생과의 연관성」 ["History and Prospect of the Spirit Movement in Korean Pentecostalism: The Origins and Developments of Pneumatology Debates"]. 「영산신학저널」 [*Youngsan Theological Journal*] 29 (2013): 7–56.

———. 「개신교 성령론의 역사」 [*History of Protestant Pneumatology*]. Anyang: Sungkyul University Publishing Department, 2003.

———. 「조용기 목사의 성령세례 교리: 1970–80년대 한국교회 성령론 논쟁의 표적」 ["Yong-gi Cho's Doctrine of Baptism of the Holy Spirit: Controversies in Pneumatological Debate Among the Korean Churches from the 1970s to the 1980s"]. 「영산신학저널」 [*Youngsan Theological Journal*] 36 (2016): 7–50.

Boff, Leonardo. *Trinity and Society*. Translated by Paul Burns. Maryknoll, NY: Orbis, 1988.

Bundy, David. "Barclay F. Buxton, A. Paget Wilkes, and the Japan Evangelistic Band: The Origins, Networks, and Theology of a Radical Holiness Mission." *World Christianity and the Fourfold Gospel* 3, no. 1 (2017): 41–64.

———. "Religion for Modernity: Martin Wells Knapp and the Radical Holiness Network of the American Progressive Era." *World Christianity and the Fourfold Gospel* 1, no. 1 (2015): 43–79.

Bundy, David, and Masaya Fujii. "Barclay Fowell Buxton, Japanese Christians and the Japan Evangelistic Band." *Journal of World Christianity* 8, no. 1 (2018): 47–74.

Byun, Seon-hwan [변선환].「Lycurgus M. Starkey Jr. 성령의 역사: 웨슬레 신학의 한 연구」「신학과 세계」["Lycurgus M. Starkey Jr. History of the Spirit: A Study of Wesley's Theology"].「세계의 신학」[*Theology and the World*] 7 (1981): 431–38.

Cho, Jong-nam [조종남].「요한 웨슬레의 신학」[*John Wesley's Theology*]. Seoul: CLSK, 1994.

Cho, Yong-gi [조용기]. *Dr. David Yonggi Cho: Ministering Hope for 50 Years*. Alachua, FL: Bridge-Logos, 2008.

———.「5중복음과 삼박자 구원」[*The Fivefold Gospel and the Threefold Blessing*]. Seoul: Youngsan Publishing, 1983.

———.「인격이신 성령」["The Holy Spirit as Person"]. In「조용기 목사 설교전집」[*Yong-gi Cho's Sermons*], 19:105–14. Seoul: SeoulMalsmSa, 1996.

———.「이성봉 목사의 사역 속에 나타난 성령」["The Holy Spirit in the Ministry of Pastor Seong-bong Lee"]. In「이성봉 목사의 부흥운동 조명」[*Understanding Pastor Seong-bong Lee's Revival Movement*], 이성봉 목사 탄신 100주년 기념 회고록 및 학술 논문집 [edited by the Committee for the 100th Anniversary of the Birth of Pastor Seong-bong Lee], 423–29. Seoul: Word of Life Publishing, 2000.

———. *The Holy Spirit, My Senior Partner: Understanding the Holy Spirit and His Gifts*. Altamonte Springs, FL: Creation House, 1989.

———.「성령과 함께 사는 삶」["Life with the Holy Spirit"]. In「조용기 목사 설교전집」[*Yong-gi Cho's Sermons*], 4:295–310. Seoul: SeoulMalsmSa, 1996.

———.「성령론」[*Pneumatology*]. Seoul: Youngsan Publishing, 1976.

Choi, Insik [최인식].「성령세례의 신학적 의의에 대한 고찰 마틴 냅 (M. Knapp) 과 윌리엄 갓비 (W. Godbey) 중심으로」["A Study of the Theological Significance of Spirit-Baptism: Focusing on Martin Knapp and William Godbey"].「한국조직신학논총」[*Journal of KSST*] 33 (2012): 37–73.

Choi, Meesaeng Lee. *The Rise of the Korean Holiness Church in Relation to the American Holiness Movement: Wesley's Scriptural Holiness and the Fourfold Gospel*. Pietist and Wesleyan Studies 28. Lanham, MD: Scarecrow Press, 2008.

Choi, Yung Hun. "Yonggi Cho's Influence on Pentecostal Theology in Korea." In *Asia Pacific Pentecostalism*. Global Pentecostal and Charismatic Studies 31, edited by Denise A. Austin, Jacqueline Grey, and Paul W. Lewis, 37–60. Leiden: Brill, 2019.

Chu, Seung-min [주승민].「한국전쟁과 성결교회: 문준경 전도사와 이판일 장로의 순교 사화를 중심하여」["The Korean War and the Holiness Church: A Study of the Martyr Narratives of Evangelist Joon-kyung Moon and Elder Pan-il Lee"].「신학과 선교」[*Theology and Mission*] 33 (2007): 329–59.

Cowman, Lettie B. *Charles E. Cowman, Missionary Warrior*. Los Angeles: Oriental Missionary Society, 1928.

Gilbertson, Richard Paul. *Baptism of the Holy Spirit: The Views of A. B. Simpson and His Contemporaries*. Camp Hill, PA: Christian Publications, 2003.

Han, Young-tae [한영태].「웨슬레의 조직신학」[*Systematic Theology of Wesley*]. Seoul: Sungkwang MunWhaSa, 1993.

Im, Hyung-geun [임형근].「역사적 배경을 중심으로 본 고전적 오순절주의의 성령침례론」["The Historical Background of Spirit Baptism in Classical Pentecostalism"].「영산신학저널」[*Youngsan Theological Journal*] 21 (2011): 83–126.

Jeon, Seoung-yong [전성용].「성령의 역사 (歷史)」["History of the Holy Spirit"]「신학과 선교」[*Theology and Mission*] 31 (2005): 1–16.

———.「성령은 누구인가: 삼위일체론적 성령론」[*Who Is the Holy Spirit? A Trinitarian Pneumatology*]. Seoul: Sebok, 2007.

Jeong, In-gyo [정인교].「이성봉 목사의 생애와 설교: 그의 부흥 설교에 대한 설교학적 분석」[*Pastor Seong-bong Lee's Life and Preaching: A Homiletical Analysis of His Revivalistic Preaching*]. Bucheon: Institute for Holiness Theology, 1998.

Kim, Hong-gi [김홍기].「성 어거스틴 은총론이 종교개혁 신학에 미친 영향」,「신학과 세계」["The Influence of St Augustine's Theology of Grace on Reformed Theology"].「세계의 신학」[*Theology and the World*] 34 (1997): 54–124.

Kim, Hong-ki, "An Interpretation of the Korean Church in the Wesleyan Perspective." In *The Global Impact of the Wesleyan Traditions and Their Related Movements*, edited by Charles Yrigoyen Jr., 201–16. Pietist and Wesleyan Studies 14. Lanham, MD: Scarecrow Press, 2002.

Kim, Ig-Jin [김익진]. *History and Theology of Korean Pentecostalism: Sunbogeum (Pure Gospel) Pentecostalism; An Attempt to Research the History of the Largest Congregation in Church History and the Theology of Its Pastor Yonggi Cho*. Zoetermeer: Boekencentrum, 2003.

Kim, Myung-yong [김명용].「개혁교회의 성령론과 오순절교회의 성령론」["Pneumatology of the Reformed Church and Pneumatology of the Pentecostal Church"].「장신논단」[*ChangShin NonDan*] 15, no. 12 (1999): 233–48.

Kim, Tae-gu [김태구].「성결과 성령세례」["Holiness and Spirit Baptism"]. In「온전한 구원, 거룩한 생활」[*Holistic Salvation and Holy Life*],「김태구 목사 설교 출판위원회 편」[edited by Publishing Committee for Pastor Tae-gu Kim's Sermons], 381–89. Seoul: Sebok, 2009.

Kim, Tong-gyu [김동규]. *Korean Pentecostal Understanding of the Holy Spirit: Focus on Rev. Dr. Yong-gi Cho's Holy Spirit Movement*. Paju-si Geonggi-do: Korean Studies Information, 2009.

Lee, Hu-jeong [이후정].「성령론」["Pneumatology"]. In「웨슬리와 감리교신학」[*Wesley and the Theology of the Methodist Church*],「한국웨슬리신학회 편」[edited by Wesleyan Theological Society of Korea], 117–41. Seoul: MTS Publishing, 1999.

———.「새 창조의 영: 존 웨슬리의 성령론적 신학」["The Spirit of New Creation: John Wesley's Pneumatological Theology"].「신학과 세계」[*Theology and the World*] 29 (1994): 77–102.

Lee, Jeong-bae [이정배].「신학의 생명화, 신학의 영성화」[*The Life of Theology and the Spiritualization of Theology*]. Seoul: Korean Christian Book Association, 1999.

———.「조직신학으로서의 한국적 생명신학」, [*Theology of Life in the Korean Context as Systematic Theology*]

(Seoul: Tosŏ Ch'ulp'an Kamsin, 1996), 332–88.
Lee, Seong-bong [이성봉].「부흥설교 진수」 [*The Heart of Revivalistic Preaching*]. Vol. 2 of 「이성봉 목사 저작전집 제2권」 [*The Works of Pastor Seong-bong Lee*]. Seoul: Word of Life, 1985.
———.「말로 못하면 죽음으로」 [*Not by Words, with Death*]. Seoul: Word of Life, 1993.
Lee, Seong-joo [이성주].「웨슬리신학」 [*Theology of Wesley*]. Seoul: Daniel Publishing, 1991.
Lee, Young-hoon. "The Holy Spirit Movement in Korea: Its Historical and Doctrinal Development." PhD diss., Temple University, 1996.
———. *The Holy Spirit Movement in Korea: Its Historical and Doctrinal Development*. Regnum Studies in Mission. Eugene, OR: Wipf & Stock, 2009.
Macarius [마카리우스].「신령한 설교」 [*Spiritual Sermons*]. Translated by [이후정 역] Hu-jeong Lee. Seoul: Eun-sung, 1993.
Menzies, William W., Wonsuk Ma, and Hyon-song Pae. *David Yonggi Cho: A Close Look at His Theology and Ministry*. Baguio City, Philippines: APTS Press, 2004.
Min, Gyeong-bae [민경배].「이성봉 목사의 부흥운동 재조명」 ["Reexamination of the Revival Movement of the Pastor Seong-bong Lee"]. In 「이성봉 목사의 부흥운동 조명」 [*Understanding Pastor Seong-bong Lee's Revival Movement*], 이성봉 목사 탄신 100주년 기념 회고록 및 학술 논문집 [edited by the Committee for Pastor Seong-bong Lee's Centennial Anniversary Works Project], 187–214. Seoul: Word of Life Publishing, 2000.
Moltmann, Jürgen. *Der Geist des Lebens: Eine ganzheitliche Pneumatologie* [*The Spirit of Life: A Holistic Pneumatology*]. München: Kaiser Verlag, 1992.
———. *God in Creation*. Translated by M. Kohl. London: SCM, 1985.
Moltmann-Wendel, Elisabeth, and Jürgen Moltmann. *Humanity in God*. London: SCM, 1983.
Moon, Myeong-seon [문명선].「조용기 목사의 오순절적 생명의 성령론」 ["Pastor Yong-gi Cho's Pneumatology of Pentecostal Life"].「영산신학저널」 [*Youngsan Theological Journal*] 26 (2012): 217–40.
———.「인격주의 성령신학으로 해석된 조용기 목사의 신학」 ["Pastor Yong-gi Cho's Theology Interpreted as a Theology of a Personal Holy Spirit"]. In 「청파 김광식 교수 고희기념논총」 허호익 편」 [*Essays for the Commemoration of Professor Kwang-sik Kim's Seventieth Birthday*], edited by [허호익] Heo Ho-ik, 302–15. Seoul: Gangnam Publishing, 2009.
Myung, Seong-hoon [명성훈].「교회성장과 성령: 여의도순복음교회의 성령역사를 중심으로」 [*Church Growth and Holy Spirit: Focused on the Work of the Holy Spirit for Yoido Full Gospel Church*]. Seoul: Seoul Book, 1992.
Myung, Sung-Hoon, and Young-Gi Hong, eds. *Charis and Charisma: David Yonggi Cho and the Growth of Yoido Full Gospel Church*. Oxford: Regnum 2003.
Oh, Sung-wook [오성욱].「만국성결교회 (International Holiness Union 1897) 전통의 성령세례 이해: 마틴 냅과 윌리엄 를 중심으로」 ["Understanding Spirit-Baptism in the Tradition of the International Holiness Union, 1897, Focusing on Martin W. Knapp and William B. Godbey"].「영산신학저널」 [*Youngsan Theological Journal*] 35 (2015): 41–76.
Outler, Albert C. "A Focus on the Holy Spirit: Spirit and Spirituality in John Wesley." *Quarterly Review* 82 (1988): 3–7.

Paik, L. George. *The History of Protestant Missions in Korea: 1832–1910*. Seoul: Christian Literature Society, 1972.

Park, Byung-Wook. *Illusion, Wirklichkeit und Ideologie im Gottesdienst: Das theologische Denken von Yonggi Cho unter besonderer Berücksichtigung seiner Theorie und Praxis vom Gottesdienst* [*Illusion, Reality and Ideology in the Church Service: The Theological Thought of Yonggi Cho with Special Consideration of His Theory and Practice of Worship*]. Frankfurt am Main: P. Lang, 1998.

Park, Hyung-ryung [박형룡]. 「성령세례와 충만」 [Baptism in the Holy Spirit and fullness of the Holy Spirit]. 「신학지남」 [*Shinhag Jinam*] 38, no. 4 (1971): 6–13.

———. 「교의신학: 구원론」, *Dogmatics: Soteriology*. Seoul: Eun-sung Munwhasa, 1972.

———. 「성령」 ["Holy Spirit"]. 「신학지남」 [*Shinhag Jinam*] 35, no. 2 (1968): 45–47.

Park, Jong-cheon [박종천]. 「하느님과 함께 기어라, 성령 안에서 춤추라」 [*Crawl with God, Dance in the Spirit! A Creative Formulation of Korean Theology of the Spirit*]. Seoul: Taehan Kidokkyo Sŏhoe, 1998.

———. "Lady-Bear Theology: The Holy Spirit and the Integrity of Creation." Paper presented at the World Methodist Evangelism Seminar, 1989.

———. 「상생의 신학」 [*Theology of Living Together*]. Seoul: Korea Theological Research Institute, 1991.

Park, Jong-ik [박종익]. 「영산 조용기 목사의 삼위일체론적 성령론 연구」 ["A Study on the Trinitarian Pneumatology of Pastor Yong-gi Cho"]. 「한세-성결 신학논단 창간호」 [*Hanse-Holiness Theology Discussion*] 1 (2004): 51–113.

Park, Myung-soo [박명수]. 「한국성결교회와 순교자, 그리고 순교기념사업」 ["The Korean Holiness Church and Martyrs, and the Memorial Project for Martyrs"]. 「성결교회와 신학」 [*Holiness Church and Theology*] 17 (Spring 2007): 243–62.

———. 「한국교회 부흥운동 연구」 [*Research on the Revival Movement of the Korean Church*]. Seoul: Korea Christian History Research Institute, 2003.

Ruether, Rosemary R. *Mary: The Feminine Face of the Church*. Philadelphia: Westminster Press, 1977.

Seong, Ki-ho [성기호]. 「사중복음과 이성봉 목사의 부흥운동」 ["The Fourfold Gospel and the Revival Movement of Pastor Seong-bong Lee"]. In 「이성봉 목사의 부흥운동 조명」 [*Understanding Pastor Seong-bong Lee's Revival Movement*], 이성봉 목사 탄신 100주년 기념 회고록 및 학술 논문집 [edited by the Committee for the 100th Anniversary of the Birth of Pastor Seong-bong Lee], 278–300. Seoul: Word of Life Publishing, 2000.

Song, Ki-sik [송기식]. 「순교자 박봉진 목사 전기」 [*Biography of Martyr Pastor Bong-jin Park*]. Seoul: Memorial Project Committee of the KEHC, 1996.

Starkey, Lycurgus M., Jr. [김덕순, 역] *John Wesley's Theology of the Holy Spirit* 「존 웨슬리의 성령신학」. Translated by Deok-soon Kim [김덕순]. Seoul: Eun-seong, 1994. Originally published as *The Work of the Holy Spirit: A Study in Wesleyan Theology*. New York: Abingdon Press, 1962.

Thornton, Wallace, Jr. *When the Fire Fell: Martin Wells Knapp's Vision of Pentecost and the Beginnings of God's Bible School*. Lexington, KY: Emeth Press, 2014.

Thorsen, Donald A. D. *The Wesleyan Quadrilateral: Scripture, Tradition, Reason and Experience as a Model of Evangelical Theology*. Nappanee, IN: Francis Asbury Press, 1990.

Wainwright, Geoffrey. *The Ecumenical Movement: Crisis and Opportunity for the Church*. Grand Rapids, MI: Eerdmans, 1983.

Wesley, John. "Minutes of Some Late Conversations Between the Rev. Mr. Wesleys and Others." In vol. 8 of *The Works of John Wesley*. Peabody, MA: Hendrickson Publishers, 1986.

———. *A Plain Account of Christian Perfection*. London: Epworth Press, 1960.

Wood, Laurence W. *The Meaning of Pentecost in Early Methodism: Rediscovering John Fletcher as John Wesley's Vindicator and Designated Successor*. Lanham, MD: Scarecrow Press, 2002.

———. *Pentecost and Sanctification in the Writings of John Wesley and Charles Wesley with a Proposal for Today*. Lexington, KY: Emeth Press, 2018.

Yi, Tŏk-chu [이덕주]. 「한국 감리 교회 역사」 [*A History of the Methodist Church in Korea*]. Seoul: KMC / Ch'op'an, 2017.

Yoo, Seung-jun [유승준]. 「태양을 삼킨 섬: 이판일·이인재 부자와 임자도의 순교자들 이야기」 [*The Island That Swallowed the Sun: The Story of Martyrs Pan-il Lee and His Son In-jae and Those of Iland Im-ja*]. Seoul: Hongseung-sa, 2017.

THEOLOGICAL ENGAGEMENT

CHAPTER 8

Baptized in the Spirit and Fire
The Relevance of Spirit Baptism for a Holiness
and Pentecostal View of the Atonement

Frank D. Macchia

The atonement is arguably the bulwark Christological doctrine of the Western church, guaranteeing the significance of Christology in counterbalance to pneumatology. More specifically, it was historically the incarnation-atonement link that gave Christology its proper place in the West. As we will see, Christology received its due in the link that was forged between the Chalcedonian Definition and Anselm's classic work on the atonement, *Cur Deus Homo*. In the linkage of incarnation and atonement the very person of Christ became the objective event of reconciliation between God and humanity. The divine Son who became flesh in the incarnation provided reconciliation between God and humanity on the cross. Given the centrality of Christ to redemption (secured by the incarnation-atonement linkage), the church in the West was thought to be protected from any subordination of Christology to pneumatology. Christ becomes more than a Spirit-anointed man (the adoptionist Christology). Christ is also more than the mere means by which the Spirit comes into the world (the problem of Christological instrumentalism).

But has this Western focus on the atonement as the chief Christological event not tilted the atonement too far in a Christological direction? I believe that it has. Anselm's massive *Cur Deus Homo* does not have much to say explicitly about the role of the Holy Spirit in the atonement. What significance does Christ's conception by the Spirit in Mary's womb and his baptism in the Spirit at the Jordan (Luke 1:35, 3:21–22) have for his later death on the cross in light of its atoning significance? More elaborately, what about John the Baptist's programmatic announcement that Christ will baptize in the Holy Spirit and fire?

THE FOCUS ON SPIRIT BAPTISM

Both Holiness and Pentecostal movements have implicitly highlighted John the Baptist's announcement by placing a unique focus on the baptism in the Holy Spirit in their understanding of Jesus's messianic mission. For example, Asa Mahan published *The Baptism of the Holy Ghost* in 1870 in which he based the sanctifying work of the Spirit on Jesus's reception of the Spirit at the Jordan as the Spirit Baptizer.[1] As is widely known, the Pentecostal Movement was born with the emphasis on Spirit baptism as the empowering work of the Spirit upon the sanctified life, though the difference between Holiness and Pentecostal traditions should not be exaggerated. One early Pentecostal author notably pointed out, "There is no difference in quality between the baptism with the Holy Ghost and sanctification. They are both holiness."[2] The Pentecostal Movement and many of their Holiness forebears gave the doctrine of the baptism in the Holy Spirit prominence as an ecumenical issue. The most significant academic works written on the topic by non-Pentecostal authors in the 1970s and beyond were written in response to the Pentecostal message.[3] The roots of the Pentecostal focus on Spirit baptism go back to John Wesley's quest for perfect love, even though he did not describe it as a Spirit baptism. Wesley understood Christian perfection as the attainment of "simplicity of intention and purity of affection," "one design in all we speak or do and one desire ruling all our tempers" by which one conforms within to the love of Christ.[4] One does not arrive thereby at absolute perfection in life but rather at a place of the complete surrender of the will to Christ that was couched within a larger journey toward conformity to Christ. As Donald W. Dayton has shown, the doctrine of Christian perfection gained popularity in American Holiness circles in the 1820s and 1830s due in part to its affinity with the optimistic utopianism of pre–Civil War America. But wedded to American revivalism, the doctrine of perfection in the Holiness Movement differed in nuance from Wesley's teaching in that perfection was now thought to be attainable by holiness advocates like Phoebe Palmer "instantaneously by the act of 'placing all on the altar.'"[5] Wedded also to this development was increased attention to pneumatology and the language of Spirit baptism drawn principally from the Book of Acts. The attainment of perfect love as a second blessing was thus called a "baptism in the Holy Spirit." Baptism in the Spirit as a second blessing spread in the nineteenth century beyond the strict boundaries of the American Holiness Movement to involve Baptists like D. L. Moody, who came to view Spirit baptism more as an empowerment for witness to Christ (following, for example, Acts 1:8) than the attainment of deeper purity through the surrender to perfect love (following, for example, Acts 15:9).[6]

It seems clear through such developments that Spirit baptism at the dawn of the Pentecostal Movement late in the nineteenth century had in certain Wesleyan and analogous revivalist circles become a bold challenge to the church to deepen its commitment to the love of Christ and its powerful victory in the spreading witness of the church. It was from this challenge that the Pentecostal Movement was born. Of course, the Pentecostals in the early decades of the movement did not all nuance the meaning of Spirit baptism the same way. Pentecostals who came from the Holiness Movement, such as William Seymour, viewed Spirit baptism as the gift of power for witness given to the human vessel that had previously received the life of God and been thoroughly cleansed within. Lest one think that Seymour was intending to leave the quest for holiness or perfect love behind in his understanding of Spirit baptism, attention should be drawn to the title he gave his remarks: "The Way into the Holiest."[7] He arguably viewed Spirit baptism as the release of perfect love in the outward witness of the believer after the believer had been justified and entirely sanctified by this love. The same could be said of many Reformed or "baptistic" Pentecostals who did not view the attainment of perfect love as a needed preparation for Spirit baptism. E. N. Bell, for example, referred to Spirit baptism as a baptism in divine love.[8] In fact, Pentecostals, both Holiness and non-Holiness in background, favored the use of Romans 5:5 (the love of God poured into our hearts) to describe Spirit baptism.[9] Spirit baptism occurred for them all on the cutting edge of a church given over in dramatic ways to the victory of divine love in the world. This view of Spirit baptism could be found also among Oneness (non-Trinitarian) Pentecostals, who viewed Spirit baptism as the empowering reception of the Spirit that was tied to Christian initiation through repentance, faith, and water baptism in Jesus's name.[10]

But at this point the question must be posed: Is Spirit baptism only an awakening or deepening experience for a spiritually withdrawn church? The ecumenical responses to the Pentecostal emphasis on Spirit baptism have maintained in different ways that Spirit baptism cannot be detached from Christian initiation or from the faith and life of the church catholic. Spirit baptism is also an ongoing challenge to the churches, calling them to ever deeper dimensions of purity and power in the love of Christ. The gift of the Spirit is eschatological in its reach, involving Christian initiation and evermore expansive experiences of Christ's love in the world.[11] In its more expanded form, Spirit baptism can indeed be a doctrine that is hospitable to Pentecostals and Wesleyans of all orientations, given the legacy of John Wesley, which puts the attainment and victory of divine love in all things at the forefront of our witness. Since sanctification and its powerful victory in the witness of the church is both a Christological and a pneumatological doctrine, the challenge before us is to link both the atonement and the reception of the Spirit at Pentecost in our understanding of Spirit baptism. The baptism in the Holy Spirit and fire is the biblical umbrella under which this link can be forged.

This focus on Spirit baptism certainly has biblical warrant. All four gospels and the Book of Acts, the narrative foundation of the New Testament, highlight Jesus's baptizing others in the Holy Spirit (Matt. 3:16; Mark 1:8; Luke 3:22; John 1:33; Acts 1:5). Luke and John note that Jesus will do this by pouring forth the Spirit upon others after his resurrection, the culmination of his Messianic mission (Luke 24:49; Acts 1:5, 2:32–36; John 20:21). The question discussed in what follows has to do with how the atonement fulfills the mission of Jesus the Spirit Baptizer, thus allowing all who wish to link the atonement to the sanctifying and empowering work of the Spirit in the world to do so in a way suggested by the biblical text.

INCARNATION, ATONEMENT, AND SPIRIT BAPTISM: THE ECUMENICAL ISSUE

Before examining the specific challenge of relating the atonement to Spirit baptism, it would help to understand more elaborately the broader problem of the neglect of the Spirit in atonement theories of the West. Helpful is the tendency of the Eastern church to view Christ's life, death, and resurrection as the means by which Christ conquers death in the resurrection so as to impart the Spirit to all flesh. In the East, Spirit Christology thus came to play a prominent role in the salvific work of Christ. Moltmann described the Eastern dependence on Spirit Christology this way: "Orthodoxy understands the history of Jesus itself pneumatologically. His incarnation, his mission, his anointing and his resurrection are the works of the Holy Spirit. The Holy Spirit is the divine subject of the history of Jesus. For that reason, the Son of God is also present in and through the Spirit in his church."[12] Moltmann added insightfully that the Western stream of thought resisted this dependence on the Spirit for understanding the significance of Jesus for salvation because it seemed to pose a danger of reducing Jesus to a mere instrument for mediating the life of the Spirit to the world. The West sought to avoid this danger in part through its emphasis on the atonement, which made Jesus's own self-giving as the eternally divine Son the objective event of reconciliation between God and humanity. Without the atonement as an objective Christological event of reconciliation, Christ was thought to be in danger of merely serving the mediation of the Spirit. Moltmann agreed with this Western conviction when he warned, "The true perception that the messianic history of Christ from his incarnation to his exaltation is the work of the eschatological Spirit must not pass by Christ's death on the cross."[13] In other words, atonement theology in the West granted Christology its due, counterbalancing it with Pentecost or with pneumatology and keeping the economies of the Son and the Spirit properly distinct and equal.

But has this "distinct and equal" been maintained in the West? I think not, although there were important theological minds who pointed in the direction of doing so. The question left unanswered in the West concerns the role of the atonement in Christ's mission of mediating the Spirit to all flesh. Unless Christ's death on the cross serves his mission of imparting new life through the Spirit, the effort at counterbalancing Christology and pneumatology will tilt the balance too far in the direction of Christology, which is what happened in the West, especially in the affirmations of the ecumenical creeds. One need not look any further in seeking to rediscover the needed balance than John the Baptist's announcement that the Messiah will baptize in the Spirit and fire (e.g., Luke 3:16). Toward that end, he himself will be Spirit baptized at the Jordan and fire baptized at his death (Luke 3:22, 12:49) so as to baptize others in the Spirit (Luke 24:49). Where is any of this in creedal Christology? The Spirit is nearly absent from both the Nicene Creed and the Chalcedonian Definition, not to mention the crowning of these statements in Anselm's atonement theory, as will be explained below.

But all is not lost when it came to the Christological creeds in the West, for the incarnation-atonement link that granted Christology dominance in relation to pneumatology also offered potential for establishing the balance between them. The unity of essence between Christ and his Father affirmed at Nicea (Nicaea) and the unity of person in Christ (who is both divine and human) at Chalcedon are important to understand what qualifies Jesus to suffer death so as to impart the Spirit on behalf of the Father to all flesh by conquering death. As Cyril of Alexandria noted, "the Son is life by nature, flowing like a river from the Father, by reason of being of the same substance as he, and thus giving life to all."[14] Though the Spirit is nearly absent from creedal Christology and its full expression in the atonement theory of Anselm, the victories won there created the potential for granting the Spirit her due. I do not use the word "victories" lightly. The incarnation-atonement linkage was intensely problematic from the beginning, despite the fact that it is suggested by texts like Hebrews 2:14 ("he too shared in their humanity so that by his death he might break the power of him who holds the power of death").[15] Since many found it enormously difficult to believe that God could suffer, the horizon of the cross made the incarnation difficult to swallow, for the capacity to suffer implied metaphysical lack, and God lacks nothing. And yet the proclamation of the gospel made the link between God and suffering impossible to avoid.

The widespread belief that God is impassible (transcends and is immune to suffering) created a crisis in the early centuries of the church and beyond when it came to deciding whether or not the divine Logos or Son was incarnated in flesh (John 1:14) and suffered and died (Heb. 2:14). As fourth-century scholars Michael Barnes and Lewis Ayres have noted, what it meant to call Jesus "God" had everything to do with how the term was being used.[16] More specifically, the meaning of the term had to do with whether or not one assumed a unity of essence between the transcendent God (typically called the true God or Father) and the Logos or Son who became flesh and suffered. Even when rhetoric was used that implied such unity of essence between them, that unity was not necessarily intended. Referring to the Son as the "second Person" of the Godhead, Barnes states the problem this way: "All sides of the early stage of the Nicene controversy could (and did) comfortably describe the production of the second Person from the first as an X from an X causal relationship. Expressions like light from light or wisdom from wisdom occur in virtually everyone's writings. Clearly, in themselves, they do not specify that the cause reproduces its own nature or identity in the product."[17]

Those who said that the Son was of the same essence of the Father (sometimes called *miahypostatic*) viewed the Son as internal to the divine self-impartation to the world, essential to the divine self-impartation for the sake of our salvation. Salvation consequently tended to be viewed as a sanctifying participation in God's presence. For those who held to two different essences between the Son and the Father (who is alone the "true God") (sometimes called *dyohypostatic*), the Son may be viewed as participating in both the divinity of the Father and creaturely existence, but not as essential to an imagined self-impartation of the true God to the world. To the contrary, the true God tended to be viewed as not involved directly in the world and salvation was consequently understood typically as a mere imitation of the Son's faithfulness, cooperation with the will of the true God as exemplified in the Son rather than receiving the divine life for a transformative participation in it.[18] We could add that Christ as the Spirit Baptizer, who overcomes sin and death on the cross to pour forth the Spirit from the Father onto all flesh, is at home in the former trajectory (*miahypostatic*) but not in the latter (*dyohypostatic*).

In the fourth century, Arius was the extreme example of the latter (*dyohypostatic*) trajectory. Arius detested those who spoke of Christ as of one essence with the Father, which in his view fractured the divine life and subjected it to the suffering of the body on the cross. Those who did this signified for Arius that Christ is "part" of God as a separate or fragmented "emanation" of God. As a result, "the Father will be according to them compounded, divided, mutable, and a body, and, as far as they are concerned, the incorporeal God suffers things suitable to the body."[19] To prevent these conclusions, Arius not only argued that the incarnate Logos was of a different essence from the Father but that he was also created before time as the means of creating all else. The problem here, however, is that a created being that is not of one essence with the Father arguably cannot in his life, death, and resurrection impart the Spirit to all flesh so as to sanctify flesh. As Athanasius wrote of Christ against the Arians, "being God, [he] later became man that instead he might deify us."[20] To this end, Athanasius noted that the impassible Logos suffered in the flesh so as to conquer sin and death as the agent of new life.[21] This affirmation of Christ's suffering and death as the means by which God sanctifies flesh in the Spirit provides the narrative arc for connecting the Spirit to the atonement. The divine Son passes through death bearing in his body the sanctifying Spirit so that, rising in the Spirit, he may grant the sanctifying Spirit to others. Viewing the affirmation of the Nicene Creed that Christ is of one essence (*homoousios*) with the Father ("true God from true God") thus allows Christ to function as the mediator of the Spirit (the Spirit Baptizer) by means of his life, death, and resurrection. The link between the atonement and the impartation of the Spirit is established.

Unfortunately, in the fifth century, Nestorius's Christology also hindered the implied connection between the atonement and the impartation of the sanctifying Spirit to all flesh. Though Nestorius affirmed Christ's full deity, he still could not allow any involvement of the divine Son in the passion of suffering flesh. For Nestorius, "God has been joined by the crucified flesh even though he has not shared its suffering."[22] So, Nestorius kept the two natures of Christ (divine and human) strictly separate, with separate functions. Moreover, Nestorius sought to avoid any view of the incarnation as a necessary divine act or an act forced on the human person of Jesus. The result is a view of the incarnation as a cooperative act of love in which both the deity and humanity of Christ are involved in mutual conjunction, interrelation, and cooperation, a "conjunction by interrelation" (*schetike synapheia*) of the two natures.[23] The scriptures note that Jesus as the divine Son incarnate communes with his Father (John 17:22–23), but the Son's humanity does not commune with the Son. The implication of saying this, contrary to Nestorius's best intentions, was a separation of two acting subjects in the one Christ. By separating the natures as much as he did, Nestorius keeps God at arm's length from humanity and humanity at arm's length from God. In Nestorius's theological vision, God does not bear death so as to grant us access to the divine life. Nestorius ends up prohibiting the humanity of Jesus from participating fully in God's self-impartation to all flesh. As Douglas Fairbairn has shown, all that we end up with in Nestorius's view of salvation is a cooperation between God and humanity, a cooperation from a distance.[24]

In opposition to Nestorius, Cyril of Alexandria was willing to say that the one Son suffers death impassibly in the flesh so as to conquer death as the mediator of life in the Spirit. "If anyone does not confess that the Word of God suffered in the flesh, was crucified in the flesh and tasted death in the flesh becoming the firstborn from the dead although as God he is life and life-giving let him be anathema."[25] This is the view that informs the Chalcedonian Definition, the one divine person of Christ acknowledged in two distinct but indivisible natures so as to grant us access to God's very life.

The debates swirling around Nicea and Chalcedon and the brilliant work connected to these accomplishments by Athanasius (after Nicea) and Cyril (before Chalcedon) linked the incarnation to the atonement in a way that made the sanctifying work of the Spirit the end result, though one would not know this by reading these creedal statements themselves. Neither would one know it by reading Anselm's classic, written in the late eleventh century, *Cur Deus Homo* (Why the God Man).[26] The creedal consensus forged from Nicea to Chalcedon concerning the incarnation cleared the way for the focus on the atonement as the crowning moment of Christology. No other thinker provided this crowning statement as significantly as Anselm. As the title of his classic suggests, Anselm had fundamentally in mind how the atonement fulfills the incarnation, especially as it was explained at Chalcedon. His goal was to demonstrate why the one who died on the cross to save us had to be both divine and human in one person. For Anselm, both God and humanity have a distinct role to play in the atonement, both of which are important to that event in different ways. It is not fitting for God alone to deliver humanity from sin and death because it is properly humanity's obligation to make atonement, for humanity is the guilty party; *they* robbed God of the honor that was due the Lord of creation. He wrote, "God was in no need of descending from heaven to conquer the devil, nor of contending against him in holiness to free mankind. But God demanded that man should conquer the devil, so that he who had offended by sin should atone by holiness."[27] Yet, humanity alone cannot atone for their sin by holiness, for they lack the ability to pay humanity's debt of honor to God and restore creation to God in the process. If God and humanity could act as one person, however, we would have our savior. For Anselm, Chalcedon grants us the precise framework for this solution. The God-Man can fulfill both roles, possessing *both* the moral obligation of guilty humanity *and* the infinite power of God. Only the God-Man described at Chalcedon can provide atonement for humanity.

Classical Christology in the West had done it. It had secured the involvement of God in the incarnation and the atonement, while also explaining the significance of Jesus Christ as in himself the great event of reconciliation between God and humanity. At the same time, the instrumentalist Spirit Christology of the East was kept at bay. And was it ever kept at bay! In addition to the near absence of the Spirit in the Nicene Creed and Chalcedonian Definition, the Holy Spirit is mentioned only once in Anselm's *Cur Deus Homo*, specifically in the context of the cross, but only to fill out a triadic designation of God. Since the Son is divine, Anselm reminds us, he restored honor to himself on the cross as well as to the Father and to the Holy Spirit.[28] Anselm did start his classic reflection on the atonement by noting that Christ died "to restore life to the world" and he assumed that this new life has cosmic breadth.[29] But more is needed to grant pneumatology its due in the context of the atonement.

What has been said by others about the Holy Spirit being the neglected "stepchild" of theology in the West has been most apparent in the area of atonement theology. In her book *The Trinity and the Paschal Mystery* Anne Hunt noted rightly that Trinitarian theology did not in the West provide a Trinitarian framework for understanding the atonement until relatively recently.[30] The atonement had been commonly viewed in a largely binitarian fashion as the culminating moment of Christ's self-offering to the Father on humanity's behalf. A role for the Spirit was implied but not granted the kind of explanation that is required by the thrust of the biblical witness. For example, even a brilliant work like Jürgen Moltmann's *Trinity and the Kingdom* concluded, "The stories of Gethsemane and Golgotha tell the history of the passion, which takes place between the Father and the Son."[31]

SANCTIFICATION AND ATONEMENT

The effort to work toward a pneumatological understanding of atonement can draw insight from both Wesleyan and Pentecostal sources, especially in viewing the atonement as the basis of both justification and sanctification, a direction that has pneumatological implications. Helpfully, Wesleyan theologians have recently reflected on the atonement as a sanctifying event.[32] The most fruitful attempt was made by Heather Oglevie, who began by noting that the Wesleyan tradition helps us to see the atonement as the basis for both justification and sanctification.[33] Indeed, even John Wesley's substitutionary model of atonement as a basis for justification (meaning Jesus takes our place and pays our debt of glory to God so that we can be acquitted of our sins and justified before God) shows that Jesus sacrificed his life for God's cause in the world, which is love for humanity. His death was the ultimate act of love and obedience to the law, the supreme act of the sanctified life.[34] In Christ's journey to the cross he shows himself to be the perfectly sanctified man, a sanctified journey that culminates at the cross for the sake of humanity. She writes that in the cross, "his holiness was not merely displayed or demonstrated but perfected: consummated and established in our race for all time."[35] Sanctification perfects human nature; Christ's perfection was earned, while ours is attained by grace.[36] His sanctified humanity unites us with God and provides the means by which we are sanctified in him.[37] Oglevie maintained insightfully that there is perfection at each stage of Christ's life, including his perfect death. So Christ had not yet achieved the totality of his perfection until death, simply because he had not yet died, an event that was needed for him to experience perfection in all that is human within the context of history.[38] At death, Christ's perfect holiness received its most severe test, and Christ passed. One could not do greater than lay down his or her life for divine love. The resurrection is the Father's vindication of Christ's perfect self-giving. Christ then imparts his life to us by pouring forth the Spirit.[39] Since Christ's self-sacrificial death was the epitome of his perfect life, our entire sanctification in him causes our lives to be living sacrifices. In this way, we share in his self-sacrificial death.[40] All of these insights are helpful, for there is much that is implicitly pneumatological in these ideas. But the linkage with the incarnation is not clear; neither is the link to Jesus's baptism in the Spirit and fire, to which Luke especially bears witness, which would make the pneumatological implication of Oglevie's work more explicit, especially in relation to the atonement.

As we will note, the classical sources from early Pentecostalism on the atonement include a mixture of motifs: forgiveness, victory over sin, healing, and self-giving love. As with Wesley, Pentecostals tended to speak of the atonement using a mixture of substitutionary and Christus victor motifs (Christus victor meaning that Christ conquers sin and death on our behalf so as to remove them as barriers between us and God). Like the Wesleyan view of atonement developed by Oglevie and others, the classical Pentecostal view of atonement was implicitly pneumatological in that they saw the victory of the spilled blood of Jesus over sin to be the victory of divine love. Oneness Pentecostal pioneer Frank Ewart wrote: "Calvary unlocked the flow of God's love, which is God's very nature, into our hearts."[41] The victory of the "river of living water" in submerging believers in divine love and resulting in entire sanctification and Spirit baptism was described by William Seymour as coming through the atonement ("all this, we get through the atonement").[42] C. H. Mason's stunning description of Spirit baptism as evidenced by groaning for the suffering and the lost out of love for them grants specificity to these early Pentecostal claims. Mason's own Spirit baptism took him to the cross where Christ groaned in the Spirit for the suffering of humanity. Mason found himself united to Christ's groaning at that moment so intimately that he heard Christ's voice in Mason's own during his groaning. This is what Mason wrote: "I surrendered perfectly to him and consented to him. He sang through me and took charge of me. It seemed I was standing at the cross and I heard him as he groaned, the dying groans of Jesus, and I groaned. It was not my voice but the voice of my beloved that I heard in me. He lifted me to my feet and then the light of heaven fell upon me and burst into me filling me. Then God took charge of my tongue. The glory of God filled the temple."[43]

However, atonement has been linked to sanctification in both Wesleyan and Pentecostal traditions in overwhelmingly Christological terms. What is the Spirit's role in all of this? As Eugene Rogers asked, what does the Spirit do that the Father and the Son cannot do better? Rogers answered that the Spirit "befriends" matter (especially human bodies) so as to turn them into the sacrament of the divine presence or of divine love, first and decisively in the incarnation, life, death, and resurrection of the Son of God, and then in us from him and in his image.[44] In my rendition of this insight, Jesus through the Spirit was baptized in the Spirit and fire as a sanctifying event in order to baptize others in the Spirit, regenerating, sanctifying, and empowering them in the journey toward the ultimate event of the Spirit and victory of divine love, the resurrection from the dead. In what follows, I will offer a sketch of my constructive pneumatological theory of atonement using the baptism in the Spirit and fire as my guide. Using John the Baptist's programmatic Christological announcement as my guide is both exegetically warranted and relevant to Holiness and Pentecostal contributions to a pneumatological understanding of the atonement.

BAPTISM IN THE SPIRIT: TOWARD A PNEUMATOLOGICAL THEORY OF ATONEMENT

Luke is a voice in the biblical canon that can help Holiness and Pentecostal theologians address the challenge of viewing Jesus's sojourn to the cross, the cross itself as a pneumatological event. He is unique among the evangelists in describing the larger significance of Christ's death as a passage through the baptism in fire to the eschatological reach of the baptism in the Spirit. Christ passed through the fire as the sanctifying event for all time so as to impart the sanctifying Spirit to all flesh. I affirm here James Dunn's conclusion that, for Luke, "the climax and proposed end of Jesus's ministry is not the cross and the resurrection, but the ascension and Pentecost."[45] The cross has its *telos* for Luke, not only at the resurrection but at Pentecost, where Christ imparts his sanctified life to people by baptizing them in the Spirit.

The point of departure is thus the programmatic announcement by John the Baptist: "I baptize you with water. But one who is more powerful than I will come, the straps of whose sandals I am not worthy to untie. He will baptize you with the Holy Spirit and fire. His winnowing fork is in his hand to clear his threshing floor and to gather the wheat into his barn, but he will burn up the chaff with unquenchable fire" (3:16–17). The immediate context of this announcement is John's baptism, which was a prophetic drama of hope that had very much to do with sanctification. This drama was connected to the Jordan's historic significance as important to the journey of the original exodus community into the Promised Land.[46] This background connects the Jordan to the exodus. In this light, John's baptism was a new exodus drama featuring a new Israel leaving its sins behind in the Jordan and reemerging from the Jordan in hopes of renewal as a sanctified, new covenant people. Under John's announcement, this baptismal drama is presented in Luke as symbolic of a people welcoming the coming era of the promised Holy Spirit as Israel had once welcomed life in the Promised Land. The coming baptism in the Holy Spirit was to fulfill these Israelite hopes by opening up a path to a new exodus but this time to the promised new covenant earmarked by a sanctified life in the Holy Spirit.

According to John's announcement, as John baptized in the Jordan, the coming Messiah will baptize in the Holy Spirit and fire. John's announcement implies that the Messiah will occasion a "river" of the Spirit and fire through which Israel must pass unto purgation or judgment, depending on their response. The promise of the coming Messiah as the Spirit Baptizer is key to John's significance as the one who foretells of the coming renewal. For Luke, the Messiah will make known the Holy Spirit through his own baptism in the Spirit and fire. The Messiah will then open a path to the Spirit at Pentecost by imparting the Spirit to all flesh on behalf of the Father. Placing Joel 2:28–32 in the background of the Messiah's future impartation of the Spirit as Luke does in Acts 2:17–21 grants Spirit baptism apocalyptic significance. There are indeed signs given at the Jordan that indicate an apocalyptic event: the heavens open, and God's voice is heard declaring Jesus as the beloved Son. And the Spirit appears in the form of a dove resting on the Messiah as the beginning of the new age, reminiscent of the Spirit's brooding on the waters of creation and the sign of new creation in the story of Noah (Gen. 1:2, 8:6–12). Kilian McDonnell noted rightly that in a very real sense for Luke, "eschatology begins at the Jordan."[47]

According to Luke, Jesus was conceived by the Spirit in the Virgin's womb as the holy Son of God (1:35). John the Baptist was filled with the Spirit in the womb (1:41), but only Jesus was conceived by the Spirit as a virginal conception. Implied here is that he stands apart from John as the one sanctified to be the Spirit Baptizer, the divine Lord of life in flesh who mediates the Spirit on behalf of the heavenly Father. As human, he was later filled with the Spirit and bore the Spirit as the one perfectly sanctified so that his embodied life became the sacrament of the Spirit to others, sanctifying them and shaping them in the image of the faithful life of Jesus, the Son incarnate. As divine, he passed on the Holy Spirit to others on behalf of the Father, something John the Baptist could never do.

According to John, the messianic baptizing in the Spirit, however, will not only lead to sanctification and renewal, it will also occasion a fire baptism of devastating judgment for those who reject it. John announced that "the winnowing fork is in his hand to clear his threshing floor and to gather the wheat into his barn, but he will burn up the chaff with unquenchable fire" (3:17). John brought together the images of wind and fire; the wind separates the repentant from the unrepentant and sweeps the unrepentant into the river of fire. For the unrepentant, the river of the Spirit becomes a river of fiery judgment (the metaphor in the text changes at this point). The devastating effects of this flood of judgment in John's announcement reminds one of texts like Isaiah 30:28: "His breath is like a rushing torrent, rising up to the neck. He shakes the nations in the sieve of destruction." Judgment is sometimes described as a mighty flood. Jonah sinks beneath the waves of death and alienation from God. He cried out to God, "I have been banished from your sight" (Jon. 2:4). Jonah's experience is especially relevant since Luke shares with Matthew a connection between Christ's fire baptism, the baptism of his death, and Jonah's sinking beneath the waves of judgment and despair. As Jonah was raised up from oblivion to proclaim God's grace to the Ninevites, so shall the Son of Man be raised to open up with eschatological finality the possibility of repentance and renewal (Jon. 2:1–6; Luke 11:29–32). As Dunn wrote, "It was the fiery πνεῦμα in which all must be immersed, as it were, and which like a smelting furnace would burn up all impurity. For the unrepentant, it would mean total destruction. For the repentant, it would mean a refining... which would result in salvation."[48] Tellingly, Luke traced Jesus's lineage to "Adam the son of God" (3:38). Just prior to this naming of Adam as the son of God, Christ as the eschatological Adam was announced the Son of God by his heavenly Father at the waters of the Jordan to fulfill the mission to Adam and Eve's seed. The waters of purgation will overflow the boundaries of Israel to reach all of humanity.

Jesus as the Spirit Baptizer in Luke means that the salvific work of Christ occurs in the presence of the Holy Spirit, the river through which all must pass, either unto purgation or final judgment. Jesus must himself pass through that river; he must himself be baptized in the Spirit and fire on the way to baptizing others in the Spirit. Little did John the Baptist know that to baptize in the Spirit and fire, the beloved Son must also endure the fire baptism in its most devastating form. Christ's victory at the Jordan was followed by his trial in the desert. Filled with the Spirit, Jesus was led by the Spirit to the desert (Luke 4:1). This temptation was only the beginning of the trial that the Messiah must endure, a trial that will take him to the garden and the cross. He endured the trial that was not only analogous to the one experienced by Israel in the desert, but also the one faced by Adam and Eve in the Garden.

For Luke, the cross is Jesus's baptism in fire, the baptism of his death. Note Luke 12:49–50: "I have come to bring fire on the earth, and how I wish it were already kindled! But I have a baptism to undergo, and what constraint I am under until it is completed." The Messiah was indeed to kindle a fire upon the Earth, just as John the Baptist foretold! He will baptize others in fire. James and John called for this fire to descend on others in Luke 9:54, but Jesus rebuked them (9:55). It was not yet time for the fire baptism. Christ must first endure this fire baptism himself, which was the baptism of his death. In Luke 12:49–50, Christ wished that the fire was already kindled on Earth and the kingdom of God already about to dawn in fullness. But his own baptism in fire had to come first. Nothing was possible without this. He will baptize in the Spirit and fire only after he proceeds through the Spirit and fire himself. To quote Joseph Fitzmyer's comments on Luke 12:49–50, Christ's fire baptism "is not one that he merely administers to others but that he must undergo; he who baptizes with fire must himself face the testing and *krisis* that the figure connotes."[49] According to Fitzmyer, the link between Jesus and Jonah in Luke is significant as well for understanding Jesus's death as the culmination of his fire baptism.[50] Jesus stated in Luke 11:29–30: "As the crowds increased, Jesus said, 'This is a wicked generation. It asks for a sign, but none will be given it except the sign of Jonah. For as Jonah was a sign to the Ninevites, so also will the Son of Man be to this generation.'" The parallel text of Matthew 12:40 explicitly ties Christ's three days in the grave to Jonah's banishment from God three days under the waves in the belly of the fish. Though Luke's account is not quite as elaborate, one can arguably make the case that Jesus's sign value in relation to Jonah's given there implies that Jesus's resurrection is to be viewed as a deliverance from a plight similar to Jonah's (cf. Matt. 12:39–40). The difference is that Jesus suffered a fate similar to Jonah's vicariously for the sake of others, as one faithful to God. He fulfilled his witness in a way that opens up a path of freedom for others. Indeed, one greater than Jonah has arrived.

Luke is not alone in highlighting Jesus as the Baptizer in the Spirit. All four gospels and the Book of Acts make this programmatic for Christology. I do not have the space to explore the other canonical voices on the role of Jesus as Spirit Baptizer. I would only highlight here the overarching point of John's Gospel that Jesus bears the Spirit so that he might impart new life to others (John 10:10). Christ is the one out of whose innermost being will flow rivers of living water unto those who believe (John 7:38). More specifically, Jesus will sanctify himself so that others may be sanctified (17:19). The cross is the place where Christ's sanctification lays the foundation for the new life that he breathes upon others, a life that follows in the way of Christ's sanctified path (John 20:22).

Relevant also is the point made in Hebrews that Christ was perfected so as to make others perfect. Note 2:10: "In bringing many sons and daughters to glory, it was fitting that God, for whom and through whom everything exists, should make the pioneer of their salvation perfect through what he suffered."

Christ's own perfect death, which with his resurrection culminated in his sanctified life, made him the mediator of the sanctified life to others. Hebrews 5:10 states the matter this way: "Son though he was, he learned obedience from what he suffered and, once made perfect, he became the source of eternal salvation for all who obey him" (5:8–9). He offers himself "by the eternal Spirit" (9:14) in fulfillment of humanity's debt of glory to the Father so as to open a path to the Spirit for sinners so that they may be living sacrifices offered through him (Rom. 12:1). Christ's self-offering by the Spirit on the cross was the attainment of perfect love, the all-determining sanctifying moment for all time. He rises in the Spirit as the one who baptizes all others in the Spirit. The fire through which he passed did not consume him; he did not lose himself as the faithful Son by entering into the fire on our behalf. The fire thus became the means by which he attained perfect love in his final act of self-giving to God on our behalf. But the self-giving directed to God was also directed to God's redemptive cause in the world. So, Christ rises from the fire in the fullness of the Spirit (as the one baptized in the Spirit) so as to pour out that Spirit (and with the Spirit the Father's love and the Son's own faithful life) upon others. Put pneumatologically, the Spirit overflows Christ's sanctified life at Pentecost (overflowing love) and comes upon the followers of Jesus. In Christ and by his Spirit, unworthy human vessels are reconciled to God and made worthy by Christ to become living vessels of the Holy Spirit. They can now offer themselves to God in a way that is worthy and in ever-increasing measure toward the attainment of that perfect love by which they were sanctified.

CONCLUSION

The long journey through creedal Christology to Anselm's atonement theory had given Christology its inherent significance in relation to pneumatology. Christ is not merely the instrument of the Spirit but is also the redemptive event for all time. But in establishing this objective significance to Christology, the tradition had neglected the significance of the Spirit in the process. This neglect is apparent in the creedal affirmations of Nicea and Chalcedon. Fortunately, the vision of God as self-imparting to flesh in incarnation and atonement was upheld in the tradition (as we noted with Athanasius and Cyril of Alexandria). All that was needed was to explicate what role the Spirit played in the incarnation and atonement so as to clarify the connection between the atonement and the impartation of the sanctifying Spirit at Pentecost. Holiness and Pentecostal movements offer us a soteriology that emphasizes the role of

Christ in providing for the sanctification of the church in his life, death, and resurrection. The question that they raise at least implicitly has to do with what the Holy Spirit has to do with the fulfillment of the mission that Christ undertakes by suffering death in his flesh on our behalf. The focus on the baptism in the Holy Spirit and fire can help in responding to this question. To facilitate this response, the constructive part of the chapter turned to John the Baptist's announcement that the Messiah will baptize in the Spirit and fire. In turning to this declaration, the Pentecostal and Wesleyan focus on the baptism in the Holy Spirit has been developed as key to the flourishing of life in the Spirit.

In developing this focus on Christ as the Spirit Baptizer, Christ's act of atonement is shown to be like a new exodus through the fire to the promised land of the sanctifying Spirit and the new creation—the era of the sanctified church as the sign and instrument of the coming kingdom. United to Christ by faith in the gospel, the church bears the Spirit and, in bearing the Spirit, has a share in Christ as well (Rom. 8:9). Water baptism dramatizes the passage of the church with him through the fire of death to the vindication of life, a vindication that is shown as it was with Christ by the descent of the Spirit upon us: "These are my sons and daughters with whom I am well pleased" (cf. Rom. 8:15–16). Those who participate in God by faith are now worthy to bear the Spirit in ever-increasing conformity to the Son. They offer themselves in self-giving love to God's cause in the world as empowered witnesses; they groan with Christ for the salvation and healing of suffering humanity; they reach with hope in the eschatological yearning of the Spirit for the liberty of the kingdom of God to come and give of themselves to realize signs of its coming in the here and now. They *experience* baptism in the Spirit in moments of awakening, deep consecration, and overflowing love in the Spirit.

NOTES

1. Asa Mahan, *The Baptism of the Holy Ghost* (New York: George Hughes, 1870), 20–36. I am grateful to Donald W. Dayton for pointing out the significance of Mahan to the focus of the Holiness Movement on Spirit baptism. Donald W. Dayton, "The Theological Roots of Pentecostalism," *Pneuma* 2, no. 1 (Spring 1980): 12–13.

2. Anonymous, "The Baptism with the Holy Ghost," *Apostolic Faith* 1, no. 11 (October 1907–January 1908): 4.

3. Frederick Dale Bruner, *A Theology of the Holy Spirit: The Pentecostal Experience and the New Testament Witness* (Grand Rapids, MI: Eerdmans, 1970); James D. G. Dunn, *Baptism in the Holy Spirit: A Re-examination of the New Testament Teaching on the Gift of the Spirit in Relation to Pentecostalism Today* (London: SCM Press, 1970); Kilian McDonnell and George Montague, *Christian Initiation and Baptism in the Holy Spirit: Evidence from the*

First Eight Centuries (Collegeville, MN: Liturgical Press, 1991).

4. John Wesley, *A Plain Account of Christian Perfection* (London: Epworth Press, 1952), 6.

5. Dayton, "Theological Roots of Pentecostalism," 9. A fuller account can be found in his book, *Theological Roots of Pentecostalism* (Metuchen, NJ: Scarecrow Press, 1987), 87–114.

6. Dayton, "Theological Roots of Pentecostalism," 9–16.

7. William J. Seymour, "The Way into the Holiest," *Apostolic Faith* 1, no. 2 (October 1906): 4.

8. E. N. Bell, "Believers in Sanctification," *Christian Evangel* (September 19, 1914): 3.

9. Besides Bell's article, note also, Anonymous, "The Old Time Pentecost," *Apostolic Faith* 1, no. 4 (September 1906): 1; Will Trotter, "A Revival of Love Needed," *Weekly Evangel* (April 3, 1915): 5.

10. Oneness Pentecostal Frank Ewart said that the Spirit baptism is the release of the flow of divine love through us: Frank Ewart, "The Revelation of Jesus Christ," in *Seven Jesus Only Tracts*, ed. Donald W. Dayton, Higher Christian Life 13 (New York: Garland, 1985), 9.

11. The major thesis of my *Baptized in the Spirit: A Global Pentecostal Theology* (Grand Rapids, MI: Zondervan, 2006). I have extended that argument into Christology in *Jesus the Spirit Baptizer: Christology in Light of Pentecost* (Grand Rapids, MI: Eerdmans, 2018).

12. Jürgen Moltmann, *The Church in the Power of the Spirit: A Contribution to Messianic Ecclesiology* (Minneapolis: Augsburg-Fortress Press, 1977), 36.

13. Ibid., 37.

14. Cyril of Alexandria, *Scolia on the Incarnation of the Only Begotten* 33, in John McGuckin, *Saint Cyril of Alexandria and the Christological Controversy: Its History, Theology, and Texts* (Crestwood, NY: St. Vladimir's Seminary Press, 2004), 328.

15. Scripture quotations are from the New International Version.

16. See Michael Rene Barnes, *The Power of God: Dynamics in Gregory of Nyssa's Trinitarian Theology* (Oxford: Oxford University Press, 2004); Lewis Ayres, *Nicaea and Its Legacy: An Approach to Fourth-Century Trinitarian Theology* (Oxford: Oxford University Press, 2004).

17. Barnes, *Power of God*, 119; quoted in Ayers, *Nicea and Its Legacy*, 23n36.

18. See Joseph Lienhard, *Contra Marcellum: Marcellus of Ancyra and Fourth-Century Theology* (Washington, DC: Catholic University of America Press, 1999), 35–46.

19. *Arius' Letter to Alexander of Alexandria* 5, in *The Trinitarian Controversy*, ed. and trans. William C. Rusch, Sources of Early Christian Thought (Philadelphia: Fortress Press, 1980), 32.

20. Athanasius, *Orations Against the Arians* 1.39, in Rusch, *Trinitarian Controversy*, 102.

21. Athanasius, *Orations Against the Arians* 3.34, in *The Christological Controversy*, ed. and trans. Richard A. Norris Jr., Sources of Early Christian Thought (Philadelphia: Fortress Press, 1980), 93.

22. *Nestorius' First Sermon Against the Theotokos*, in Norris, *Christological Controversy*, 130.

23. McGuckin, *Saint Cyril of Alexandria*, 161.

24. Douglas Fairbairn, *Grace and Christology in the Early Church*, Oxford Early Christian Studies (Oxford: Oxford University Press, 2003), 14.

25. *The Third Letter of Cyril to Nestorius* 12, in McGuckin, *Saint Cyril of Alexandria*, 275.

26. The text used in this chapter is St. Anselm, *Cur Deus Homo*, in *St. Anselm: Basic Writings*, trans. S. N. Deane (La Salle, IL: Open Court, 1968). For the significance of Chalcedon to Anselm's *Cur Deus Homo*, see Michael J. Deem, "The Christological Renaissance: The

Chalcedonian Turn of St. Anselm of Canterbury," *St. Anselm Journal* 2, no. 1 (Fall 2004): 42–51. For insight into Anselm's understanding of atonement as the source of salvation by grace, see D. Bentley Hart, "A Gift Exceeding Every Debt: An Eastern Orthodox Appreciation for Anselm's *Cur Deus Homo*," *Pro Ecclesia* 7, no. 3 (Summer 1998): 333–49.

27. Anselm, *Cur Deus Homo* 2.19, in *St. Anselm: Basic Writings*.

28. Anselm, *Cur Deus Homo* 2.28.

29. Anselm, *Cur Deus Homo* 1.1.

30. Anne Hunt, *The Trinity and the Paschal Mystery: A Development in Recent Catholic Theology* (Collegeville, MN: Liturgical Press, 1997).

31. Jürgen Moltmann, *The Trinity and the Kingdom: The Doctrine of God* (Minneapolis: Fortress Press, 1990), 76.

32. This interest is shown by the theme of the 2014 meeting of the Wesleyan Theological Society: the atonement. Besides Oglevie's article cited below, see, for example, Hank Spaulding, "Sanctifying Atonement: Womanist Theology, Wesleyan Ethics, and the Future of Nazarene Atonement Theology," *Wesleyan Theological Journal* 50, no. 1 (Spring 2015): 162–86.

33. Heather Oglevie, "Entire Sanctification and the Atonement: A Wesleyan Demonstration," *Wesleyan Theological Journal* 50, no. 1 (Spring 2015): 38.

34. Ibid., 52.

35. Ibid., 40.

36. Ibid.

37. Ibid., 41.

38. Ibid., 45.

39. Ibid., 46.

40. Ibid., 49.

41. Ewart, "Revelation of Jesus Christ," 5.

42. William J. Seymour, "River of Living Water," *Apostolic Faith* 1, no. 3 (November 1906): 2.

43. C. H. Mason, "Tennessee Evangelist Witnesses," *Apostolic Faith* 1, no. 7 (April 1907): 7.

44. Eugene Rogers, *After the Spirit: A Constructive Pneumatology from Resources Outside the Modern West* (Grand Rapids, MI: Eerdmans, 2005), 19–32.

45. Dunn, *Baptism in the Holy Spirit*, 44.

46. Colin Brown, "What Was John the Baptist Doing?," *Bulletin for Biblical Research* 7 (1997): 37–50.

47. Kilian McDonnell, *The Baptism of Jesus in the Jordan: The Trinitarian and Cosmic Order of Salvation* (Collegeville, MN: Michael Glazer, 1996), 148.

48. Dunn, *Baptism in the Holy Spirit*, 13–14.

49. Joseph Fitzmyer, *The Gospel According to Luke: X–XXIV*, The Anchor Bible 18A (New York: Doubleday, 1970), 995.

50. Ibid., 929–32.

BIBLIOGRAPHY

Anonymous. "The Baptism with the Holy Ghost." *Apostolic Faith* 1, no. 11 (October 1907–January 1908): 4.

Anonymous. "The Old Time Pentecost." *Apostolic Faith* 1, no. 4 (September 1906): 1.

Anselm, St. *Cur Deus Homo*. In *St. Anselm: Basic Writings*. Translated by S. N. Deane. La Salle, IL: Open Court, 1968.

Arius' Letter to Alexander of Alexandria. In *The Trinitarian Controversy*, edited and translated by William C. Rusch, 31–32. Sources of Early Christian Thought. Philadelphia: Fortress Press, 1980.

Athanasius. *Orations Against the Arians*, book 1. In *The Trinitarian Controversy*, edited and translated by William C. Rusch, 61–129. Sources

of Early Christian Thought. Philadelphia: Fortress Press, 1980.
———. *Orations Against the Arians*, book 3. In *The Christological Controversy*, edited and translated by Richard A. Norris Jr., 83–101. Sources of Early Christian Thought. Philadelphia: Fortress Press, 1980.
Ayres, Lewis. *Nicaea and Its Legacy: An Approach to Fourth-Century Trinitarian Theology*. Oxford: Oxford University Press, 2004.
Barnes, Michael Rene. *The Power of God: Dynamics in Gregory of Nyssa's Trinitarian Theology*. Oxford: Oxford University Press, 2004.
Brown, Colin. "What Was John the Baptist Doing?" *Bulletin for Biblical Research* 7 (1997): 37–50.
Bruner, Frederick Dale. *A Theology of the Holy Spirit: The Pentecostal Experience and the New Testament Witness*. Grand Rapids, MI: Eerdmans, 1970.
Cyril of Alexandria. *Scolia on the Incarnation of the Only Begotten*. In *Saint Cyril of Alexandria and the Christological Controversy: Its History, Theology, and Texts*, by John McGuckin, 294–335. Crestwood, NY: St. Vladimir's Seminary Press, 2004.
———. *The Third Letter of Cyril to Nestorius*. In McGuckin, *Saint Cyril of Alexandria and the Christological Controversy*, 266–75.
Dayton, Donald W. "The Theological Roots of Pentecostalism." *Pneuma* 2, no. 1 (Spring 1980): 3–21.
———. *Theological Roots of Pentecostalism*. Metuchen, NJ: Scarecrow Press, 1987.
Deem, Michael J. "The Christological Renaissance: The Chalcedonian Turn of St. Anselm of Canterbury." *St. Anselm Journal* 2, no. 1 (Fall 2004): 42–51.
Dunn, James D. G. *Baptism in the Holy Spirit: A Re-examination of the New Testament Teaching on the Gift of the Spirit in Relation to Pentecostalism Today*. London: SCM Press, 1970.
Ewart, Frank. "The Revelation of Jesus Christ." In *Seven Jesus Only Tracts*, edited by Donald W. Dayton. Higher Christian Life 13. New York: Garland, 1985.
Fairbairn, Douglas. *Grace and Christology in the Early Church*. Oxford Early Christian Studies. Oxford: Oxford University Press, 2003.
Fitzmyer, Joseph. *The Gospel According to Luke: X–XXIV*. The Anchor Bible 28A. New York: Doubleday, 1970.
Hart, D. Bentley. "A Gift Exceeding Every Debt: An Eastern Orthodox Appreciation for Anselm's *Cur Deus Homo*." *Pro Ecclesia* 7, no. 3 (Summer 1998): 333–49.
Hunt, Anne. *The Trinity and the Paschal Mystery: A Development in Recent Catholic Theology*. Collegeville, MN: Liturgical Press, 1997.
Lienhard, Joseph. *Contra Marcellum: Marcellus of Ancyra and Fourth-Century Theology*. Washington, DC: Catholic University of America Press, 1999.
Macchia, Frank D. *Baptized in the Spirit: A Global Pentecostal Theology*. Grand Rapids, MI: Zondervan, 2006.
———. *Jesus the Spirit Baptizer: Christology in Light of Pentecost*. Grand Rapids, MI: Eerdmans, 2018.
Mahan, Asa. *The Baptism of the Holy Ghost*. New York: George Hughes, 1870.
Mason, C. H. "Tennessee Evangelist Witnesses." *Apostolic Faith* 1, no. 7 (April 1907): 7.
McDonnell, Kilian. *The Baptism of Jesus in the Jordan: The Trinitarian and Cosmic Order of Salvation*. Collegeville, MN: Michael Glazer, 1996.
McDonnell, Kilian, and George Montague. *Christian Initiation and Baptism in the Holy Spirit: Evidence from the First Eight Centuries*.

Collegeville, MN: Liturgical Press, 1991.

Moltmann, Jürgen, *The Church in the Power of the Spirit: A Contribution to Messianic Ecclesiology*. Minneapolis: Augsburg-Fortress Press, 1977.

———. *The Trinity and the Kingdom: The Doctrine of God*. Minneapolis: Fortress Press, 1990.

Nestorius' First Sermon Against the Theotokos. In *The Christological Controversy*, edited and translated by Richard A. Norris Jr., 123–30. Sources of Early Christian Thought. Philadelphia: Fortress Press, 1980.

Oglevie, Heather. "Entire Sanctification and the Atonement: A Wesleyan Demonstration." *Wesleyan Theological Journal* 50, no. 1 (Spring 2015): 38–52.

Rogers, Eugene. *After the Spirit: A Constructive Pneumatology from Resources Outside the Modern West*. Grand Rapids, MI: Eerdmans, 2005.

Seymour, William J. "River of Living Water." *Apostolic Faith* 1, no. 3 (November 1906): 2.

———. "The Way into the Holiest." *Apostolic Faith* 1, no. 2 (October 1906): 4.

Spaulding, Hank. "Sanctifying Atonement: Womanist Theology, Wesleyan Ethics, and the Future of Nazarene Atonement Theology." *Wesleyan Theological Journal* 50, no. 1 (Spring 2015): 162–86.

Trotter, Will. "A Revival of Love Needed." *Weekly Evangel*, April 3, 1915, 5.

Wesley, John. *A Plain Account of Christian Perfection*. London: Epworth Press, 1952.

CHAPTER 9

The Presence of the Kingdom
Optimism of Grace in the Holiness and Pentecostal Movements

Henry H. Knight III

The linkage between Wesleyanism, the Holiness Movement, and Pentecostalism has long been recognized. Sociologist David Martin concluded his 2002 survey of global Pentecostalism, suggestively titled *Pentecostalism: The World Their Parish*, with this observation: "Pentecostalism tells tales of Methodist paternity, but fatherhood is only rarely acknowledged."[1] This echoes the 1970 comment by Frederick Dale Bruner that "Pentecostalism is primitive Methodism's extended incarnation," although Bruner, a theologian in the Reformed tradition, did so only to point out Pentecostalism's questionable parentage.[2]

The story of how Wesley's Methodism eventually led to Pentecostalism has been ably told, most notably by Vinson Synan (whose 1971 book on the subject begins with the words "John Wesley") and in Donald Dayton's groundbreaking theological account in 1987.[3] These studies and others like them do not gloss over the fierce disagreements between and within these various movements.[4] Nor should they. Acknowledging differences are important, not only in the case of theological disputes but also in describing the changes that happen when those theologies take root in, say, African American or Latino contexts, and even more so in varied cultures throughout the world.

Yet what has intrigued me the most are the commonalities. While acknowledging the theological differences, we should not lose sight of the family resemblance. For this really is an extended family—whose internal squabbles cannot erase all that is held in common. What, then, are the traits that mark this distinctive theological family? I propose at least three, one eschatological, another pneumatological, the third epistemological, all intertwined.

ANTICIPATING HEAVEN BELOW

We can begin with the eschatological, more particularly with an inaugurated eschatology. To put it simply, either explicitly or implicitly, these movements have a firm belief that in a multitude of ways the life of the coming kingdom of God is already becoming manifest in this present age. There is a yearning for the life of heaven, and for God's will to be done on Earth as in heaven. Using language from several hymns by Charles Wesley, these movements anticipate heaven below.[5]

One example of Charles Wesley's usage of the term is found in his well-known hymn "O For a Thousand Tongues to Sing," which has as its focus justification and the new birth. Jesus is the speaker:

> *With me your chief, ye then shall know,*
>   *Shall feel your sins forgiven;*
> *Anticipate your heaven below,*
>   *And own that love is heaven.*[6]

He could also use related language as in this description of the new birth:

> *When thou dost in my heart appear,*
>   *And love erects its throne,*
> *I then enjoy salvation here,*
>   *And heaven on earth begun.*[7]

John Wesley did not use the term "heaven below," but he did use other eschatological language to describe the present Christian life, especially sanctification, calling it "the beginning of heaven," "walking in eternity," and "tasting the powers of the world to come."[8] Others did occasionally use "heaven below" to describe sanctification, including John Fletcher, Francis Asbury, and Phoebe Palmer.[9]

The term was not limited to the Christian life but could describe worship as well. The early American preacher William Waters speaks of a 1780 Love Feast as "a little heaven below"; in 1906, an unnamed Pentecostal said the same of worship at the Azusa Street Revival.[10] These comments seem so representative of the larger ethos of early Methodism and Pentecostalism that they, respectively, inspired two book titles: Lester Ruth's *A Little Heaven Below: Worship at Early Methodist Quarterly Meetings* and Grant Wacker's *Heaven Below: Early Pentecostals and American Culture*. The term "heaven below" is richly descriptive of each of these movements, and it is also one of the familial links that they have in common. From Wesley on, the movements were eschatological through and through.

This claim that they anticipate heaven below may seem counterintuitive, especially for those in the late nineteenth-century Holiness Movement and the early Pentecostals who were caught up in premillennial urgency. After all, the impetus for Charles Parham's missional vision was that the gospel must be preached to the nations prior to the return of Jesus in glory.[11] But while their language often echoed that of the dispensationalism of John Nelson Darby, theirs was no premillennial escapism. Their hope in the return of Jesus was for justice and peace on this Earth. Then, said the Holiness theologian H. C. Morrison, "the earth will not be owned and dominated by a few people of vast wealth but will be amicably divided up among the people."[12] As William Kostlevy has argued, these Holiness premillennialists "anticipated a fundamentally altered social order," a this-worldly apocalypticism that was shared by Pentecostals such as Parham.[13] This sounds less like the dispensational premillennialism of Dwight Moody, who proclaimed God would destroy this world but will save the church by taking them out of it, and more like John Wesley's vision of the world renewed in holiness.[14]

As both Donald Dayton and Larry McQueen have shown, the premillennialism of early Pentecostals was actually quite different in a multitude of ways from the Darby-Scofield variety.[15] Most especially, their latter rain theology led Pentecostals, in McQueen's words, to experience "an immediate sense of 'heaven below,'" with the baptism of the Holy Spirit as "a foretaste of heaven."[16] In fact, from Wesley on, these movements were a witness to a new reality: the reign of God manifest in their lives, churches, and in their world.

THE TRANSFORMING POWER OF THE HOLY SPIRIT

The second trait is pneumatological, which can be described as their "optimism of grace." The term "optimism of grace" was coined by E. Gordon Rupp in 1952 to describe the inner dynamic of Wesley's theology. He contrasted it on one hand with the "pessimism of nature" of both Catholics and Reformation

Protestants, in which the effects of sin limit the salvation we can expect in this age, and on the other the "optimism of nature of the Enlightenment, in which original sin is denied and reason leads humanity out of ignorance and into unending progress."[17]

Wesley insisted on the traditional teaching on original sin—his longest essay was on that subject—but even more he insisted on grace overcoming sin.[18] Grace for him was not only the death of Christ *for us*, but also the work of the Holy Spirit *in us*.[19] Indeed, grace for Wesley most often meant the work of the Spirit. This was much more than a shift in emphasis. Wesley argued that the goal of salvation was to restore people to the image of God in this life, such that love would fill and fully govern the heart, what Wesley called Christian perfection. Salvation, he said, is "a present deliverance from sin, a restoration of the soul to its primitive health, its original purity; a recovery of the divine nature; the renewal of our souls after the image of God."[20] There was no way to get from a thoroughgoing Protestant understanding of original sin to this Wesleyan goal of Christian perfection except by way of the transformative power of the Holy Spirit.

In developing this exceptionally powerful pneumatology, Wesley was going theologically where no Protestant had gone before—although the Pietists had come close. The catalyst for this theology was the eighteenth-century awakening itself. In it Wesley found, as he would say, abundant experimental evidence of the power of the Spirit at work. In this he was not alone. Charles Wesley and John Fletcher developed similarly high pneumatologies. Jonathan Edwards, although not going so far as to expect Christian perfection in this life, also produced a pneumatology with far more expectancy as to what the Spirit can do than had either John Calvin or his Puritan predecessors.[21]

It is no wonder that Frank Whaling argued that Wesley was "working with a distinctive pneumatology that has no exact equivalent" in 'Western spirituality' up to that time," and Albert Outler called Wesley's way of salvation a "pneumatocentric soteriology."[22] This is an apt description, provided it does not imply a diminished Christology. What it should suggest instead is a robust economic Trinitarianism, one in which the life and especially the atonement of Christ is both the foundation and criterion for the Christian life, and the Spirit is the power that enables the love revealed in Christ to govern the believers' heart and life. It is this Trinitarianism, with its powerful pneumatology, that Wesley bequeathed to his Methodist, Holiness, and Pentecostal descendants.

Thus, John Wigger's observation that "it may not be an exaggeration to say that this quest for the supernatural in everyday life was the most distinctive characteristic of early American Methodism" can be extended to cover the Holiness and Pentecostal movements as well.[23] The spirituality in these movements can be called openness to the presence of transcendence to distinguish it from the later liberal theologies that emphasized divine immanence. This is not a discovery of the God already within us. It is more an in-breaking from without, an encounter with a God who is other than us—an experience that cannot leave us unchanged. By in-breaking or encounter is not only meant a kind of suddenness; it can, as Wesley said, be instantaneous or gradual.[24] The emphasis here is entering into, and growing in, a transforming relationship with God in and through means of grace such as the Lord's Supper, scripture, prayer, and serving others, as well as dreams and visions, experiences of healing, speaking in tongues, and the like. It is through these Spirit-enabled encounters that we come to know God experientially, analogous to how we know another person, and then grow in the knowledge and love of God.

Through the presence and power of the Holy Spirit, the adherents in these movements saw themselves as witnesses to a new eschatological reality, of which its content was in continuity with the love revealed in Jesus Christ. This eschatological linkage may have not been always explicit but it has been certainly present in the movements. What pervaded and shaped these movements is a distinctive spirituality, in which love is the governing motivation and goal, expectant faith undergirds a firm reliance on God, and hope as optimism of grace not only makes one receptive to the work of the Spirit but propels one into mission.[25]

The most important manifestation of this new eschatological reality for all these movements is sanctification. It was for them not a by-product of salvation but the point of salvation, and not a partial renewal but a thoroughgoing renovation of the heart. Wesley described it as the kingdom of God in the heart.[26] The radicality of this eschatological soteriology is seen in the insistence that one can be entirely sanctified in this life through the power of the Spirit. With this Christian perfection, the image of God that was lost in the fall into sin is fully restored, such that love fully governs the desires, motivations, and dispositions of the heart. For Wesley, however, Christian perfection is more than a recovery. It is a present anticipation of the new creation itself, in which people not only love as God loves but do so more fully than what was possible for Adam and Eve, for we know that love revealed is at its greatest depth in the cross of Jesus Christ.[27]

The eschatological nature of sanctification and Christian perfection was not often as explicit among Wesley's descendants as was its Pentecostal nature as a work of the Spirit. But, from Phoebe Palmer to William Seymour, it was described as a thoroughly transformed heart, something not for the life to come but a gift to be received in the present. While soteriology was the major focus of these movements, it was by no means the only one. There was also a deep concern with ecclesiology and mission. In fact, for Wesley, soteriology, ecclesiology, and mission were intertwined. The true church, he argued, was defined by neither membership nor by the proper practice of word and sacrament but by people seeking or growing in holiness.[28] The organization of his movement—preachers, conferences, societies, classes, bands, and spiritual discipline—was to facilitate growth in the Christian life and "to reform the nation, especially the church, and to spread scriptural holiness over the land."[29] Put differently, the organization was shaped for formation and by mission.

Wesley was quite clear that a church renewed in holiness by the Holy Spirit would be much like the church depicted in Acts 2, except that it would be free of the sins that compromised the primitive church, such as the Ananias and Sapphira incident and the discrimination against Hellenistic widows. It would be governed solely by love and would faithfully seek to do God's will on Earth as it is in heaven.[30] There are many examples in the Holiness and Pentecostal movements of similar ecclesial visions, such as the Wesleyan Methodist quest for holy and egalitarian churches in the early nineteenth century.[31] Three examples will be given here that help illustrate "heaven below" from different angles.

The first is the story of B. T. Roberts's fight against pew rentals that led to Free Methodism. Roberts was an early figure in the Holiness Movement who was committed to the doctrine of entire sanctification, itself a manifestation of heaven below. A Methodist minister in upstate New York, Roberts was appalled at the wealthy lifestyles of the upwardly mobile clergy and laity, and most especially of their readily adopting pew rentals as a funding mechanism for local churches. While prominent families would sit in the more expensive pews at the front, the poor would be relegated to the gallery or to standing in the back.

In "New School Methodism," published in the *Northern Independent* in 1857, Roberts argued that this practice and the deeper problem of cultural accommodation were not only not Wesleyan but also clearly not Christian.[32] After forming the Free Methodist Church in 1860, Roberts continued to argue, in the words of Howard Snyder, that it compromises the fundamental mission of the church to not "preach the gospel to the poor" and "maintain the Bible standard of Christianity."[33] "The true church," Roberts said, must be "holy; not in name merely but in reality."[34] In other words, he was arguing for a church that would manifest in its own life something of the holiness of heaven. As a result of such advocacy, Roberts was expelled from his conference in the Methodist Episcopal Church and became one of the leaders in founding the Free Methodist Church, which upheld holiness and prohibited pew rentals.

The second example draws upon the analysis of African American Methodism by James H. Cone, who argued that a "black congregation is an eschatological community that lives as if the end of time is already at hand." This is because, in worship, the Holy Spirit empowers the participants "with courage and strength to bear witness in their present existence to what they know is coming in God's own eschatological future."[35] In other words, in the church they live out not who white society says they are but their actual identities in the kingdom of God.

A third example comes from William Seymour and the congregation that formed at Azusa Street. Seymour had been profoundly influenced by the interracial and egalitarian Holiness ministries of the late nineteenth century, including the Evening Light Saints and God's Bible School.[36] Now at Azusa Street, he was experiencing a radically inclusive community built by the power of the Spirit. As Cecil Robeck has noted, "the Azusa Street Mission was one of the most racially inclusive, culturally diverse groups to gather in the city of Los Angeles at that time."[37] The Azusa Street periodical, the *Apostolic Faith*, said that it was the blood of Jesus and the power of Pentecost that "makes all races and nations into one common family in the Lord and makes them satisfied to be one."[38] "One token of the Lord's coming," it noted, "is that He is melting all races and nations together, and they are filled with the power and glory of God. He is baptizing by one Spirit into one body and making up a people that will be ready to meet Him when He comes."[39] Thus this was seen as both an anticipation of, and preparation for, the coming of Jesus Christ.

Of course, prevailing norms have a way of reasserting themselves. As Holiness and Pentecostal movements navigated their way through the culture of the time, they began to increasingly conform to it, especially with regard to race. This is not to say that race relations were idyllic even in the early days of Pentecostalism. For example, Charles Parham, often identified as the founder of the Pentecostal Movement, exhibited the features of white paternalism, later mixed with more overt racism; William Carothers, his chief deputy, was an ardent segregationist.[40] Early Pentecostalism, like its Holiness antecedents, was not free from cultural assumptions about race, especially among white participants.

But that should not discount the witness of those relatively and at times radically egalitarian Holiness and Pentecostal meetings during an era of Jim

Crow laws, pervasive racism, lynchings, and stringent restriction of non-Western European immigrants. Whatever the internal tensions over race, the main threat was external. The overtly racist attacks by the mainstream press on the Azusa Street Revival are just one example of how interracial ministry was seen as abhorrent and a threat to society.[41]

Almost as controversial was the frequent violation of gender norms. Both Holiness and Pentecostal bodies commonly (although not universally) supported women preachers, in sharp contrast to both mainline Protestants and more Reformed or Baptist evangelicals.[42] For example, the predominantly northern Methodist Episcopal Church was moving in the opposite direction. While conferences had given several women licenses to preach as early as 1869 and permitted them to pastor churches, at the 1880 General Conference the denomination voted not only to not ordain women but to rescind women's licenses to preach.[43] On the whole, women found more opportunities to preach and even lead within the Holiness and Pentecostal movements.

It was difficult enough to be simply a witness to the kingdom of God in the midst of a hostile culture. But these movements were missional to the core. They not only sought to manifest holiness in their lives and congregations but also to proclaim the promises of the gospel to both the wider church and world. This could only incite greater opposition. Randall Stephens has shown how as northern and western Holiness and Pentecostal evangelists moved into the Southern United States, the interracial character of their meetings, led by preachers who could be black or white, male or female, drew furious and often violent reaction.[44]

The heart of the missional impetus, beginning with Wesley, was to proclaim a salvation of which its goal is to have hearts perfected in love in this life. What Holiness and Pentecostal adherents made explicit was that with that entire sanctification came an empowerment for ministry. The ensuing controversy between the Holiness and Pentecostal movements was not over whether there was an empowerment but how such power was received. For the Holiness Movement, it was linked to Christian perfection, itself seen as Spirit baptism; for Pentecostals, it was received in a Spirit baptism experience subsequent to that of Christian perfection. Yet Pentecostals could also describe this subsequent baptism of the Spirit as "when you sum it up, . . . just more of God's love. If it does not bring more love, it is simply a counterfeit. . . . Pentecost makes us love Jesus more and love our brothers more. It brings us all into one common family."[45]

With love as the motive and empowered by the Spirit, these movements became missional dynamos. In addition to the proclamation of the promise of a full salvation, they engaged in a wide range of ministries, just like Pietists before them. Wesley's Methodists made care for the poor and dispossessed a driving concern, as well as visiting the sick and those in prison, feeding the hungry, and establishing Strangers Friends Societies to meet the needs of desperate people who were forced off rural lands and streaming into cities and mining areas looking for work.[46] Large segments of the Holiness Movement in nineteenth-century America fought slavery, racism, discrimination against women, class prejudice, and later the ravages of alcohol.[47] All this they saw as their participation in the work of God in the world, such that God's will was actually being done on Earth as in heaven.

It is no accident that the nineteenth century also saw the emergence of a healing movement within segments of the Holiness Movement, which would in the twentieth century become a hallmark of Pentecostalism. Although largely forgotten by then, John Wesley had been a strong advocate of healing through both medicine and prayer: "God has more than one method of healing either the soul or body," he said.[48] While many of the early Holiness and Pentecostal proponents of divine healing would initially see reliance on medicine as lack of faith and have a more formulaic way of appropriating divine healing, they would be helpfully counteracted by others who continued to emphasize miraculous healing but in ways that took more account of divine freedom and were, though often unknown to them, more in agreement with Wesley's theology.[49] The most striking example of this is R. Kelso Carter, who wrote a book in 1884 arguing that divine healing has been accomplished in the atonement and can be always and instantly received by faith, only to write a second book almost twenty years later correcting the first. There he said that not being healed did not mean there was a lack of faith, nor did the use of doctors and medicine indicate lack of faith.[50] But whatever their theological differences, for Wesley and his descendants, belief in divine healing was one of the most striking examples of an optimism of grace, even if it was sometimes taken too far by some.

ENCOUNTERING THE TRANSCENDENT GOD

There is one more aspect of Christian witness to be highlighted concerning these movements, one that points to their distinctive epistemology. For the most part, they were in the Enlightenment world but not of it. Their witness to the presence of transcendence, and of a future reality already made manifest, was in sharp contradiction to the immanent world being constructed by modernity. Theirs was a reality governed by God's purposes and suffused with the presence and power of the Holy Spirit. This does not mean that they were premodern holdovers. Wesley—here again like Jonathan Edwards—was an appreciative appropriator of new learning. But both Wesley and Edwards read Enlightenment thought with a critical eye. They could see in Deism the direction all this might take, and neither was willing to let the Enlightenment frame reality in purely natural or material terms.

With regard to Edwards, Avihu Zakai aptly summarized the goal of his writing as the "reenchantment of the world by demonstrating the infinite power of God's absolute sovereignty in both the 'order of nature' and the 'order of time.'"[51] In his reflection on the order of time, Edwards was not only going against the Enlightenment tide, which increasingly understood history solely in terms of human actors, but was in contrast to his own Puritan forebears who depicted history as being moved forward by great and godly rulers. Instead, in a series of sermons on "A History of the Work of Redemption," Edwards emphasized the power of the Holy Spirit as the agent of revival, and revival as the engine of history. These were the seeds of a later work that Edwards never was able to write.

John Wesley did not have such an ambitious writing project with regard to salvation history. But in a series of sermons published later in his life, he delineated in detail both the purpose of creation and the goal toward which it is moving, with Christ at the center and the Spirit as the primary agent of change and renewal.[52]

What Wesley and Edwards were presenting was a way of understanding the world from the standpoint of the God revealed in Jesus Christ, giving it quite a different meaning and purpose than Enlightenment-inspired naturalism. But they were not so much interested in arguing for this construal than inviting people through conversion to enter into this way of seeing and living in this world. This occurred through the gift of faith by the Holy Spirit, enabling a person to encounter experientially the reality of God. For both of them, faith was only minimally assent to that which we know about God; it was most centrally knowing and trusting in God.

The intellectual world of Edwards and Wesley was heavily influenced by the empiricist epistemology of John Locke. Both were aware that Locke's reliance on the five senses for knowledge, if absolute, would make knowing God an impossibility. One could still believe that God exists and was encountered in the past based on the reliability of the scriptural witnesses. We would then have true information *about* God but we would not have a transformative encounter *with* God.

Drawing on an older tradition of spiritual senses, Edwards and Wesley developed their responses to Locke by arguing that faith itself is a spiritual sense, a supernaturally given sense analogous to our natural senses. Faith is the spiritual perception of God through scripture and, at least for Wesley, all other means of grace, including prayer, the Eucharist, Christian conferencing, and works of mercy to the neighbor.[53] In Wesley's theology, faith enables people to experience what God has done throughout salvation history. Thus, past events such as the cross and future events such as feasting in the new creation are experienced through faith as present realities, just as much as the present work of God.[54]

One implication of this emphasis on the Holy Spirit and faith is that ordinary people become the primary vehicles of God's work in the world. Edwards observed that "in pouring out his Spirit chiefly on the common people, and bestowing his greatest and highest favours on them, God is admitting them nearer to himself than the great, the honorable, the rich and the learned."[55] Likewise Wesley, in describing how in the awakening God was renewing the church in holiness, argued that in carrying out this work:

> God will observe the same order which he hath done from the beginning of Christianity. "They shall all know *me*," saith the Lord, not from the greatest to the least (this is that wisdom of the world which is foolishness with God) but "from the least to the greatest," that praise may not be of men, but of God. Before the end even the rich shall enter into the kingdom of God. Together with them will enter in the great, the noble, the honourable; yea, the rulers, the princes, the kings of the earth. Last of all the wise and learned, the men of genius, the philosophers, will be convinced that they are fools; will "be converted and become as little children, and enter into the kingdom of God."[56]

The Holiness and Pentecostal descendants of Wesley lost his spiritual sense epistemology due to the increasing cultural presence in America of the commonsense philosophy of Francis Hutcheson and Thomas Reid with its distinctively different anthropology. Their emphasis, in different ways, on an innate universal common sense negated the need for a grace-given faith as a spiritual sense.[57] While most Protestant traditions adopted this view early on, Methodism, with its Wesleyan emphasis on universal prevenient grace, was able to resist its spell into the early nineteenth century. Eventually mainline Methodist theologians readily adopted it. The Holiness Movement adopted it in a more nuanced way, qualifying it with more traditional Wesleyan and biblical emphases, yet nonetheless having a trust in natural human abilities that was considerably different from Wesley and earlier Methodism.[58]

What they and the Pentecostals maintained was Wesley's emphasis on knowing God experientially and on the transforming power of the Spirit. Jackie David Johns's description of Pentecostalism would apply as well to the Holiness Movement: at the heart of their "world-view is transforming experience with God." This "becomes the normative epistemological framework," changing the way people interpret the world. As a result, the "Spirit-filled believer has a predisposition to see the transcendent God at work in, with, through, above, and beyond all events."[59] Like Wesley before them, they see the world with new eyes, and have an expectancy to both experience and see the effects of what God is doing in the world.

CONCLUSION

The Holiness and Pentecostal movements consisted largely of ordinary people who were renewed, empowered, and led by the Spirit. They proclaimed the promise that God could be encountered and known, hearts and lives changed, and that every person had a role to play in God's work in the world. Their message had credibility when their own lives and communities showed evidence of the transformation they proclaimed.

Because the promise of both holiness and power was to all, this gave them an egalitarian tendency that put them in tension with the dominant cultural norms of the time. While themselves not immune to cultural pressures, they nonetheless often stood out as present witnesses to an alternative, eschatological reality.

This also made them theologically distinct. Their emphasis on the in-breaking power of a transcendent God led them to firmly reject liberal theologies that either took God out of the world entirely or limited an immanent God to natural historical processes. Because of their optimism of grace, they also rejected a Calvinistic scholasticism that was long on rational apologetics but short on recognizing the present power of the Spirit.

Theirs instead is a third trajectory through modernity, one that calls into question the basic assumptions of Enlightenment thought as well as the cultural status quo. In the Western world, the tendency of Enlightenment thought was to remove divine agency from the world and divine purpose from history. With their expectant faith and testimonies to God's present activity, the Holiness and Pentecostal movements instead give witness to an in-breaking of an eschatological reality through the power of the Holy Spirit, and of a God who does not rest until history reaches its goal and God's reign comes in fullness.

NOTES

1. David Martin, *Pentecostalism: The World Their Parish* (Oxford: Blackwell, 2002), 167.

2. Fredrick Dale Bruner, *A Theology of the Holy Spirit: The Pentecostal Experience and the New Testament Witness* (Grand Rapids, MI: Eerdmans, 1970), 37.

3. Vinson Synan, *The Holiness-Pentecostal Movement in the United States* (Grand Rapids, MI: Eerdmans, 1971); Donald W. Dayton, *Theological Roots of Pentecostalism* (Metuchen, NJ: Scarecrow Press, 1987).

4. See Henry H. Knight III, ed., *From Aldersgate to Azusa Street: Wesleyan, Holiness, and Pentecostal Vision of the New Creation* (Eugene, OR: Pickwick Publications, 2010).

5. I argue this at length in Henry H. Knight III, *Anticipating Heaven Below: Optimism of Grace from Wesley to the Pentecostals* (Eugene, OR: Cascade, 2014).

6. John Wesley, *A Collection of Hymns for the Use of the People Called Methodists*, vol. 7 of *The Works of John Wesley*, ed. Franz Hildebrandt and Oliver A. Beckerlegge (Nashville: Abingdon Press, 1983), 81, hymn 1.

7. Charles Wesley, "Rejoicing in Hope," in *Hymns and Sacred Poems* (1742), 182, available via the Center for Studies in the Wesleyan Tradition, Duke Divinity School, http://divinity.duke.edu/initiatives-centers/cswt/wesley-texts/charles-wesley.

8. See the following by John Wesley: "On God's Vineyard," in *Sermons III*, vol. 3 of *The Works of John Wesley*, ed. Albert C. Outler (Nashville: Abingdon Press, 1986), 514–15; "Walking by Sight and Walking by Faith," in *Sermons IV*, vol. 4 of *The Works of John Wesley*, ed. Albert C. Outler (Nashville: Abingdon Press, 1987), 57; "The Case of Reason Impartially Considered," in *Sermons II*, vol. 2 of *The Works of John Wesley*, ed. Albert C. Outler (Nashville: Abingdon Press, 1985), 595; "A Word to a Sabbath-Breaker," in *The Works of the Rev. John Wesley*, ed. Thomas Jackson (repr., Grand Rapids, MI: Baker Book House, 1996), 11:165; "A Word to a Swearer," ibid., 11:168.

9. See John Fletcher, "An Equal Check to Pharisaism and Antinomianism," in *The Works of John Fletcher* (Salem, OH: Schmul, 1974), 1:69; Francis Asbury, "Letter to Henry Smith," in *The Journal and Letters of Francis Asbury*, ed. Elmer T. Clark, J. Manning Potts, and Jacob S. Payton (Nashville: Abingdon Press, 1958), 3:440; Phoebe Palmer, *Faith and Its Effects* (New York: Foster & Palmer, Jr., n.d.), 38, and her hymn, "The Cleansing Stream."

10. Cited in Lester Ruth, *A Little Heaven Below: Worship at Early Methodist Quarterly Meetings* (Nashville: Kingswood Books, 2000), 154; *Apostolic Faith*, December 1906, cited in Grant Wacker, *Heaven Below: Early Pentecostals and American Culture* (Cambridge: Harvard University Press, 2001).

11. On Parham's missional vision, see D. William Faupel, *The Everlasting Gospel: The Significance of Eschatology in the Development of Pentecostal Thought* (Sheffield: Sheffield Academic Press, 1996), 165–76; Gary B. McGee, *Miracles, Missions, and American Pentecostalism* (Maryknoll, NY: Orbis, 2010), 73–76; Douglas Jacobsen, *Thinking in the Spirit: Theologies of the Early Pentecostal Movement* (Bloomington: Indiana University Press, 2003), 25–26.

12. H. C. Morrison, *Will God Set up a Visible Kingdom on Earth?* (Louisville, KY: Pentecostal Publishing, 1934), 75–76.

13. William C. Kostlevy, *Holy Jumpers: Evangelicals and Radicals in Progressive Era America* (Oxford: Oxford University Press, 2010), 8–9.

14. Quoted in W. H. Daniels, *Moody: His Word, Work, and Workers* (New York: Hitchcock & Walden, 1877), 475–76. See John Wesley, "The General Spread of the Gospel," in *Sermons II*, 2:485–99.

15. Dayton, *Theological Roots*, 147; Larry McQueen, "Early Pentecostal Eschatology in Light of *The Apostolic Faith*, 1906–1908," in *Perspectives in Pentecostal Eschatologies: World Without End*, ed. Peter Althouse and Robby Waddell (Eugene, OR: Pickwick Publications, 2010), 139–54.

16. McQueen, "Early Pentecostal Eschatology," 150–51.

17. E. Gordon Rupp, *Principalities and Powers: Studies in the Christian Conflict in History* (Nashville: Abingdon-Cokesbury, 1952), 91–92.

18. John Wesley, "The Doctrine of Original Sin: According to Scripture, Reason and Experience," in *Doctrinal and Controversial Treatises I*, vol. 12 of *The Works of John Wesley*, ed. Randy Maddox (Nashville: Abingdon Press, 2012), 155–481.

19. John Wesley, "Justification by Faith," in *Sermons I*, vol. 1 of *The Works of John Wesley*, ed. Albert C. Outler (Nashville: Abingdon Press, 1984), 186; Wesley, "The Great Privilege of Those That Are Born of God," in *Sermons I*, 1:431–32.

20. John Wesley, "A Farther Appeal to Men of Reason and Religion," pt. 1, in *The Appeals to Men of Reason and Religion and Certain Related Open Letters*, vol. 11 of *The Works of John Wesley*, ed. Gerald R. Cragg (Nashville: Abingdon Press, 1989), 106. Theodore Runyon called salvation as our renewal in the image of God "the indispensable key to Wesley's whole soteriology," in *The New Creation: John Wesley's Theology Today* (Nashville: Abingdon Press, 1998), 12.

21. For a recent study of John Wesley's pneumatology, see Joseph W. Cunningham, *John Wesley's Pneumatology: Perceptible Inspiration*, Ashgate Methodist Studies Series (Burlington, VT: Ashgate, 2014). For how Charles Wesley understood the work of the Spirit in relation to Christian perfection, see John R. Tyson, *Assist Me to Proclaim: The Life and Hymns of Charles Wesley* (Grand Rapids, MI: Eerdmans, 2007), 233–34; for a broader view, see Jason E. Vickers, "Charles Wesley's Doctrine of the Holy Spirit: A Vital Resource for the Renewal of Methodism Today," *Asbury Journal* 61, no. 1 (Spring 2006), 47–60. For a discussion of the significance of John Fletcher's identifying a separate dispensation of the Spirit, see J. Russell Frazier, *True Christianity: The Doctrine of Dispensations in the Theology of John William Fletcher* (Eugene, OR: Pickwick Publications, 2014), 158–210; Melvin E. Dieter, "The Development of Holiness Theology in Nineteenth Century America," *Wesleyan Theological Journal* 20, no. 1 (1985): 61–77. For Jonathan Edwards's unprecedented emphasis on the Spirit in the Reformed tradition, see W. Ross Hastings, *Jonathan Edwards and the Life of God: Toward an Evangelical Theology of Participation* (Minneapolis, MN: Fortress Press, 2015); Robert W. Caldwell, *Communion in the Spirit: The Holy Spirit as the Bond of Unity in the Theology of Jonathan Edwards* (Milton Keynes: Paternoster Press, 2006).

22. Frank Whaling, ed., *John and Charles Wesley: Selected Prayers, Hymns, Journal Notes, Sermons, Letters and Treatises* (New York: Paulist Press, 1981), xv. Albert C. Outler, in Wesley, *Sermons I*, 1:81.

23. John H. Wigger, *Taking Heaven by Storm: Methodism and the Rise of Popular Christianity in America* (New York: Oxford University Press, 1998), 110.

24. Among Wesley's many references to this are "The Repentance of Believers," in *Sermons I*, 1:346; "On Patience," in *Sermons III*, 3:176–77; "On Working Out Our Own Salvation," in *Sermons III*, 3:204; "On God's Vineyard," in *Sermons III*, 3:516; "Minutes of Some Late Conversations, 1768," in *The Methodist Societies: The Minutes of Conference*, vol. 10 of *The Works of John Wesley*, ed. Henry D. Rack (Nashville: Abingdon Press, 2011), 363–64; "A Plain Account of Christian Perfection," in *Doctrinal and Controversial Treatises II*, vol. 13 of *The Works of John Wesley*, ed. Paul Wesley Chilcote and Kenneth J. Collins (Nashville: Abingdon Press, 2013), 106, 187–88.

25. I argue this at length in Knight, *Anticipating Heaven Below*.

26. John Wesley, "The Way to the Kingdom," in *Sermons I*, 1:224–25.

27. John Wesley, "God's Love to Fallen Man," in *Sermons II*, 2:423–35.

28. John Wesley, "Of the Church," in *Sermons III*, 3:55–56. Wesley took issue with the Church of England definition of the church as where the pure word is preached and the sacraments are rightly administered not only because it is insufficient but it excludes from the church catholic the Church of Rome along with other bodies of Christians with deficient doctrine or practice (52).

29. John Wesley, "Minutes of Several Conversations" (Q.3), in *The Works of John Wesley*, 8:299.

30. Wesley, "The General Spread of the Gospel," in *Sermons II*, 2:495. See also Wesley, "Of the Church," in *Sermons III*, 3:50–56; and Wesley, "The Mystery of Iniquity," in *Sermons II*, 2:452–66.

31. See Douglas M. Strong, *Perfectionist Politics: Abolitionism and the Religious Tensions of American Democracy* (New York: Syracuse University Press, 1999).

32. "New School Methodism," *Northern Independent* 2, no. 2 (August 20, 1857): 2; and no. 3 (August 27, 1857): 2, referenced in Howard A. Snyder, *Populist Saints: B. T. and Ellen Roberts and the First Free Methodists* (Grand Rapids, MI: Eerdmans, 2006), 383.

33. Snyder, *Populist Saints*, 800. For further discussion of Roberts's concern to preach the gospel to the poor, see William C. Kostlevy, "Benjamin Titus Roberts and the 'Preferential Option for the Poor' in the Early Free Methodist Church," in *Poverty and Ecclesiology: Nineteenth-Century Evangelicals in the Light of Liberation Theology*, ed. Anthony C. Dunnavant (Collegeville, MN: Liturgical Press, 1992), 51–67; Donald W. Dayton, "'Good News to the Poor': The Methodist Experience After Wesley," in *The Portion of the Poor*, ed. M. Douglas Meeks (Nashville: Abingdon Press, 1995), 83–86.

34. B. T. Roberts, *Fishers of Men; or Practical Hints to Those Who Would Win Souls* (Rochester, NY: G. L. Roberts, 1878), 322; cited in Snyder, *Populist Saints*, 795.

35. James H. Cone, "Sanctification and Liberation in the Black Religious Tradition," in *Sanctification and Liberation*, ed. Theodore Runyon (Nashville: Abingdon Press, 1981), 175.

36. For the impact of the Evening Light Saints on Seymour, see Cecil M. Robeck Jr., *The Azusa Street Mission and Revival: The Birth of the Global Pentecostal Movement* (Nashville: Thomas Nelson, 2006), 29–31; Vinson Synan and Charles R. Fox Jr., *William Seymour: Pioneer of the Azusa Street Revival* (Alachua, FL: Bridge-Logos Foundation, 2012), 40–46. For the impact of God's Bible School, see Robeck, *Azusa Street*, 31–35; Wallace Thornton Jr., *When the Fire Fell: Martin Wells Knapp's Vision of Pentecost and the Beginnings of God's Bible School* (Wilmore, KY: Emeth Press, 2014), 145–46.

37. Robeck, *Azusa Street*, 88.

38. *Apostolic Faith* 1, no. 7 (April 1907): 3.

39. *Apostolic Faith* 1, no. 6 (February–March 1907), 7.

40. On Parham and Carothers, see Wacker, *Heaven Below*, 231–32; Robeck, *Azusa Street*, 44–49.

41. Robeck, *Azusa Street*, 125–26; Gaston Espinosa, *William Seymour and the Origins of Global Pentecostalism* (Durham: Duke University Press, 2014), 139.

42. For a study of the autobiographies of women preachers in the Holiness Movement, see Susie C. Stanley, *Holy Boldness: Women Preachers' Autobiographies and the Sanctified Self* (Knoxville: University of Tennessee Press, 2002). For a discussion and analysis of the ambiguous situation of women preachers in early Pentecostalism, see Wacker, *Heaven Below*, 158–76.

43. Jean Miller Schmidt, *Grace Sufficient: A History of Women in American Methodism, 1760–1939* (Nashville: Abingdon Press, 1999), 179–93.

44. Randall J. Stephens, *The Fire Spreads: Holiness and Pentecostalism in the American South* (Cambridge: Harvard University Press, 2008), 82–89, 213–14, 238–39. See also Espinosa, *William Seymour*, 96–142.

45. *Apostolic Faith* 2, no. 13 (May 1908): 3. Contemporary Pentecostal theologians have picked up on the centrality of love in early Pentecostalism in different ways. See Steven J. Land, *Pentecostal Spirituality: A Passion for the Kingdom* (Sheffield: Sheffield Academic Press, 1993); and Frank D. Macchia, *Baptized in the Spirit: A Global Pentecostal Theology* (Grand Rapids, MI: Zondervan, 2006).

46. On Wesley and his Methodists, see Richard P. Heitzenrater, ed., *The Poor and the People Called Methodists, 1729–1999* (Nashville: Kingswood Books, 2002); Manfred Marquardt, *John Wesley's Social Ethics: Praxis and Principles*, trans. John E. Steely and W. Stephen Gunter (Nashville: Abingdon Press, 1992); Stephen W. Rankin, "The People Called Methodists," in Knight, *From Aldersgate to Azusa Street*, 36–44; Knight, *Anticipating Heaven Below*, 183–228.

47. On the Holiness Movement, see Donald W. Dayton with Douglas M. Strong, *Rediscovering an Evangelical Heritage: A Tradition and Trajectory of Integrating Piety and Justice*, 2nd ed. (Grand Rapids, MI: Baker Academic, 2014); Dayton, "Good News to the Poor"; Strong, *Perfectionist Politics*; Knight, *Anticipating Heaven Below*, 183–228.

48. John Wesley, *Journal*, May 18, 1772, in *Journals and Diaries V (1765–1775)*, vol. 22 of *The Works of John Wesley*, ed. W. Reginald Ward and Richard P. Heitzenrater (Nashville: Abingdon Press, 1993), 323–24. For discussions of Wesley's views on healing, see Deborah Madden, *"A Cheap, Safe and Natural Medicine": Religion, Medicine and Culture in John Wesley's Primitive Physick* (Amsterdam: Rudopi, 2007); Deborah Madden, ed., *"Inward and Outward Health": John Wesley's Holistic Concept of Medical Science, the Environment and Holy Living* (London: Epworth Press, 2008); E. Brooks Holifield, *Health and Medicine in the Methodist Tradition: Journey Toward Wholeness* (New York: Crossroad, 1986); Knight, *Anticipating Heaven Below*, 144–56.

49. Among the studies of the divine healing movements that show this tension are Kimberly Ervin Alexander, *Pentecostal Healing: Models in Theology and Practice* (Blandford Forum, UK: Deo, 2006); Heather D. Curtis, *Faith in the Great Physician: Suffering and Divine Healing in American Culture, 1860–1900* (Baltimore: Johns Hopkins University Press, 2007); Dayton, *Theological Roots*, 115–41; Nancy A. Hardesty, *Faith Cure: Divine Healing in the Holiness and Pentecostal Movements* (Peabody, MA: Hendrickson, 2003); James Robinson, *Divine Healing: The Formative Years, 1830–1890* (Eugene, OR: Pickwick Publications, 2011); James Robinson, *Divine Healing: The Holiness-Pentecostal Transition Years*,

1890–1906 (Eugene, OR: Pickwick Publications, 2013).

50. See both books reprinted in Donald W. Dayton, ed., *Russell Kelso Carter on "Faith Healing"* (New York: Garland, 1985).

51. Avihu Zakai, *Jonathan Edwards's Philosophy of History* (Princeton: Princeton University Press, 2003), 32. Besides this book by Zakai, which is an extended argument that Edwards was responding to Enlightenment thought in the areas of creation, history, and ethics, see Michael J. McClymond, *Encounters with God: An Approach to the Theology of Jonathan Edwards* (New York: Oxford University Press, 1998). McClymond argued that Edwards undertook an "audacious form of mediation" between tradition and modernity, seeking to reconstruct intellectual disciplines "so as to make them congruent with Christian truth as he understood it" (7). His discussion of Edwards on *"The History of Redemption"* is on pp. 65–79.

52. See especially sermons 54–64 in Wesley, *Sermons II*.

53. On Wesley's understanding of means of grace, see Henry H. Knight III, *The Presence of God in the Christian Life: John Wesley and the Means of Grace* (Lanham, MD: Scarecrow Press, 1992); Runyon, *New Creation*, 102–45; Randy L. Maddox, *Responsible Grace: John Wesley's Practical Theology* (Nashville: Kingswood Books, 1994), 192–229; Kenneth J. Collins, *The Theology of John Wesley: Holy Love and the Shape of Grace* (Nashville: Abingdon Press, 2007), 237–70.

54. For a discussion of Edwards's understanding of faith as a spiritual sense that enables us to know God, see McClymond, *Encounters with God*, 9–26. For a discussion of Wesley on this topic, see Runyon, *New Creation*, 72–81, 149–60, and Knight, *Anticipating Heaven Below*, 30–36.

55. Jonathan Edwards, "History of the Work of Redemption," cited in Zakai, *Philosophy of History*, 251.

56. Wesley, "The General Spread of the Gospel," in *Sermons II*, 493–94.

57. For critical engagement of Wesley and Edwards with the philosophy of Hutcheson, see the analysis in Richard B. Steele, *"Gracious Affections" and "True Virtue" According to Jonathan Edwards and John Wesley* (Metuchen, NJ: Scarecrow Press, 1994), 316–40.

58. This story is told in detail in Mark A. Noll, *America's God: From Jonathan Edwards to Abraham Lincoln* (New York: Oxford University Press, 2002), 93–113, 233–38, 330–64. See also Randy L. Maddox, "Reconnecting the Means to the Ends: A Wesleyan Prescription for the Holiness Movement," *Wesleyan Theological Journal* 33, no. 2 (1998): 29–66.

59. Jackie David Johns, "Yielding to the Spirit: The Dynamics of a Pentecostal Model of Praxis," in *The Globalization of Pentecostalism: A Religion Made to Travel*, ed. Murray W. Dempster, Byron D. Klaus, and Douglas Petersen (Oxford: Regnum, 1999), 74–75.

BIBLIOGRAPHY

Alexander, Kimberly Ervin. *Pentecostal Healing: Models in Theology and Practice*. Blandford Forum, UK: Deo, 2006.

Apostolic Faith. Reprinted in *Like as of Fire*, edited by E. Myron Noble. Washington, DC: Middle Atlantic Regional Press, 1991.

Asbury, Francis. *The Journal and Letters of Francis Asbury*. Edited by Elmer T. Clark, J. Manning Potts, and Jacob S. Payton. 3 vols. Nashville: Abingdon Press, 1958.

Bruner, Fredrick Dale. *A Theology of the Holy Spirit: The Pentecostal Experience and the New Testament Witness*. Grand Rapids, MI: Eerdmans, 1970.

Caldwell, Robert W. *Communion in the Spirit: The Holy Spirit as the Bond of Unity in the Theology of Jonathan Edwards*. Milton Keynes: Paternoster Press, 2006.

Collins, Kenneth L. *The Theology of John Wesley: Holy Love and the Shape of Grace*. Nashville: Abingdon Press, 2007.

Cone, James H. "Sanctification and Liberation in the Black Religious Tradition." In *Sanctification and Liberation*, edited by Theodore Runyon, 174–92. Nashville: Abingdon Press, 1981.

Cunningham, Joseph W. *John Wesley's Pneumatology: Perceptible Inspiration*. Ashgate Methodist Studies Series. Burlington, VT: Ashgate, 2014.

Curtis, Heather D. *Faith in the Great Physician: Suffering and Divine Healing in American Culture, 1860–1900*. Baltimore: Johns Hopkins University Press, 2007.

Daniels, W. H. *Moody: His Word, Work, and Workers*. New York: Hitchcock & Walden, 1877.

Dayton, Donald W. "'Good News to the Poor': The Methodist Experience After Wesley." In *The Portion of the Poor*, edited by M. Douglas Meeks, 65–96. Nashville: Abingdon Press, 1995.

———, ed. *Russell Kelso Carter on "Faith Healing."* New York: Garland, 1985.

———. *Theological Roots of Pentecostalism*. Metuchen, NJ: Scarecrow Press, 1987.

Dayton, Donald W., with Douglas M. Strong. *Rediscovering an Evangelical Heritage: A Tradition and Trajectory of Integrating Piety and Justice*. 2nd ed. Grand Rapids, MI: Baker Academic, 2014.

Dieter, Melvin E. "The Development of Holiness Theology in Nineteenth Century America." *Wesleyan Theological Journal* 20, no. 1 (1985): 61–77.

Espinosa, Gaston. *William Seymour and the Origins of Global Pentecostalism*. Durham: Duke University Press, 2014.

Faupel, D. William. *The Everlasting Gospel: The Significance of Eschatology in the Development of Pentecostal Thought*. Sheffield: Sheffield Academic Press, 1996.

Fletcher, John. *The Works of John Fletcher*. 4 vols. Salem, OH: Schmul, 1974.

Frazier, J. Russell. *True Christianity: The Doctrine of Dispensations in the Theology of John William Fletcher*. Eugene, OR: Pickwick Publications, 2014.

Hardesty, Nancy A. *Faith Cure: Divine Healing in the Holiness and Pentecostal Movements*. Peabody, MA: Hendrickson, 2003.

Hastings, W. Ross. *Jonathan Edwards and the Life of God: Toward an Evangelical Theology of Participation*. Minneapolis, MN: Fortress Press, 2015.

Heitzenrater, Richard P., ed. *The Poor and the People Called Methodists, 1729–1999*. Nashville: Kingswood Books, 2002.

Holifield, E. Brooks. *Health and Medicine in the Methodist Tradition: Journey Toward Wholeness*. New York: Crossroad, 1986.

Jacobsen, Douglas. *Thinking in the Spirit: Theologies of the Early Pentecostal Movement*. Bloomington: Indiana University Press, 2003.

Johns, Jackie David. "Yielding to the Spirit: The Dynamics of a Pentecostal Model of Praxis." In *The Globalization of Pentecostalism: A Religion Made to Travel*, edited by

Murray W. Dempster, Byron D. Klaus, and Douglas Petersen, 70–84. Oxford: Regnum, 1999.

Knight, Henry H. III. *Anticipating Heaven Below: Optimism of Grace from Wesley to the Pentecostals.* Eugene, OR: Cascade, 2014.

———, ed. *From Aldersgate to Azusa Street: Wesleyan, Holiness, and Pentecostal Visions of the New Creation.* Eugene, OR: Pickwick Publications, 2010.

———. *The Presence of God in the Christian Life: John Wesley and the Means of Grace.* Lanham, MD: Scarecrow Press, 1992.

Kostlevy, William C. "Benjamin Titus Roberts and the 'Preferential Option for the Poor' in the Early Free Methodist Church." In *Poverty and Ecclesiology: Nineteenth-Century Evangelicals in the Light of Liberation Theology*, edited by Anthony L. Dunnavant, 51–67. Collegeville, MN: Liturgical Press, 1992.

———. *Holy Jumpers: Evangelicals and Radicals in Progressive Era America.* Oxford: Oxford University Press, 2010.

Land, Steven J. *Pentecostal Spirituality: A Passion for the Kingdom.* Sheffield: Sheffield Academic Press, 1993.

Macchia, Frank D. *Baptized in the Spirit: A Global Pentecostal Theology.* Grand Rapids, MI: Zondervan, 2006.

Madden, Deborah. *"A Cheap, Safe and Natural Medicine": Religion, Medicine and Culture in John Wesley's Primitive Physic.* Amsterdam: Rodopi, 2007.

———, ed. *"Inward and Outward Health": John Wesley's Holistic Concept of Medical Science; The Environment and Holy Living.* London: Epworth Press, 2008.

Maddox, Randy L. "Reconnecting the Means to the Ends: A Wesleyan Prescription for the Holiness Movement." *Wesleyan Theological Journal* 33, no. 2 (1998): 29–66.

———. *Responsible Grace: John Wesley's Practical Theology.* Nashville: Kingswood Books, 1994.

Marquardt, Manfred. *John Wesley's Social Ethics: Praxis and Principles.* Translated by John E. Steely and W. Stephen Gunter. Nashville: Abingdon Press, 1992.

Martin, David. *Pentecostalism: The World Their Parish.* Oxford: Blackwell, 2002.

McClymond, Michael J. *Encounters with God: An Approach to the Theology of Jonathan Edwards.* New York: Oxford University Press, 1998.

McGee, Gary B. *Miracles, Missions, and American Pentecostalism.* Maryknoll, NY: Orbis, 2010.

McQueen, Larry. "Early Pentecostal Eschatology in Light of *The Apostolic Faith*, 1906–1908." In *Perspectives in Pentecostal Eschatologies: World Without End*, edited by Peter Althouse and Robby Waddell, 139–54. Eugene, OR: Pickwick Publications, 2010.

Morrison, H. C. *Will God Set up a Visible Kingdom on Earth?* Louisville, KY: Pentecostal Press, 1934.

Noll, Mark A. *America's God: From Jonathan Edwards to Abraham Lincoln.* New York: Oxford University Press, 2002.

Palmer, Phoebe. *Faith and Its Effects.* New York: Foster & Palmer, Jr., n.d.

Rankin, Stephen W. "The People Called Methodists." In *From Aldersgate to Azusa Street: Wesleyan, Holiness, and Pentecostal Visions of the New Creation*, edited by Henry H. Knight III, 36–44. Eugene, OR: Pickwick Publications, 2010.

Robeck, Cecil M., Jr. *The Azusa Street Mission and Revival: The Birth of the Global Pentecostal Movement.* Nashville: Thomas Nelson, 2006.

Roberts, B. T. *Fishers of Men; or Practical Hints to Those Who Would Win Souls*. Rochester, NY: G. L. Roberts, 1878.

Robinson, James. *Divine Healing: The Holiness-Pentecostal Transition Years, 1890–1906*. Eugene, OR: Pickwick Publications, 2013.

Runyon, Theodore. *The New Creation: John Wesley's Theology Today*. Nashville: Abingdon Press, 1998.

Rupp, E. Gordon. *Principalities and Powers: Studies in the Christian Conflict in History*. Nashville: Abingdon-Cokesbury, 1952.

Ruth, Lester. *A Little Heaven Below: Worship at Early Methodist Quarterly Meetings*. Nashville: Kingswood Books, 2000.

Schmidt, Jean Miller. *Grace Sufficient: A History of Women in American Methodism, 1760–1939*. Nashville: Abingdon Press, 1999.

Snyder, Howard A. *Populist Saints: B. T. and Ellen Roberts and the First Free Methodists*. Grand Rapids, MI: Eerdmans, 2006.

Stanley, Susie C. *Holy Boldness: Women Preachers' Autobiographies and the Sanctified Self*. Knoxville: University of Tennessee Press, 2002.

Steele, Richard B. *"Gracious Affections" and "True Virtue" According to Jonathan Edwards and John Wesley*. Metuchen, NJ: Scarecrow Press, 1994.

Stephens, Randall J. *The Fire Spreads: Holiness and Pentecostalism in the American South*. Cambridge: Harvard University Press, 2008.

Strong, Douglas M. *Perfectionist Politics: Abolitionism and the Religious Tensions of American Democracy*. New York: Syracuse University Press, 1999.

Synan, Vinson. *The Holiness-Pentecostal Movement in the United States*. Grand Rapids, MI: Eerdmans, 1971.

Synan, Vinson, and Charles R. Fox Jr. *William J. Seymour: Pioneer of the Azusa Street Revival*. Alachua, FL: Bridge-Logos Foundation, 2012.

Thornton, Wallace, Jr. *When the Fire Fell: Martin Wells Knapp's Vision of Pentecost and the Beginnings of God's Bible School*. Lexington, KY: Emeth Press, 2014,

Tyson, John R. *Assist Me to Proclaim: The Life and Hymns of Charles Wesley*. Grand Rapids, MI: Eerdmans, 2007.

Vickers, Jason E. "Charles Wesley's Doctrine of the Holy Spirit: A Vital Resource for the Renewal of Methodism Today." *Asbury Journal* 61, no. 1 (Spring 2006): 47–60.

Wacker, Grant. *Heaven Below: Early Pentecostals and American Culture*. Cambridge: Harvard University Press, 2001.

Wesley, Charles. "Rejoicing in Hope." In *Hymns and Sacred Poems* (1742), 182. Available via the Center for Studies in the Wesleyan Tradition, Duke Divinity School. http://divinity.duke.edu/initiatives-centers/cswt/wesley-texts/charles-wesley.

Wesley, John. *The Works of John Wesley*. Vol. 1, *Sermons I*. Edited by Albert C. Outler. Nashville: Abingdon Press, 1984.

———. *The Works of John Wesley*. Vol. 2, *Sermons II*. Edited by Albert C. Outler. Nashville: Abingdon Press, 1985.

———. *The Works of John Wesley*. Vol. 3, *Sermons III*. Edited by Albert C. Outler. Nashville: Abingdon Press, 1986.

———. *The Works of John Wesley*. Vol. 4, *Sermons IV*. Edited by Albert C. Outler. Nashville: Abingdon Press, 1987.

———. *The Works of John Wesley*. Vol. 7, *A Collection of Hymns for the Use of the People Called Methodists*. Edited by Franz Hildebrandt and Oliver A. Beckerlegge. Nashville: Abingdon Press, 1983.

———. *The Works of John Wesley*. Vol. 10, *The Methodist Societies: The Minutes of Conference*. Edited by Henry D. Rack. Nashville: Abingdon Press, 2011.

———. *The Works of John Wesley*. Vol. 11, *The Appeals to Men of Reason and Religion and Certain Related Letters*. Edited by Gerald R. Cragg. Nashville: Abingdon Press, 1989.

———. *The Works of John Wesley*. Vol. 12, *Doctrinal and Controversial Treatises I*. Edited by Randy L. Maddox. Nashville: Abingdon Press, 2012.

———. *The Works of John Wesley*. Vol. 13, *Doctrinal and Controversial Treatises II*. Edited by Paul Wesley Chilcote and Kenneth J. Collins. Nashville: Abingdon Press, 2013.

———. *The Works of John Wesley*. Vol. 22, *Journals and Diaries V (1765–1775)*. Edited by W. Reginald Ward and Richard P. Heitzenrater. Nashville: Abingdon Press, 1993.

———. *The Works of the Rev. John Wesley*. Edited by Thomas Jackson. 14 vols. Reprint, Grand Rapids, MI: Baker Book House, 1996.

Whaling, Frank, ed. *John and Charles Wesley: Selected Prayers, Hymns, Journal Notes, Sermons, Letters and Treatises*. New York: Paulist Press, 1981.

Wigger, John H. *Taking Heaven by Storm: Methodism and the Rise of Popular Christianity in America*. New York: Oxford University Press, 1998.

Zakai, Avihu. *Jonathan Edwards's Philosophy of History*. Princeton: Princeton University Press, 2003.

Fulfilling the Full Gospel
The Promise of the Theology of the Cleveland School

Chris E. W. Green

In a recent Festschrift for John Christopher Thomas, Kenneth J. Archer describes the Cleveland School (CS) as "a community of scholars who embrace and work from a particular school of Pentecostal thought and praxis."[1] He briefly sketches the history of the school, stating that it began in the mid-1980s as a "creative synergistic convergence" among scholars at the Church of God Theological Seminary (now Pentecostal Theological Seminary) in Cleveland, Tennessee. He identifies Cheryl Bridges Johns, Steve Land, Rickie Moore, and Chris Thomas as the "foundational four," explaining how their shared responsibilities at the seminary, teaching and learning together alongside mentoring figures like R. Hollis Gause, James Beaty, and French Arrington, provided a fecund environment in which their mutually inspired and mutually influenced works could mature. Archer describes this as the gestation period.

Following the line of Archer's thought, one might say that the school's birth came in the early 1990s, as the first seminal CS works were published, each of which originated as a PhD dissertation, and were written while these figures worked closely together: in 1991, Thomas's *Footwashing in John 13 and the Johannine Community*, and in 1993, both Land's *Pentecostal Spirituality: A Passion for the Kingdom* and Bridges Johns's *Pentecostal Formation: A Pedagogy Among the Oppressed*.[2] In the intervening year, around the same time, Thomas, Land, and Moore founded the *Journal of Pentecostal Theology*. The first two issues

TOP TO BOTTOM

Fig. 10.1 Steven J. Land speaking at the 2018 Society for Pentecostal Studies meeting. Courtesy of Society for Pentecostal Studies.

Fig. 10.2 Cheryl Bridges Johns. Courtesy of Carrie Workman Photography.

Fig. 10.3 Rickie D. Moore at the 2018 Society for Pentecostal Studies meeting. Courtesy of Society for Pentecostal Studies.

Fig. 10.4 John Christopher Thomas. Courtesy of John Christopher Thomas.

included seminal articles by Moore, Thomas, and Land as well as Bridges Johns and her husband, Jackie.[3] As it matured, it became more and more recognizable as a school of thought dedicated to the articulation of a distinctly Pentecostal way of being in the world. Inarguably, CS theology is still maturing, not least through the ongoing work of the foundational figures. But already, thirty-plus years on from its beginnings, the influence of the Cleveland School is wide and deep.

It is worth noting that Bridges Johns, Land, Moore, and Thomas did not label themselves "the Cleveland School." Amos Yong seems to have been the first to use the term.[4] Others have followed suit, including Archer, Michael Frost, Jacqueline Grey, Wolfgang Vondey, William Oliverio, Marty Mittelstadt, James Smith, and Hannah Mather.[5] No doubt, reasonable minds will differ on the "essence" of CS thought. Is it defined by an insistence on Pentecostal distinctives? Is it defined by an affirmation of the fivefold gospel? Is it defined by a commitment to Wesleyan theology/spirituality more broadly construed? Is it defined by a retrievalist methodology, which privileges the first ten years of the Pentecostal Movement? Is it defined by a confessional hermeneutic? Is it defined by a "paramodern" epistemology? Is it defined by a holistic liberationist soteriology and "progressive" concern for social justice and peacemaking?[6] All of the above? Some set of the above?

I am not sure how these questions should be answered to everyone's satisfaction, even if they can be answered. All that notwithstanding, it remains possible to speak meaningfully about the CS, I believe—possible and beneficial—so long as allowance is made for significant differences of opinion within the school itself, and significant agreements with those outside of it. In a volume exploring the intertwined histories, present, and future of the Holiness and Pentecostal traditions, this task appears worthwhile. So, in the following paragraphs, I offer a beginning of that work through engagement with a few characteristic sources, convictions, concerns, and techniques that mark the CS as a distinctive "style" of Pentecostalism.[7] Along the way, I also offer a few programmatic suggestions for the development of both the CS and the larger Pentecostal scholarly traditions.

THE (IM)POSSIBILITY OF A BLACK WESLEYAN-HOLINESS PENTECOSTALISM

In the inaugural issue of the *Journal of Pentecostal Theology*, Land published an essay, "A Passion for the Kingdom: Revisioning Pentecostal Spirituality," which reads as an abbreviated form of his then soon-to-be published monograph.[8] In the opening lines, he asserted that a dramatic "revisioning" of the Pentecostal tradition is needed, agreeing with Grant Wacker that contemporary Pentecostals need to return to their beginnings. Wacker stated:

> In crucial respects, the Pentecostal movement is less mature today than it was in the early years. Modem Pentecostals do not need to romanticize their past in order to learn from it. The first generation resisted the blandishments of secular society in order to preach a gospel that challenged the culture in more than superficial ways. Modern Pentecostals might recover that vision. They might discover as church historian George Marsden has put it, that grace is not cheap and forgiveness is more than good manners. They might discover that in the beginning, the movement survived not in spite of the fact that it was out of step with the times, but precisely because it was.[9]

Land contended that Pentecostals need to return to their roots in black/holiness theology/spirituality because only then can they learn again how to be "out of step with the times" and "in step" with the Spirit.[10] Or, to say the same thing another way, the Pentecostal Movement cannot be true to itself—that is, it cannot be faithful to its God-given charism and vocation—unless and until it recovers its "black roots": its wholly embodied spirituality and spiritualized embodiment, its orality and narrativity, its concern with "maximum participation" and reconciliatory community, and its appreciation for the iconic power of dreams and visions.[11] This "blackness," fused with Wesleyan theology and Holiness spirituality, gave rise to the peculiar sensibilities and convictions, beliefs and practices of "Pentecostalism."[12] And so Pentecostals cannot now be Pentecostal apart from a reignition of this fusion.

It is not for no reason that Thomas favors the metaphor of the "black gospel choir" in his construal of biblical interpretation. He explains his use of the image in a paper presented to the World Council of Churches Consultation on Healing in Mission in Santiago, Chile, and published later in *International Review of Mission*:

> I would like to suggest that Scripture be likened to a choir; not just any choir—but a black gospel choir. Those familiar with this musical style and tradition will immediately recognize why I have chosen this metaphor. If you have ever been to a black gospel choir practice and heard the individual notes which are rehearsed, you come away with the firm belief that there is simply too much dissonance for all these notes to be sung together. The end result, one is certain, will be a horribly offensive noise. But when the music starts,

unbelievably the dissonance is extraordinarily beautiful. The temptations in the choir practice to make the notes sound more similar, or change the music to suppress artificially the dissonance are based on a misunderstanding of the music's intent and function. One of the many other aspects of this metaphor worthy of comment is the moment in a black gospel song when the choir goes silent and the person, seemingly with the smallest, softest voice takes the lead for a stanza or chorus. In some choirs this person would not even find a place, but in a black gospel choir this small voice is occasionally given the lead. The lessons for a view of scripture are not hard to see. Temptations to force the diversity of scripture into an artificial unity are illegitimate and do the canon a disservice. It is only through allowing the dissonance to be heard in all its intensity that the scripture can have its full impact. In addition, this approach to scripture makes it possible for even the smallest and seemingly most insignificant voice to take the lead at the appropriate moment.[13]

There is more here than meets the eye because this metaphor is not drawn at random but arises naturally from a core CS conviction: Pentecostalism is essentially "black."[14]

This leads to a first programmatic suggestion: the CS needs to do more than celebrate its black church inheritance; it needs to continue to *be* "black," both in the sense that honors its heritage in the black church tradition and in the sense that it is intentionally resistant to "whiteness." The interracial character of Azusa Street Revival services prefigures the future that the Spirit desires not only for the Pentecostal Movement but also for the church catholic and the world.[15] In the same way, it must continue to be "Wesleyan."[16] Allowing, of course, for indigenization and adaptation in various ministerial contexts, CS theology, in order to be true to itself, needs to be affectively and imaginatively, doctrinally and practically black and Wesleyan, and in this way "Catholic," drawing on the wisdom of those traditions and working out the possibilities embedded in the beliefs and practices they have mediated.[17]

It has to be acknowledged that Pentecostals, as a group, from the first failed to fulfill this calling. And not only in North America.[18] As Moore says, "It is beyond dispute that Pentecostalism, particularly in its North American context, soon lost much of the revolutionary social vision and eschatological urgency that imprinted and propelled the movement's infancy."[19] But Pentecostals continue to fail—even to attempt to fulfill this vision, or acknowledge it as desirable.[20] Before the so-called Memphis Miracle, in an interview with the *Los Angeles Times*, Harvey Cox praised the dismantling of the all-white forty-six-year-old Pentecostal Fellowship of North America and the formation of the interracial Pentecostal and Charismatic Churches of North America.[21] But a couple of years later, Leonard Lovett grieved it. "In hindsight what took place in Memphis was no more than cosmetic to say the least. . . . [R]acial reconciliation within the Pentecostal movement is nowhere near realization in our time. The dialogue was no more than a temporary 'peak of progress,' a short lived miracle that will eventually slide into irrelevance as racial patterns within the Pentecostal-Charismatic movement adapt in ways that maintain and give credence to white dominance."[22] The work of racial conciliation requires the effort of exposing racism's sinister substructures, doing what can be done to overthrow them.[23] To that end, the CS needs to reaffirm its indebtedness to the black tradition and reignite its blackness. And this is inseparable from its reaffirmation of its indebtedness to the Jewish people, their story, their scriptures. "We must remember this truth from scripture: We joined the story of another people, of Israel, and in this way learned of our God."[24]

RETRIEVALISM, SECTARIANISM, AND THE DEVELOPMENT OF A MATURE PENTECOSTALISM

Land agrees with Walter Hollenweger that the first ten years of Pentecostalism were "the heart and not the infancy of the movement," precisely because in those years Pentecostals fused black theology/spirituality and Wesleyan theology/spirituality. But Yong, in the article in which he first referred to the "Cleveland School," questioned Land's approach:

> At one level, the "Cleveland School" of pentecostal studies has led the way in arguing that the theological heart and soul of modern pentecostalism lies in the first ten years of the revival as it emerged in and across North America. At stake here are both historiographical issues related to the "proper" genealogy of the movement and theological and philosophical matters related to defining the "essence" of pentecostalism. If the Cleveland School is right, then pentecostalism is essentially delimited in North American terms, and the proper missiological response is to find ways to take the North American version and contextualize that in the global south.[25]

Yong's critique raises important concerns. But it is worth noting that Hollenweger, who was not an American, based his claim on studies of global Pentecostal/ Charismatic movements and with explicit concern both for "traditional and independent churches in the Third World" and ecumenical conversations.[26] Land shared these concerns.[27] Moreover, Cheryl Bridges Johns also opened her presidential address to the Society for Pentecostal Studies with a remark about the significance of the Pentecostal Movement for the global future: "Most of us have heard of the late president of Princeton Theological Seminary, John McKay's prophetic statement, 'America's future will abide in a reformed Catholicism and a mature Pentecostalism.' I believe that the statement may be broadened to include the future of the world."[28]

Both Bridges Johns and Land, like Hollenweger, sought to define Pentecostalism not in "North American terms" but in terms of a prophetic, antiestablishment black spirituality that emerged at the margins of American society and in protest of it.[29] Precisely so, the Pentecostalism they envision remains open to other traditions in their various contexts. They desire a "mature sectarian identity" for the sake of a "mature Pentecostal ecumenism."[30]

Interestingly, Mark Cartledge discerns a distinction between those scholars who emphasize ecumenical engagement and those who emphasize a retrieval of early Pentecostal sources, placing Thomas in the retrievalist camp.[31] This is a helpful observation, but Cartledge himself would be the first to say that it should not be overplayed. That is, it would be a mistake to claim that Thomas is retrievalist as opposed to ecumenical. It would be better to say that his ecumenism depends upon his retrievalist work, which also holds true for the other foundational figures.

In particular, Thomas's work as senior editor of *Journal of Pentecostal Theology*, alongside Moore and Land, confirms his ecumenical openness. As made clear in the first editorial, the journal was designed from the beginning to serve the broader Pentecostal and Charismatic movements in ecumenical and international academic conversations.[32] The first few issues proved the seriousness of this commitment, including pieces by prominent non-Pentecostal scholars (including Walter Hollenweger, Jürgen Moltmann, Harvey Cox, Clark Pinnock, and James Dunn[33]) as well as Pentecostals and Charismatics not identified with the CS (including Frank Macchia, Murray Dempster, Mark Cartledge, Henry [Hal] Knight, and Ralph Del Colle).[34]

In his Society for Pentecostal Studies presidential address, Thomas, much as Bridges Johns had done, encouraged Pentecostal scholars to do their work unapologetically, without feeling compelled to work in the categories important to other traditions. Yet he also talks about Pentecostal answerability in dialogue with those outside the tradition, while warning against both "emperor worship" and "house-servant" attitudes:

While most Pentecostals would want to believe that God has done and is doing something special within their particular branch of the Christian tree, it seems to me that few of us would want to suggest that what is taking place outside our movement is without merit or God's blessing. In order for Pentecostal theology to function as it should in the next century, we must be willing to dialogue with a wide variety of theological partners. What is called for is not the kind of "emperor worship" that on occasion results when Pentecostals receive the attention of a major figure within the circle of academic theology. There has sometimes been a tendency for Pentecostals to turn such opportunities into times of affirmation for the views of the scholar in question, whether or not they accurately represent the views and ethos of the movement. Nor is this a call for the accommodating "house-servant" attitude that on occasion is exhibited when those in wider ecumenical circles invite this or that Pentecostal to participate in some consultation. Who of us involved in such work has not had the experience at one time or another of eventually understanding that the purpose of our presence was simply to sign off on the work of others rather than be given or take the opportunity to play an active role in the deliberations? Rather, what is needed is honest, sometimes even hard-hitting exchanges where theological differences and similarities may be fully appreciated. The goal, it would seem, is to testify to others about what we know to be true and to reexamine our faith in the light of the testimony of fellow travelers who have a genuine desire for dialogue. Sadly, not all who claim such a desire for dialogue live up to their promise. However, it is only through such honest exchanges that we can hope to draw nearer a more perfect understanding of the Kingdom, while at the same time avoiding the temptation of falling into the trap of letting other groups and their agenda (both stated and hidden) define who we are and what we are about.[35]

Expanding the discussion further, Yong contrasted the CS and Springfield School with the Birmingham School and its thesis, which, he argued, maintains "a much more dynamic view of pentecostal origins in terms of its initial flourishing in multiple locales around the world," and is more self-critically aware of "the thoroughly contextual nature of all theological reflection."[36] He admitted his sympathies lie with the Birmingham thesis but that he believes "the processes of contextualization" are "even more convoluted" than the thesis admits. "Thus, for example, there is no direct rereading of the Bible from any contextual perspective; rather, there is a complicated back-and-forth dialogue and interaction between various contexts (e.g., between Cleveland and Springfield and Birmingham, as these discussions are negotiated in North America vis-à-vis Princeton, New Haven, and Boston, etc., and in Europe with Oxford, Amsterdam, Heidelberg, Rome, etc.), shaped by the plurality of needs, wants, and goals with which communities of readers approach scripture, and always unpredictably informed by the work of the Spirit in the reading and interpreting community."[37]

Perhaps the issues are even more convoluted than Yong acknowledges. The CS builds upon Hollenweger's work, arguably no less rigorously than the Birmingham School does. Moreover, the CS is also profoundly influenced by Walter Brueggemann's postcritical approach, which reinforces Hollenweger's contextualist theology. It follows then that Land, Thomas, Bridges Johns, and Moore speak as they do of early Pentecostalism not because they believe it should be paradigmatic for all Pentecostals everywhere—much less all Christians—but because they recognize in it the best and worst of their own Appalachian Pentecostal experience. In other words, they speak of it because they know it, and because they are too well schooled in contextual theology—thanks in no small part to Hollenweger and Brueggemann—to try to speak for Pentecostalisms in other contexts.[38] What is more, at least a few academics in various global contexts have shown appreciation for CS theology.[39] In any case, the distinctions between these hypothetical schools are blurred, both by collaboration—for example, Thomas's and Macchia's *Revelation* commentary[40]—and by the fact that scholars identified with one school actually serve at institutions identified with another.

That said, CS Pentecostals can aspire to embody in their work, as well as in their lives, an even wider openness to others, an even deeper hospitality.[41] This then leads to a second programmatic suggestion: CS scholars, and those who share affinities with the CS, should continue to speak unapologetically, undefensively, without rancor or bitterness, without feeling the need to prove their legitimacy either as scholars or as Christians. Precisely for such reason, CS theology needs to be Marianized; Mary, the Mother of God, embodies the hospitable life in ways all other disciples must learn to follow.

A Marian theology casts the life of faith as a life of self-effacing cooperation with God and deferential care for others. As Luke makes clear, Mary is chosen because she is "lowly"—impoverished, powerless, and frightened. And not in spite of this but because of it, she, like the void, like Sinai, like the mercy seat, becomes the site of God's self-revelation. This truth is demonstrated publicly at the wedding of Cana, as her alarm that the celebrants have no wine provokes Jesus to enact the first of his signs.

Mary's entire life, as presented to us in the gospels, is a life of preferring others, a life of caring for her neighbors in delighted collaboration with God. Through her, Jesus baptizes Elizabeth in the Spirit. And at the cross, she assumes responsibility for the Beloved Disciple as if he were her own. But hers is also a life of deep and persistent sorrow, as Simeon had prophesied in the beginning it would be. Her consent to the Spirit—itself, of course, a gift of the Father—opened not only her womb but also the womb of all creation to Christ. But it also opened her wounds. A Marianized Pentecostal theology, therefore, speaks the "full gospel" boldly, but never triumphalistically; it enters into critical self-reflection and dialogue without illusions, unassumingly open to surprise.

PNEUMATIC APOCALYPTICISM AND THE END OF PENTECOSTALISM

The CS is obviously retrievalist and restorationist, even if it is also ecumenical. And all retrievalisms and restorationisms run the risk of hagiographic distortion. Like it or not, the truth is that early Pentecostals did, far too often, speak in triumphalist terms, never realizing their vision had been determined, without their consent, by the "crusading mind" of colonialism.[42] Historically, restorationist theologies are overwhelmingly exceptionalist and adversarially sectarian. As already said, all of this should be repudiated in no uncertain terms for both theological and pastoral reasons.[43] But it arguably remains possible to develop a chastened restorationism, one that is marked by Marian (that is, Christlike) modesty, humility, and radical openness to others.

In 2000, Moore, Thomas, and Land dedicated an issue of *Journal of Pentecostal Theology* to the spirit of reconciliation and the answerability of Pentecostals to other traditions. They explained their reasoning in a brief editorial:

> It has been customary to begin each issue of *JPT* with an article by or a scholarly exchange with an "outside dialogue partner," that is, someone who comes from outside the ranks of Pentecostalism. This issue interrupts our usual pattern with another kind of exchange—one that is perhaps more venturesome than any we have yet tried. Perhaps it is one that goes the furthest yet in fulfilling the promise mentioned in the editorial of our inaugural issue, namely, to publish "less conventional offerings, such as testimonies—the poetry of the Pentecostal tradition."
>
> The following "Collection of Words" reflects a diversity of forms: a testimony, two letters, and two confessions.... But beyond all these words, perhaps there is a deeper connection to consider—one that goes beyond

words themselves; one that has to do with a common spirit, indeed, a spirit of reconciliation that has been blowing through our society in these last (few) days.

We offer the following "collection of words" in this same, common spirit. And we do so in the hope and the belief that these words may bear witness to the *Uncommon* Spirit of reconciliation, indeed, the *Holy* Spirit, who is surely the most "outside dialogue partner" of all.[44]

This theme of pneumatic transcendence—the Spirit as the true outsider in all dialogue—appears everywhere in the early CS writings. For example, in the conclusion of her presidential address, Bridges Johns remarked that Pentecostals need to remember that "the same fire which birthed the movement . . . has the capacity to devour it."[45] "God is larger than the Pentecostal movement, and is sovereign and is Lord over the whole earth, Pentecostals know that they cannot tame, domesticate or contain the Creator Spirit."[46]

In a 1997 essay on Jonah, Moore warned about "a God who comes at us armed with questions," contending that all believers, like Jonah, are inclined to flee from such a presence. "Yet the ending of Jonah is open, and it thereby *functions to open*. It denies closure not only to Jonah but also to the reader. For what is a reader to do with a biblical book that ends like no other, with a question?"[47] As Moore reads it, the end of the book of Jonah generates an openness toward God who is our end—not the end we fear, but the end too good for us to imagine.

The same holds true for the book of Habakkuk as Moore reads it, although Habakkuk, unlike Jonah, entered into lament. At the end of his journey, he finds his own limitations and the limitlessness of God. As Moore notes, "The prophet comes to this final step, the end of himself, only to discover 'the Lord God is my strength; he makes my feet like deer's feet and makes me walk on my lofty hills' (3:19). Freshly revealed to his faithful lamenter, God is the end of the lament." Habakkuk laments, but laments *to* God—much as Job did—and so comes to find that "when followed with tenacious faithfulness to the end, indeed the end of ourselves, leads us to the revelation of God as the true end, highest joy, and lasting praise of our life."[48]

The same theme appeared earlier in Moore's oeuvre, in a justly celebrated essay on Deuteronomy, which concludes with a reflection on what it means to read scripture theologically from "inside" a Pentecostal experience:

> The voice that comes to claim central position on the inside of this confession comes from the outside, from the wilderness, from "otherness" itself.

It comes from the margin and then marginalizes all who claim it, who are claimed by it. It will ever put marginal voices in a totally and radically new light—the voices of widows, orphans and aliens. Without the experience of the voice which comes from the midst of the fire, as it did on the day of Pentecost and as it did at Azusa Street, we may never become critical enough to affirm as we should the other voices from the margins.[49]

And it appeared again much later in a recent essay entitled "Altar Hermeneutics," which described biblical interpretation as "a confrontational encounter" with "the God of the altar," an encounter that lays bare "our vested interests, the fears beneath them, and the deep, unresolved wounds underlying and underwriting these fears."[50] So, drawing on Brueggemann's categories, Moore articulates:

In the church, particularly in its studious quarters, we have reached for *a high view of Scripture*, but *a deep view of Scripture*, it seems to me, has scarcely crossed our minds. We have wanted a Scripture that is high enough to give us high authority, but not one that is deep enough to reveal the secrets of our hearts. And in the academy, even in its faith based precincts, we have championed *a critical view of the Bible* that emphasizes its broad diversity, but perhaps our broad and critical view of the Bible, in its stress on seeing the hands of multiple authors and the voices of many "others," *has not been nearly broad and diverse and critical enough*—broad enough so that "no one [not even we ourselves] can cross it" and diverse enough to host, amid and even beyond all the human "others," the very otherness of God and critical enough so that it becomes the most searching source of our own self-criticism.[51]

As is clear from these examples, Moore reads confessionally as a Pentecostal. But his reading always calls Pentecostal*ism* into question. Not only Pentecostal theology and spirituality, but also *faith itself*, including his own faith, and indeed his very existence. This is the opposite of triumphalism, and it is integral to the gestalt of CS theology, which leads to my third programmatic suggestion: in this historical moment, amid the resurgence of ultranationalism, xenophobia, and racism, as well as the exposure of widespread sexual abuse in the churches and wider societies, and the patriarchalism that by default protects the abusers, the CS needs to affirm, even more forcefully than it has done before, the apocalyptic transcendence of the Spirit, and so the precariousness of all our experiences and activity, especially those deemed "religious" or "spiritual."

PENTECOST, SOCIAL HOLINESS, AND THE COMMON GOOD

Dale Coulter contends that Pentecostalism is a nonconformist and folk-driven outworking of the Wesleyan vision. This is true, he said, not only of Charles Parham's Bible School in Topeka and Seymour's Azusa Street Mission, but of all the centers of the movement around the globe.[52] On the basis of this assertion, he called for a revival of nonconformist, folk Wesleyanism among Pentecostals.

As Coulter described it, the Wesleyan vision of Christianity is a "storied way" that leads to "full union with God" through a "crisis-process dynamic" to the forging of "a new people" who work together with God "for the renewal of all things."[53] The Wesleyan way, Coulter maintains, empowers people to live together differently, to live together as "an extension of divine *philanthropia*, transforming the folk cultures of societies by liberating men and women to become agents of the kingdom." "In short, as we are caught up in God's story, we proclaim a gospel way through revival that calls us to embody holiness as a form of dissenting piety and recover the apostolic insistence that the age of the Spirit has come, and it calls us to work toward the eighth day when God will wipe away every tear."[54]

Coulter reminds us that Wesleyans, rightly, believe their work in the world matters. They are persuaded, as they should be, that a faithful Christianity is as concerned with worldly responsibility as it is with personal conviction: holiness must be "brought to bear on personal *and* social realities."[55] With this in mind, Coulter repeatedly, rightly, held up the work of the global women's movement as both evidence and example. But he did not talk about the widespread resistance to the Civil Rights Movement, the indifference to the bombings of civilians and the internment of Japanese American citizens during World War II, or recent support for inhumane immigration regulations. Other examples could be given, but the point is clear: Pentecostalism, if it is to be true to itself as a black Wesleyan-Holiness Christian tradition, must take social responsibility seriously. There is no "being right with God" separate from "doing right by others." And it is impossible to do right by others—to love them, as God does, with God's love, which has been shed abroad in our hearts—without taking seriously the social and cultural, economic and political conditions in which they live. And that calls for a fourth programmatic suggestion: the CS needs to take prophetic initiative in challenging Pentecostals, perhaps especially in the United States and the United Kingdom, to confront their own failures, and to begin again to take seriously their answerability for what happens in the world—politically, economically, culturally, ecologically—as witnesses of the hope of the coming kingdom of God. Daniela Augustine is right: Pentecostals, like all Christians, are called to serve the common good, empowered by the healing Spirit for the work of "world-mending." "The Spirit uplifts the Christified human life as the visible means of invisible grace toward peace building and reconciliation, economic justice, sociopolitical inclusion, and ecological renewal. Indeed, the healing of the entire cosmos starts from within hallowed, Spirit-saturated humanity."[56]

There is a need for what Coulter calls "Christian realism," which, he believes, premillennialism made possible for early Pentecostals:

> Premillennialism also fueled a kind of Christian realism among Pentecostals that checked a particular interpretation of the Wesleyan optimistic view of grace. Admittedly, this realism could take extreme forms, such as the initial pentecostal rejection of ecumenism based on its being an organization and institution. Yet, Christian realism also recognized the need for ongoing renewal because history itself was tragic—the body will decay, strength will fail, life will disappoint, nations will fall.... Premillennialism forced Pentecostals to grapple with the natural limits of human freedom and historical processes. It also, however, grounded Christian hope that fuels the optimism of grace and the pursuit of justice in the temporal orders of society.[57]

As Coulter sees it, premillennialism generated a healthy, holy suspicion of the "establishment," including a suspicion of ecclesial establishments, whether state-sponsored or culturally hegemonic.[58] But perhaps more needs to be said. When it goes wrong, premillennialism's historical pessimism tends to engender twisted forms of social irresponsibility, either fatalistic quietism or cynical realpolitik, insinuating baseless suspicions that make it impossible to love one's neighbors, especially those known as strangers. At least in many Pentecostal circles, premillennialism has gone wrong in exactly these ways.[59] As Moore says, "Much of the movement has now given way to the *stasis* of Western middle-class culture. Lament has been virtually silenced by a consumerist ideology of uninterrupted blessing; salvation in terms of the Spirit's formation of a prophetic community and ongoing transformation of world structures has been mostly replaced by the promise of individual materialism and well-being within a framework of accommodation to the world's cultural and social (dis)arrangements."[60]

APOCALYPTIC AFFECTIONS AND THE HEART OF PENTECOSTAL THEOLOGY/ SPIRITUALITY

As his book's subtitle shows, the heart of Land's work is his account of the "apocalyptic affections," which constitute the "integrating core" of Pentecostal spirituality. No one in the CS has done more with this insight than Lee Roy Martin. For example, his reading of Psalm 63 describes the faithful life as, above all, a life of passion for God. The Psalms, as Martin reads them, call us to move ever closer toward the God who has already moved toward us, and encourages us to let ourselves be moved by his nearness.[61]

But as Martin himself makes clear, these affections are *apocalyptic*. They arise from the innate creaturely need for God, and from the effects of his uncreated presence, which turns out again and again to be more than we need, and not at all what we imagined we wanted. An affectivity that is not apocalyptic in this sense distorts knowing, diminishing the life of faith to a shadow of itself. Simeon Zahl has suggested that contemporary Pentecostal anthropologies as a rule are too optimistic, as well as too voluntarist.[62] But the answer is not a more pessimistic view of human nature. It is a more hopeful view of God, the kind of hopefulness born of mystical experience and theological reflection on that experience.[63]

Again, Zahl is not entirely wrong to say Pentecostal doctrines of grace are sometimes too "optimistic." This can be seen in "overrealized," and "Kingdom-now" theologies, as well as in accounts of sanctification that construe "perfection" as absolute sinlessness. For example, I have heard more than a few ministers and academics critique liturgical prayers of confession as denials of the reality of sanctification, criticisms that betray profound confusion and misapprehension about both Wesleyan doctrine and the spiritual life. But the roots of that confusion and misapprehension are not primarily in the doctrine of human being but in the doctrine of God—and in the praying that shapes and is shaped by that doctrine. So, here is a final programmatic suggestion: the CS needs to continue to press for a more robust Pentecostal doctrine of God, one that goes beyond biblicism and does not suppose that the experience of God is self-interpreting.

The "New Issue" controversy, and the resultant split into Trinitarian and Oneness traditions, uncovered deep insufficiencies in the theology of the early Pentecostal Movement, insufficiencies that have not yet been adequately addressed. Early Pentecostal theology was populist, pragmatic, experientialist, and biblicist, undergirded both by a profound distrust of liturgy and dogma, and an even more profound confidence in "common sense" and the leading of the Spirit. But it was not anti-intellectual, and its passionate spirituality arose from and gave rise to rigorous theological reflection. It is possible, even necessary, to recapture that rigor and passion. And it is also possible and necessary to do so in discerning conversation with the larger Christian liturgical and dogmatic traditions.[64]

CONCLUSION

In conclusion, a few words about my programmatic suggestions and the future of the CS. First, I have suggested that the CS needs not only to honor its roots in the black church tradition but also to *be* "black" in the sense that they hold to and bring forth a spirituality and theology shaped by the experience of "outsider," marginalized communities. Second, I suggested that the CS needs to be "Marianized," so that it embodies its identity with divine hospitality, marked by a radical openness to God and to neighbor that welcomes the unexpected, and resists traditionalistic ways of thinking that stymie Spirit-led theological innovation and development. Third, I suggested that the CS needs to affirm, even more forcefully, the Spirit's apocalyptic transcendence because only that belief can keep a tradition from eventually closing in on itself. Fourth, I suggested that the CS needs to take prophetic initiative to challenge Pentecostals, especially in the United States and the United Kingdom, to face their own theological and ministerial failures, and to take up their God-given worldly responsibilities again. Fifth and finally, I suggested that the CS needs to continue to press for a more robust doctrine of God, one that goes beyond biblicism and does not suppose that the experience of God is self-interpreting.

These are, I believe, true developments and not deviations; they represent enlargements, advancements, and elaborations of themes already present in the DNA of the CS. And they are inextricably bound up together, each depending on the others for wholeness and intelligibility. Prophetic critique, for example, divorced from a sense of the Spirit's apocalyptic transcendence, is mere scolding. And any attempt to perform "blackness" that is not energized by divine hospitality is just appropriation. But these developments are needed not as ends in themselves but in order to continue the widening and deepening of Christian tradition in its mission. That can happen only in serious, lasting dialogue that is itself wide and deep. Thankfully, as the chapters in this volume testify, at least some of those conversations are already underway.

NOTES

1. Kenneth J. Archer, "The Cleveland School: The Making of an Academic Pentecostal Theological Tradition," in *Spirit and Story: Pentecostal Readings of Scripture; Essays in Honor of John Christopher Thomas*, ed. Blaine Charette and Robby Waddell (Sheffield: Sheffield Phoenix Press, 2020), 186.

2. John Christopher Thomas, *Footwashing in John 13 and the Johannine Community* (Sheffield: Sheffield Academic Press, 1991); Steven J. Land, *Pentecostal Spirituality: A Passion for the Kingdom* (Sheffield: Sheffield Academic Press, 1993); Cheryl Bridges Johns, *Pentecostal Formation: A Pedagogy Among the Oppressed* (Sheffield: Sheffield Academic Press, 1993).

3. Rickie D. Moore, "Canon and Charisma in the Book of Deuteronomy," *Journal of Pentecostal Theology* 1, no. 1 (1992): 75–92; John Christopher Thomas, "The Devil, Disease, and Deliverance: James 5:14–16," *Journal of Pentecostal Theology* 1, no. 2 (April 1993): 25–50; John Christopher Thomas, "Women, Pentecostals, and the Bible: An Experiment in Pentecostal Hermeneutics," *Journal of Pentecostal Theology* 2, no. 5 (October 1994): 41–56; Steven J. Land, "A Passion for the Kingdom: Revisioning Pentecostal Spirituality," *Journal of Pentecostal Theology* 1, no. 1 (1992): 19–46; Jackie David Johns and Cheryl Bridges Johns, "Yielding to the Spirit: A Pentecostal Approach to Group Bible Study," *Journal of Pentecostal Theology* 1, no. 1 (1992): 109–34.

4. Amos Yong, "Salvation, Society, and the Spirit: Pentecostal Contextualization and Political Theology from Cleveland to Birmingham, from Springfield to Seoul," *Pax Pneuma: The Journal of Pentecostals and Charismatics for Peace and Justice* 5, no. 2 (2009): 22–34.

5. Kenneth J. Archer, "The Making of an Academic Pentecostal Tradition: The Cleveland School," paper presented at the Society for Pentecostal Studies meeting in March 2016; Michael J. Frost, *The Spirit, Indigenous Peoples and Social Change*, Global Pentecostal and Charismatic Studies Series 30 (Leiden: Brill, 2018), 70; Jacqueline Grey, "When the Spirit Trumps Tradition: A Pentecostal Reading of Isaiah 56:1–8," in *Constructive Pneumatological Hermeneutics in Pentecostal Christianity*, ed. Blaine Charette and Robby Waddell (New York: Palgrave Macmillan, 2016), 143–58; Wolfgang Vondey, *Pentecostal Theology: Living the Full Gospel*, Systematic Pentecostal and Charismatic Theology Series 1 (London: Bloomsbury, 2017), 6; L. William Oliverio Jr., "Contours of a Constructive Pentecostal Philosophical-Theological Hermeneutics," *Journal of Pentecostal Theology* 29, no. 1 (April 2020): 1–22. In personal correspondence, Marty Mittelstadt shared with me that although he has not yet used the term in print, he frequently makes use of it in his teaching. He also suggested that the categorization is not helpful when it is adversarially overstating or weaponizing differences between "Wesleyan" and "Reformed" Pentecostals. James K. A. Smith, *Thinking in Tongues* (Grand Rapids, MI: Eerdmans, 2010), 6; Hannah Ruth Katharine Mather, "Pneumatic Interpretation in the Renewal Tradition: The First 50 Years" (PhD thesis, Middlesex University, 2019), 112–48.

6. Archer, "Making of an Academic Pentecostal Tradition," 192. Archer states, "The particularity of Pentecostal spirituality and theology, a Pentecostal hermeneutic, contextuality, narrativity, affectivity, the Fivefold Gospel or variations on the themes associated with the Full Gospel, peacemaking, and a concern for ecumenism are all noticeable features of this school of thought."

7. For one interpretation of this "style," see Kenneth J. Archer, *The Gospel*

Revisited: Towards a Pentecostal Theology of Worship and Witness (Eugene, OR: Pickwick Publications, 2011), 1–17.

8. Land, "Passion for the Kingdom," 20.

9. Grant Wacker, "Wild Theories and Mad Excitement," in Pentecostals from the Inside Out, ed. H. B. Smith (Wheaton, IL: Scriptum Press, 1990), 27.

10. Land, "Passion for the Kingdom," 20.

11. Ibid.

12. Ibid., 23.

13. John Christopher Thomas, "The Spirit, Healing and Mission: An Overview of the Biblical Canon," International Review of Mission 93, nos. 370–71 (July–October 2004): 422–23. See also "'What the Spirit Is Saying to the Church'—The Testimony of a Pentecostal in New Testament Studies" and "Discerning Dialogue," in Spirit and Scripture: Examining a Pneumatic Hermeneutic, ed. Kevin L. Spawn and Archie T. Wright (New York: T&T Clark, 2012), 115–29, 183–85.

14. Blackness is not the equal opposite of whiteness. It is a protest against it, a creative form of life raised up in defiance against oppression. Blackness is natural and graced. Whiteness is unnatural and satanic. See Willie Jennings, "Overcoming Racial Faith: How Christianity Became Entangled with Racism," Divinity 14, no. 2 (Spring 2015): 4–9.

15. Bridges Johns, Pentecostal Formation, 69.

16. See Kimberly Ervin Alexander, "'The Almost Pentecostal': The Future of the Church of God in the United States," in The Future of Pentecostalism in the United States, ed. Eric Patterson and Edmund Rybarzyk (Lanham, MD: Rowman and Littlefield, 2007), 137–56.

17. Land, Pentecostal Spirituality, 26; see also Leonard Lovett, "Black Origins of Pentecostalism," in Aspects of Pentecostal-Charismatic Origins, ed. Vinson Synan (Plainfield, NJ: Logos, 1975), 145–58; Cheryl J. Sanders, "Wanted Dead or Alive: A Black Theology of Renewal," Pneuma 36, no. 3 (2014): 407–16; Dale M. Coulter, "Toward a Pentecostal Theology of Black Consciousness," Journal of Pentecostal Theology 25, no. 1 (2016): 74–89.

18. Allan Anderson, "Pentecostals and Apartheid in South Africa During Ninety Years: 1908–1998," Cyberjournal for Pentecostal-Charismatic Research 9 (February 2001), http://www.pctii.org/cyberj/cyberj9/anderson.html.

19. Rickie D. Moore, "Joel," in The Book of the Twelve, ed. John Christopher Thomas, Pentecostal Commentary Series (Leiden: Brill, 2020), 133.

20. See Chris Green, "The Spirit that Makes Us (Number) One: Racism, Tongues, and the Evidences of Spirit Baptism," Pneuma 41, nos. 3–4 (2019): 1–24.

21. Larry B. Stammer, "Era of Racial Separation Ending for Pentecostals," Los Angeles Times, October 17, 1994, https://www.latimes.com/archives/la-xpm-1994-10-17-mn-51344-story.html.

22. Leonard Lovett, "Looking Backward to Go Forward," Pneuma 18, no. 1 (Spring 1996): 122–25.

23. See Jennings, "Overcoming Racial Faith," 9.

24. Ibid., 8.

25. Yong, "Salvation, Society, and the Spirit," 23.

26. Walter Hollenweger, "Pentecostals and the Charismatic Movement," in The Study of Spirituality, ed. Cheslyn Jones, Geoffrey Wainwright, and Edward Yarnold, SJ (New York: Oxford University Press, 1986), 552.

27. Land, "Passion for the Kingdom," 42–44.

28. Cheryl Bridges Johns, "The Adolescence of Pentecostalism: In Search of a Legitimate Sectarian Identity," Pneuma 17, no. 1 (Spring 1995): 3.

29. See Zachary Michael Tackett, "As a Prophetic Voice: Liberationism as a Matrix for Interpreting American Pentecostal Thought and Praxis," Journal of the European Pentecostal Theological Association 33, no. 1 (2013): 42–57.

30. Bridges Johns, "Adolescence of Pentecostalism," 16–17. Bridges Johns is a leading ecumenist. She was a participant in the International Roman Catholic-Pentecostal Dialogue and the Mennonite (USA)-Church of God Dialogue. She was also a long-term member of Evangelicals and Catholics Together (ECT), and active in the Commission on Faith and Order for the National Council of Churches (1992–96), serving on its Executive Committee. She has participated in a number of World Council of Churches initiatives and delivered plenary addresses at the Global Christian Forum meeting in Kenya (2007) and at a National Meeting for Christian Churches Together (2014).

31. Mark Cartledge, "Renewal Ecclesiology in Empirical Perspective," *Pneuma* 36, no. 1 (2014): 15.

32. See *Journal of Pentecostal Theology* 1, no. 1 (1992): 3.

33. Walter Hollenweger, "The Critical Tradition of Pentecostalism," *Journal of Pentecostal Theology* 1, no. 1 (1992): 7–17; Jürgen Moltmann, "A Response to My Dialogue Partner," *Journal of Pentecostal Theology* 2, no. 4 (April 1994): 59–70; Harvey Cox, review of *Pentecostal Spirituality: A Passion for the Kingdom*, by Steven J. Land, *Journal of Pentecostal Theology* 2, no. 5 (October 1994): 3–12; Clark Pinnock, "The Work of the Holy Spirit in Hermeneutics," *Journal of Pentecostal Theology* 1, no. 2 (April 1993): 3–23; James D. G. Dunn, "Baptism in the Spirit: A Response to Pentecostal Scholars on Luke-Acts," *Journal of Pentecostal Theology* 1, no. 3 (October 1993): 3–27.

34. Frank D. Macchia, "Sighs Too Deep for Words: Toward a Theology of Glossolalia," *Journal of Pentecostal Theology* 1, no. 1 (1992): 47–73; Murray W. Dempster, "Christian Social Concern in Pentecostal Perspective: Reformulating Pentecostal Eschatology," *Journal of Pentecostal Theology* 1, no. 2 (April 1993): 51–64; Mark Cartledge, "Charismatic Prophecy: A Definition and Description," *Journal of Pentecostal Theology* 2, no. 5 (October 1994): 79–120; Henry H. Knight III, "God's Faithfulness and God's Freedom: A Comparison of Contemporary Theologies of Healing," *Journal of Pentecostal Theology* 1, no. 2 (April 1993): 65–89; Ralph Del Colle, "Spirit-Christology: Dogmatic Foundations for Pentecostal-Charismatic Spirituality," *Journal of Pentecostal Theology* 1, no. 3 (October 1993): 91–112.

35. John Christopher Thomas, "Pentecostal Theology in the Twenty-First Century," *Pneuma* 20, no. 1 (1998): 9.

36. Yong, "Salvation, Society, and the Spirit," 24.

37. Ibid.

38. In a well-known passage in his *Pentecostal Spirituality*, Land situated Pentecostalism in paradoxical relation to other Christian traditions:

> Pentecostalism flows in paradoxical continuity and discontinuity with other streams of Christianity. Insofar as it retains similarity to the first ten years of the movement, it is more Arminian than Calvinist in its approach to issues of human agency and perseverance. It is more Calvinist than Lutheran in its appreciation of the so-called 'third use of the Law' to guide Christian growth and conduct. It is more Eastern than Western in its understanding of spirituality and participation in the divine life (theosis).... It is both ascetic and mystical... more Catholic than Protestant in emphasizing sanctification transformation more than forensic justification, but more Protestant than Catholic in the conviction that the Word is the authority over the church and tradition for matters of faith, practice, government, and discipline. (18)

An unfriendly critic might say those who hold such a view are neither Arminian nor Calvinist, neither Calvinist nor Lutheran, neither Eastern nor Western, neither Catholic nor Protestant. Perhaps Land's Pentecostalism does not so much hold the middle ground between the various traditions as it is "off in left field." But one might also make the case that this theological eclecticism, whatever its flaws, inconsistences, and incoherencies, holds serious ecumenical promise.

39. See Wilmer Estrada-Carrasquillo, "The Latino/a Pentecostal Response to the McDonaldization Process of the Church in the United States," in *Pentecostals and Charismatics in Latin America and Latino Communities*, ed. Sammy Alfaro and Néstor Medina (New York: Palgrave Macmillan, 2015), 199–210; Wilmer Estrada-Carrasquillo, "¿Y los pentecostales? ¡Presentes! Public Theological Contributions from Latin America," *Journal of Pentecostal Theology* 24, no. 2 (2015): 231–40; Wilmer Estrada-Carrasquillo, "The Relational Character of Wesley's Theology and Its Implications for an Ecclesiology for the Other: A Latino Pentecostal Testimony," *Asbury Journal* 73, no. 1 (2018): 105–20; Marius Nel, "Pentecostals and the Marginalised: A Historical Survey of the Early Pentecostal Movement's Predilection for the Marginalised," *HTS Teologiese Studies* 75, no. 1 (2019): 1–8; Miguel Alvarez, "The South and the Latin American Paradigm of the Pentecostal Movement," *Asian Journal of Pentecostal Studies* 5, no. 1 (2002): 135–53.

40. John Christopher Thomas and Frank D. Macchia, *Revelation*, Two Horizons New Testament Commentary (Grand Rapids, MI: Eerdmans, 2016).

41. Vondey, *Pentecostal Theology*, 55–57.

42. Kosuke Koyama, *Waterbuffalo Theology* (Maryknoll, NY: Orbis, 1974), 32.

43. See David Courey, *What Has Wittenberg to do with Azusa? Luther's Theology of the Cross and Pentecostal Triumphalism* (London: Bloomsbury, 2015). In my judgment, Courey is right to challenge triumphalism, but I think he mistakenly reads it into Archer's *Pentecostal Hermeneutics*. In the end, he, like Archer, calls for a critical reaffirmation of early Pentecostal theology/spirituality.

44. Rickie D. Moore, John Christopher Thomas, and Steven J. Land, "A Collection of Words Bearing Witness to the Spirit of Reconciliation," *Journal of Pentecostal Theology* 8, no. 17 (October 2000): 5–6. The issue included a testimony of a Church of God of Prophecy pastor washing the feet of a Catholic priest, a confession of Catholic sins against Pentecostals by Killian McDonnell and a responding confession of Pentecostal sins against Catholics by Frank Macchia, an article on patristic conceptions of initiation, two articles on missions and missiology, an article on abuse, an article on postmodernism, and two articles on Pentecostalism in Latin America.

45. Bridges Johns, "Adolescence of Pentecostalism," 17.

46. Ibid., 16.

47. Rickie D. Moore, "'And Also Much Cattle?!' Prophetic Passions and the End of Jonah," *Journal of Pentecostal Theology* 5, no. 11 (October 1997): 48.

48. Rickie D. Moore, "The Prophetic Path from Lament to Praise: Tracking the Burden of Habakkuk," *Living Pulpit* 11, no. 4 (October–December 2002): 27. See also Rickie D. Moore, "Raw Prayer and Refined Theology: 'You Have Not Spoken Straight to Me, as My Servant Job Has,'" in *The Spirit and the Mind: Essays in Informed Pentecostalism*, ed. Terry L. Cross and Emerson B. Powery (Lanham: University Press of America, 2000), 35–48.

49. Rickie D. Moore, "Deuteronomy and the Fire of God: A Critical Charismatic Interpretation," *Journal of Pentecostal Theology* 3, no. 7 (1995): 33.

50. Rickie D. Moore, "Altar Hermeneutics: Reflections on Pentecostal Biblical Interpretation," *Pneuma* 38, no. 1–2 (2016): 156.

51. Ibid., 159.

52. Dale M. Coulter, "Recovering the Wesleyan Vision of Pentecostalism: 5 Theses," *Pneuma* 40, no. 4 (2018): 457.

53. Ibid., 460, 465, 470, 475, 480.

54. Ibid., 488.

55. Ibid., 487; emphasis added.

56. Daniela Augustine, *The Spirit and the Common Good: Shared Flourishing in the Image of God* (Grand Rapids, MI: Eerdmans, 2019), 200.

57. Coulter, "Recovering the Wesleyan Vision," 482–83.

58. Ibid., 487.

59. See Robby Waddell, "The Coming of the Son of Man in Mark's Gospel," in *Spirit and Story: Pentecostal Readings of Scripture; Essays in Honor of John Christopher Thomas*, ed. Blaine Charette and Robby Waddell (Sheffield: Sheffield Phoenix Press, 2020), 42–60; Robby Waddell, "Apocalyptic Sustainability: The Future of Pentecostal Ecology," in *Pentecostal Eschatology: World Without End*, ed. Peter Althouse and Robby Waddell (Eugene, OR: Pickwick Publications, 2010), 95–110; Robby Waddell, "A Green Apocalypse: Comparing Secular and Religious Eschatological Visions of Earth," in *Blood Cries Out: Pentecostals, Ecology, and the Groans of Creation*, ed. A. J. Swoboda (Eugene, OR: Pickwick Publications, 2014), 133–51.

60. Moore, "Joel," 178.

61. See Lee Roy Martin, *The Spirit of the Psalms: Rhetorical Analysis, Affectivity, and Pentecostal Spirituality* (Cleveland, TN: CPT Press, 2018).

62. See Simeon Zahl, *Pneumatology and Theology of the Cross in the Preaching of Christoph Friedrich Blumhardt: The Holy Spirit Between Wittenberg and Azusa Street*, T&T Clark Studies in Systematic Theology (New York: T&T Clark, 2010).

63. For an example of this kind of reflection, see especially Daniel Castelo, *Pentecostalism as a Christian Mystical Tradition* (Grand Rapids, MI: Eerdmans, 2017).

64. Land (*Pentecostal Spirituality*, 18) suggested three decades ago that this is best done in company of Wesley because of Wesley's integration of sources—Eastern and Western, ancient and modern, doctrinal and mystical—in his theology and ministry.

BIBLIOGRAPHY

Alexander, Kimberly Ervin. "'The Almost Pentecostal': The Future of the Church of God in the United States." In *The Future of Pentecostalism in the United States*, edited by Eric Patterson and Edmund Rybarzyk, 137–56. Lanham, MD: Rowman and Littlefield, 2007.

Alvarez, Miguel. "The South and the Latin American Paradigm of the Pentecostal Movement." *Asian Journal of Pentecostal Studies* 5, no. 1 (2002): 135–53.

Anderson, Allan. "Pentecostals and Apartheid in South Africa During Ninety Years: 1908–1998." *Cyberjournal for Pentecostal-Charismatic Research* 9 (February 2001). http://www.pctii.org/cyberj/cyberj9/anderson.html.

Archer, Kenneth J. "The Cleveland School: The Making of an Academic Pentecostal Theological Tradition." In *Spirit and Story: Pentecostal Readings of Scripture; Essays in Honor of John Christopher Thomas*, edited by Blaine Charette and Robby Waddell, 182–200. Sheffield: Sheffield Phoenix Press, 2020.

———. *The Gospel Revisited: Towards a Pentecostal Theology of Worship and Witness*. Eugene, OR: Pickwick Publications, 2011.

———. "The Making of an Academic Pentecostal Tradition: The Cleveland

School." Paper presented at the Society for Pentecostal Studies meeting, March 2016.

Augustine, Daniela. *The Spirit and the Common Good: Shared Flourishing in the Image of God.* Grand Rapids, MI: Eerdmans, 2019.

Bridges Johns, Cheryl. "The Adolescence of Pentecostalism: In Search of a Legitimate Sectarian Identity." *Pneuma* 17, no. 1 (1995): 3–17.

———. *Pentecostal Formation: A Pedagogy Among the Oppressed.* Sheffield: Sheffield Academic Press, 1993.

Cartledge, Mark. "Charismatic Prophecy: A Definition and Description." *Journal of Pentecostal Theology* 2, no. 5 (October 1994): 79–120.

———. "Renewal Ecclesiology in Empirical Perspective." *Pneuma* 36, no. 1 (2014): 5–24.

Castelo, Daniel. *Pentecostalism as a Christian Mystical Tradition.* Grand Rapids, MI: Eerdmans, 2017.

Coulter, Dale M. "Recovering the Wesleyan Vision of Pentecostalism: 5 Theses." *Pneuma* 40, no. 4 (2018): 457–88.

———. "Toward a Pentecostal Theology of Black Consciousness." *Journal of Pentecostal Theology* 25, no. 1 (2016): 74–89.

Courey, David. *What Has Wittenberg to do with Azusa? Luther's Theology of the Cross and Pentecostal Triumphalism.* London: Bloomsbury, 2015.

Cox, Harvey. Review of *Pentecostal Spirituality: A Passion for the Kingdom*, by Steven J. Land. *Journal of Pentecostal Theology* 2, no. 5 (October 1994): 3–12.

Del Colle, Ralph. "Spirit-Christology: Dogmatic Foundations for Pentecostal-Charismatic Spirituality." *Journal of Pentecostal Theology* 1, no. 3 (October 1993): 91–112.

Dempster, Murray W. "Christian Social Concern in Pentecostal Perspective: Reformulating Pentecostal Eschatology." *Journal of Pentecostal Theology* 1, no. 2 (April 1993): 51–64.

Dunn, James D. G. "Baptism in the Spirit: A Response to Pentecostal Scholars on Luke-Acts." *Journal of Pentecostal Theology* 1, no. 3 (October 1993): 3–27.

Estrada-Carrasquillo, Wilmer. "The Latino/a Pentecostal Response to the McDonaldization Process of the Church in the United States." In *Pentecostals and Charismatics in Latin America and Latino Communities*, edited by Sammy Alfaro and Néstor Medina, 199–210. New York: Palgrave Macmillan, 2015.

———. "The Relational Character of Wesley's Theology and Its Implications for an Ecclesiology for the Other: A Latino Pentecostal Testimony." *Asbury Journal* 73, no. 1 (2018): 105–20.

———. "¿Y los pentecostales? ¡Presentes! Public Theological Contributions from Latin America." *Journal of Pentecostal Theology* 24, no. 2 (2015): 231–40.

Frost, Michael J. *The Spirit, Indigenous Peoples and Social Change.* Global Pentecostal and Charismatic Studies Series 30. Leiden: Brill, 2018.

Green, Chris. "The Spirit that Makes Us (Number) One: Racism, Tongues, and the Evidences of Spirit Baptism." *Pneuma* 41, nos. 3–4 (2019): 1–24.

Grey, Jacqueline. "When the Spirit Trumps Tradition: A Pentecostal Reading of Isaiah 56:1–8." In *Constructive Pneumatological Hermeneutics in Pentecostal Christianity*, edited by Blaine Charette and Robby Waddell, 143–58. New York: Palgrave Macmillan, 2016.

Hollenweger, Walter. "The Critical Tradition of Pentecostalism." *Journal of Pentecostal Theology* 1, no. 1 (1992): 7–17.

———. "Pentecostals and the Charismatic Movement." In *The Study of Spirituality*, edited by Cheslyn Jones, Geoffrey Wainwright, and Edward Yarnold, SJ, 549–53. New York: Oxford University Press, 1986.

Jennings, Willie. "Overcoming Racial Faith: How Christianity Became

Entangled with Racism." *Divinity* 14, no. 2 (Spring 2015): 4–9.

Johns, David Jackie, and Cheryl Bridges Johns. "Yielding to the Spirit: A Pentecostal Approach to Group Bible Study." *Journal of Pentecostal Theology* 1, no. 1 (1992): 109–34.

Knight, Henry H., III. "God's Faithfulness and God's Freedom: A Comparison of Contemporary Theologies of Healing." *Journal of Pentecostal Theology* 1, no. 2 (April 1993): 65–89.

Koyama, Kosuke. *Waterbuffalo Theology*. Maryknoll, NY: Orbis, 1974.

Land, Steven J. "A Passion for the Kingdom: Revisioning Pentecostal Spirituality." *Journal of Pentecostal Theology* 1, no. 1 (1992): 19–46.

———. *Pentecostal Spirituality: A Passion for the Kingdom*. Sheffield: Sheffield Academic Press, 1993.

Lovett, Leonard. "Black Origins of Pentecostalism." In *Aspects of Pentecostal-Charismatic Origins*, edited by Vinson Synan, 145–58. Plainfield, NJ: Logos, 1975.

———. "Looking Backward to Go Forward." *Pneuma* 18, no. 1 (Spring 1996): 122–25.

Macchia, Frank D. "Sighs Too Deep for Words: Toward a Theology of Glossolalia." *Journal of Pentecostal Theology* 1, no. 1 (1992): 47–73.

Martin, Lee Roy. *The Spirit of the Psalms: Rhetorical Analysis, Affectivity, and Pentecostal Spirituality*. Cleveland, TN: CPT Press, 2018.

Mather, Hannah Ruth Katharine. "Pneumatic Interpretation in the Renewal Tradition: The First 50 Years." PhD thesis, Middlesex University, 2019.

Moltmann, Jürgen. "A Response to My Dialogue Partner." *Journal of Pentecostal Theology* 2, no. 4 (April 1994): 59–70.

Moore, Rickie D. "Altar Hermeneutics: Reflections on Pentecostal Biblical Interpretation." *Pneuma* 38, no. 1–2 (2016): 148–59.

———. "'And Also Much Cattle?!' Prophetic Passions and the End of Jonah." *Journal of Pentecostal Theology* 5, no. 11 (October 1997): 35–48.

———. "Canon and Charisma in the Book of Deuteronomy." *Journal of Pentecostal Theology* 1, no. 1 (1992): 75–92.

———. "Deuteronomy and the Fire of God: A Critical Charismatic Interpretation." *Journal of Pentecostal Theology* 3, no. 7 (1995): 11–33.

———. "Joel." In *The Book of the Twelve*, edited by John Christopher Thomas, 123–84. Pentecostal Commentary Series. Leiden: Brill, 2020.

———. "The Prophetic Path from Lament to Praise: Tracking the Burden of Habakkuk." *Living Pulpit* 11, no. 4 (October–December 2002): 26–27.

———. "Raw Prayer and Refined Theology: 'You Have Not Spoken Straight to Me, as My Servant Job Has.'" In *The Spirit and the Mind: Essays in Informed Pentecostalism*, edited by Terry L. Cross and Emerson B. Powery, 35–48. Lanham: University Press of America, 2000.

Moore, Rickie D., John Christopher Thomas, and Steven J. Land. "A Collection of Words Bearing Witness to the Spirit of Reconciliation." *Journal of Pentecostal Theology* 8, no. 17 (October 2000): 5–6.

Nel, Marius. "Pentecostals and the Marginalised: A Historical Survey of the Early Pentecostal Movement's Predilection for the Marginalised." *HTS Teologiese Studies* 75, no. 1 (2019): 1–8.

Oliverio, L. William, Jr. "Contours of a Constructive Pentecostal Philosophical-Theological Hermeneutics." *Journal of Pentecostal Theology* 29, no. 1 (April 2020): 1–22.

Pinnock, Clark. "The Work of the Holy Spirit in Hermeneutics." *Journal of Pentecostal Theology* 1, no. 2 (April 1993): 3–23.

Sanders, Cheryl J. "Wanted Dead or Alive: A Black Theology of Renewal." *Pneuma* 36, no. 3 (2014): 407–16.

Smith, James K. A. *Thinking in Tongues*. Grand Rapids, MI: Eerdmans, 2010.

Stammer, Larry B. "Era of Racial Separation Ending for Pentecostals." *Los Angeles Times*, October 17, 1994. https://www.latimes.com/archives/la-xpm-1994-10-17-mn-51344-story.html.

Tackett, Zachary Michael. "As a Prophetic Voice: Liberationism as a Matrix for Interpreting American Pentecostal Thought and Praxis." *Journal of the European Pentecostal Theological Association* 33, no. 1 (2013): 42–57.

Thomas, John Christopher. "The Devil, Disease, and Deliverance: James 5:14–16." *Journal of Pentecostal Theology* 1, no. 2 (April 1993): 25–50.

———. *Footwashing in John 13 and the Johannine Community*. Sheffield: Sheffield Academic Press, 1991.

———. "Pentecostal Theology in the Twenty-First Century." *Pneuma* 20, no. 1 (1998): 3–19.

———. "The Spirit, Healing and Mission: An Overview of the Biblical Canon." *International Review of Mission* 93, nos. 370–71 (July–October 2004): 421–42.

———. "'What the Spirit Is Saying to the Church'—The Testimony of a Pentecostal in New Testament Studies" and "Discerning Dialogue." In *Spirit and Scripture: Examining a Pneumatic Hermeneutic*, edited by Kevin L. Spawn and Archie T. Wright, 115–29, 183–85. New York: T&T Clark, 2012.

———. "Women, Pentecostals, and the Bible: An Experiment in Pentecostal Hermeneutics." *Journal of Pentecostal Theology* 2, no. 5 (October 1994): 41–56.

Thomas, John Christopher, and Frank D. Macchia. *Revelation*. Two Horizons New Testament Commentary. Grand Rapids, MI: Eerdmans, 2016.

Vondey, Wolfgang. *Pentecostal Theology: Living the Full Gospel*. Systematic Pentecostal and Charismatic Theology Series 1. London: Bloomsbury, 2017.

Wacker, Grant. "Wild Theories and Mad Excitement." In *Pentecostals from the Inside Out*, edited by H. B. Smith, 19–28. Wheaton, IL: Scriptum Press, 1990.

Waddell, Robby. "Apocalyptic Sustainability: The Future of Pentecostal Ecology." In *Pentecostal Eschatology: World Without End*, edited by Peter Althouse and Robby Waddell, 95–110. Eugene, OR: Pickwick Publications, 2010.

———. "The Coming of the Son of Man in Mark's Gospel." In *Spirit and Story: Pentecostal Readings of Scripture; Essays in Honor of John Christopher Thomas*, edited by Blaine Charette and Robby Waddell, 42–60. Sheffield: Sheffield Phoenix Press, 2020.

———. "A Green Apocalypse: Comparing Secular and Religious Eschatological Visions of Earth." In *Blood Cries Out: Pentecostals, Ecology, and the Groans of Creation*, edited by A. J. Swoboda, 133–51. Eugene, OR: Pickwick Publications, 2014.

Yong, Amos. "Salvation, Society, and the Spirit: Pentecostal Contextualization and Political Theology from Cleveland to Birmingham, from Springfield to Seoul." *Pax Pneuma: The Journal of Pentecostals and Charismatics for Peace and Justice* 5, no. 2 (2009): 22–34.

Zahl, Simeon. *Pneumatology and Theology of the Cross in the Preaching of Christoph Friedrich Blumhardt: The Holy Spirit Between Wittenberg and Azusa Street*. T&T Clark Studies in Systematic Theology. New York: T&T Clark, 2010.

CONTRIBUTORS

Kimberly Ervin Alexander is Director of Online Education at Ramp School of Ministry and an Honorary Research Fellow at the Manchester Wesley Research Centre. Alexander is a past president of the Society for Pentecostal Studies. She serves on several editorial boards for Wesleyan and Pentecostal publications. She is the author of *Pentecostal Healing: Models in Theology and Practice* as well as numerous books, articles, and chapters on healing, women in Pentecostalism, and early Pentecostal spiritual experience.

David Bundy is Associate Director of the Manchester Wesley Research Centre. He is a specialist in Methodist, Holiness, and Pentecostal history, focusing primarily on issues outside of North America as well as on early Asian and East African Christianities. He is the author of *Keswick: A Bibliographic Introduction to the Higher Life Movements*, *Visions of Apostolic Mission: Scandinavian Pentecostal Mission to 1935* and numerous scholarly articles. He has served as librarian and historian at Asbury Theological Seminary, Christian Theological Seminary, and Fuller Theological Seminary.

Insik Choi is Professor of Systematic Theology, Seoul Theological University, and Director of the Global Institute for the Fourfold Gospel Theology. He has served as Graduate Dean of Seoul Theological University and Chairman of Korean Systematic Theology. He received his doctorate at Kirchliche Hochschule Berlin (currently Berlin Humboldt University).

Robert A. Danielson is the Scholarly Communications Librarian at Asbury Theological Seminary in Wilmore, Kentucky. He is a missiologist with a PhD in intercultural studies and teaches in the E. Stanley Jones School of World Missions and Evangelism at Asbury Theological Seminary as an affiliate faculty.

Chris E. W. Green is Professor of Theology at Southeastern University in Lakeland, Florida, a Teaching Pastor at Sanctuary Church in Tulsa, Oklahoma, and Canon Theologian for the Diocese of St Anthony in the Communion of Evangelical Episcopal Churches.

Geordan Hammond is Senior Lecturer in Church History and Wesley Studies at Nazarene Theological College, Manchester and Director of the Manchester Wesley Research Centre. He is author of *John Wesley in America: Restoring Primitive Christianity* and coeditor of *George Whitefield: Life, Context, and Legacy*; *Religion, Gender, and Industry: Exploring Church and Methodism in a Local Setting*, and the journal *Wesley and Methodist Studies*.

David Sang-Ehil Han is Dean of the Faculty/Vice President for Academics and Professor of Theology and Pentecostal Spirituality at Pentecostal Theological Seminary. He is an Honorary Fellow of the Manchester Wesley Research Centre and Publisher of Aldersgate Press (the publication arm of the Wesleyan Holiness Connection). Dr. Han has published articles and chapters in various journals and books on theological issues such as sin and salvation, Jesus and the Spirit, the Spirit and life, Pentecostalism in Asia, Christian hospitality, and pastoral practices.

Henry (Hal) H. Knight III is Donald and Pearl Wright Professor of Wesleyan Studies and E. Stanley Jones Professor of Evangelism, Saint Paul School of Theology, Leawood, Kansas. He is the author of *The Presence of God in the Christian Life: John Wesley and the Means of Grace, Anticipating Heaven Below: Optimism of Grace from John Wesley to the Pentecostals, John Wesley: Optimist of Grace*, and editor of *From Aldersgate to Azusa Street*.

Frank D. Macchia is Professor of Christian Theology at Vanguard University of Southern California and Associate Director of the Centre for Pentecostal and Charismatic Studies at Bangor University, Wales. His most recent books are *The Spirit-Baptized Church: A Dogmatic Inquiry* and *Jesus the Spirit Baptizer: Christology in Light of Pentecost*. He has written extensively on various systematic loci in the light of pneumatology.

Luther Oconer is Associate Professor of Global Wesleyan Theology at Asbury Theological Seminary, Florida Dunnam Campus in Orlando. He is an ordained elder from the United Methodist Church in the Philippines. He is also the author of *Spirit-Filled Protestantism: Holiness-Pentecostal Revivals and the Making of Filipino Methodist Identity*.

Cheryl J. Sanders is Professor of Christian Ethics at Howard University School of Divinity and Senior Pastor of Third Street Church of God in Washington, DC. She is a former President of the American Theological Society and is a member of the American Academy of Religion and the Society of Christian Ethics. Her publications include *Saints in Exile: The Holiness-Pentecostal Experience in African American Religion and Culture, Ministry at the Margins: The Prophetic Mission of Women, Youth, and the Poor*, and *Empowerment Ethics for a Liberated People: A Path to African American Social Transformation*.

Daniel Woods is Professor of History Emeritus at Ferrum College (Virginia) and School of Ministry Director for the North Carolina Conference of the International Pentecostal Holiness Church. In 2017, he coauthored *Fire Baptized: The Many Lives and Works of Benjamin Hardin Irwin* with Vinson Synan.

INDEX

Italicized page references indicate illustrations. Endnotes are referenced with "n" followed by the endnote number.

abolitionism, 4, 55, 139, 146–47
Abrams, Minnie, 53
active holiness, theologies of, 170–71
Acts of the Holy Ghost (Woodworth-Etter), 58
Adams, Archie, 125
Adams, T. L., 128
addiction, 34–35
adoptionist Christology, 187
Advent Christian, 56
Africa, 32, 68n29, 142
    African religions, 140
African Americans 4, 36, 46n48
    and Holiness, 5, 13–14, 34, 40, 129
    and Methodism, 3, 214
    and Pentecostalism, 208, 231–34
    women, 138–58
African Methodist Episcopal Church, 138, 147
Akola, India, 57
alcohol, 34, 126, 139, 216
Aldersgate, London, England, 166
Alexander, Estrelda, 141, 142
Alexander, Kimberly, 13, 18n21, 72–95, 253
All Aboard (Orwig), 123, 125–26
All Saints Church (Sunderland, England), 72, 75, 79
Almont, Michigan, 56
Amanda Berry Smith (Israel), 141
AME Church. *See* African Methodist Episcopal Church
American Academy of Religion, 11
American Board of Foreign Missions, 67n22
Americanism, 3
Ames, Iowa, 99
Amsterdam, Netherlands, 237
Autobiography, An (Smith), *142*

Anderson, Allan, 86n2
Anglican Church, 3, 67n13, 77, 90n54
    and John Wesley, 222n28
    Pentecostalism in, 80, 85–86, 87–88n12
    See also Episcopal Church
Anselm, Saint, 187, 191–92, 194–95, 202, 204–5n26
Anti-Christ, theologies of, 126
Anticipating Heaven Below (Knight), 11
antislavery, 55, 216
apocalypticism, theologies of, 15, 199, 210, 238, 243–44
    and transcendence, 239, 244
Apostles' Creed 162
Apostolic Faith, 42, 59, 76, 142–43, 214
Apostolic Faith Church in England, 77
apotheosis, 161, 202
Appalachian region, United States, 36, 46n47, 119, 237
Appenzeller, Henry, 159
Archer, Kenneth, 229, 231, 245n6, 248n43
Arkansas, 5
Arminian theology, 247–48n38
Arnold's Practical Sunday-school Commentary (ed. Morrow), 37
Arrington, French, 229
Asbury, Francis, 3, 209
Asbury College (Wilmore, KY), 13, 96, 99, 104, 105, 111, 127, 128
Asbury Theological Seminary (Wilmore, KY), 8–11, 96
ascension, theologies of, 198
asceticism, 39, 247n38
Asia, continent, 12–13, 96, 100, 107, 110, 111, 112
Aspects of Pentecostal-Charismatic Origins (Synan), 8
Assam Province, India, 109
Assemblies of God, 16n5, 130, 131
    Korean, 168–69
    World Assemblies of God Congress, *170*
Athanasius, 193, 194, 202

atonement, theologies of, 1, 12, 14–15, 187–207
Augustine, Daniela, 242
Augustine, Saint, 161, 172
Austin, Texas, 150–51
Australia, 53
Awrey, Daniel, 127
Azusa Street Revival and Mission, 6, 11, 14, 41–42, 52–53, 59, 72, 99, 123, 125, 133n18, 134n29, 138, 140, 141, 142–43, 145–46, 155, 168, 209–10, 214–15, 233, 240–41

Bahraich, India, 59
Baltimore, Maryland, 150–51
Baltimore and Ohio Railroad (B.&O.), 128
Bangalore, India. *See* Bengaluru, India
Bareilly, India, 100
Barnes, Michael, 192
Baroda (Vadodara), India, 100
baptism
    and atonement, 14–15, 187–207
    and biblical narrative, 169–70
    and Christian unity, 213–15
    and eschatology, 199
    and fire, 123–25, 187–207
    in Korean Christianity, 168
    and natality, 187–88
    Spirit baptism: defined, 170–71; doctrinal centrality, 172–73, 187–207; practice of, 1, 6, 12, 16n5, 30–31, 38–39, 72, 75, 77–78, 82, 109–10, 111, 119, 121–22, 125, 133n11, 139, 143, 152, 154, 155, 162–63, 166, 198–202
    and theological language: use of "receiving," 166, 168, 215; use of "with," 98
    water baptism: 122, 166, 187–88, 197, 198, 199, 203
Baptism of the Holy Ghost, The, (Mahan), 188
Baptists, 2, 4, 28, 53, 80, 90n50, 100, 140, 143–44, 149, 154, 189, 214
    Holiness and Radical Holiness movements influences, 5, 30, 40, 56, 147
    Missionaries, 53, 100
Barratt, Thomas Ball, 72, 82–83, 90n55

Barth, Karl, 162–63, 166
Bartleman, Frank, 125
Battle River Railway (B. R. R.), 127
Baxter, Elizabeth, 39, 54, 57
Baxter, Michael, 57
Beaty, James, 229
Bell, E. N., 189
Bengaluru (Bangalore), India, 100, 107
Bethel Bible School (Topeka, KS), 241
Bethshan (London), 39, 44n11, 57
Bethune, Mary, 142, 146, 149, 152, 155
Bethune-Cookman University (Daytona Beach, FL), 152
Beulah Bible School (Whitley City, KY), 32
Bhusawal, India, 64
Bible Bands, 143
Bible naming, in Korea, 176n49
binitarian theology, 195
Birmingham School, theological, 236–37
blackness, 233, 244, 246n14
Bluefield, West Virginia, 129–30
Bluegrass region, Kentucky, 128
Boardman, Mary Morse, 39
Boardman, William E., 3, 4, 31, 39
Boddy, Alexander A., 13, 72–95, *73*
    genealogy, 76–77
Boddy, Jane Vazeille, 72, *73*, 73–74, 80, 88n12
    genealogy, 76–77
Boddy, Mary, 72, *73*, 73–74, 80, 82, 86
    genealogy, 76–77
Bombay (Mumbai), India, 57, 59, 60, 62, 64, 66, 68n29, 100, 101
Bombay Guardian, 56, 57, 61, 65
Booth, Catherine, 55, 56, 82
Boston, Massachusetts, 5, 129, 237
Bowen, George, 56, 67n22
Boy's Christian Home (Dhond, India), 59, 62
Bradford, Sarah, 151
Brethren movements, Protestant
    English, British, 31, 42
    German, 3
Brethren of the Common Life, 2
Bridegroom's Magazine, 89n31, 133n11
Bridges Johns, Cheryl, 10, 18n21, 229, *230*, 231, 235, 237, 239, 247n30

British Brethren. *See under* Brethren movements
Brooklyn, New York, 146
Brown, A. C. M., 37
Brueggeman, Walter, 237, 240
Bruner, Frederick, 208
Buldana Berar, India, 64
Bundy, David, 1–24, 27–51, 253
 scholarship, 8–9, 10–11, 12, 18n21, 97
Burgin, Kentucky, 127
Burning Bush, 5
Burroughs, Nannie, 153–54
Butler, Anthea, 140, 143, 144–45, 146, 148–49, 150, 154
Byun, Seon-hwan, 160, 162, 163

Calcutta (Kolkata), India, 67n21, 100
California, 6, 42, 59, 99–100, 142–53
Calvin, John, 2, 211
Calvinism, 219, 247–48n38
Calvinistic Methodists, 109
Cambridge, England, 74
camp meetings, 48n67, 53, 58, 59, 66n3, 77, 127, 128, 141
Canada, 42, 99, 109, 151
card games, 139
Carothers, William, 214
Carpenter, Mary, 55
Carradine, Beverly, 124, 129
Cartledge, Mark, 73, 82, 92n94, 235
cartoons, 33
Cartwright, Desmond, 83
Cary, Clement, 125, 133n24
Cary, Thurman, 127
Casselberry, Judith, 141, 146, 154
Castelo, Daniel, 249n63
Catherine of Siena, 2
Catholicism, 123, 210–11, 235, 247–48n38
 and ecumenism, 247n30, 248n44
 monasticism, 2
 Pentecostal influences, 43
 scholarship, 2–3
 and J. Wesley, 222n28
catholicity, universality, 233
"Celestial Railroad, The" (Hawthorne), 123
Chalcedonian Christianity, 187, 191–92, 194–95, 202, 204–5n26

Chambers, Oswald, 40, 84
Chapell, Colin, 139
chaplaincy, military, 168
Chapman, Diana, 82–83, 91n77
charisma, theologies of, 170–71
Charismatic Movements, 7–8, 170–71, 234–35
 and psychological testing, 9
Chesapeake & Ohio Railroad, 119
Chesnut, Arthur, 168
chi, Korean concept of wind, 163
chi-pneumatology, 163
Chicago, Illinois, 5, 47n57, 99, 165
Chicago & Eastern Railroad (C. E. R.), 127
Chi-Ho, Yoon, 159–60
children, African American, 153
 and revivalism, 53, 56
Chile, 232
China, 100, 101, 106, 107, 110, 143, 159–60, 163
 China Inland Mission, 80
Cho, Yong-gi, 167, 169–71, *170*, 176n49, 177n64
Choi, Byung-heon, 168
Choi, Insik, 14, 159–83, 253
Christ and Culture (Niebuhr), 14, 145–46
Christian Alliance Mission (Bhusawal, India), 64
Christian and Missionary Alliance, 5, 56, 57, 58, 66n3
Christiana Revival (Norway), 72, 76
 See also Barratt, Thomas Ball
Christian Churches Together, 247n30
Christian Herald, 57
 Christian Herald Office, publisher, 57
Christian Lay Churches, 77
Christian Science, 129
Christian's Manual (Merritt), 4
Christian Witness and Advocate of Bible Holiness, 5
Christian Women of India, 54
Christology
 adoptionist, 187
 binitarian, 195
 Chalcedonian, 188, 191–92, 194–95, 203
 dyohypostatic, 192–93
 and *homoousious*, 193
 and incarnation, 187–88, 190–203

Christology (*continued*)
   and logos, 192–93
   and Mariology, 238
   metaphysics of, 192
   miahypostatic, 192–93
   Nicaean, 191–94, 203
   Pentecostal, 15, 36
   schetike synapheia (conjunction by interrelation), 194
   and Spirit baptism, 187–207
   typologies of, 145–46
Church Missionary Society, 67n13
Church of England. *See* Anglican Church
Church of God (Anderson, IN), 5
   See also Evening Light Saints
Church of God (Cleveland, TN), 41–42, 129, 135n48, 247n30
Church of God in Christ, 7, 14, 140–41, 143–44, 146–49, 153–54
   Women's Convention, 149
Church of God of Prophecy, 41–42, 248n44
Church of God Theological Seminary. *See* Pentecostal Theological Seminary
Church of Our Lord Jesus Christ, 141, 146, 154
Church of the Nazarene, 6–7, 42
Cincinnati, Ohio, 5, 12, 27, 29, 32, 33, 37, 38, 39, 43n6, 119, 127, 128, 143, 165
Cincinnati Southern Railway (C. S.), 127
Civil Rights Movement, USA, 241
Civil War, USA, 3–5, 96, 188
Clarke, Charles, 87n12, 88n25
Clarke, Harry, 131
class, 6, 7, 8, 14, 15, 32, 36, 76–78, 88n22, 138, 139, 141, 142, 146, 147, 148, 149, 155, 216, 242
Cleveland, Tennessee, 8–11, 229
Cleveland School, theological, 15, 229–52
coal mining, 129
Coffey, Lillian, 14, 138, 141, 143–45, *144*, 146, 148–49, 152, 154
COGIC. *See* Church of God in Christ
Collegeville, Minnesota, 10
Collier-Thomas, Bettye, 141
colonialism, 238
communalism, theologies of, 39
Communion rails, 75

Confidence, 72, 75, 76, 82, 83, 85
Confucianism, 163
Congregationalists, 2, 3, 4, 28, 40, 100
conversion, theologies of, 30–31, 41, 55, 145–46, 169
COOLJC. *See* Church of Our Lord Jesus Christ
Cottret, Bernard, 2
Coulter, Dale, 18n21, 241–42
Courey, David, 248–49n43
Cowman, Charles, 38, 42, 165
Cowman, Lettie, 38, 42, 102
Cowman & Kilbourne Mission. *See* Oriental Missionary Society
Cox, Harvey, 233–34, 235
Cox, Phebe, 59
Crawl with God, Dance in the Spirit (Park), 162
creeds, Christian, 187, 191–93, 202–3
Creffield, Franz, 6
Crisp, Eleanor, 91n78
cross, Christian symbol, 191, 195, 200–201
CS. *See* Cleveland School
Cullis, Charles, 31
Cur Deus Homo (Anselm), 187, 194–95, 204–5n26
Cyril of Alexandria, 191, 194, 202

Dalton, Illinois, 58
Danielson, Robert, 12, 13, 52–71, 253
Daniel the Prophet (Harris), 74
Darby, John, 210
Dardar, India, 62
Darlington, England, 83
Dasehra meetings, 101, 109, 113n29
Dashiel, E. H., 35
Daund, India, 53, 58–59, 61, 62
Dayton, Donald, 8–9, 10, 18n21, 139, 146, 188, 203n1, 208, 210
Daytona Beach, Florida, 152
Deism, 217
Delaware, 151
Del Colle, Ralph, 235
deliverance, theologies of, 86
Dempster, Murray, 235
Des Plaines, Illinois, 99
Detroit, Michigan, 149
devil. *See* Satan

Index

Devonshire, England, 83–84
Dharangaon, India, 64
Dhond, India, 59, 62, 64
Die Heils Fuelle (Orwig), 123
Dieter, Melvin, 9
disability, in Christianity, 151, 157n40
dispensation, theologies of, 39
divine healing. *See* healing
Dixie Flyer (train), 135n52
doctors, missionary, 109
dogma, Pentecostal critique of, 243–44
Dow, Lorenzo, 3, 16nn6–7, 77
drugs, 34
dualism, in Christian metaphysics, 164
Dudley, Lula, 128, 134n32
Duke University (Durham, NC), 11
Dunn, James, 198, 200, 235
Durham, William, 135n52
Durham County, England, 77
Durham Road Wesleyan Church (Sunderland, England), 77
Durham University (England), 74
Dyer, Alfred Saunders, 67n21
Dyer, Alfred S., 54, 55, 56–58, 61, 67–68n24
Dyer, Helen S., 54, 56–58, 62
dyohypostatic theology, 192–93

Earnest Christian (Roberts), 4
East Tennessee Holiness Association, 126
Eastern Christianity. *See* Orthodox Churches
Eastern Pentecostal Mission (Buldana Berar, India), 64
Ebony, 149
ecclesiology, 14, 32, 139–41, 145–47, 154, 171–72, 213
Echoes from Bharatkhand (Ward), 60
ecological pneumatology, 163–64, 172
economic justice. *See under* justice
ecumenism, 10, 245n6, 247n30
    and the global South, 234–35
    and missions, 107
    and pneumatology, 159–83
Edict of Nantes, Revocation, 2
Edwards, Jonathan, 211, 217–18, 221n21, 224n51, 224n54, 224n57

egalitarianism, in the Holiness Movement, 32, 39, 145–46, 148, 214
Egypt, 42
Elaw, Zilpha, 141
Electric Message, 103–4
Ellichpur (Achalpur), India, 59
Emory University (Atlanta, GA), 8, 10
emperor worship, 235–36
Empiricism, British, 161
England, Pentecostalism in, 12–13, 72–95, 99–100, 108, 241–42
    Royal Artillery, 101
English Brethren. *See under* Brethren movements
English language, 28, 63
Enlightenment era, 216–20, 224n51
enthusiasm, Wesleyan, 77
Episcopal Church (USA), 56, 107
epistemology, 209, 231
    Wesleyan, 161
eschatology
    and baptism, 199
    and railroads, 121–25
    theologies of, 37, 82, 106–7, 209–16, 219–20, 243–44
    and weather, 121–22
establishment churches, 78
Eswatini (Swaziland), 42
Ethiopia, 143
Europe, 42, 72, 74, 78, 79, 85, 86n2, 90n55, 108, 237
evangelicalism, 85
    defined, 30
    dialogue with Catholicism, 247n30
Evangelist Speaks, The, 144
Evans, Mrs., 142–43
Evanston, Illinois, 58
Evening Light Saints, 143, 214, 222n36
Ewart, Frank, 197, 204n10
Ewesley Road Wesleyan Church (Sunderland, England), 78, 82
exile, theologies of, 14, 140, 141–42, 145–47, 155, 156n7
experience
    and hermeneutics, 239–40
    and mysticism, 243, 249nn63–64
    theologies of, 31, 75, 80, 108, 164–65, 166, 203, 211–12, 218, 243–44

faith healing. *See* healing
famine, 58–59, 60–61
Fairbairn, Douglas, 194
Farrow, Lucy, 142
Faupel, D. William, 8, 9, 10, 18n21
feminism, 147–48
Fénelon, François, 2
Ferguson, E. A., 124
Fetter Lane, London, England, 166
Finney, Beatrice, 28, 37
Finney, Charles, 3, 57
fire, as symbol, 14, 31, 105, 122, 124–25, 187–207
Fire-Baptized Holiness Church, 127
First Church (Wonsan, N. Korea), 109–10
fivefold gospel, 15, 82, 85, 169, 231, 245n6
Fivefold Gospel and the Threefold Blessing, The (Cho), 169
Fletcher, John, 9, 81, 172, 209, 211, 221n21
Florida, 129, 152
Flower Pentecostal Heritage Center (Springfield, MO), 73, 144, *170*
footwashing, practices of, 248n44
Footwashing in John 13 and the Johannine Community (Thomas), 229
Foucault, Michel, 45n27
fourfold gospel, 41, 164, 167–68, 172
Fox, Daniel, 107
France, 2, 99–100
Frank Leslie's Illustrated Newspaper, 54
Franklin, Louise, 154
Franklin Springs, Georgia, 8, 9
Franklin Springs College, 8
fraternal orders, 126
 See also Freemasonry
Free Church of Scotland, 66n14
Free Methodist Church, 4–5, 6–7, 42, 56, 58, 68n27, 123, 214
 foreign missions, 58–60, 64, 100, 107
Freemasonry, 36
Friends' Association for the Abolition of the state Regulation of Vice, 56–57
From Aldersgate to Azusa Street (Knight, ed.), 11
Frost, Michael, 231
Fukuoka, Japan, 100
Fuller, Jennie, 57, 58, 66n3
Fuller, Marcus, 55, 57, 66n3

full gospel, theologies of, 1, 12, 165, 229–52, 245n6
 Korean, 165, 167–71, 173

Galax, Virginia, 129
Garrett Biblical (Theological) Seminary, 58, 165
Gause, R. Hollis, 8, 9–10, 229
gender, 14, 15, 32, 38, 40, 139, 147–48, 215
 See also African Americans: women; Pentecostal Movement: and women's ministry; Radical Holiness Movements: and women; sex trafficking; United States of America: and black women; womanism; women
genealogy
 of Jesus, 200
 of John Wesley, 76–77
Genesee County, New York, 58
Georgia, 5, 8, 9, 135n52
German Brethren. *See under* Brethren movements
Gilbertson, Richard, 173
Gilded Age, 27, 40
Gilkes, Cheryl, 140, 148, 149
gi-pneumatology, 172
Gladden, Washington, 153
Global Christian Forum, 247n30
"Global" Holiness. *See under* Holiness Movement
glossolalia, 5, 16n5, 40–41, 42, 52, 83–84, 142–43, 146
 necessity of, 41
Godbey, William, 12, 37, 40, 52, 59, 64–65, 69n55, 106, 125, 127
God's Bible School (Cincinnati, OH), 12, 27–51, *29*, 143, 165, 214
God's Revivalist, and *God's Revivalist and Bible Advocate*. See *Revivalist*
Gohr, Glenn, 132n
Gojong of Korea, King and Emperor, 159
Goreh, Nehemiah, 55, 67n13
gospel music, 232–33
Goss, Howard, 130
Gourley, Thomas, 135n52
grace
 imputation, 161–62

optimism, 208–20
prevenient, 163, 218–19
and spiritual senses, 161, 218, 224n54
theologies of, 1, 13, 204–5n26
universal, 163
Great Celestial Railroad, The (Owen), 122, 123–24
Great Indian Revival. *See under* India
Greek Americans, 129
Green, Chris, 15, 229–52, 253
Greensboro, NC, 119
Gregersen, Dagmar, 82
Gregson, Joseph, 53
Grey, A. L., 102
Grey, Jacqueline, 231
Guide to Christian Perfection (Merritt), 4
Gujerat, India, 58
Guyon, Madame, 2

hagiography, 238
Hammond, Geordan, 1–24, 253
  scholarship, 11
Han, David Sang-Ehil, 1–24, 254
  scholarship, 11, 18n21
Hardie, Robert, 109–10
Harding, U. E., 42
Hardy, Clarence, 147
Harper, Frances, 147
Harper, Michael, 80, 86n2, 87n12, 90n54
Harriet Tubman (Bradford), 151
Harris, Mary, 73, 80, 86
Harris, Reader, 13, 73, 74, 78–86
Hartford-Battersby, Canon T. D., 56
Haslam, William, 55, 56
Hawthorne, Nathaniel, 123
healing, 4, 5, 31, 36–37, 56, 57, 72, 82, 89n31, 96, 106, 111–12, 125, 145–46, 164, 167, 168, 172, 197, 203, 212, 216, 242
Heaven Below (Wacker), 210
Heidelberg, Germany, 237
Henck, F. W., 126
Heong, Huh, 168–69
Hepburn Act, USA, 130–31
hermeneutics, 231, 236–39, 244, 245n6
  "altar hermeneutics," 240
  apocalyptic, 243
Hero of Faith and Prayer, A (Hills), 32

High Bridge, Kentucky, 128
Higher Christian Life, The (Boardman), 4
Higher Life Movement, 8, 56, 57, 65
  See also Keswick Convention
Hills, A. M., 32, 40
Hindi language, 63
Hinduism, 55
Hirst, Mabel, 38
Hirst, William, 38
holiness, theologies of, 30–31, 63–64, 78, 80–82, 84, 85–86, 108–10, 121–22, 147–48, 156n7, 219–20
  "A-B-C typology" of, 173
  active and passive, 170–71
  and baptism practices (*see* baptism)
  and Charismatic Movements, 7–8, 170–71, 234–35
  defined, 52–53
  optimism of grace, 208–20
  racism implicit, 231–34
Holiness Movement, 2–8, 29–30, 34, 58, 60, 62–66, 87n4, 98–99, 107, 111–12, 120, 123, 129, 132, 132n3, 138–44, 146, 152, 168, 188, 189, 208, 210, 213–16, 218–19
  and African Americans, 13, 138–58, 231–34
  biblical interpretation, 32–33, 39, 41, 42
  and Charismatic Movements, 7–8, 170–71, 234
  and class, 32, 36, 39–40
  critique of establishment religion, 34–37, 124–25, 166, 175n32
  and ecumenism, 8–11, 159–83
  and education, 32
  and egalitarianism, 32, 39, 145–46, 148, 214
  and grace, 161–63, 204–5n26, 208–20
  "global" Holiness (theology), 13, 32, 43, 97, 107–12, 208
  healing, centrality of, 216
  in India, 52–71
  and Keswick (*see* Keswick Convention)
  in Korea, 159–83
  leadership, 59, 138–58
  and mainline Protestantism, 146–47
  missionaries, 32, 38–41, 42, 58

Holiness Movement (*continued*)
  music, 32–33
  Pentecostalism, relation and comparisons to, 1–7, 12, 13, 52–53, 80–81, 85–86, 121–22, 208–20
  and premillennialism, 4–5, 210
  as "protest Protestantism," 140
  publishing, 33, 35, 44n11, 57–58, 64, 106–7, 124, 126–27, 129, 130–31, 133n11, 133n18
  race, 32, 33, 139, 141–42, 146–47, 231–34 (*see also* racism)
  Radical Holiness, relation and comparisons to, 1–7 (*see also* Pentecost networks; Radical Holiness Movements)
  scholarship, 1–3, 7–12, 33, 53; in Korea, 177n64
  and socialism, 39–40
  spirit baptism, centrality of, 187–207 (*see also under* baptism)
  and trains, 119–37
  and wealth, 32
  and Wesleyan Christianity, relation to, 3, 81, 85–86
  See also mission: self-supporting; National Camp Meeting Association for the Promotion of Holiness; National Holiness Association; Pentecost networks; Radical Holiness Movements; Radical Holiness Networks; Sanctified Churches
Holiness-Pentecostal Movement in the United States, The (Synan), 8–9, 208
Holiness School (Meridian, MS), 128
Holiness Union, 97–99, 119
Hollenweger, Walter, 92n94, 234, 235, 237
Holy Boldness (Stanley), 141
Holy Spirit movement, Korean, 168
home missions, 130, 143, 149
homoousios, theologies of, 193
Hope, 143
hospitality, spiritual practice, 237
Hotle, Frank, 61, 62
Howard, Victor, 4
Hudson, Neil, 74

Hughes, Hugh, 81
Hughes, John, 105
Hundley, Cheryl, 132n
Hungarian Americans, 129
Hunt, Anne, 195
Hurston, Zora, 140
Hutcheson, Francis, 218, 224n57
Hutchins, Julia, 142
Hutchinson, William, 77, 78
Hypes, J. W., 129

If It Wasn't for the Women (Gilkes), 140
Illinois, 58, 59, 127, 149
Illustrator, The (ed. Morrow), 37
immanence, theologies of, 164, 216–17
  See also transcendence
impassability, of God, 192
incarnation, theologies of, 187–88, 190–203
India, 12–13, 38, 52–71, 96, 100, 105–10, 114n67, 143
  caste system, 68
  Great Indian Revival, 109–10
Indiana, 143
Indianapolis, Indiana, 40, 143
Indian Holiness Association, 60
India's Millions, 58
India Vanguard, 64, 65, 69n51
industrialism, theologies of, 34–35
Industrial Workers of the World, 12, 36
Ingersoll, Robert, 123
initiation, Christian theologies of, 189–90, 248n44
In Search of Our Mothers' Gardens (Walker), 147–48
Inskip, John, 141
interfaith dialogue, 160
International Holiness Union (Cincinnati, OH), 165
International Review of Mission, 232
International Roman Catholic-Pentecostal Dialogue, 247n30
Iowa, 5, 99
Irish Americans, 37
Israel, 100, 198–200, 234
Israel, Adrienne, 141
Is the World Growing Better (Morrison), 106

Italian Americans, 129
Italy, 99–100

Jabalpur (Jubblepur), India, 100, 101
Japan, 13, 38, 96, 99, 100, 101, 103–4, 107, 110, 159, 165
Japanese Americans, 241
Jehovah's Witnesses, 56
Jeon, Seong-yong, 166
Jesus, Jobs, and Justice (Collier-Thomas), 141
Jesus People, 7
Jewish Americans, 129
Jim Crow laws, 40, 214–15
John of the Cross, Saint, 2
John the Baptist, 14, 188, 191, 198–202, 203
Johns, Cheryl. *See* Bridges Johns, Cheryl
Johns, Jackie, 219, 231
Jones, Charles E., 123, 132n
Journal of Pentecostal Theology, 229–30, 231–32, 235, 238–49, 248n44
Juillerat, L. Howard, 129
Junction City, Kentucky, 127
justice
  economic, 4, 40
  social, 13–14, 39, 55, 56, 138–58, 231
justification, doctrine of, 169–70, 196, 209, 247–48n38

Kaesong (Songdo), North Korea, 100, 109–10
Kangwon Province, South Korea, 109–10
Kansas City, Missouri, 11
Kedgaon, India, 52, 58, 62, 64, 109
KEHC. *See* Korean Evangelical Holiness Church
Kempis, Thomas à, 2
Kentucky, 5, 8, 9, 28, 32, 37, 96, 104, 127, 128, 131
Kenya, 247n30
Kerin, Dorothy, *73*
Keswick Convention (England), 8, 53, 74–76, 83, 84, 88n22, 91n58
  movement and influences, 8, 55, 56, 57, 72–73, 75–76, 82, 87n4, 87n5, 104–5, 107, 108–9, 111
  theology, 81, 88n15
  See also Higher Life Movement

Khasi Hills, India, 53, 109
Kilbourne, Ernest, 102, 103–4, 105, 165
Kim, Hong-gi, 160, 161–62
Kim, Tae-gu, 166
KKK. *See* Ku Klux Klan
Klassen, Pamela, 147
Knapp, John, 125
Knapp, Lucy, 37
Knapp, Martin Wells, 12, 27–28, 30, 31–40, *32*, 42–43, 43n6, 44n11, 46n42, 46n47, 54n48, 47–48n49, 48n67, 119–25, *120*, 128, 132, 132–33n6, 133n7, 133n12, 165
Knapp, Minnie, 37
Knapp, Octavia, 37
Knight, Henry, 8, 10, 11, 18n21, 20n40, 208–28, 235, 254
Knox Memorial Methodist Episcopal Church (Manila, Philippines), *99*
Kobe, Japan, 100
koinonia, 10
Kolkata, India. *See* Calcutta, India
Korean Empire, 14, 100, 106, 107, 109–10, 159–60, 162
Korean Evangelical Holiness Church, 165–68, *167*, 171, 173
Korean Methodist Church, 160, 171
Korean Pentecostal Church, 168
Korean Revivals, 160, 168
  Korean Pentecost revival (Pyongyang, N. Korea), 100, 106, 109–10
Korean Theology of Life, The (Lee), 163
Korean War, 160, 169
Korku tribe, India, 59
Kostlevy, William, 5, 10, 18n21, 132n, 210
Ku Klux Klan, 40
Kuosmanen, Juhani, 2

Labor of Faith, The (Casselberry), 141
labor unions, 126
Land, Steven, 8, 10, 229, *230*, 231–32, 234–35, 237, 238–39, 247–48n38, 248n44, 249n64
Lankford, Sarah Worrall, 3
Lanowli (Lonalva), India, 100, 107
  camp meeting and convention, 53, 66n3, 107
Latin America, 248n44

Latino Americans, 208
Latour, Bruno, 34
Lee, Hu-jeong, 160–61
Lee, Jarena, 141
Lee, Jeong-bae, 160, 162, 163, 175n32
Lee, Myung-heon, 165
Lee, Myung-jik, 165
Lee, Seong-bong, 166–68, *167*, 176n48
Lee University (Cleveland, TN), 8
Lexington, Kentucky, 127
liberation, theologies of, 15, 36, 231
licentiate degrees, 74
Life for God in India, A (Dyer), 57
Life of Theology and the Spiritualization of Theology, The (Lee), 163
life theology, Korean, 163–64
Lightning Bolts from Pentecostal Skies, 120
Lillian Brooks Coffey Rest Home (Detroit, MI), 149
Lindley, Susan, 140–41, 152–53, 154
Little Heaven Below, A, (Ruth), 210
liturgy, Pentecostal critique of, 243–44
Liverpool, England, 99
Living in the Spirit (Gause), 8
Locke, John, 161, 217–18
logos, theologies of, 161–62, 192
London, England, 39, 44n11, 47n57, 57, 79, 85, 166
Los Angeles, California, 6, 42, 59, 72, 99, 123, 142–43, 168, 214
    Los Angeles Times, 233–34
Louisville, Kentucky, 5, 114n58, 131
    Louisville Institute, 11
Louisville and Nashville Railroad (L. & N. R. R.), 127
Louisville Southern Railroad (L. S.), 127
Love Feast, practice, 209
Loveland, George, 132n
Lovett, Leonard, 234
Lucknow, India, 100, 101, 108
Lutheran Churches, 42, 247–48n38
Lyon, Jo Anne, 10, 18n21

Macarius, 160–61, 162, 172
Macchia, Frank, 14, 187–207, 235, 237, 248n44, 254
Maclay, Robert, 159
Mahan, Asa, 3, 4, 188, 203n1

Malaysia, 100, 101, 108
Manchester, England, 77, 78
Manchester Courier, 83
Manchester Wesley Research Centre, 11, 86
Manila, Philippines, 99, 100, 101–2, 107, 110–11
    Manila Healing Revival, 111
Mantle, J. Gregory, 55, 56
Mariology, doctrine of, 162–63, 187–88, 237–39, 244
    Theotokos, 163, 227–28
Marshall, Texas, 127
Martin, David, 208
Martin, Lee Roy, 243
Martinsburg, West Virginia, 127–28
Marston, Leslie, 7
Marty, Martin, 20n36
Maryland, 141, 151
Mason, Charles, 140, 143–44, 147, 149, 197
Mather, Hannah, 231
McAlister, Robert, 42
McClurkan, J. O., 106
McDonnell, Kilian, 199, 248n44
McGonigle, Herbert, 8–9
McKay, John, 235
McQueen, Larry, 210
Memphis, Tennessee, 143–44, 233–34
    the Memphis Miracle, 233
Mennonite Churches, 64, 247n30
    Mennonite Mission (Sunderganz, India), 64
    Mennonite (USA)-Church of God Dialogue, 247n30
Meridian Women's College (Meridian, MS), 128, 134n46
Merritt, Timothy, 3, 4
Methodism and Methodist movements
    and African Americans, 3, 5, 40, 152, 154
    Calvinistic Methodists, 109
    Chapels, 78
    in England, 72, 77–78
    German "Methodist" Brethren, 3
    and higher education, 8
    and Holiness and Pentecostalism, 2–3, 5, 28, 36, 111, 141–42, 208–9, 218–19
    and indigenous religions, 163
    in Korean peninsula, 159–83

Mission Halls, 78, 83, 85
"New School Methodism" (Roberts),
 213–14
 and primitivism, 3, 77
 and Radical Holiness, 96–107, 165
 sects and denominations (*see individual institutional names*)
 theological distinctions, 195–96, 140
  (*see also* Wesleyan Christianity)
Methodist Boy's School (Pune, India), 62
Methodist Episcopal Church, 3, 5, 35–37,
 68n39, 214–15
 Annual Conferences: Bombay Annual
  Conference, 100; Northwest India
  Conference, 103; Philippine Islands
  Annual Conference, 99, 111
 bishops, 58; missionary bishops, 108
 and conferencing, 106
 General Conferences: 1880, 215; 1891,
  98–99; 1904, 98; 1908, 98
 and the Holiness Union, 97–99
 in Japan, 159–60
Methodist Episcopal Church, South, 8, 40
 foreign mission 100, 107, 109, 159–60
 and Holiness Union, 97
Methodist Episcopal Girls' School (Seoul,
 S. Korea), 100, 107
Methodist Times, 81
Mexico, 143
miahypostatic theology, 192–93
Michigan, 37, 56, 149
Miller, J. R., 55, 56, 67n15
Milwaukee, Wisconsin, 129
minjung theology, 163, 172
mission, faith mission, 58, 59
 See also Pentecost Bands; Vanguard
  Mission
mission, self-supporting, 5, 32, 67n22, 107
 See also Pentecost Bands; Vanguard
  Mission
mission, theologies of, 31–32, 38–42
Missionary Training Home (Cincinnati),
 165
 See also God's Bible School
Missionary Training Home (New York
 City), 39
Mission Hall (Seoul, S. Korea), 165
Missouri, 11, 38, 60

Mitchell, George, 6
Mittelstadt, Marty, 231, 245n5
modernity, philosophical, 231, 248n44,
 249n64
Moltmann, Jürgen, 162, 163, 175n32,
 190–91, 195, 235
Monasticism, 2
Mong, Ra Woon, 168
Monkwearmouth, England, 75, 83, 84
Montreal, Canada, 99
Moody, Dwight, 57, 152, 189, 210
Moody Bible Institute (Chicago, IL), 30,
 39, 152, 165
Mooers, New York, 99
Moore, Joanna, 143, 149
Moore, Rickie, 229, *230*, 231, 233, 235, 237,
 238–40, 242, 248n44
Moravians, 2
Morgan, Louis, 132n
Morrison, Henry, 13, 95–116, *99*, 124, 131,
 133n18, 210
Morrow, Abbie C., 37–38, 47n57
Morrow, T. J., 47n56
Moule, Handley, 81
Mukti Mission and Revival, 12, 52–71, 109
Müller, George, 58
Mumbai, India. *See* Bombay, India
Murray, Andrew, 31, 44n11, 87n5
music, in worship, 32–33, 83
 theologies of, 232–33
Muttra (Mathura), India, 100, 103
Myanmar, 100, 107
mysticism, 243, 249nn63–64

Nagasaki, Japan, 100, 102
Nakada, Juji, 38, 42, 47n63, 165
Nanjing (Nanking), China, 100, 102
National Association of Evangelicals, 6–8
National Camp Meeting Association for
 the Promotion of Holiness, 4
 See also National Holiness Association
National Council of Churches, 247n30
National Council of Negro Women, 146,
 152, 155
National Holiness Association (NHA),
 4–5, 36–37, 113n14
 See also Holiness Movement; Radical
  Holiness Movements

Nazarene Theological College (Manchester, England), 11
"'Neglected Voices' and 'Praxis' in the Social Gospel" (Lindley), 152–53
Nestorius, 193–94
Netherlands, The, 83, 86n2, 237
Networks, Holiness. *See* Radical Holiness Networks
New England Fellowship, 6, 17n19
New England region, United States, 128
Newton, Richard, 55, 56
New York City, New York, 39, 47n57, 47n62, 72, 141, 146, 150–51
New York state, 57, 58, 99, 123, 139, 213
NHA. *See* National Holiness Association
Nicaean Christianity and Creed, 191–95, 202
Nicholasville, Kentucky, 127
Niebuhr, H. Richard, 14, 138, 145–46
non-denominational Christianity, 30
Norfolk and Western Railroad (N.&W.), 129
North America, continent, religious movements, 3–4, 6, 72, 73, 134n29, 233, 237
North Carolina, 119
North Carolina and Virginia Railroad (N.C.V.A.), 129
North Chili, New York, 57
Northern Independent, 213–14
North Korea, 100, 109–10
North Park Theological Seminary (Chicago, IL), 9
North Star (Darlington, England), 83
Northwestern University (Evanston, IL), 58
Norton, Albert B., 12, 52, 58–59, 61, 62, 64, 65, 68n28
Norton, Mary, 57, 58, 65
Norway, 72, 82
    See also Barratt, Thomas Ball; Christiana Revival

Oakland, California, 143
Oberlin College (Oberlin, OH), 40, 57
Ockenga, Harold, 7
Oconer, Luther, 13, 95–116, 254
"O For a Thousand Tongues to Sing" (C. Wesley), 209

Oglevie, Heather, 196–97
Ohio, 28, 29, 98, 123, 124, 143, 149
Ohio Wesleyan University (Delaware, OH), 108
Oldham, William, 97–110
Oliverio, William, 231
OMS. *See* Oriental Missionary Society
Oneness Pentecostalism, 6, 16n5, 189, 197, 204n10, 243–44
    See also Trinitarian theology: "New Issue" controversy; Trinitarian theology: non-trinitarianism
opium, 56
optimism
    and theology, 14–15
    of grace, 208–20
Optimism of Pre-Millennialism, The (Morrison), 106
Oriental Missionary Society, 42, 99, 100, 102, 103–4, 107, 111, 165
original sin, theologies of, 211
orphans, and orphanages, 36, 42, 53, 55, 57, 59, 61, 62–64, 65, 153, 240
Orthodox Churches, 161, 190, 247–48n38, 249n64
Orwig, Aaron, 123, 125–27, 134n33
Orwig, William, 123
Oslo, Norway, 72
    See also Christiana Revival (Norway)
Outler, Albert, 160–61, 211
Owen, Olin, 122, 123–25, 133n15
Oxford, England, 237

Pacific Ocean, 110
pacifism, 85, 139
Padmanji, Baba, 55, 66n14
Palestine, 83, 99–100
Palmer, Phoebe, 3, 4, 188, 209, 213
Pandita Ramabai (Dyer), 57
pantheism, 164
Parham, Charles, 2, 16n1, 169, 210, 214, 241
Park, Gui Im, 168
Park, Jong-cheon, 160, 162–63
Parousia, theologies of, 37, 82, 106–7, 172
passive holiness, theologies of, 170–71
Paton, John, 55, 56, 67n16
patristic theology, 248n44
Paul, John, 135–36n59

Peabody, Nettie, 28, 37
peacemaking, 231, 245n6
Pewee Valley Suburban railroad, 131
Peniel Mission (Dharrangon, India), 64
Penn-Lewis, Jesse, 54, 57, 58
Penn State University Press, 15
Pennsylvania, 141
Pentecost, biblical narrative, 31–32, 39, 41, 42, 169–70, 188–89, 191, 199, 202, 213
Pentecostal and Charismatic Churches of North America, 233–34
Pentecostal Assemblies of Canada, 42
Pentecostal Assemblies of the World, 7
Pentecostal Convention (Louisville, KY), 131
Pentecostal Fellowship of North America, 233–34
Pentecostal Formation (Bridges Johns), 229
Pentecostal Herald, 5, 61, 62, 96, 106, 133n18, 135n48
Pentecostal Holiness Church, 125
Pentecostal Holiness Union. *See* Holiness Union
Pentecostal League of Prayer, 13, 72–95
Pentecostal Missionary Union, 80, 90n55, 91n78
Pentecostal Movement
　and African Americans, 231–34
　in Anglican Church, 80, 85–86, 87–88n12
　and baptism (*see* baptism)
　and "blackness," 233–34, 244
　and Charismatic Movements, 7–8, 170–71, 234
　and economic class, 15
　comparison between American and British, 72–73
　culto Pentecostal, Philippine, 111
　defined, 52–53
　in England, 12–13, 72–95, 99–100, 108, 241–42
　and ecumenical dialogue, 247n30
　and foreign missions, 80; in Asian continent, 13, 96; in India, 13; in Korean peninsula, 13, 96, 159–83; in Japan, 13, 96
　and the "French Prophets," 16n2
　and geography, 15
　and hermeneutics, 231, 236–40, 243–44, 245n6
　Holiness Movement, relation and comparisons to, 1–7, 12, 13, 52–53, 80–81, 85–91, 121–22, 208–20
　history: early, 214–15; proliferation of sects, 98–100
　and Keswick (*see* Keswick Convention)
　and lament, 242
　leadership, 12, 15, 30, 41–42
　and psychological testing, 9
　and racism, 6, 231–34
　and Radical Holiness, 3–7, 52–53, 95–116 (*see also* Radical Holiness Movements)
　scholarship, 7–10, 53, 229–52, *230*, 248n44
　Spirit baptism (*see under* baptism)
　theology, 92n94, 197–8, 247–48n38: "distinctives," 5–6, 232–33; and dogma, 243–44; ecumenical pneumatology, 159–83; missiology, 248n44; optimism of grace, 208–20; premillennialism, 210, 242
　and trains, 119–37
　and women's ministry, 82–83, 215
Pentecostal Spirituality (Land), 10, 229, 247–48n38
Pentecostal Theological Seminary (Cleveland, TN), 8, 9–10, 11
theological legacy, 229–52
Pentecost Bands, 5, 12, 52, 59, 60–61, 62–64, 65, 68n40, 69n50
　See also Free Methodist Church; mission, faith mission; mission, self-supporting
Pentecost for England (Boddy), 76
Pentecost networks, 13, 30–33, 53, 76, 78, 80, 81–84, 86, 123, 188–89
　See also Radical Holiness Movements; Radical Holiness Networks
perfection, theologies of, 30–31, 45n23, 105–6, 108, 161, 188–89, 196–97, 199, 201–2, 209–12, 215, 221n21, 243
　"second blessing," 121–22, 124, 125, 166, 171, 188–89
　See also sanctification

Philadelphia, Pennsylvania, 150–51
Philippines, 99, 100, 101–2, 107, 108, 110–12
Pickett, L. L., 106, 127
Piercy, Jehu, 99–100, 101, 107
Pietism, 2, 211
Pilgrim Holiness Church, 119
Pilgrim's Progress (Orwig, rev.), 123–24
Pine Bluff, Arkansas, 143
Pinnock, Clark, 235
PLP. *See* Pentecostal League of Prayer
pluralism, religious, 160
Plüss, Jean-Daniel, 74, 86n2
Pneuma, 8
Pneumatology
    and atonement, 187–207
    and diversity, 164
    ecological, 163–64, 172
    and ecumenism, 159–83
    and eschatology, 14, 209–13, 221n21, 243–44
    in-breaking of the Spirit, 211–12
    ontology and, 173
    in Pentecostal and Holiness movements, 1, 3, 13–14, 30–31, 38, 82, 105–6, 109–10, 124, 142–43, 155, 209; *chi*-pneumatology, 163; *gi*-pneumatology, 172
    and process theology, 163
    and transcendence, 239–40, 244
    and the Trinity, 162–63
Polhill, Cecil, 78, 80, 90n54, 91n78
polity, theologies of, 31
Polman, Gerritt, 83
Polman, Mrs., 83
Pope-Levison, Priscilla, 82
populism, 27, 28, 34, 43, 243–44
Portland, Oregon, 6, 10
postmillennialism, 37
postmodernism, philosophical, 248n44
poverty, and theology, 35, 36, 37, 38, 39–40, 45n30, 46n43, 139, 143, 145, 149, 155, 173, 213, 216, 222n33
Powar, Soonderbai, 62
power, theologies of, 4, 14, 34–37, 86, 105, 121, 123, 124–25, 133n18, 163–71, 173, 188, 189–90, 197–98, 210–12, 214, 215, 216–17, 219–20, 232, 241, 242
"Powerhouse in the Sky" (Knapp), 33

"prayer mountain" movement, Korean, 168
premillennialism, 4–5, 31, 37, 46n48, 96–97, 106–7, 112, 210, 242
Presbyterians, 2, 3, 4, 30, 56, 100, 107, 109, 110, 152, 154, 159, 168
Primitive Methodist Church, 3, 77
primitivism, Christian, 3, 77, 139, 213
Princeton, West Virginia, 129–30
Princeton Theological Seminary (Princeton, NJ), 146, 235, 237
Principles of the Interior or Hidden Life (Upham), 4
prisons, 216
process theology, 163
progressivism, theological, 231
    Progressive Era, 13, 27, 30, 34
prosperity gospel, 146
prostitution, 126
Protestantism, 43, 81, 146, 218, 247–48n38
    and Korean Christianity, 159–83
    mainline Protestantism, 6, 140–41, 215, 218
    and original sin, 211
    Reformation, 2, 161, 172, 210–11
Providence, Rhode Island, 128
Pulaski, Virginia, 129–30
Pune (Poona), India, 52, 62, 107
Puritanism, 211, 217
Pyongyang, North Korea, 100, 109–10
    Revival (*see under* Korean Revivals)

Quakers (Society of Friends), 2, 4, 5, 28, 30, 38, 40, 42, 56, 57, 67–68n24, 141
Queen, Bessie, 37

racism, 32, 34, 40, 139, 141–42, 146–47, 150, 153, 155, 214–16, 231–34, 240, 241, 246n14, 246n20
Radical Holiness Movements, 1, 5–7, 27–51, 64–65, 99, 111–12, 138–58
    defined, 4–5, 30–38, 96–97, 105, 111–12, 139
    ecclesiology, 139–41, 145–47, 154
    healing, 5, 31, 36, 44n11, 96, 105–6, 111–12
    "Holy Rollers," 6, term, 17n17
    and Methodism, 3–7, 34–37, 98–99, 165

missions, 31–32, 38, 59–65, 95–116
origins, 27
"Pauline holiness," 103–4
and periodical publishing, 5, 27, 44n11, 57, 65, 130, 133n11, 133n18
and premillennialism, 4–5, 31, 37, 46n48, 96–97, 112
Radical Holiness "theory," 41
and Social Gospel, 36, 138, 145–46, 152–54
and women, 13–14; black women, 138–58
See also Christian and Missionary Alliance; Evening Light Saints; Holiness Movement; Keswick Convention; National Holiness Association; Pentecost Bands; Pentecost networks; Radical Holiness Networks; Sanctified Churches; mission, self-supporting; Vanguard Mission
Radical Holiness Networks, 2, 4–5, 27, 30–31, 33, 38–40, 42, 43, 53, 59, 66n10, 165
Radical Holiness theology. See fourfold gospel; healing; mission, faith mission; mission, self-supporting; perfection, theologies of; premillennialism; sanctification
Rail-Ways, Inc. (R. W. I.), 127
Raj Nandgaon, India, 60–61, 63, 64
Ramabai, Pandita, 12, 52–71, 54, 109
Randall, Ian, 72–73, 78, 80, 81, 82
Rangoon, Myanmar, 100, 107
Ransom, Reverdy, 153–54
Rauschenbusch, Walter, 36, 153
realism, Christian, 146–47
realpolitik, 242
Rees, Annie, 90n50
Rees, Byron, 38
Rees, Seth, 40, 42, 120, 128, 132, 135n48, 165
Reeves, Edward, 129–30
Reformation. *See under* Protestantism
Reformed Christianity, 30, 159, 166, 170, 208, 215, 221n21, 245n5
scholarship, 2–3

Reid, Clarence, 159–60
Reid, I., 35
Reid, Thomas, 218
Religion on the American Frontier (Sweet), 33
religious education, 42, 56
restorationism, Christian, 139–40, 172
resurrection, theologies of, 197–98, 201–3
Reuther, Rosemary, 162, 163
Revelation (Thomas and Macchia), 237
revisionist history, 66n7
revival bands, 111
Revivalist, 5, 28, 31–32, 37–38, 40, 43–44n6, 119, 124, 129
"Railroad editions," 121–22, 132–33n6, 134–35n46
Richmond, Nicholasville, Irvine, & Beattyville Railroad (R. N. I. & B. R. R.), 127
Roanoke, Virginia, 129
Robeck, Cecil, 214
Roberts, B. T., 3, 4, 55, 56, 57, 58, 68n27, 213–14, 222n33
Roberts, Evan, 57, 75, 79, 90nn49–50
Robinson, Lizzie, 14, 138, 141, 143–44, *144*, 149–50, 155
Robinson, Martin, 74, 77, 80, 87n5, 87n7, 87–88n12, 90n54, 90n56
Rochester, New York, 57, 58
Roebuck, David, 8, 18n21
Rogers, Eugene, 197–98
Roman Catholicism. *See* Catholicism
Rome, Italy, 237
Roosevelt, Franklin, 152
Rose, Delbert, 9
Rose, Susan, 8
Roy, Ram, 55
Rumsey, Mary, 168
"Runaway Ranters," 77
Rupp, E. Gordon, 210–11
Ruskin Cave College (Dickson, TN), 128
Russell, Charles, 56
Ruth, Lester, 210
Rutland, Erica, 132n

Salem, Virginia, 129
salvation. *See* soteriology

Salvation Army, 5, 7, 36, 56, 82, 168
sanctification
 and atonement, 196–98
 and Christology and pneumatology, 190, 192–94, 198–203
 and "Finished work," 5
 and music, 32
 Pentecostal and Holiness experiences and theologies of, 3–4, 5, 6, 14, 16n5, 30–31, 32, 34, 38, 41, 53, 56, 64–65, 78, 79, 80–82, 96–98, 101–6, 108, 110, 111, 121, 122, 124, 125, 126, 128, 131, 133n10, 138–45, 146, 148–50, 154–55, 161–62, 166, 167, 171–73, 188–90, 193, 197, 209, 212–13, 215, 243; comparisons, 247–48n38
 teleological, 161
 See also perfection, theologies of
Sanctified Church, The (Hurston), 140
Sanctified Churches, 16n5, 138–41, 145, 149–50
Sanders, Cheryl, 13–14, 138–58, 254
San Francisco, California, 100
Sanjan, India, 62, 64, 68n44
Sankey, Ira, 57
Santiago, Chile, 232
Santiago de Compostela, Spain, 10
Satan, 34, 83–85, 104, 106, 129, 132, 195, 246n14
Scandinavian region, 73
schetike synapheia (conjunction by interrelation), theologies of, 194
Schmelzenbach, Harmon, 42
Schmelzenbach, Lula, 42
Scofield, C. I., 210
Scotland, 56, 72, 99–100
Scott, Orange, 3, 4
Scriptural Doctrine of Christian Perfection, The (Mahan), 4
Scudder, Vida, 153
Seattle, Washington, 6
 Seattle Pacific University, 11
Second Coming, of Christ. *See* Parousia
Second Coming of Christ, The (Morrison), 106
secret societies, 34, 36
Seneca Falls, New York, 139

Seoul, South Korea, 100, 107, 109–10, 165, 167, 168, 169, 170, 176n49
Seoul Bible School, and Theological Seminary, 165, 166–67
sex trafficking, 46n45, 56
Seymour, Jennie, 142
Seymour, William, 2, 6, 40, 41, 42, 138, 140, 142–43, 169, 189, 197, 213, 214, 222n36, 241
Shanghai, China, 100
Sherman, Bessie, 60, 64
Sherman, C. W., 60, 61–62, 64
Short Circuit, The, (Bundy, ed.), 9
Simpson, Albert B., 39, 41, 57, 58, 165
Singapore, 100, 101, 107–8
Sisson, Elizabeth, 82
Slater, Charles, 42
slavery, 4, 139, 143, 146–47, 149, 151, 216
Smith, Amanda, 14, 138, 141–42, *142*, 145, 147, 150–52, 155
Smith, James, 231
Smith, Jennie, 126
Smith, Joseph, 98
Smith, Timothy, 4, 9, 19n33
smoking, 107, 139
social change, 163–64
 as divine *philanthropia,* 241–42
social ethics, 138, 141–42, 145–47, 152, 154, 155
Social Gospel movement, 36, 138, 152–54
socialism, 40
social justice. *See under* justice
Society for Pentecostal Studies, 7–10, *230,* 235–36
sociology, academic discipline, 208
Soltau, George, 42
Songdo, North Korea. *See* Kaesong, North Korea
soteriology
 and apotheosis, 161, 211
 and eschatology, 212–14, 219–20, 242
 full salvation, 123, 128, 129, 215–16
 and Christology, 169–70, 202–3, 204–5n26
 and race, 150–51, 214
 salvation history, 218
South Africa, 37, 47n62
South Carolina, 128

Southern Holiness Association. *See* Holiness Union
Southern Pentecostal Mission (Vasind, India), 64
South Korea, 100, 167, 170, 176n49
Spain, 10
Sparkling Water from Bible Fountains (ed. Morrow), 37
Spirit and Story (eds. Charette and Waddell), 229
Spirit baptism. *See under* baptism
Springfield School, theological, 236–37
Stalker, Charles H., 38, 40
Stanley, Susie, 10, 141
Starkey, Lycurgus, 161
Stephens, Randall, 132n, 215
St. John's Abbey, and University (Collegeville, MN), 10
St. Louis, MO, 38, 60
Stockmayer, Otto, 31, 44n11
Storey, Mary, 37–38
St. Paul School of Theology (Kansas City, MO), 11
St. Paul's Cathedral (Calcutta, India), 67n21
Strong, Douglas, 4
Sunday schools, 37, 144
Sunday travel, 126
Sunderganz, India, 64
Sunderland, England, 72, 75, 76, 77, 78, 79, 85, 86n2, 89nn44–45, 90n49
  revival and conventions, 80–82, 83, 84, 86n2, 89n44, 90n50
Sunderland, La Roy, 3
Sungkiang, China, 100
supernaturalism, 105–6, 111–12
Suzhou (Soochow), 100
Swaziland. *See* Eswatini
Sweet, William Warren, 33
Synan, Vinson, 8, 9, 18n21, 208
Snyder, Howard, 9, 60, 213
Syria, 160

Taylor, G. F., 125
Taylor, John, 87n12, 89n34
Taylor, William (Bishop), 31–32, 37–38, 41, 58–59, 67n22, 68n29, 107
Taylor University, 7

technology, and religion, 33–34, 120–21
temperance, alcohol, 34, 55, 89n35, 126, 216
Tennessee, 8, 9, 10, 11, 126, 127, 128, 129, 143–44, 229, 233–34
Terry, Neely, 142
Texas, 127, 147, 150–51
Thelle, Agnes, 82
Theological Roots of Pentecostalism (Dayton), 9
theological suspicion, 243–44
theology
  theological anthropology, 161, 164–65, 187, 194, 242–43
  theological language, 32–33
  See also individual topics
Theology of Living Together (Park), 162
theosis, 161, 211, 242
Theotokos, theologies of, 163, 237–38
Thoburn, James, 108
Thomas, John, 229, *230*, 231–32, 235–36, 237, 238, 248n44
Thy Healer, 44n11
tobacco, 34, 107
Tokyo, Japan, 99, 100, 102, 103–4, 111, 165
  Tokyo Bible School of Nakada, 165
Tomlinson, A. J., 41–42, 135n58
Tongues of Fire, 78–79, 81, 82, 84
tongues, theologies of, and practice. *See* glossolalia
Topeka, Kansas, 241
tracts, 123–24, 126–27
trains, and railroads, 13, 33–34, 119–37
  and clergy bureaus, 130, 135n57
  and music, 33
transcendence
  apocalyptic, 244
  and immanence, 164, 212, 216–17
  pneumatic transcendence, 239–40, 244
  theologies of, 216–17
Trasher, Lillian, 42
tribulation, in theology, 124
Trinitarian theology
  binitarian critique, 195
  doctrine of Trinity, 160, 162–63, 171, 192–93, 211, 243
  and "New Issue" controversy, 243–44
  (*see also* Oneness Pentecostalism)
Trinitarian theology (*continued*)

non-trinitarianism, 189 (*see also* Oneness Pentecostalism)
theological perspectives of: *dyohypostatic and miahypostatic* theologies, 192–93; *homoousious*, 193; and sovereignty, 217; *schetike synapheia*, 194; theological anthropology, 194
Trinity and the Kingdom (Moltmann), 195
Trinity and the Paschal Mystery, The (Hunt), 195
True Wesleyan, The (Scott), 4
Truth, Sojourner, 147
Tubman, Harriet, 151, 157n40
Turner, H. G., 127
typology, 145–46, 173

Underwood, Horace, 159, 168
Union Seminary (Seoul, S. Korea), 109
Unitarianism, 55
United Methodist Church, 10
    General Commission on Archives and History, 133n10
United States of America
    Black Cabinet, 152
    and black women, 138–58
    Civil Rights Movement, 241
    Hepburn Act, 130–31
    Holiness and Pentecostalism in, 2, 3–7, 12, 40–41, 52, 54, 58, 60–61, 65, 72, 96, 100, 107–9, 169, 188, 212, 241–42
    Holiness critique of, 124–25, 234–35
    historical scholarship, 30
    Interstate Commerce Commission, 135n56
    military, 168
    and populism, 27, 34
    and the Progressive Era, 27, 34
    and rail transportation, 119–37
    racial segregation in, 40, 214–15
    and social hierarchies, 147–48
    White House, 148
unity, Christian, 80, 138–58
University of Cambridge (England), 74
University of Chicago (Illinois), 9
University of Georgia (Athens, GA), 8–9
University Park, Iowa, 5
Upham, Thomas, 3, 4

Vanguard Mission (St. Louis, MO and Sanjan, India), 5, 38, 59, 60, 62, 64
Vasind, India, 64
vaudou, Haitian, 140
Vazeille, Mary (Molly), 76
Vicar's Testimony, A (Boddy), 75, 81–82
Victorian Era, 150
Virginia, 128, 129–30
Vondey, Wolfgang, 231
voodoo. *See vaudou*, Haitian
Vuilleumier, Henri, 2

Wacker, Grant, 210, 231–32
Wainwright, Geoffrey, 162–63
Wakefield, Gavin, 74–75, 77, 82–83, 88n25
Wales, 78, 79, 90nn49–50, 109
    Welsh Revival, 52, 53, 57, 65–66, 80, 90n49
Walker, Alice, 138, 147–48, 151–52
Walker, T., 107
Ward, C. B., 61
Ward, E. F., 12, 38, 52, 57, 59–62, *60*, 64, 65
Ward, Ethel, 68
Ward, Phebe, 12, 38, 52, 57, 59–62, *60*, 64, 65
Ward, W. R., 2
Ware, Steven, 139
Warne, Francis, 108
War on the Saints (Penn-Lewis), 58
Waters, William, 209–10
Watson, G. D., 40
Waukesha, Wisconsin, 5
Way of Holiness, The (Palmer), 4
weather, and eschatology, 121–22
Webb-Peploe, H. W., 81
Wells, Ida, 147
Welsh Revival. *See under* Wales
Wesley, Charles, 209, 211, 221n21
Wesley, John
    bicentenary, 77; holiness, 81, 85–86, 103–4, 210
    and the Church of England, 222n28
    denominational legacy (*see individual institutional names*)
    and enthusiasm, 77
    and epistemology: synergistic, 160–61, 171–72, theological, 160–61, 217–18
    genealogy and family, 76–77 (*see also* Boddy, Alexander A.; Boddy,

Jane; Boddy, Mary; Vazeille, Mary (Molly); Wesley, Charles)
  influence: upon Korean Methodism, 160–62, 166
  and Jonathan Edwards, 217–19, 224n57
  and Karl Barth, 166
  and Macarius, 160–61
  and Pentecostalism 2–3, 73, 76–78, 81, 166, 171, 197, 208–13, 218–19, 243 (*see also* Methodism; Wesleyan Christianity)
  theological sources, 249n64
  theology: conferencing, 218; grace, 161–62, 218–19, 224n53; sanctification, 161–62, 166, 171, 188, 190, 210–12, 215–16, 243; soteriology, ecclesiology, mission, 213; quadrilateral, 172; theological anthropology, 161; Trinitarian theology, 160
Wesleyan Christianity and movements
  and blackness, 232, 233, 244, 246n14
  and the Cleveland School, 231
  denominations of (*see individual institutional names*)
  in England, 72–95
  and enthusiasm, 77
  and epistemology, 160–61, 171–72
  folk Wesleyanism, 241
  history, 3–4, 159–60
  in Korean peninsula, 159–83
  and Orthodoxy, 161, 249n64
  and Reformed Christianity, 245n5
  theology: divine *philanthropia*, 241; eschatology, 209–13, 219–20; grace, 1, 14, 161–63, 204–5n26, 208–20; Wesleyan quadrilateral, 172; sanctification and atonement, 196–8; theological anthropology, 161, 242–43; "Wesleyan-Holiness-Pentecostal pneumatology," 159
  relation to J. Wesley, 3, 81
Wesleyan Church (in the UK), 77, 78
Wesleyan Methodist Church (later Wesleyan Church)
  in the US, 4–5, 10, 213
  in Seneca Falls, NY, 139
Wesleyan Pentecostals, 8, 16n5, 85–86

Wesleyan quadrilateral, 172
Wesleyan studies and scholarship, 7–10, 15, 53, 229–52, *230*
  and womanism, 148–49
Wesleyan Theological Society, 7, 9–11, 19n33, 205n32
Western Theological Seminary (Portland, OR), 10
West Virginia, 127–28, 129–30
Whaling, Frank, 211
whiteness, 147, 153, 233, 246n14
Whitsuntide Conference (Sunderland, England), 80
Widmeyer, Charles, 42
Wigger, John, 211–12
Wigglesworth, Smith, 78
Willard, Frances, 55
Wilmore, Kentucky, 8, 9, 96, 127, 128
Wimberly, C. F., 131
Wisconsin, 5, 129, 149
Wobblies. *See* Industrial Workers of the World
womanism, 147–52
women, 35, 132, 135n57
  education, 55–56
  in ministry, 4, 5, 37–38, 40–41, 82–83, 130, 215
  and Radical Holiness, 13–14, 138–58
  theological writings of, 54–55, 223n42
  See also gender
Women in the Church of God in Christ (Butler), 140
Women of Azusa Street, The (Alexander), 141, 142
Women Preachers (Godbey), 37
Women's Christian Temperance Union, 55, 126, 141, 154
Wonsan Revival (N. Korea), 109–10
Woods, Daniel, 13, 119–37, 254
Woodworth-Etter, Maria, 55, 56, 58
World Conference on Faith and Order, 10
World Council of Churches, 232, 247n30
World Tour of Evangelism (Morrison), 96, 97–98
World War I, 106
World War II, 160, 241
World War in Prophecy, The (Morrison), 106

Worrell, Adolphus, 55, 56
Wray, Newton, 35
Wright, J. Elwin, 6–7, 17n19
Wrongs of Indian Womanhood, The (Fuller), 57

Yale University (New Haven, CT), 41
Yangon, Myanmar. *See* Rangoon, Myanmar
Yeakley, M. L., 127–28
Ye Are Men Now Serve Him (Chapell), 239–40
Yeotmal, India, 62, 64
YMCA, 77, 100, 107
　National Railroad YMCA, 126
YMCA Magazine, 77
Yoido Full Gospel Church (Seoul, S. Korea), 167, 169, 171, 173, 177n64

Yong, Amos, 231, 234–37
Yoon, Seong-beom, 162, 163
York, H. Stanley, 132n
"You Have Stept out of Your Place" (Lindley), 140–41
Young, Brigham, 3, 16n7
Young, Lorenzo Dow, 16n7
Young Men's Christian Association. *See* YMCA

Zahl, Simeon, 243
Zakai, Avihu, 217, 224n51
Zenana Training Home (Pune, India), 62
zi-chi, zi-ri Korean theologies of Ultimate Doing and Ultimate Being, 163

www.ingramcontent.com/pod-product-compliance
Lightning Source LLC
Chambersburg PA
CBHW022042290426
44109CB00014B/948